31.95

The International Economy and Industrial Development

The International Economy and Industrial Development:

The Impact of Trade and Investment on the Third World

Robert H. Ballance
SENIOR INDUSTRIAL DEVELOPMENT OFFICER,
UNITED NATIONS INDUSTRIAL DEVELOPMENT ORGANISATION

Javed A. Ansari
LECTURER IN INTERNATIONAL ECONOMICS,
CITY UNIVERSITY, LONDON

Hans W. Singer
PROFESSOR OF ECONOMICS,
INSTITUTE OF DEVELOPMENT STUDIES, UNIVERSITY OF SUSSEX

ALLANHELD, OSMUN   Publishers

ALLANHELD, OSMUN & CO. PUBLISHERS, INC.

Published in the United States of America in 1982
by Allanheld, Osmun & Co. Publishers, Inc.
(A Division of Littlefield, Adams & Company)
81 Adams Drive, Totowa, New Jersey 07512

Copyright © 1982 by Robert H. Ballance,
Javed A. Ansari and Hans W. Singer

All rights reserved. No part of this publication may
be reproduced, stored in a retrieval system, or
transmitted in any form or by any means, electronic,
mechanical, photocopying, recording, or otherwise,
without the prior permission of the publisher.

Library of Congress Cataloging in Publication Data

Balance, Robert H.
  The international economy and industrial development.

  Includes index.
  1. Underdeveloped areas—industries.
  2. Underdeveloped areas—commerce.
  I. Ansari, Javed A. II. Singer, Hans Wolfgang, 1910-.
  III. Title
  HC 59.7.B297   338.09172'4   82-6651

ISBN 0-86598-086-1   AACR2

82 83 84/10 9 8 7 6 5 4 3 2 1
Printed in Great Britain

Contents

List of Tables	viii
List of Figures	x
List of Abbreviations	xi
Preface	1

Part I
The Role of the External Sector in the Industrialization Process

Preface		3
I	Strategies for Industrialization in Advanced Countries	7
1.1	Classical economic theory and British industrialisation in the nineteenth century	8
1.2	German industrialization and the economics of Frederick List	16
1.3	The great industrialization debate and Soviet industrial development	25
1.4	The lessons of history	32
II	Strategies for Trade and Industrialization in the Post-War Era	39
2.1	Import substitution in the Third World	39
2.2	Export orientation in the Third World	48
2.3	Export performance in the Third World	53
2.4	Western trade strategies and their consequences for Third World industrialization	60
2.5	The consolidation of neo-protectionism — international consequences	73
2.6	Recent attempts at international reform	77

Contents

Part II
Structural Relationships between Industry and Trade

Preface		91
III	Structural Changes in World Industry	95
3.1	The Spread of World industry	95
3.2	Estimating the pattern of industrial growth	107
Annex to Chapter III		123
IV	Structural Changes in World Trade in Manufactures	130
4.1	Determinants of export performance	130
4.2	Estimating changes in comparative advantage	140
4.3	The contribution of exports to growth	152
Annex to Chapter IV		170
V	Policies and Prospects for Industrial Development in the Third World	172
5.1	Iron and steel	173
5.2	Chemicals and petrochemicals	183
5.3	Textiles	194
5.4	Food processing	206

Part III
Agents for Industrialization in the Negotiating Process

Preface		223
VI	The Transnational Corporation as an Agent for Industrialization	225
6.1	TNC objectives and Third World industrialization	226
6.2	The developmental impact of investment by TNCs	231
6.3	Policies of transnational corporations: an empirical investigation	239
6.4	Conclusions	259

Contents

VII	The Public Manufacturing Enterprise as an Agent for Industrialization	268
7.1	Growth of public manufacturing enterprises in LDCs	269
7.2	The public manufacturing enterprise as an agent of industrialization	271
7.3	Policies of Indian public manufacturing enterprises: an empirical study	276
7.4	Problems and prospects of co-operation between transnationals and public manufacturing firms	285
VIII	Industrial Restructuring and International Negotiations	297
8.1	The institutional setting and industrial realities	298
8.2	Structural change and interest group behaviour in western countries	302
8.3	Structural change and interest group behaviour in the Third World	305
8.4	Industrial restructuring and international negotiation	310
Index		321

List of Tables

Chapter I
I.1 British growth in the eighteenth century 11

Chapter II
II.1 Imports of manufactures by end-use in western countries and LDCs, 1968 and 1974 44
II.2 Sources of growth by end-use in selected LDCs 56
II.3 The United States' contribution to world industrial output and trade, various years 63
II.4 Structural changes in manufacturing in selected western countries and years 75

Chapter III
III.1 Estimated shares of world output in manufacturing by various country groupings, selected years 96
III.2 The structure of net manufacturing output in selected western countries, 1963 and 1975 100
III.3 The structure of net manufacturing ouput in selected LDCs, 1963 and 1975 102
III.4 Kendall's coefficient of concordance between the rankings of industrial branches (value added) across countries, 1963, 1970, 1975 105
III.5 Absolute and relative gaps in *per captia* GDP and MVA, 1960 and 1977 106
III.6 The distribution of growth rates of MVA by income level and market orientation, 1960–77 108
III.7 Estimated coefficients of logistic equation (2) for samples from four different country groups 112
III.8 Income levels corresponding to maximum rates of structural change in industry 118

List of Tables

Annex to Chapter III
A.III.1 Estimated coefficients of quadratic equation (4) for samples from four different country groups (annual pooled cross-section for 1974–7)   127

Chapter IV
IV.1   A constant market share analysis for major exporters of manufactures (SITC 5 to 8 less 688), 1966–76   134
IV.2   Spearman rank correlation coefficients in export performance indices of seventy-nine industries, 1966–7 and 1975–6   143
IV.3   Average increase in export performance indices by country sample and by product characteristics, 1966–7 to 1975–6   146
IV.4   Exports with a marked RCA as a share of exports of manufactures, 1966–7 and 1975–6   151
IV.5   Contribution to the growth of manufactured exports (1966–7 and 1975–6) by country group   153
IV.6   Spearman rank correlation coefficients between exports and output growth in LDCs, 1968–74   154
IV.7   A constant market share analysis of the LDCs' labour-intensive exports, 1967–8 to 1973–4   157

Annex to Chapter IV
A.IV.1 Composition of four country samples used in estimating comparative advantage   170
A.IV.2 Country samples used in the computation of Spearman rank correlation coefficients for exports and growth   171

Chapter V
V.1   Iron and steel production in industrialized countries, 1870–1975   173
V.2   Distibution of world iron and steel exports   177
V.3   Distribution of world MVA in textiles   195

List of Tables

Chapter VI
VI.1	Distribution of subsidiaries and affiliates of companies in the UK sample	242
VI.2	Average rates of growth of firms in different size classes: India	246
VI.3	Transition matrix for measuring Indian subsidiaries' internal mobility	247
VI.3	Impact of growth on profitability	250
VI.5	Investment behaviour of TNCs and subsidiaries	254
VI.6	Profitability and size: the regression analysis	255

Chapter VII
VII.1	Relationship between opening size and growth of fifty Indian PMEs, 1972–9	279
VII.2	Transition matrix for measuring firms' mobility: Indian PMEs, 1972–9	280
VII.3	Investment behaviour of Indian PMEs: a summary of regression results	281
VII.4	Relationship between size and profitability, Indian PMEs, 1972/73–1978/79	282

List of Figures

Chapter III
1.	Illustrative growth paths for manufacuring	111
2.	Estimated growth paths of manufacturing for four country groups	116

Annex to Chapter III
A.1	Graph of the logistic function of equation (5)	128

List of Abbreviations

ACP	African, Caribbean and Pacific States
ASEAN	Association of South-East Asian Nations
CACM	Central American Common Market
CMS	constant market share
DR	direct reduction
ECDC	economic co-operation among developing countries
EEC	European Economic Community
FAO	Food and Agriculture Organization
GATT	General Agreement on Tariffs and Trade
GDP	Gross Domestic Product
GNP	Gross National Product
GSP	Generalized System of Preferences
IC	industrialized countries
IDS	International Development Strategy
ILO	International Labour Office
IMF	International Monetary Fund
ITO	International Trade Organization
LDC	less developed country
MFA	Multifibre Arrangement
MFN	most favoured nation
MTN	multinational trade negotiations
MVA	manufacturing value added
NEP	New Economic Policy
NIC	newly industrializing country
NIEO	New International Economic Order
NTB	non-tariff barriers
OECD	Organization for Economic Co-operation and Development
OPEC	Organization of Petroleum Exporting Countries

List of Abbreviations

OTC	Organization for Trade Co-operation
PME	public manufacturing enterprise
R and D	research and development
RCA	revealed comparative advantage
RDC	recently developed country
SITC	Standard International Trade Classification
TNC	transnational corporation
UK	United Kingdom
UN	United Nations
UNCTAD	United Nations Conference on Trade and Development
UNCTC	United Nations Centre on Transnational Corporations
UNIDO	United Nations Industrial Development Organization
US	United States (of America)
USSR	Union of Soviet Socialist Republics
VER	voluntary export restraints

Preface

Third World industrialization has been the subject of extensive research. In recent times growing attention has been paid to the impact of trade strategies on industrial development. This book seeks to make an empirical and an analytical contribution to that debate. It draws together evidence on the external sector's role in restructuring world industry, as well as the implications for investment and employment in the Third World. An attempt is made to spell out the policies of the main agents of industrial development—including transnational corporations, public manufacturing enterprises, domestic interest groups and governments—and to assess the realism and usefulness of proposals made in the New International Economic Order debates and by the Brandt Commission in this field.

The book has been written both for policy makers in government, industry and international organizations and for advanced undergraduate and graduate students. It may serve as a text for courses in economic development, industrial economics and international economics. Although the results of original empirical research have been presented, the technical discussion was kept to a minimum in the hope that this will increase the accessibility of the book to the large number of people who are becoming increasingly concerned about Third World development.

Robert Ballance and Javed Ansari were employed at the United Nations Industrial Development Organization during the time the book was written. The views expressed here do not in any way represent those of UNIDO.

Economists who undertake studies that cut across a range of subject matter and methodologies are fortunate indeed if they have the benefit of advice from others who are specialists in given fields.

Preface

In our case the high standards of competence and ready cooperation of colleagues were invaluable. We should specifically mention Susanna Seeling, Helmut Forstner, Constantin Gaganas and Laura Iansiti of the Regional and Country Studies Branch of UNIDO. Margit Atanasiu and Angelika Kaiser provided typing and editorial assistance. Others who helped in a variety of ways during the book's preparation include Ronald Dore, Susan Joekes, David Evans and Raphael Kaplinksy of the Institute of Development Studies, University of Sussex, Tim Tutton, Jonathan Court, Saib Saah and Geoff Kay of the City University, London, John Salter of the University of Manchester, Dieter Stentzel of the Munich Centre for Advanced Training in Applied Statistics for Developing Countries (Carl Duisberg-Gesellschaft E.V) and Robert Anderson of the International Institute for Applied Systems Analysis. Finally, Subrahmanjan Nanjundan, Head of Regional and Country Studies Branch, UNIDO, gave encouragement and was instrumental in maintaining a genuine research atmosphere in which such work can be carried out.

Part I

The Role of the External Sector in the Industrialization Process

Preface

Industrial development is a multifaceted process affecting many important and influential groups within society. In advanced societies these groups include a wide spectrum of interest: suppliers of labour, capital and industrial inputs, consumers of industrial products, managers of firms, government planners and policy makers. In the Third World the portion of a society having a vested interest in industrial development may be relatively small, although it is almost always politically influential. The momentum and character of industrial development is determined, to a great extent, by how these vested interests react to different sets of changing conditions of production. Some conditions may be regarded as 'internal' to an economy, i.e. they are dependent, to varying degrees, on the economic, political and social characteristics that affect relationships of domestic producers and consumers. Others are external in nature and have consequences for both domestic and foreign interest groups. This book attempts to analyse the importance of such 'external conditions' on the pace and orientation of industrial development in the Third World.

Our overriding concern pertains to international shifts in industrial capacity and how this phenomenon is related to changing external conditions. We have used the term 'industrial restructuring' to refer to the international spread of production capacity and manufacturing activity. Within the context of a single economy, industrial restructuring is closely related to changes in the composition of manufactured output and to the corresponding use of various factors of production. As factors of production move out of one industrial branch and into another, structural changes occur. Some activities contract when measured in terms of their shares in production, employment, investment and exports. These contractions are often accompanied by an expansion elsewhere in manufacturing or in other sectors of the economy. For example, a contraction in one industrial branch (e.g. textiles) may be accompanied by an expansion in another (e.g capital goods) or in another sector (e.g. services).

At the international level similar patterns of growth and change are often observed simultaneously in different countries at comparable levels of development. Consequently, the contraction of an industrial branch can be common to several countries and may be preceded by a corresponding expansion of that same branch in other countries. The restructuring process inevitably establishes some link between interest groups in different countries and influences their motivations and respective patterns of behaviour. Clearly then the external sector plays an important role in facilitating or hindering a country's ability to restructure its manufacturing sector.

Part I discusses three alternative 'models' for industrial development in advanced countries and then reviews industrialization strategies in the Third World. In each case the choice of a model, or strategy, circumscribed the impact of the external sector. This choice usually reflects the wishes of influential interest groups within the country. It is the balance of political and economic forces within a society that will ultimately determine the role that will be assigned to foreign trade and investment as instruments of the national industrialization strategy. The relationship between interest group behaviour on the one hand and accepted economic theory on the other is central to this book's theme.

Conventional economic theory—both neo-classical and neo-Marxist—stresses the scientific character of economic analysis. Others have noted that such analysis may reveal the operation of supra-historical standards or rules that determine, or at least circumscribe, the feasible policy options available to economic practitioners. Economic schools of thought differ in their identifica-

Preface

tion of supra-historical rules. Neo-classical economists, for example, stress the consequences of changes in the money supply on the level of economic activity as a supra-historical economic law. Neo-Marxists identify modified forms of the Law of the Tendency of the Rate of Profit to Fall as a persistent economic constraint in all societies where capital accumulation occurs. There is general recognition, however, that policy cannot modify the operation of these laws. In fact, the efficacy of policy is determined to a significant degree by the extent to which it is consciously based on such laws.

What are the 'laws' determining the impact of the external sector—the flow of goods and inputs across national boundaries—on the process of industrialization and to what extent can they unambiguously be called 'economic'? How does their operation circumscribe and synthesize the policies of different industrial actors? How—and to what extent—can these laws be manipulated, modified or suspended in order to achieve the objectives of the policy makers?

To what degree are the operations of these laws dependent upon other 'laws' determining the pace and direction of social activity? What, for example, is the impact of a modification of property relationships, through nationalization or through a policy of encouraging local capitalist farmers, *à la* Stolypin, on the need for foreign investment or foreign export markets for rapidly growing industries? To what extent does a need for foreign resources stimulate a change in the balance of domestic political and economic power?

We do not expect that a new comprehensive theory of the role of trade and foreign investment in industrialization will emerge but we hope that the exercise may suggest a new synthesis of elements in diffferent theoretical approaches which permits a better understanding of the interplay between economic 'laws' and economic policies in the field.

Chapter I

Strategies for Industrialization in Advanced Countries

This chapter discusses the role of economic theory in a society's adoption of an industrial strategy and its impact on the role of the external sector. Three countries—Britain, Germany and the USSR—are chosen for discussion. Conventional economic theory—both neo-classical and Neo-Marxist—has put great emphasis on the 'scientific' character of ecomonic analysis. This interpretation does not necessarily deny the importance of the ideological perspective—what Schumpeter would call 'vision'—in determining the economic questions that we choose to ask in any given historical epoch. It does suggest that analysis transcends Schumpeterian vision when applied to any concrete historical circumstance. Economic analysis inevitably reveals the operation of 'suprahistorical standards and rules'.[1] This relevance of such rules for the efficiency of policy has been noted above.

In reviewing the industrial development process of industrialized countries, we describe the changes that took place in the industrial structure and the factors responsible for initiating and sustaining structural change. An attempt will be made to identify the social and economic forces that were instrumental in shaping national policy during crucial periods of industrial restructuring. In particular, we will try to show the part these forces played in determining the role of the external sector in the industrialization process. The attitude to foreign trade and investment was determined not so much on the basis of developments within the field of economic theory, but reflected the need to preserve the economic and political interests of the stronger and more influential social classes. The prevalent economic orthodoxy of a given historical period was invariably dependent on the interests of the dominant groups. This is most clearly evident when we examine the evolution of British industrial and trade policies in the eighteenth and early nineteenth centuries.

1.1 Classical economic theory and British industrialization in the nineteenth century

The leading British classical economists—particularly Smith and Ricardo—put a great deal of emphasis on the contribution that international trade could make to the development process. Early on in his writings Smith asserted that the division of labour was limited by the extent of trade.[2] His main target of criticism was the teaching of the Mercantilist School. He argued that foreign trade provided producers with special opportunities. 'By opening a more extensive market for whatever part of the produce of their labour may exceed the home consumption it encourages them to improve its productive powers and to augment its annual produce to the utmost and thereby to increase the real revenue and wealth of the Society.'[3] The mercantilist writers had stressed the importance of maintaining trade surpluses and sustaining monopoly positions in export markets through the use of commercial policy.[4] In an attempt to show the shortsightedness of such policy, Smith was no narrow theoretician. He was as deeply concerned with issues of national economic policy as the mercantilist authors.

There are important differences between the social environment of the Continental mercantilist writers and that of the British classical economists. Britain was less affected by the religious wars and the political upheavals of the sixteenth and seventeenth centuries. It suffered no invasions and its ruling aristocracy did not develop the power and social ascendency of comparable classes in Europe. In Britain the medieval constitution survived and the State's dominance over civil society was less extended than in the Continent. Economic activity—including economic enterprise related to colonial expansion—remained mainly outside the domain of state authority. Although protectionist policies were pursued, and enthusiastically advocated (by Child and Petty, among others), they were less restrictive and applied with greater laxity than in the other major European countries. The abandonment of these regulatory policies was a relatively painless affair. 'With the rapid economic development towards the end of the eighteenth century the English State easily became the minimal or laissez-faire "nightwatchman" state of the Industrial Revolution that presided over the most dramatic initial phase of the world industrialization.'[5]

In a vitally important sense this 'low profile' state structure depended upon the successful colonial enterprise that had been launched by the British as early as the sixteenth century. It was this success which enabled a spontaneously emergent merchant class to create such a state and to maintain control over it. Moreover, this relationship was legitimately equated with the dominance of 'civil society' over the 'state'—for its maintenance did not require an extension of social coercion or political authoritarianism. The merchants' success in colonial ventures spilled over into the pockets of other social groups. Thus Marx notes that 'the colonies provided a market for the budding manufacturers which was guaranteed by the mother country's monopoly of the market. The resources captured outside Europe flowed back into the mother country and were turned into capital there.'[6] The easily available capital made it possible to achieve a working synthesis between the economic interests of the landed gentry and the town merchants. This complementarity of interests was sustained until the nineteenth century when manufacturing capital assumed a pre-eminent position in the British economy.

Adam Smith recognized the importance of colonial trade as an instrument for accelerated growth in the seventeenth century:

> By opening a new and inexhaustible market to all commodities of Europe it [i.e. colonization of the Americas] gave occasion to a new division of labour and improvements of art, which in the narrow circle of ancient commerce would never have taken place for want of a market. . . . One of the principal effects of these discoveries has been to raise the mercantile system to a degree of splendour and glory which it could never otherwise have attained. It is the object of that system to enrich a great nation rather by trade and manufacture than by the improvement and cultivation of land, rather by the industry of the towns than by that of the country.[7]

The International Economy and Industrial Development

The impact of colonial trade on British industrialization during the seventeenth and eighteenth centuries has been regarded as of crucial importance. According to Williams,

> this triangular trade [pattern] gave a triple stimulus to British industry. The Negroes were purchased with British (and Oriental) manufactures, transported to the plantations, they produced sugar, cotton, indigo, molasses, and other tropical products, the processing of which created new industries in England, while the maintenance of the Negroes and their owners in the plantations provided another market for British industry. By 1750 there was hardly a trading or manufacturing town in England which was not in some way connected with the triangular or direct colonial trade. The profits obtained provided one of the mainstreams of that accumulation of capital in England which financed the Industrial Revolution. It was the capital accumulated in the West Indies trade that financed James Watt and the steam engine. Boulton and Watt received advances from Low, Vere, Williams and Jennings.[8] [9]

The overall importance of trade in British industrialization may be gauged from the fact that, in 1688, English exports constituted about 5 per cent of national income. A hundred years later this figure had risen to 15 per cent and by the early 1880s the value of exports constituted over 30 per cent of national income.[10] Similarly Mandell has estimated that 'for the period 1760–80 the profit from India and the West Indies alone more than doubled the accumulation money available for investment in industry (in Britain).'[11] Estimates have also been made for the relative importance of export demand in the stimulation of specific branches of industrial production. For wool manufacturers, Landes finds that 'at the end of the seventeenth century English exports of wool cloth probably accounted for 30 per cent of the output of that industry . . . by 1771–72 the proportion had apparently risen to something under a half.'[12] Similar trends prevailed in the cotton manufacturers industry which, according to Hobsbawm, 'was launched like a glider by the pull of the colonial trade to which it was attached.'[13]

Deane and Cole have also provided estimates of growth of different sectors of the British economy for the eighteenth century as shown in Table I.1.

Strategies for Industrialization in Advanced Countries

Table I.1. British growth in the eighteenth century
(1700 = 100)

Year	National income	Export industries	Domestic industries	Agricultural production
1700	100	100	100	100
1760	147	222	114	115
1780	167	246	123	126
1800	251	544	152	143

Source: Deane and Cole, 'British Economic Growth 1688–1959', in *Cambridge Economic History of Europe*, Cambridge University Press, London, 1967, Vol. VI, p. 78.

The marked difference in the growth performance of the export oriented industries compared with agriculture and domestic manufacturing is noteworthy. Output of the former increased by a factor of five during this period whereas agricultural output and domestic manufacturing output increased only by about 50 per cent. The rate of growth of the agricultural sector was a constraint on the expansion of domestic manufacturing. Export oriented manufacturing was less limited by this factor; in the years 1780–1800 it experienced very rapid expansion. The cotton industry grew at an annual rate of 14 per cent while iron and steel and metal working industries grew at a pace exceeding 5 per cent per annum.[14] In aggregate terms British foreign trade grew at a rate of about 2 per cent per annum during the seventeenth century. In the period 1700–14 growth accelerated to over 13 per cent.[15] To some extent this acceleration may be explained by changes in trade policy. In the eighteenth century protectionism was widespread. Cotton imports from Asia were prohibited to protect the English wool industry. After 1774 when this prohibition was removed, the 'free trade' movement gained momentum. In 1807 the British slave trade was made illegal and the monopoly privileges of the East India Company were restricted. In 1846 the Corn Laws were repealed and adherence to the Free Trade 'doctrine' became enshrined as an important principle of state economic policy.

Although Smith was a champion of free trade, it must be remembered that he was writing at a time when the overall

The International Economy and Industrial Development

consequences of the Industrial Revolution could only be dimly perceived. The British economy was primarily agrarian and the seventeenth and eighteenth century had witnessed a series of profound changes in the structure of agricultural production—both in terms of ownership patterns and application of production technology. Large-scale enterprises outside the agricultural sector continued to confine themselves mainly to the financial and commercial spheres. Manufacturing industry was organized around relatively small production units, managed by master craftsmen. This made it possible for many eighteenth century economists—including 'occasionally Adam Smith—to class the manufacturer with the workmen'.[16] Smith did not foresee the organizational innovations that would accompany the Industrial Revolution, believing 'that the corporate form of enterprise was an anomaly except in such cases as canals and the like'.[17] At other points in the *Wealth of Nations*, however, Smith writes of 'merchants and master manufacturers who live on profit.'[18] It is important to realize that this condemnation of the 'class of merchants and manufacturers'[19] is part of a general attack on the whole network of restrictive regulations embodied in the mercantilist system representing, in his view, individual and sectional interests and constituting an obstruction to the general process of capital accumulation and industrial expansion.[20] Removing these obstructions and dismantling protectionist regulations would pave the way to accumulation and industrial expansion—and thus international trade and investment had a vital role in sustaining these processes.[21] Smith's thesis was that the extent of the industrial division of labour could be extended by specializing in accordance with Britain's existing absolute advantage in manufacturing and by removing mercantilist restrictions on the import of primary goods.

In contrast, Ricardo was writing at a time when the demand for manufactures had fallen off and prices of agricultural products had risen in the wake of the Napoleonic Wars. According to him the significant contribution of trade to national development lay in its impact on agricultural prices. If a policy of free trade were adopted it would be possible to import cheap agricultural goods. This would arrest the tendency towards diminishing returns in domestic agriculture, prevent an increase in food prices and the real wage rate

Strategies for Industrialization in Advanced Countries

and ensure high levels of industrial profitability and capital accumulation. Moreover, adherence to a policy of free trade would be as much in the interests of Britain's trading partners, for they would be able to procure efficiently produced manufactures from Britain. Specialization in accordance with the existing international division of labour would be of mutual advantage. This argument is based upon a number of important assumptions 'which in conformity with his practice he never expressly states.'[22] Critics, on the other hand, have argued that 'the international division of labour associated with the "law" of comparative advantage has never been "natural" but was manufactured by the very British industrial interests and their overseas allies who then enshrined this division as a supposed natural law.'[23] The international division of labour, which according to Ricardo made it advantageous for Portugal to specialize in the production of wine and for England to specialize in the production of cloth,[24] had emerged as a direct consequence of English trade and colonial policy during the seventeenth and eighteenth centuries.[25] The enactment of the Treaty of Methuen in 1703 meant the virtual exclusion of German and Dutch exports from Portuguese markets. Fifty years earlier Portugal had granted commercial privileges to England in exchange for military assistance against Spain.[26] 'By 1754 . . . England had become mistress of the entire commerce of Portugal; all the trade of this country was carried by her [i.e. English] agents.'[27] Smith had believed that 'the Methuen Treaty was evidently advantageous to Portugal.'[28] But the impact of trade liberalization on the Portuguese economy was the emergence of

> a strong dependence of Portugal on England. . . . By guaranteeing the supremacy of Portugal's landed interests, the Methuen Treaty established a permanent link between those interests and England—a link which (was) at the core of Portugal's independence. The large and chronic deficit created by the type of international division of labour in the Portuguese balance of payments caused Brazilian gold to outflow entirely from Portugal and to be directed mainly to England, where given the different conditions it contributed to the industrialization of that country much more than it had done in Portugal whose manufacturing sector had been sacrificed to the production of wine.[29]

The International Economy and Industrial Development

In Ricardo's texts and pamphlets there is no recognition of these developments. Indeed the subsequent extension of his analysis suggests that the smaller country (i.e. Portugal) would get the larger share of the gains from trade.[30] If, however, Portugal were to specialize in the production of agricultural goods as a result of adopting free trade policies then, in the long run Ricardian analysis may be interpreted as suggesting that free trade is not in Portugal's national interest. For Ricardo believed that the 'law' of diminishing returns applied with particular force to agriculture,[31] and specialization would enhance rents, reduce profits and the rate of capital accumulation. He was quite aware that there was considerable value in making a clear distinction between the gains to a particular country and the gains to the 'world' from the pursuit of a particular trade policy. Thus in his analysis of colonial trade, for example, Ricardo argued that 'the trade of a colony may be so regulated that it shall at the same time be less beneficial to the colony and more beneficial to the mother country than a perfectly free trade.'[32] He never extended the argument to recognize that the pattern of product specialization may determine the long-run impact of free trade on the domestic economy of the colonial or smaller trading partners.[33]

As against this, Ricardo was emphatic in asserting the importance of free trade policy as an instrument for English industrialization and capital accumulation. 'Let (food and vegetables) be supplied from abroad in exchange for manufactured goods and it is difficult to say what the limit is at which you cease to accumulate wealth and derive profit from its employment.'[34] 'While trade is free and corn cheap profits will not fall however great the accumulation of capital.'[35]

Ricardo was writing when British industrialization had been ongoing for well nigh a century. Agriculture had been established on a capitalist basis. Britain had also 'established a decisive lead over France, her nearest rival, as a manufacturing and trading nation.'[36] A new industrial and commercial bourgeoisie had become a significant force in British politics. Ricardo's economics were affected by and eminently suited to an analysis of the issues and problems of early nineteenth century British economy.[37] He was seriously concerned about the impact of the Napoleonic Wars

Strategies for Industrialization in Advanced Countries

on the British economy. As Winch has stated,

> The period marked out by the last edition of the Wealth of Nations in Smith's lifetime in 1789 and Ricardo's death in 1823 . . . encompasses one of the crucial phases in Britain's process of industrialization . . . in the course of dealing with the economic problems associated with these developments classical political economy acquired many of its leading characteristics.[38]

In Ricardo's scheme the agricultural sector is a primary determinant of the level of economic development a nation can sustain. In this, his analysis is very close to Smith's. Unlike Smith, however, Ricardo does not lay any great emphasis on improvement in manufacturing productivity,[39] and does not concern himself with an analysis of the evolution of the forms of industrial organization. Ricardo's advocacy of a free trade policy—as against, for example, Thomas Malthus who argued for limited protection to sustain agricultural income and investment[40]—clearly represents a fusion of the interests of the commercial and industrial bourgeoisie. As we have seen, in Smith's time such a coincidence of class interest was nascent but not explicit and his attitude to the capitalist classes could be interpreted as being somewhat ambiguous. In particular, Smith condemned their tendency towards monopoly and 'cartelization' as detrimental to the extension of the division of labour and to capital accumulation. In Ricardo's time the organizational structure of industrial enterprise was undergoing a rapid and fundamental metamorphosis. The 'putter out' system was being replaced and dominated by the 'factory system' of industrial organization in the more technologically advanced industries. This development rendered 'guild type' association unnecessary and paved the way for the active competitive search for internal and external markets which would characterize most of the nineteenth century. Ricardo, therefore, argued it was the capitalists alone who could be the focus of an economic expansionist policy. If profits rose as a share of national product, so would the rate of capital accumulation, and this would be in the interest of the majority of the population which now constituted the industrial labour force. A policy of free trade could serve as an important instrument for promoting the national ascendency of British capitalists and accelerating the pace of

The International Economy and Industrial Development

economic development.

Classical political economy thus identified a set of supra-historical laws—the impact of the increasing division of labour, the distribution of the gains from trade, the operation of the law of diminishing returns in agriculture, the relation between the share of capital, labour and land, etc.—which determined the rate of economic progress. The attitude of the classical political economist to industrial development and industrial organization was deeply influenced by their perception of these laws. They believed that economic policy should be modified to promote certain economic tendencies and counter others. They were not concerned with the advocacy of Utopian solutions but pragmatically related their theory to proposals that were politically realistic. The articulation of the theory in the realm of policy making in particular was based upon a perception of an identification with the interests of an influential group of policy makers. It was this coincidence of perspectives—of a shared 'vision' of Britain's present and future—that endeared the classical theory to industrialists, bankers and civil servants and that was responsible for its enthronement as the 'conventional wisdom' on the basis of which British economic policy sought to justify itself from the abolition of the Corn Laws in 1847 till the turn of the century.

1.2 *German industrialization and the economics of Frederick List*

List enjoyed in Germany a much greater popular appeal than either Smith or Ricardo in Britain. List was, of course, much more than an economist. He was a patriot and a visionary and intimately associated with the long and painful struggle for German independence and unification. He 'entertained a grand vision of [Germany's] national situation.... [He] saw a nation that struggled in the fetters imposed by a miserable immediate past but he also saw its economic potentialities.'[41] To realize these economic potentialities was his main preoccupation. He saw Germany's condition in the early nineteenth century as transitory. He argued for a radical change in economic policy—a change that would not augment existing dominant trends but transcend them. Thus, he opposed a continuation of the status quo in Germany and was concerned with the short-run welfare implications of the policies he advocated. He constructed a 'stages' theory of economic development, identifying hunting, agriculture, agriculture plus manufacturing and agriculture plus manufacturing plus commerce as necessary stages which must be encountered in the development process. This rather vague and loose formation of a stages theory[42] emphasized the point that 'economic policy has to do with changing economic structure and therefore cannot consist of a set of unchanging recipes.'[43]

List is seen as a champion of the German customs union—the Zollverein—established in the early nineteenth century. His main argument for the necessity of its establishment was what we now term 'the infant industry argument'.[44] This break with classical political economy was by no means of a fundamental nature. Neither List's nor Hamilton's formulation of the 'infant industry' argument ran counter to the main propositions of classical trade theory. Accordingly, J. S. Mill 'accepted the infant industry theory realizing that it ran within the free trade logic.'[45]

At the same time it must be emphasized that List was deeply influenced by his study of mercantilist policy. He approvingly quotes, 'England's prohibitions [of] . . . the silk and cotton goods of the East—[46] articles competing with those of her *own factories* . . . England's ministers obeyed the theory of productive power when they determined upon their industrial policy.'[47] According to List, the choice of trade policy should be determined by the relative international competitiveness of the country concerned.[48]

Compared to nineteenth century Anglo-Saxon writers, the distinguishing feature of List's work is an explicit recognition of the 'intimate relations existing between politics and political economy'.[49] Free trade, though an important means for achieving an optimum allocation of resources domestically,[50] could not serve as an instrument for enhancing international competitiveness of weak and relatively under industrialized nation states. Hence, international trade and investment policies of such countries should eschew free trade and institutionalize state protection of domestic industry.

'Mercantilism' had exerted an important influence on German economic policy since the seventeenth century.[51] Early German

The International Economy and Industrial Development

mercantilist theory is to be distinguished from the work of English mercantilists in that 'the German Mercantilists serving a less productive economy without a strong export trade had to concentrate all their attention on the domestic market.'[52] Reality demanded that they address a closed system of national economics; the doctrine of political economy called commercialism.'[53] German mercantilists assumed that the international economy was on the whole static—'that the world holds a supposedly stable quantity of commodities and that a growing national economy can acquire a greater share of this only in economic conflict at the expense of another country.'[54] They believed that the State had an obligation to facilitate the development and marketing of manufactures in international markets—this was regarded as a concern of the State by the spokesman of the merchants of Ulm in 1677.[55] This insistence on the role of the State as a stimulant and an organizer of productive activity led Wilson to define mercantilism 'as a policy of economic management meeting the needs alike of the State and of the national economy.'[56]

The peculiar role of the State in the process of Germany's industrialization owes itself above all to the historical development of the country. At the beginning of the eighteenth century some parts of what is now West Germany were already among the most advanced of Europe. By the early nineteenth century half of Prussia's exports consisted of manufactured products—grain accounted for only 8 per cent of all exports.[57] In Eastern Germany the level of industrialization was meagre and feudal modes of production and distribution predominated. However, industrial potential, even in these Eastern States, was considerable. Germany had developed close commercial links with both France and Britain. British, French and Belgian entrepreneurs brought in the new technology and helped in its adaptation to German conditions. German entrepreneurs purchased the new untried technology and procured the services of foreign skilled labour on a relatively large scale.

In the early nineteenth century there were formidable obstacles to German industrialization. 'These obstacles were removable by administrative action, by political change in the country itself and by the pressure of political and economic change in neighbouring

Strategies for Industrialization in Advanced Countries

countries.'[58] The most important obstacle to development was Germany's 'balkanization' into more than 350 mini principalities, in the Treaty of Westphalia.[59] Political unification was perceived as a fundamental pre-requisite of economic development. Each attempt at economic rationalization during the seventeenth and eighteenth centuries was frustrated by political fragmentation. Nationalism and patriotism—the unification of a great European heartland in conflict with France and Britain which sought to deny it unity—was at the heart of the programme of German industrial development. The political unification of Germany took place during 1814–70,[60] a period of consolidation of German industrialization.

In the early nineteenth century the desire for political unification found expression in the establishment of the Zollverein, a customs union embracing most German States. Emphasis was also placed on building a system of effective road communication linking the states to each other. The Common Market arrangement sought to maintain the advantages that Napoleon's unification of Central Europe had bestowed on the merchants and the manufacturers of the Rhineland, while other European nations were increasingly turning towards protectionism.

The main instrument chosen for economic unification was the harmonization of tariff structures. In 1816 and 1817 Prussia abolished all internal tariffs in Prussian territory and devised a common external tariff for all the provinces. This policy sought to integrate the local markets and to permit the Eastern and Western provinces to specialize in commodities in which they enjoyed comparative cost advantages—the grain of East Prussia could move to the West, and the textiles and coal of the Rhineland Duchies could be sold to the Eastern provinces. There were, of course, interest groups which resisted economic integration—the Southern States producing uncompetitive manufactures, the small principalities drawing a large proportion of their public revenue from excise duty and the northern ports interested in the preservation of unrestricted trade with the rest of Europe, etc. However, from 1822 onwards—when France increased her tariff levels substantially—more and more States joined the Prussian Zollverein. Rival customs unions of Central German States, headed by Hanover and Electoral Hesse, were also set up in 1829 and 1830. By 1834 these had been

The International Economy and Industrial Development

absorbed into the Zollverein and—although Hanover did not join until 1851—effective German economic unification can be said to have been accomplished in that year. 'From January 1st, 1834 (the Zollverein) included about 23.6 million consumers and stretched from the French frontiers to towns that are now in the Soviet Union and from the mouths of the Elbe and the Oder to the Alps.'[61] Its establishment was accompanied by important innovations in railway construction which made for greater market accessibility. The extension of the domestic market was also as important as foreign trade in the period 1834–40—but with accelerated industrialization export growth rates tended to decline. Significant increase in export was achieved only after 1863, almost thirty years after the effective consolidation of the Zollverein and after about twenty-five years of rapid industrial development.

Initially, mining and metallurgy were the leading industrial sectors and 'growth pace setters'. Textiles were of much less significance to Germany than to Britain or France. Prior to the mechanization of the textile industry in the second half of the nineteenth century, it was dominated by the linen industry[62] which had an organizational structure that retarded the incorporation of technical change. Export demand was an insignificant source of growth for the German linen industry.

In contrast, the woollen industry, stimulated by extension of the Zollverein, was export oriented. In the 1830s German woollen exports captured important segments of the American market. In the 1850s Eastern Europe became another important outlet. Mechanization began early in the 1820s, and by the middle 1840s, large-scale production enterprises were common. Indeed some sections of the woollen industry—for example the worsted industry—had no tradition of small-scale production in Germany.

The metallurgical industries experienced substantial technological change in the late 1840s. Until then the iron industry had remained very backward and outmoded. Over the period 1840–70 it expanded rapidly and became the most dynamic sector in the German economy. The extraordinary growth of the iron industry was due to the sudden increase in demand for railway construction and the stimulus this provided for exploration.

Initially, the iron industry was mainly local and Germany had to import rail from Britain to undertake the first phase of railway construction. By 1870 the country was capable of meeting almost all its domestic requirements in this area. This was largely due to the switch from charcoal to coke smelting technique in the 1850s which permitted Germany to increase domestic production dramatically and reduce import requirements for iron products. Coke smelting techniques were developed by enterprises destined to become leading German metallurgical manufacturers. These techniques were obtained from England and Wales and the entrepreneurs and workers who initially employed them in Germany were frequently British and Belgian. The availability of easy marketing opportunities facilitated the development of the new technology in the German steel industry. The very rapid growth of the metallurgical and associated engineering industries meant that by the 1870s Germany was becoming increasingly dependent on imports of iron ore.

Such a rapid sophistication of steel and engineering production between 1820 and 1870—from nuts and bolts to locomotives and steamships—would not have been accomplished without profound organizational developments. 'The remarkable changes in the methods of company foundation and in the methods of manipulating capital . . . altered almost beyond recognition the framework in which production had previously taken place.'[63] The transition from the older production structure—centred on the self-employed, part-time craftsman—to the modern factory oriented system was extraordinarily swift in both the textile and metallurgical industries. In the older production ventures, even when common access to a production technique was necessary, the individualized character of the production process was not lost.[64] In mining and steel making enterprises there was collective ownership by the workers themselves who worked the mines for different groups of miners at different times. The capital employed was limited by the miners' income and the enterprise was clearly not geared towards capital accumulation and expansion. Up to 1840 the State vested ultimate management responsibility in the person of a 'mining captain' for each enterprise. This individual, though a state employee, was also accountable to the miners themselves.

The State played an important role in the transition from craft and guild controlled industrial enterprises to modern joint stock ventures. From 1811 onwards, state restrictions on entry into various industries were progressively removed in Prussia and Bavaria. The artisans and master craftsmen felt threatened by the new organizational forms and the high level of competition. They resisted liberalization of state restrictions and were sometimes successful in reversing state policy.[65] In the period 1815–36 there was a fierce struggle between the guilds and the artisans on the one hand and the newly emerging large-scale firms and the liberalizing reformers on the other. The latter group made only limited progress, for the guilds had considerable political power and, unlike their French and Belgian counterparts, they had not been weakened in the last quarter of the nineteenth century. From 1848, however, liberalization proceeded rapidly. This appears surprising for the 1848 revolutions were largely made by the artisans and the peasants who demanded the abolition of feudalism and the state regulation of industry. Many German Governments were responsive to these demands—thus the Bavarian Law of 1853 was more restrictive than that of 1834. However, industries outside the control of the guilds—particularly engineering—grew at a very rapid rate during the two decades following 1848. It was this unprecedented expansion which induced the German States to liberalize Commercial Laws—Nassau in 1860, Wuttenberg in 1862, Saxony in 1861 and Prussia in 1868.

State ownership of industry had been a feature of German economic life since the eighteenth century. The State owned coal mines and blast furnaces in Prussia, smelting works and gun foundries in Silesia, iron ore mines and foundries in Bavaria, metallurgical works in Wuttenberg and blast furnaces in Hanover. Many State officials are included in the lists of German founders of large industrial enterprises. In the early nineteenth century the State was also an important source of capital for industrial entrepreneurs in the wool and engineering industries. German state industrial policy in the early nineteenth century has been aptly described as 'mercantilist policy (but) changed from the rather unsophisticated policy of direct subsidization of desirable manufactures to a policy of where the Government's role was seen as providing the necessary basis for development, the social overhead

Strategies for Industrialization in Advanced Countries

capital, as providing the right atmosphere and, then, as withdrawing from the arena.'[66] Although such a 'retreat' did take place in some areas, the State retained effective control in others such as the coal and ore fields and the railways until well into the 1860s.

State support of private enterprise necessitated the institutionalization of joint ventures. These were particularly conspicuous in the field of banking. The newly established German banks played an important role in the financing of industry. These banks issued secured mortgages to landowners who thus had funds for direct investment in industrial enterprises. The typical German firm was a relatively large enterprise dependent on loan capital. This was particularly true of metallurgical industries. (Textile industries on the other hand were mainly self financing.) After 1850 a network of large joint stock banks became directly interested in railway construction and metal industries. During the period 1850–70 important foreign investments were also made in German industry. Very often this foreign capital was channelled through German banks and a variety of forms of collaboration between domestic and foreign capital sprang up.

It has sometimes been argued that Germany's rapid industrial expansion in this period was caused by the development of new banking institutions. Certainly the relationship between the development of commercial and industrial organizations was close. The German banks had limited liability and a large proportion of their profits originated in industry. They responded to the accelerated demand for industrial capital very successfully and they quickly integrated themselves into a nationwide financial system assisted by the policy of economic unification that was being pursued by the German States. Close links were formed between the banks and individual industries. The mode of establishment of enterprises known as 'company foundation'—whereby a bank put capital into an industrial enterprise and then sold the shares of the enterprise to the public—became legal in Germany in the 1850s. It became common for German bankers to sit on boards of directors of industrial firms. The links between finance and industry were thus very strong.

The marriage of industrial and commercial interests was fostered by state policy. The State frequently had a share in both types of

The International Economy and Industrial Development

enterprises and its attitude was crucial. The country's 'reformed' mercantilism of the nineteenth century found expression in policies that nurtured domestic industries through harmonization of tax structures, unification of tariff systems and progressive dismantling of internal barriers of trade. The external tariffs levied on most imports were modest and in the case of many manufacturers became unnecessary in the 1870s. Indeed the Zollverein rapidly permitted Germany to overcome the disadvantage of being denied access to colonial markets by allowing the development of a powerful Central European market. By the mid-1870s German exports, led by manufactures, were about 10 per cent higher than France. By 1913 Germany had overtaken Britain as a manufacturing producer.[67] At that time Germany had acquired colonial possessions of her own and commercial links had been established with China and East Africa. Much of this colonial expansion was rendered necessary by the need to secure raw materials. German industry was more dependent in the 1870s on the home market than either the British or the French. The ability of the domestic economy to sustain rapid industrialization was being fully stretched. Supply scarcities were an important factor leading to the crisis of 1873. It was to relieve these crises that Germany sought to expand her economic links with the less developed nations of Europe and Africa.

In the early stages of German industrialization the liberalization of trade between what were then separate state entities did play an important part. This liberalization was a consequence of a political movement which sought Germanic unity and the creation of a strong Central European State. Hence trade liberalization within the Zollverein implied a change in the relationship of Zollverein members and third countries. In general, however, trade discrimination against these outside nations was modest. The inflow of foreign capital and foreign technology was encouraged and they played an important part in accelerating the pace of German industrialization. The emphasis upon the overcoming of political obstacles to integration ensured that the role of state authorities and state institutions became crucial in the field of industrial development. The German State of the nineteenth century was not like the 'nightwatchman state' that presided over the process of British industrialization a century ago. It was an interventionist State which was expected to create industrialization potential within the economy. The 'reformed' mercantilism of List and of some members of the Historical School sought to provide a theoretical basis for a revision of the role of state policy as an instrument of national economic organization. Although there was considerable resistance to these ideas in the 1840s and 1850s,[68] the unprecedented expansion of heavy industries in the third quarter of the nineteenth century paved the way for the acceptance of the teachings of List. Germany's industrial development thus provides us with an example of state sustained industrialization where the inititative for expansion remained in the hands of a national bourgeoisie. This bourgeoisie made effective use of the external sector as a source of capital and technology. But it was possible for it to do so precisely because national political integration had strengthened its hand vis-à-vis its foreign trading and investment partners.

1.3 The great industrialization debate and Soviet industrial development

The 1920s were a period of great economic controversy within the USSR. Lenin's New Economic Policy (NEP), adopted in 1921, had created the possibility of achieving industrial growth through a strategy that permitted what was described as 'the small commodity producing sector', covering the bulk of peasant households, to remain predominant within the Soviet economy. Emphasis was placed on the development of trade between town and country. In 1922 the Government renounced its monopoly on grain and introduced free trade on all agricultural products.[69] The principal purpose of the NEP was to consolidate the economic and political alliance between the peasants and the ruling Bolshevik party. This required that Soviet industry should be capable of producing light manufactured goods which could be purchased by the peasants. Private capital was allowed to play an important part in the reorganization of inter-sectoral trade and in the production of light consumer goods in the early 1920s.

This growth of the private sector alarmed sections within the Bolshevik party. Lenin himself described the NEP as a 'retreat' in 1922 and argued that 'On behalf of the party we must now call a

The International Economy and Industrial Development

halt.'[70] It was argued that the NEP had rendered industrial development seriously dependent on the position of peasant agriculture. By 1925 when 'building Socialism in one country' and 'catching up with the most advanced capitalist countries' had become important goals of Soviet state policy, the institutional framework created by the NEP was seen by many economists as clearly unsuitable for sustaining rapid industrialization. It was argued in particular that all 'pre capitalist and capitalist modes of production' in agriculture and small industry must be liquidated. The systematic elimination of market relationships within the economy was necessary for it was assumed that the free market relationship even in secondary sectors must sustain forces hostile to the Bolshevik regime.

Preobrazhenskii was the leading theorist of the school which argued for accelerated industrialization in the 1920s. He constructed a six sector model[71] on the basis of Marx's scheme of expanded reproduction. In this model the state sector producing capital goods is regarded as being of crucial importance in determining the overall pace of economic growth. Preobrazhenskii shows that higher capital accumulation in this sector requires an increase in the extraction of surplus from peasant agriculture—this he terms 'primitive socialist accumulation'. This argument was in principal accepted by the Left Opposition within the Bolshevik party[72] which called for the establishment of 'the dictatorship of industry' within the Soviet economy. The Left Opposition argued that state support of the industrial sector should be considerably extended. Favourable inter-sectoral terms of trade should be maintained and retooling should be encouraged. This retooling required a massive increase in investment within the capital goods sector of state industry. In Preobrazhenskii's view a high rate of capital accumulation should be accompanied by a high level of concentration of investment. He advocated the introduction of capital-intensive methods of production and believed that large-scale production was more efficient. It is only after the producer goods sector had become fully modernized that a radical transformation of agriculture and of small-scale industry could be attempted. Preobrazhenskii classified the historical epoch during which the productivity of Soviet industry would lag behind that of

Strategies for Industrialization in Advanced Countries

the most developed capitalist economy (i.e. the United States during the 1920s) as 'the infant stage of development of Soviet industry'. Throughout this period—which Preobrazhenskii saw as being a long one—maximum protection must be provided to industry and socialist accumulation must depend on a large diversion of savings (surplus) from agriculture to industry. Preobrazhenskii believed that the expansion of the capital goods sector was not constrained by demand. The state sector had the ability to effectively deploy the output of the capital goods industries and peasant demand was of secondary importance in determining industrial growth. Furthermore, Preobrazhenskii believed that potential savings substantially exceeded actual (i.e. realized) surplus of the agricultural sector. Finally, Preobrazhenskii's proposed strategy reflected a disillusionment with the international trade mechanism as a mobilizer of surplus for investment within the Soviet economy. It was regarded as unwise to rely on a policy of exporting agricultural products and importing capital equipment; for exposing the Soviet economic system to international market pressures would inevitably endanger the Communist regime. For these reasons Preobrazhneskii and the Left Opposition insisted that top priority be given to the task of achieving rapid industrial development through the mobilization of domestic resources.[73]

Preobrazhenskii's views were strongly contested by Bukharin, Shanin and a host of other Soviet authors. These economists stressed the importance of sustaining high levels of agricultural output and peasant demand for consumer goods produced in the industrial sector. They argued that priority ought to be given to strengthening the 'worker-peasant' alliance that had carefully been constructed during the days of the NEP. This required that primary emphasis be placed on the development of agriculture and of the light manufacturing industrial branches which could provide consumer goods for the peasants. In the early 1920s Shanin argued for the postponement of heavy industrial investment. He asserted that, due to the relatively low capital output ratio obtained in the agricultural sector, investment in this sector was likely to be more productive than investment in capital goods industries. Shanin advocated a strong stimulation of foreign trade. This would lead to a stocking of manufactured goods which would relieve the 'goods

The International Economy and Industrial Development

famine' the USSR was experiencing in the wake of the 'Scissors Crisis' of 1923. In Shanin's view the USSR should industrialize by first developing agriculture and the expansion of agricultural based manufactured exports. This would open the way to import substitution in the light consumer goods industry, and the eventual expansion of the capital goods industry should be in response to the growth in demand by agriculture and the consumer goods industries for investment goods. Shanin and Bukharin both envisaged a concern for the adequacy of effective demand as an important factor sustaining Soviet industrialization.[74]

Up to 1925 when the Fifteenth Party Conference was convened, Bukharin's reformulation of Shanin's thesis received official support.[75] Subsequently these views fell into disfavour. The extreme isolation of the USSR from the international economy, the need for militarily surpassing the advanced capitalist states and the growing reluctance of the peasants to market larger and larger amounts of grain, convinced Stalin that reliance on the rapid development of heavy industry was his only option if the aim of 'building socialism in one country' was to be pursued. He ruthlessly purged the Right Opposition (Bukharin was 'liquidated' in the early 1930s[76]), and declared in 1928, 'We will now proceed from the premise that a fast rate of development of the means of production is the key to the industrialization of the country . . . what does a fast rate of development of industry involve? It involves the maximum capital investment in industry.'[77]

In 1928 the USSR adopted the First Five Year Plan. Its principal aims were

> firstly to build a modern highly developed industry and thus make it possible to lay the foundations for the economic independence of the USSR and strengthen its defence capacity; secondly to make a big step towards radically reorganizing the small individual peasant economy into a large scale collective economy . . . and thirdly to oust capitalist elements from all branches of the economy.[78]

An investment programme of 64,600 million roubles, more than twice the level of public investment over the period 1923/24–1927/28, was approved. About 78 per cent of total industrial investment was allocated to the capital goods sector which was expected to grow

Strategies for Industrialization in Advanced Countries

at an annual rate of about 47 per cent. According to official Soviet estimates, investment and output targets were generally met during the First Five Year Plan. Output of the producer goods sector grew at a rate of 28 per cent per annum. Industry's share in gross output increased from 48 per cent in 1928 to 70 per cent in 1932. There was a substantial increase in the concentration of production. The industrial units established during this period were by far the largest in terms of capital employed, volume of output and number of workers. By 1933 the Central Committee of the CPSU was already claiming that 'the USSR can now produce the greater part of the necessary equipment at its own enterprises.'[79] The Plan concentrated on the development of certain key industrial branches—steel, machine tools, electricity and transport equipment. The light consumer goods industries lagged behind. The textile industry did not fulfil its plan targets. Food manufacturing also faced problems of raw material shortages and grew relatively slowly. The industrial branches related to the agricultural sector experienced serious difficulties in obtaining industrial raw materials and supplies.

It was realized in 1928 that this programme of accelerated industrialization depended crucially upon the ability of the agricultural sector to generate a large surplus and to countenance the diversion of this surplus to capital goods industry. During 1923–24—in the days of the 'Scissors Crisis' which had sparked off the 'Great Industrialization Debate'—peasants and kulaks had reacted vigorously to a decline in agriculture's inter-sectoral terms of trade. The level of grain marketed during these years fell substantially.[80] It was felt that a tight control of agricultural and industrial prices during the period of the First Five Year Plan would not itself be sufficient to sustain a high rate of surplus extraction from the rural sector. This required significant acceleration and extension of the 'collectivization' movement within agriculture. The rapid development of 'collectives' enabled the State to directly determine the mixture of crops produced, the portion of production that was marketed and the level of agricultural prices. The First Five Year Plan aimed at achieving collectivization in 20 per cent of the total sown area of the USSR. By 1930 the Central committee of the Bolshevik Party was already predicting that 'we shall be able to collectivize the bulk of the peasant households.'[81] By 1933 it was claimed that over the period 1928–32 the proportion of 'collectivized peasant households to total peasant households increased from 0.8 per cent to 61.5 per cent.'[82] Collectivization was pushed through brutally. In some parts there was fierce resistance, and it has been estimated that more than 3 million people perished as a consequence of these struggles.[83] Today the Bolshevik Party itself admits that serious mistakes were made during this period and argues that these excesses were mainly responsible for stagnant output level and declining livestock population. It is argued, however, that 'in agriculture during the first five year plan period prerequisites were created for its subsequent development through the radical reorganization of the entire socio-economic pattern of the countryside.'[84] The performance of the agricultural sector did improve gradually during the Second Five Year Plan.

Resources extracted from agriculture and surpluses generated within large-scale production were the main sources of industrial investment in the early years of Soviet industrialization. The external sector was of relatively minor significance. In Tsarist times foreign investment had been an important source of industrial investment. Foreign trade with West European countries was also flourishing. Russia had also made some headway in exporting manufactures.[85] The Bolshevik revolution and the civil war—during which the Allies actively supported the Whiteguards—disrupted these foreign trade and investment links, whereas foreign investment remained virtually frozen. Throughout the interwar years trade levels fluctuated. At the beginning of the NEP period trade agreements were signed with Austria, Czechoslovakia, Germany, Great Britain, Italy, Norway and Sweden.[86] Foreign trade was a government monopoly from the earliest days of the revolution. Lenin had written, 'Trade is the link in the historical chain of events in the transitional forms of our socialist construction which we the proletarian government must grasp with all our might.'[87] Throughout the NEP period emphasis was placed on the conclusion of bilateral trade agreements. By 1925 such agreements had been reached with almost all European countries. An explicit aim of foreign trade policy was to 'protect the rising socialist economy against the economic offensive of the captialist powers.'[88] It is, therefore, not surprising that despite the many bilateral agreements

Strategies for Industrialization in Advanced Countries

trade levels increased only moderately. In 1925–26 total external trade (exports plus imports) amounted to less than 1 billion roubles; in 1913 the external trade volume had been three times greater than this.[89] These trends persisted during the years 1928–32. Soviet exports consisted mainly of farm products such as grain and butter. Exports of manganese ore, timber and pelts were also important as earners of foreign exchange. The main imports were machines, lathes, capital equipment and industrial raw materials. There was a strong emphasis on the acquisition and transfer of advanced production technology. Capital goods accounted for 93 per cent of the total import bill in 1931. The USSR's main trading partners during this period were Germany, Great Britain, Italy and the United States.[90] The industrialization strategy made it impossible to envisage penetration of manufactures in exports markets. Foreign trade was a mechanism for procuring the advanced technology that could not locally be produced. No attempt was made to relocate industrial investment in order to explore possibilities from changing comparative advantages in international markets.

The Soviet industrialization strategy may therefore be summarized as follows:

1. The State under the leadership of the Communist Party was the main agent of industrial resource mobilization. The private sector was seen as a dangerous rival of the Communist Party. It was ousted from both industry and agriculture. By 1932 the share of the private sector in Soviet industry had dropped to 0.5 per cent[91] and by that year 84 per cent of state procurements of grain came from collective and state farms.[92]
2. Emphasis was placed on the rapid expansion of the capital goods sector. A small set of key industrial branches developed very rapidly. The light manufacturing sector failed to keep pace and a productivity gap emerged between these industries and the producer goods sector. The expansion of this sector was sustained not by the growth of the consumer goods industries, but by the State itself. The resources for investment in this sector were extracted primarily from agriculture and were also obtained from the surpluses generated within the producer goods sector.

The International Economy and Industrial Development

3. The external sector was not an important source of direct industrial investment. Trade, which revived moderately after the civil war, contributed towards industrial development by enabling the Soviet authorities to import advanced technological equipment. Soviet industrialization remained geared to the expansion of domestic demand and to import substitution. Expansion of manufacturing exports was not attempted and Soviet exports were either farm products or mineral raw materials.

4. The costs of such a strategy have been high. We have already noted that the forced collectivization movement of the early 1930s caused immense human suffering. Moreover the industrial structure that was built remains an extraordinarily inefficient one. This is in part due to the autarchic economic policies of the Soviet regime. Soviet industrial enterprises have simply not been adequately exposed to the ruthless competitive pressures of international product markets. The planning mechanisms and procedures of the 1930s attached little importance to the achievement of high levels of industrial efficiency. The overriding concern was the achievement of the fastest possible expansion in the key industrial sectors—steel, coal, machinery, electricity. These procedures have contributed towards a growth of inflexibility within the Soviet industrial system. Industrial inefficiency has persisted and it has proved extremely difficult to alter significantly planning priorities.

1.4 *The lessons of history*

The British, German and Soviet industrialization strategies provide contrasting models of industrial development for the countries of the Third World. In Britain, a 'nightwatchman' state facilitated industrial transformation by permitting a domestic bourgeoisie to seize the economic opportunities provided by a successful colonialist policy. It was recognized that expanded international trade could play a crucial role in allowing Britain to restructure her industry in accordance with her changing international comparative advantages. Thus, the British example established the classical pattern of industrial expansion: specialization initially in light manufactured

Strategies for Industrialization in Advanced Countries

goods, then in intermediates and finally in heavy capital equipment. This 'classical' pattern evolved in Britain not in response to State initiatives but as a consequence of changing international opportunities. The State's level of direct intervention in international markets declined throughout the period of the post-Napoleonic Pax Britannica.

In Germany, on the other hand, national political forces were important in initiating and sustaining the industrialization process. Political cohesion was an essential pre-requisite of economic recovery and industrial growth. The movement for political unification had an impact upon the economy. National political forces encouraged economic integration, stimulated trade and investment and provided support for domestic businessmen and industrialists. The role of the State was particularly vital in the heavier industries. These industries developed behind protectionist barriers and contained significant proportions of public investment. Moreover, the State played a crucial role in bulding an institutional network which consciously sought to relate financial and industrial developments. As time passed, German industry became competitive in a wide range of international markets. Protectionism became unnecessary and pressure built up for the adoption of more liberal trade policies.

In the case of the Soviet Union concern with international competitiveness was not an important issue. The Bolshevik regime was committed to rapid industrial transformation. During the days of the 'Great Industrialization Debate' the economists of the Right within the Bolshevik Party argued that industrial development required the encouragement of private initiative, the consolidation of the 'worker-peasant' alliance which had sustained the NEP and increasing involvement in international trade. Such a strategy was seen as politically dangerous by the dominant faction, the Centre, within the Communist Party. It was felt that the private sector, particularly within agriculture, was a political rival and, in alliance with external forces, could destroy the Soviet revolution. The regime, therefore, opted for an autarchic industrialization strategy which maximized the exploitation of agriculture and concentrated investment in the industrial branches whose expansion served best the purpose of 'surpassing the most advanced capitalist states' and 'building socialism in one country'.

The Third World's quest for industrialization in the modern world must be based on appreciation of the historical experiences of the industrialized countries as well as on existing opportunities. The preference for the British, German or Soviet 'model' within the Third World is determined jointly by the balance of political forces on these countries and the material conditions—the mode of production—that circumscribe their ability to achieve economic objectives. In our analysis of the role of the external sector in the industrialization process in less developed countries (LDCs), we analyse the constant interplay of these two sets of forces. Our analysis is concerned with changes in the material conditions that influence the international distribution of industrial production, investment and trade and the identification of the political forces that, in given circumstances, facilitate or retard international industrial restructuring in accordance with changing material conditions.

This chapter has outlined three different foreign trade and investment strategies adopted by political élites to restructure their national economies in response to changing material conditions. It suggests that large and/or potentially resource-rich countries such as Brazil, China, India and Indonesia have a wider range of policy choices than small and/or modestly endowed countries such as Ghana, Singapore and Taiwan. The former groups can, if they so desire, choose to ignore internal opportunities and achieve industrialization through the pursuit of autarchic—import substituting—policies. This choice is simply not available to the smaller, poorer countries. Isolation from international trade and international investment has made industrial restructuring impossible for Burma, Kampuchea and Laos. Such isolation is not, however, an 'irrational choice' on the part of the policy makers of these countries. It has proved to be a crucial factor in sustaining the dominance of the existing political élite within these countries.

The majority of Third World countries have attempted to achieve industrial growth and restructuring. In Chapter II we analyse the policies pursued by Third World governments to achieve these aims and attempt to identify the forces that sustain these policies.

Industrial restructuring may be conceived of as a process whereby the rate of growth of different industrial branches differs systematically in such a way that the production structure undergoes significant modifications. Britain, a predominantly agrarian economy in the late eighteenth century, became an industrial country specializing in the production of light consumer goods by 1830. By 1870 it was a large-scale producer of heavy capital equipment. Structural change within the USSR involved a direct transition from an agrarian to a heavy capital goods producing economy.

Changes in the output mix of an economy reflect changes in its modes of production. For example, peasant farming was replaced by the 'putter out' system initially, and the factory eclipsed 'cottage industries' as the industrial sector matured. In the 'de-industrializing' societies of the West, the office is fast replacing the factory as the main unit of production organization. This change in the organization of production serves as a mechanism for the emergence of new social and economic forces which acquire greater influence over national policy making.

Finally, changes in the structure of production have an impact on the international position of the industrializing economy. Some countries—such as Britain in the nineteenth century and Germany in the twentieth—gear their industrialization strategies to changing opportunities in international markets. In such cases, industrial restructuring may become a direct consequence of changing comparative advantages. An export promotion strategy suggests that LDCs will gain if international industrial restructuring takes place in accordance with changes in comparative advantages. Such restructuring is, however, likely to be resisted by economic and political forces operating in the 'threatened' industries. These forces have in recent years been conspicuously successful in promoting 'neo-protectionist' tendencies within the West. The consequences and the potential of the neo-protectionist movement are assessed in Chapter II.

Notes

[1] M. Dobb, *Theories of Value and Distribution since Adam Smith*, Cambridge University Press, London, 1975, p. 4.
[2] According to Dobb, this view had already been developed by Smith prior to his tour of France and Switzerland in 1764–66. Dobb; *op. cit.*, pp. 41–2.

The International Economy and Industrial Development

[3] A. Smith, *An Enquiry Into the Nature and Causes of the Wealth of Nations*, Methuen (complete in one volume), London, 1826, p. 411.
[4] For a discussion of these policies, see J. Schumpeter, *A History of Economic Analysis*, Allen and Unwin, London, 1967, p. 338–62.
[5] T. Nairn, 'The twilight of the British state', *New Left Review*, 101–2, February–April 1977, p. 14.
[6] K. Marx, *Capital Vol. I*, Pelican, Harmondsworth, 1971, p. 918.
[7] Smith, *op. cit.*, p. 432.
[8] E. Williams, *Capitalism and Slavery*, Capricorn, New York 1966, pp. 51–2, 102–3.
[9] These were trading companies with large investments in West Indian trade.
[10] *Cambridge Economic History of Europe*, Vol. IV, Cambridge University Press, London, 1967, p. 51.
[11] Quoted in A. G. Frank, *Dependent Accumulation*, Vol. 1, Macmillan, London, 1979, p. 47.
[12] *Cambridge Economic History*, *op. cit.*, Vol. IV, Part 1, pp. 287–8.
[13] E. J. Hobsbawn, *The Age of Revolution 1789–1848*, Mentor, New York, 1964, p. 52.
[14] Frank, *op. cit.*, p. 74.
[15] W. Schlote, *British Overseas Trade from 1700 to the 1930s*, Oxford University Press, Oxford, 1952, pp. 42–3.
[16] Schumpeter, *op. cit.*, p. 150.
[17] *Ibid*.
[18] Adam Smith, *op. cit.*, p. 246.
[19] Expressed more vehemently in *ibid.*, p. 436–7.
[20] Dobb, *op cit.*, p. 55.
[21] It should be remembered that in the eighteenth century more than 70 per cent of British foreign exports went to the Third World. See Frank, *op. cit.*, p. 74.
[22] These include free competition, a two-country, two commodity model of analysis, constant labour costs and implications of adherence to his formulation of the labour theory of value. Moreover, Ricardo's formulation is ambiguous about the distribution of the gains from trade between England and Portugal. In his example, the commodities exchange after trade in a ratio half way between their domestic comparative cost ratios in the two countries, but he does not indicate how the international price ratio is to be derived from his model. These assumptions have been modified by a host of neo-Ricardian and neo-Classical authors. J. Viner, *Studies in the Theory of International Trade*, Allen and Unwin, London, 1960, p. 444.
[23] Frank, *op. cit.*, pp. 94–5.
[24] The famous example by D. Ricardo, *Principles of Political Economy and Taxation*, Penguin, 1971, pp. 153–60.
[25] F. List, *National Systems of Political Economy*, Lippincott, Philadelphia, 1856, pp. 113–17.
[26] This was agreed in the Treaty of London signed in 1654.
[27] Marquis de Pombal, Prime Minister of Portugal, remarks quoted in Manchester, U.K. *British Preeminence in Brazil, its Rise and Fall*, North Carolina U.P., Chapel Hill, 1933, p. 39.
[28] Quoted in S. Sideri, *Trade and Power: Informal Colonization in Anglo French*

Strategies for Industrialization in Advanced Countries

Relations, Rotterdam University Press, Rotterdam, 1970, p. 5.
[29] *Ibid.*, p. 13.
[30] Viner, *op. cit.*, p. 448.
[31] Dobb, *op. cit.*, pp. 67–8.
[32] Saraffa, *Works and Correspondence of David Ricardo*, Vol. I, Cambridge University Press, London, 1966, p. 343.
[33] See, in particular, D. Winch, *Classical Political Economy and the Colonies*, Bell, London, 1965, pp. 39–51 and 74–7. One is under the impression that Ricardo's analysis of colonial questions is entirely from the perspective of the mother country.
[34] Quoted in Dobb, *op. cit.*, p. 90.
[35] P. Saraffa, *op. cit.*, Vol. VIII, p. 208.
[36] D. Winch, *The Emergency of Economics as a Science, 1750–1870*, Fontana, London, 1971, p. 26.
[37] *Ibid.*, p. 28.
[38] *Ibid.*
[39] On Smith's study of manufacturing productivity, see M. Dobb, *op. cit.*, pp. 38–64.
[40] D. Winch, *op. cit.*, p. 38.
[41] J. Schumpeter, *op. cit.*, 504–5.
[42] Severely criticized by Knies quoted in Schumpeter, *op. cit.*, p. 442.
[43] *Ibid.*
[44] As formulated in the famous Report on Manufacture, first published in 1791.
[45] Schumpeter, *op. cit.*, p. 505.
[46] During the seventeenth and eighteenth centuries.
[47] F. List, *National System of Political Economy*, Lippincott and Co., Philadelphia, 1856, pp. 117–18 (emphasis in original).
[48] List, *op. cit.*, pp. 79, 69.
[49] List quoted in Frank, *op. cit.*, p. 97.
[50] That is, the 'national principle' on the basis of which trade and commerce should be organized within the German union.
[51] I. Bog. 'Mercantilism in Germany', in D. C. Coleman, (ed.), *Revisions in Mercantilism*, Methuen, London, 1969, Chapter 7, pp. 162–89.
[52] 'Child and Man' had been much more concerned with balance of trade propositions.
[53] I. Bog, *op. cit.*, p. 169.
[54] J. C. van Dillen quoted in I. Bog, *op. cit.*, p. 169.
[55] *Ibid.*, p. 170.
[56] C. Wilson, 'Mercantilism: some vicissitudes of an idea', *Economic History Review*, 1957, pp. 74–86.
[57] A. Milward and S. Saul, *The Economic Development of Continental Europe 1780–1870*, Allen and Unwin, London 1973, p. 366.
[58] *Ibid.*, p. 367.
[59] Signed in 1648.
[60] That is, from the defeat of Napoleon Bonaparte to the defeat of Louis Napoleon III.
[61] Milward and Saul, *op. cit.*, p. 376.
[62] Which, according to Dieterice, accounted for about 30 per cent of non-agricultural

The International Economy and Industrial Development

output in Prussia in 1835. Quoted in Milward and Saul, *op. cit.*, p. 391.
[63] *Ibid.*, p. 411.
[64] T. C. Banfield, *Industry of the Rhine*, Series 2, Methuen, London, 1848, pp. 98–9.
[65] Thus, in 1834, Bavaria tightened restrictions on entry in a number of relatively small-scale artisan dominated industries.
[66] Milward and Saul, *op. cit.*, p. 417.
[67] *Ibid.*, pp.60–1.
[68] See above.
[69] *Resolutions and Decisions of the CPSU Congresses*, Part 1, Progress Publishers, Moscow, 1954, p. 563.
[70] V. I. Lenin, *Collected Works*, Vol. 33, Progress Publishers, Moscow, 1951, p. 280.
[71] Described in N. Spulber, *Soviet Strategy for Economic Growth*, Indiana University Press, Bloomington, 1964, pp. 44–6.
[72] Headed by Leon Trotsky.
[73] This is a summary of the arguments presented in E. Preobrazhenskii, *The New Economics*, Clarendon Press, London, 1965, pp. 70–110.
[74] This is a summary of Skanin's position presented in D. Yaffe, *Soviet Industrialization: Planned Economic Development and the World Economy*, Institute of Development Studies, University of Sussex, Brighton, 1972, (mimeo) pp. 21–4.
[75] B. N. Ponomaroyov, *et al.*, *History of the Communist Party of the Soviet Union*, Moscow Foreign Language Publishing House, 1960, p. 410.
[76] The left opposition had been eliminated in the middle 1920s. Preobrazhenskii shared Bukharin's fate a few years later.
[77] J. V. Stalin, *Collected works*, Vol. XI, Foreign Language Publishing House, Moscow, 1954, p. 256.
[78] A. Podkolzin, *A Short Economic History of the U.S.S.R.*, Progress Publishers, Moscow, 1968, p. 149.
[79] Quoted in Podkolzin, *ibid.*, p. 153.
[80] M. Lipton, *Why Poor People Stay Poor*, Temple, London, 1977, p. 130.
[81] Quoted in Podkolzin, *op. cit.*, p. 157.
[82] *Ibid.*, p. 158.
[83] M. Levin, *Russian Peasants and Soviet Power*, Allen and Unwin, London, 1968.
[84] Podkolzin, *op cit.*, p. 117.
[85] M. Dobb, *Soviet Economic Development*, Routledge and Kegan Paul, London, 1967, Chapter 2.
[86] Podkolzin, *op. cit.*, p. 117.
[87] Lenin, *Collected Works*, Vol. 33, p. 113 (emphasis in original).
[88] CPSU resolution adopted in 1923 quoted in Podkolzin, *op. cit.*, p. 134.
[89] *Ibid.*, p. 134.
[90] *Ibid.*, p. 163.
[91] *Ibid.*, p. 150.
[92] *Ibid.*, p. 160.

Chapter II

Strategies for Trade and Industrialization in the Post-war Era

This chapter begins with a review of trade strategies in the Third World. Our knowledge of these alternatives—import substitution and export promotion—is limited in comparison with what we know of the industrialized countries' approaches as discussed in Chapter I. For example, very little is actually known about the behaviour of domestic interest groups and how they have reacted to changes in the industrial structure. Following a review of these trade strategies, the discussion turns to export performance in the Third World. For an LDC, the appropriate choice of policies depends to a great degree upon the policies followed by the world's major trading nations. Thus, the trade strategies of western countries are considered in light of their consequences for industrialization in the Third World. Revisions in the West's approach to trade issues, occurring largely in response to structural changes and the spread of industrial capacity, are examined. The final section examines the recent consolidation of neo-protectionist forces in the West with a view to the international consequences of this development.

2.1 *Import substitution in the Third World*

International circumstances prevailing in the period 1913–50 are the most commonly cited explanation for the emergence of import substitution as an industrial strategy in the LDCs.[1] The legacy of two world wars and an interim depression led to a break in the long-term relationship between industry and trade. This period was atypical from a historical standpoint. For almost any terminal dates

The International Economy and Industrial Development

within the last century and a half, the growth of world trade equalled or exceeded that of production, provided that the years of war and depression are excluded.[2] The advanced LDCs with relatively large manufacturing sectors felt the disruption in the industry-trade relationship most acutely. Manufacturing activity of the Third World was largely concentrated in these countries and they opted for a policy of import substitution, in part to offset declining trade levels.

For policy makers, one aspect of the interrelationship between industrialization and trade—the level of imports—became a focal point for their efforts to alter the industrial structure. Imports were taken as a guide in identifying those industrial activities where policy encouragement might hasten the replacement of imports by domestic production. Thus, the strategy depended heavily upon the characteristics of domestic demand rather than income redistribution, employment maximization, etc. for the selection of industries to be favoured by policy initiatives.

Although exceptions can be found, policy makers generally conceded that the import substitution process must begin with the production of consumer goods.[3] In the long term, economists thought of import substitution as a sequential process working its way from light consumer goods to heavy industry and capital goods. This line of thought was in contrast to that in some more recently industrialized countries—such as the USSR—where immediate emphasis had been placed upon heavy industry.

Conditions in the LDCs made their experiences with import substitution quite different from those of more advanced countries. First, the impetus for import substitution was spurred mainly by a reduction of previously available imports. Imports largely consisted of 'luxury' consumer goods—a consequence of the inequitable distribution of income and wealth in the Third World. In contrast, the import substitution experience of Germany, Japan or the USSR was initiated under conditions of expanding income partially derived from exports. Major consuming sectors of these economies were not cut off from supplies, either domestic or foreign. Second, the industrialized countries, even when they were predominantly producers of light consumer goods, were also producing capital goods for the same industries, if only by artisan means. Thus, they gained immediate experience in matching technology to available supplies of inputs, and in overcoming technical problems in the use of these products. The LDCs, in contrast, imported relatively complex technologies, but without the sustained experimentation in technological development and innovation that had been associated with the original emergence of these industries. There was no experience nor vested producer interest groups arguing for the protection of capital goods.

The importance of moving into the domestic production of capital goods was not lost on Latin American economists and policy makers, however. The following quote is typical of the position held by supporters of an import substitution approach:

> If, for example, substitution were confined to final consumer goods, the import schedule might be virtually limited to the imports needed to maintain current production, with no margin left for the entry of new products and in particular, of the capital goods essential for the expansion of production capacity. To prevent this happening, it is imperative to embark promptly on substitution in respect of additional categories, especially of intermediate products and capital goods, before an excessively rigid import structure jeopardizes the very continuation of the process.[4]

Thus, the sequence of import substitution pictured by economists implied the existence of a systematic body of measures to encourage the development of different types of industries in different phases of the development process. In other words, the growth process was to be spurred first by consumer goods industries, followed by an expansion of the production of supplies and intermediates and, later, capital goods. The relative protection accorded each category should have changed accordingly, favouring first one set of industries and then another. With few exceptions, this pattern of tariff setting failed to materialize.

In practice, once LDCs imposed tariffs, their levels were not later reduced. The protection of consumer goods eventually became a permanent feature of industrial policy. The approach ran counter to the original concept of a sequential process moving from consumer goods into intermediates and then capital goods. Although the application of protective measures was broadened to include industries other than consumer goods, this amounted to reducing—not eliminating—the privileged position enjoyed by the producers of consumer goods relative to other manufacturers. The absolute level of tariffs accorded to consumer goods remained higher than those accorded to other groups of producers.

In retrospect, this approach to tariff setting altered the pattern of economic activity and domestic resource allocation in two ways. First, it prompted a movement of resources out of agriculture and mining into the import-competing manufactures. This shift resulted in a 'home market' bias due to its discrimination against exporters.[5] Eventually, much of the manufacturing sector received some degree of protection, the main effect of which was to raise domestic prices of manufactured products. Furthermore, when policy makers discriminated in favour of one industry or sector they necessarily discriminated against some other activity. Most of those LDCs that vigorously pursued an import substitution strategy had a large agricultural sector which was the main loser. Where the manufacturing sector was relatively small compared to the agricultural sector, the cost of protection could be spread over a large number of farmers.[6] Countries like Argentina, Brazil, Egypt, India and Pakistan were most closely identified with the strategy and have a relatively large agricultural sector. Many smaller countries (e.g. Hong Kong, Israel, Singapore and Taiwan) with relatively small agricultural sectors quickly abandoned their import substitution strategies. The structure of the economy—perhaps more than the opinions of its policy makers—may be identified as an important determinant of the extent to which import substitution was actively pursued.

Second, there were parallel although less pronounced consequences for different types of industries in the manufacturing sector. The pattern of protection led to a shift of resources out of unfavoured lines of manufacturing, often potential exporters or producers of capital goods and industrial intermediates. Thus, import substitution exhibited a 'consumer goods' bias similar to its home market bias.

Given the high levels of protection accorded to consumer goods, the impact on investment, pricing policies and firm behaviour was substantial. Clearly, it was well worth the industrialist's effort to go to any length in the way of lobbying, bribery or political protection in order to achieve such levels of protection. The main beneficiaries were industries hampered by high operating costs due to small-scale production methods imposed by limited domestic markets, the use of inferior technology and organization or the simple failure to minimize costs given the available technology. Protectionism often led to very high profits (and possibly overinvestment) and an inefficient use of resources.[7]

At least two troublesome consequences may be directly attributed to the prevailing pattern of effective protection in LDCs. First, the production of manufactures for export was considerably discouraged. The economic rent accruing to domestic producers who sold in protected home markets was substantially greater than the returns from exports which could only be sold at internationally competitive prices. Thus, the earnings-to-cost ratio associated with import substitution[8] was often much larger than that from exporting, and firms behaved accordingly. Second, the high rates of protection recorded in LDCs led to unexpected (but rational) forms of behaviour on the part of industrialists which did not coincide with the intended objectives of an import substitution strategy. Industrialists who benefited from highly profitable operations in protected markets were reluctant to encourage an expansion of the domestic production of supplies, equipment and other inputs since they feared that this might lead to the emergence of new competitors.[9] Their ability to maximize profits also depended upon the existence of a large difference in the effective rate of protection for their own products and those levied on their industrial inputs. Thus, they had a vested interest in discouraging the establishment of industries providing inputs since these producers, in turn, might become eligible for protection at levels similar to that accorded to established firms selling the final goods.[10]

LDCs have remained heavily dependent on capital goods imports and industrial inputs. Table II.1 summarizes the results of an extensive compilation of imports by end-use. A comparison of the two years 1968 and 1974[11] is somewhat marred by the erratic jump in the share of fuels and lubricants which was largely due to price increases and not to changes in production structure or demand patterns. The corresponding shares of all other imports are lower

The International Economy and Industrial Development

Table II.1 Imports of manufactures by end-use in western countries and LDCs, 1968 and 1974 (percentages)

Country grouping (number of countries)[a]	Imports by End-use[b]			
	Capital goods	Industrial inputs	Fuels and lubricants	Consumer goods
Western countries				
1968 (14)	12.4	53.6	10.9	23.1
1974 (20)	11.6	46.8	21.8	19.8
LDCs of which:				
per capita GDP of > $900				
1968 (7)	18.1	52.6	9.8	19.5
1974 (7)	16.4	53.6	17.0	13.0
per capita GDP of $300 to $900				
1968 (7)	23.8	52.7	8.8	14.7
1974 (15)	20.0	53.7	13.4	12.8
per capita GDP of < $300				
1968 (. . .)	. . .	. . .	. . .	. . .
1974 (12)	17.2	62.5	6.9	13.4

Source: United Nations, *Commodity Trade Statistics*, Series D, various issues.
Notes: [a] LDCs were grouped according to *per capita* GDP in 1974.
[b] The definitions of imports by end-use were based on United Nations, 'External trade statistics, draft classification by broad economic categories' (E/CN.3/408).

than they otherwise would have been. The figures, nevertheless, reveal some interesting results. In each instance the LDCs' imports of consumer goods constituted a smaller share of the total than that observed in western countries. For purposes of the present discussion the most relevant sub-group of LDCs comprises those with a *per capita* GDP exceeding $900. These countries actively pursued import substitution during the 1960s and the reduction in the import share of consumer goods was substantial (19.5 per cent to 13.0 per cent).

Industrial inputs accounted for more than one half the LDCs imports of manufactures and increased over time. Although the time period may be too short to reveal the extent of structural change, this type of shift obviously does not conform with the changing import pattern originally contemplated by economists favouring import substitution. Clearly, there has been a rising dependence upon foreign suppliers as import substitution continues. The share of capital goods imported by LDCs declined modestly but remained substantially higher than the corresponding values in western countries. In summary, with the possible exception of consumer goods imports by the more advanced LDCs, there is little evidence that their import pattern changed significantly.[12] On the contrary, increased dependence on foreign suppliers occurred not only for fuels and lubricants but also for industrial inputs. The declining share of capital goods must be discounted to some extent in view of the rapid increase in the prices of fuels and lubricants.

While import substitution is currently out of favour, it is necessary to exercise some caution in writing off this strategy as a total failure. There are many conceptual problems involved in developing an overall assessment of such policies. Import substitution has sometimes been viewed as a set of policy measures resulting in the acceleration of the natural replacement process. This rather vague definition leaves open many questions that pose problems when attempting a quantitative assessment of the strategy. First, ambiguities occur when economists wish to apply some notion of optimality to the country and period in question. If policy (current or past) results in a substantial misallocation of resources, the difference between actual import substitution and import substitution with 'optimal' policies may be great. The gap may prevail in the beginning year of the exercise, the terminal year or both, and a decision is required as to which combination of actual and/or optimal substitution is to be measured. Second, questions of a statistical nature arise. If directly observable ratios of imports to total availabilities are used, the results will differ from indirect measures which compare actual growth in imports to a norm such as the growth in output with no change in the import availability ratio.[13] Finally, the direction of causation between import substitution and economic growth is not clearly discernible. Some economists have treated import substitution as a cause of growth while

The International Economy and Industrial Development

others have concluded that the import content of supplies tends to decline as industrialization progresses.[14] Thus, it is not clear whether import substitution is rightly regarded as a cause of economic growth or a consequence. It is sufficient here to simply note that the measurement of import substitution raises many difficult questions, not all of which can be answered given our present state of knowledge.

On the whole, however, there is now a general concensus that the strategy led to disappointing results. As we have seen, the highest tariffs were imposed on imports of consumer goods often produced by the 'least' essential industries. Although the relative importance of consumer goods in the LDCs' imports was reduced, imports of industrial supplies, fuels and capital goods became more important both relatively and absolutely. The perverse result was that domestic industries (including those which were heavily protected) became more dependent upon foreign suppliers. Subsequent foreign exchange crises forced the curtailment of these imports and, in turn, domestic production. Often, the dependence on foreign imports was not lessened and the strategy succeeded only in altering the type of imports in question.

The importance that we attach to the composition of imports also relates to a second explanatory aspect—the nature and pace of structural change. Generally, the sequential pattern of substitution that economists envisaged, moving from consumer goods to heavy industry and capital goods, was highly compressed. Experience suggests that broad structural changes of the type contemplated here are to be measured over a span of several decades. For example, in the period 1960–71 the share of intermediate goods in total manufacturing output rose, at most, 4–5 per cent in individual LDCs.[15] Recognizing that other growth sources (e.g. growth in domestic demand) contributed to these shifts, the contribution of import substitution could not be great.

Evidence from another source is provided in studies of structural change. Many capital goods and the principal industrial intermediates have been described as 'late industries', meaning that they are a major growth stimulus at relatively high levels of *per capita* income. On average, the share of these branches rose from 40 per cent of manufacturing vaue added (MVA) to 50 per cent as *per capita* GDP

Strategies for Trade and Industrialization in the Post-War Era

rose from $300 to $1000.[16] Although this fact says nothing about the extent of import substitution, experience suggests that the time required for a transition of this magnitude would be considerable. Many politicians (and, perhaps, other policy makers) often seemed to expect that import substitution would, within a decade or so, alleviate foreign exchange constraints and take hold in branches other than consumer goods. These aspirations may have been encouraged, in part, because the strategy was originally popularized in response to balance of payments problems that were immediate and urgent. One should also add, however, that few advocates of the strategy qualified their enthusiasm by stressing the long-term nature of such structural changes.

Finally, we have referred earlier to the role which vested producer interests exerted on policy formulations. Producers of consumer goods dominated the manufacturing sectors of LDCs engaged in import substitution. They accounted for an average of 54 per cent of MVA in a large sample of countries in the 1950s.[17] Political influence accompanied industrial prominence. Brazil provides a good case in point. Here, Bergsman observed that 'policies concerning tariffs, exemptions from tariffs for certain importers, lines of credit, etc., owed their design at least as much to the entrepreneurs who stood to gain or lose from them as to public official's view.'[18] He goes on to indicate that the practice of consultation and accommodation was widespread in both the 1950s and 1960s.

In general, industrialists who were active in policy deliberations had often been previously tied to importing interests. Subsequently, they erected plants of their own to apply the 'last touches' to imported inputs and thereby maintain levels of consumption that would otherwise have been reduced by war or balance of payments difficulties. They had little inclination to further extend the substitution phase into intermediate goods and supplies, a step which would sever their foreign contacts and accentuate domestic competition.

Once established, this industrial class realized substantial profits through their protected position and had good reasons to discourage the establishment of domestic suppliers. These included fears that the local product would be inferior, the fact that they might be restricted to only one supplier after domestic sources emerged and

The International Economy and Industrial Development

the threat of additional competition if a domestic producer of industrial inputs should decide to move into production of the final goods.

The development of import substitution industries in the LDCs did not lead to the type of industrial restructuring capable of exploiting the economic potential of these countries. A general disillusionment with this strategy became gradually evident and export promotion policies gained favour.

2.2 Export orientation in the Third World

Both national and international developments favoured a shift towards export promotion policies in the 1960s. The international spread of manufacturing capacity extended the degree of interdependence and specialization among countries. In fact, few, if any, manufactures produced in industrialized countries were not dependent in some way on foreign economies, being reliant on imported raw materials or intermediate inputs, imported capital equipment and technology, or consumers in foreign markets. The rapid expansion of international trade was, therefore, a concomitant of the spread in manufacturing capacity.

Changes in international economic policy accompanied the shifts in the pattern of industrial specialization. Progress in the liberalization of trade was substantial. Tariffs on manufactures were considerably reduced as a result of agreements reached in the Dillon and Kennedy round of tariff negotiations. Simultaneously, western firms, ranging from retail chains to transnational corporations (TNCs), became active in seeking favourable production sites abroad to take advantage of low-cost labour.[19] Their efforts were spurred by the slow growth of the labour force and rising real wages in the West as well as declining transport costs, new organizational structures and related innovations and a favourable international policy environment.

At the national level, shifts in the allocation of funds for research and development (R and D) had a dramatic impact upon the industrial structure in western countries. By the 1970s, capital goods, electrical engineering industries, chemistry and petrochemistry, aerospace and the automobile industry absorbed between

76 and 92 per cent of the R and D funds allocated to industry in France, Italy, Japan, the United Kingdom, the United States and West Germany.[20] A further example of the impact of technological change on industrial structure was the growth in the share of research-oriented activities in the total ouput of the engineering industry. In West Germany such activities accounted for 8 per cent of industrial output in 1950 and for 27 per cent in 1975. The corresponding figures for Japan were 1 and 48 and, for the United States, 22 and 50 per cent.[21] The efficiency of western countries in science-intensive industries increased greatly by comparison with their efficiency in other industrial activities.

Structural changes such as these altered some of the basic conditions faced by potential exporters in LDCs. The West's demand for light manufactures like consumer goods rose, spurred by a rapid growth in income. At the same time the resource claims of other sectors and activities such as science-intensive industries received a higher priority. Under these circumstances it is not surprising that the West's technological and innovative lead in traditional industries such as textiles, clothing, footwear, leather products, etc. was reduced while predominance in many science-intensive activities was extended. These structural changes, in conjunction with the adjustments in international policy, made the shift to export promotion a more feasible alternative in the 1960s.

Structural changes within LDCs also provided a major impetus for the transition to export promotion. The growth of commercial and industrial experience, managerial know-how, a skilled labour force and the acquisition of transport and communication facilities in a limited number of LDCs meant that exporting became a feasible alternative. As Maizels has argued, 'the product of home manufacturing industry tends to spill over into the export market.'[22]

During the period 1960–75 manufacturing output in the Third World grew at 7.4 per cent per annum—a rate far exceeding the pace of other sectors. Accordingly, an increasing portion of total income (GDP) was accounted for by the manufacturing sector. This was most noticeable in the case of countries at intermediate levels of *per capita* income ($520–$1075) where the sector's share in GDP rose from 17 to 23 per cent. Changes took place at the branch level of manufacturing, reducing the predominance of the food, textiles and clothing branches. Heavy industry's contribution to MVA rose from 38 to 51 per cent during 1960–76.[23] These types of structural changes, in turn, altered the composition of LDCs' exports. The share of manufactures in total exports jumped from 20 per cent in 1960 to 45 per cent in 1976. Equally significant is the fact that a rising proportion of these exports was subjected to varying degrees of local processing prior to export. Between 1968 and 1974 the share of unprocessed exports to be transformed after shipment fell from 38 to 24 per cent of LDCs' exports. The corresponding share of finished manufactures exported for final consumption rose from 41 to 50 per cent, respectively.[24]

While the Third World's successes in exporting manufactures were dramatic in the 1960s and 1970s, the experience of Asian countries was particularly striking. By 1977 they accounted for 73 per cent of all the Third World's exports of manufactures. The relative performance of a few Asian countries is so prominent as to suggest that dynamic export performance in the 1960s and 1970s was largely a regional affair. Notably, most Asian exports were intended for western markets. In 1960 they supplied only 39 per cent of the Third World's exports of manufactures to the West, but by 1977 the Asian share reached 73 per cent.[25]

It is not difficult to identify plausible economic reasons for the Asian countries' success. The abundance of unskilled labour and relatively low wage levels in many Asian countries gave them an advantage over competitors in other LDCs, although policy initiatives were probably more aggressive in this region than elsewhere. There are other equally compelling explanations for this success that do not pertain to considerations of factor endowment, policy or economic efficiency. For political reasons several successful Asian exporters such as Korea, the Philippines and Taiwan maintained close trade relations with the United States. Others, including Hong Kong, Malaysia and Singapore, had a preferential status with the United Kingdom and the Commonwealth. Although difficult to quantify, these relationships undoubtedly played a role in facilitating the Asian export drive. An important implication is that insofar as external political/economic considerations served to boost the Asian export performance, they were not necessarily aimed at labour-intensive manufacturers or at specific industries with obvious comparative advantages. Certainly, the employment and distributional effects of exports gains might have been greater had this been the case.

Latin American export performance contrasts markedly with that of Asian countries. Although Latin America is the most industrialized of the developing regions, its present share of the Third World's exports of manufactures is about the same as in 1960. There are two explanations for the region's laggardly export performance. First, the tradition of import substitution and the consequent industrial structure was more firmly established than elsewhere. A second factor was the region's inability to penetrate western markets.

Political considerations have also exerted a substantial influence on export performance in Latin America. The overriding political circumstance has been the foreign policy objective of the United States—dating back to the nineteenth century—to secure the western hemisphere from external influence. Paradoxically, the United States' own trade interests shifted away from Latin America in the post-war period as that country grew more dependent on far-flung suppliers to meet its increased need for imports of particular commodities.[26] Meanwhile, the United States urged Latin American governments to 'discard tariffs, encourage private capital and ban state enterprises: measures which would facilitate United States trade and investment'.[27] Trade difficulties were further compounded by the formation of the European Community.[28]

Mexico and Brazil took the lead in trying to extricate the region from excessive dependence on the United States. However, Mexico's border industries, its border trade and the importance of remittances from Mexican workers in the United States have maintained a unique set of relations between the two countries. Brazil has, perhaps, been more successful, although the domination of transnational corporations is thought by some to have perpetuated the country's external dependence.

In broad terms, the relatively advanced state of industrialization in Latin America after the war may have limited the region's ability to adapt to changes in the international environment. Unlike Asia, many industrial sectors were well developed and already oriented towards the home market. Latin American countries had, in reality, little choice but to accede to other pressures exerted by strongly entrenched domestic group interests in the industrial sector.

Among specific LDCs there are many instances where governments sought to introduce export-oriented policies in the last two decades. However, there is only scanty information on the extent to which incentives encourage or subsidize export programmes. During the late 1960s South Korea's programme was estimated to have a subsidy equivalent of about 12 per cent of the value added in exports of manufactures; Brazilian incentives carried a subsidy element varying from 6 to 38 per cent of the export value depending on the product. A roughly comparable figure for Argentina was 20 per cent but applied only to non-traditional exports. Corresponding figures for Colombia and Mexico were lower and were also restricted to particular product types.[29] Policy adjustments to complement export incentive programmes were also introduced. The most prominent measures have aimed at rescheduling import tariffs with a view to reducing the overall level of effective protection as well as the range of dispersion between industrial branches.

A precise comparison of the net effect associated with export subsidies/incentives and discrimination through protection cannot be made since quantitative estimates are not available. However, it is unlikely that either the subsidy element for exports or the reduction in home markets bias have been sufficient to provide equal rewards for exports as for home production in most LDCs. Despite partial evidence which indicates an improving trend, the overriding qualitative impression is that a bias remains, favouring production intended for the home market.[30]

The export successes of some LDCs are the result of policy revisions that are more basic than the simple introduction of export incentives. Specifically, many governments have taken steps to re-enforce the impact of an incentive system by altering the economic role played by the state. For example, the shift in industrial strategies has sometimes been accompanied by a reduction in the previously large number of ministries and state supervisory organs charged with the responsibility of dealing with foreign trade.[31] Increased activity by the State often reflects the new emphasis on exports by preserving low wage levels to maintain a country's cheap labour advantage, by offering guarantees against strikes and by giving assurances against expropriation. These and other initiatives are usually dependent upon a greater concentration or centralization of political power—an essential factor which can often reflect the underlying conflict between established vested interests geared to serve the home market and a new, outward-looking class of entrepreneurs.

In conclusion, the successful export of manufactures was not a widespread phenomenon, although it led to a vast literature calling for a general application of such an industrialization strategy throughout the Third World. An important distinction between this strategy and its predecessor, import substitution, concerns the supposedly static nature of export promotion as it was usually pictured during the 1960s. Its proponents made little mention of the possibility that structural changes or shifts in comparative advantage would occur as industrialization continued. Thus, little attention was paid to the LDCs' prospects for production of capital goods. Advocates of import substitution had stressed dynamic considerations, including internal and external economies of scale. Although they were not particularly concerned with the concept of comparative advantage, hindsight has shown that they overemphasized the extent and rapidity of structural change which was expected to result from import substitution. In their extreme forms, import substitution strategies visualized an ever changing industrial structure moving from consumer goods to capital goods, while export promotion prophesied a growing share of labour-intensive manufactures in domestic production. In the next section we examine some consequences of these strategies by estimating their contribution to industrial growth attributable to import substitution, export expansion and domestic demand.

2.3 Export performance in the Third World

Preceding sections of this chapter have discussed the interaction between changes in trade policy and industrial structure. There were obvious implications for industrial growth in these discussions but, so far, we have said little about the relative significance of export-led growth. Methods of estimating sources of growth begin with an identity between supply and demand and proceed to decompose increases in output between two years into demand factors (domestic demand and exports) and import substitution. The concept may be expressed as follows:

$$D = d_1 \triangle (F + I) + d_1 \triangle E + (d_2 - d_1) S_2$$

where D = domestic production, F = final demand, I = intermediate demand, E = exports, S = total supply, d = proportion of domestic production to total supply, and subscripts 1 and 2 refer to the beginning and ending year of the period studied. The first term on the right side of the equation represents the growth in domestic demand. The second term is a similar expression for export promotion. The third term, assuming a constant proportion of total supply is imported, measures the difference between actual imports in year 2 and hypothetical imports if their proportion to total supply had remained equal to that in the base year.

The approach employed here is to compare actual changes in the three components with hypothetical values that would have occurred if exports, imports and industrial output had grown at the same rate as aggregate domestic demand. This method assumes that 'proportionate growth' is the norm and compares deviations or non-proportional increases in each of the three growth sources.[32]

Before continuing, we should alert the reader to the fact that subsequent refinements and variations on the approach briefly described here provide alternative and, sometimes, more extensive information on the sources of growth. First, total measures of growth (rather than the direct measures used here) may be employed and would take account of technological change or, more specifically, changes in input coefficients, that could then be treated as a separate source of growth.

Second, the original method, as defined above, prompted extensive discussion of conceptual differences in the treatment of import substitution. We have already referred to one aspect of this discussion which concerned the relationship between actual import substitution and an 'optimal' situation.[33] Another aspect of the debate concerns the fact that the definition of import substitution does not take into account indirect imports such as intermediate inputs. Import substitution at the final stages of production may mean large increases in the imports of intermediate inputs used by the domestic industry. A more extreme definition of import substitution was proposed to measure the domestic production necessary to substitute completely for imports including intermediates.[34] Related to this argument is the fact that most approaches assume that domestic and imported goods are perfect substitutes although this is obviously not the case.

Third, economists have pointed out that results are sensitive to the length of time involved. An improvement may be had by dropping the practice of estimating growth sources between two specific years and replacing it by a series of successive and fairly brief intervals of estimation.[35] Finally, inconsistent estimates are obtained when comparing aggregated and disaggregated measures of growth sources. Results are sensitive to structural changes within a given industry over time and the practice of aggregating estimates to arrive at measures of the growth contributions of sub-groups such as consumer goods, intermediates, etc. may not capture interindustry effects.[36]

These qualifications all suggest that the techniques for measuring sources of growth are still at a preliminary stage. Several of the refinements entail severe data requirements and information for only a very few LDCs is adequate to meet such needs. Users of cross-country data such as is available in UN sources must adopt methods with less stringent data requirements, however. Furthermore, we are not so much concerned with precise estimates of growth sources for a particular country as with the relative importance (or unimportance) of import substitution and export promotion in the Third World.

Table II.2 summarizes our main evidence. With very few exceptions domestic demand is the most significant component of industrial growth. The predominance of this component is most pronounced in the case of intermediate industries. Among the four product categories the relative importance of export expansion is greatest in the case of consumer non-durables as would be expected. The highest (positive) values for import substitution are mainly observed for capital goods and consumer durables.

Turning to the observations within each of the four product categories, other general tendencies may be observed. Among basic

The International Economy and Industrial Development

Table II.2. Sources of growth by end-use in selected LDCs[a]   (percentages)

		Basic consumer goods			Intermediate industries		
Country	Period	Domestic demand	Export expansion	Import substitution	Domestic demand	Export expansion	Import substitution
Libya	1968–75	150.5[b]	2.0[b]	–52.5[b]	109.0[c]	–	–9.0[c]
Iran	1968–74	111.5	19.1	–30.6	96.4[e]	1.3[e]	2.3[e]
Iraq	1972–75	154.8	–1.9	–52.9	260.9	9.7	–170.6
Panama	1967–75	64.4	4.7	30.9	125.6[g]	0.9[g]	–26.5[g]
Fiji	1968–74	213.5[h]	—	–173.5[h]	101.8	3.0	–4.8
Brazil	1968–74	92.4	8.6	–1.0	100.7[j]	2.6[j]	–3.3[j]
Cyprus	1970–76	38.7	50.1	11.2	27.0[k]	29.0[k]	44.0[k]
Turkey	1968–75	91.9	8.6	–0.5	106.5	2.2	–8.7
Tunisia	1968–75	103.2	34.7	–37.9	115.4	18.5	–33.9
Chile	1969–74	–92.7	0.2	–7.5	175.5[l]	30.3[l]	–105.8[l]
Ecuador	1969–74	95.1	8.1	–3.2	179.9	4.3	–84.2
Guatemala	1968–72	77.7	28.7	–6.4	58.8	13.7	27.5
Colombia	1968–75	84.4	16.5	–0.9	95.7	13.9	–9.6
South Korea	1968–75	71.9[m]	18.1[m]	10.0[m]	85.7	10.4	3.9
Ghana	1968–72	17.3	2.6	80.1	47.9[l]	3.4[l]	48.7[l]
Zambia	1967–73	49.8[n]	—	50.2[n]	41.8[o]	–0.1[o]	58.3[o]
El Salvador	1968–72	69.2	12.4	18.4	88.3	0.3	11.4
Jordan	1967–75	181.0	15.5	–96.5	112.2[o]	17.8[o]	–30.0[o]
Nigeria	1967–75	72.5[p]	–0.0[p]	27.5[p]	134.6[q]	3.0[q]	–37.6[q]
Honduras	1968–75	50.5	3.4	46.1	72.3	10.3	17.4
Philippines	1968–74	86.3	8.8	4.9	103.9	7.4	–11.3
Thailand	1968–70	57.6	0.2	42.2	91.1[g]	8.2[g]	0.7[g]
Egypt	1968–73	83.4	17.7	–1.1	81.9	8.2	9.9
Sri Lanka	1968–74	69.7[r]	3.5[r]	26.8[r]	25.9[s]	8.7[s]	65.4[s]
Madagascar	1968–74	40.2	4.3	55.5	52.1[u]	7.8[u]	40.1[u]
Indonesia	1970–75	80.9	1.0	18.1	113.3[g]	1.6[g]	–14.9[g]
India	1968–74	88.1[t]	11.7[t]	0.2[t]	94.5	2.6	2.9
Malawi	1968–73	81.3[m]	1.2[m]	17.5[m]	45.3	0.3	54.4

Strategies for Trade and Industrialization in the Post-War Era

Capital goods and consumer durables			Other industries			Total		
Domestic demand	Export expansion	Import substitution	Domestic demand	Export expansion	Import substitution	Domestic demand	Export expansion	Import substitution
...	...	...	69.5^d	—	30.5^d	134.1	1.3	−35.4
97.8	1.5	0.7	105.4^f	0.0^f	−5.4^f	100.2	4.3	−4.5
275.0	0.1	−175.1	130.0	−1.0	−29.0	221.2	2.9	−124.1
...	...	...	83.4	1.9	14.7	91.6	2.5	5.9
81.8	0.3	17.9	103.4^l	1.1^i	−4.5^i	96.3	1.8	1.9
^{j}	^{j}	^{j}	97.7	2.2	0.1	99.3	3.4	−2.7
5.4	19.6	75.0	83.9	9.3	6.8	37.8	32.9	29.3
109.0	1.0	−10.0	90.2	0.4	9.4	102.9	3.3	−6.2
149.3	2.6	−51.9	90.5	4.3	5.2	114.2	19.0	−33.2
−40.6	1.5	−60.9	−117.0	30.7	−13.7	−35.1	16.4	−81.3
79.7	1.2	19.1	72.3	—	27.7	108.8	3.8	−12.6
41.4	5.5	53.1	65.8	6.1	28.1	59.7	13.0	27.3
64.5	3.1	32.4	96.1	3.3	0.6	84.6	10.3	5.1
52.4	15.1	32.5	94.3	9.1	−3.4	76.2	13.2	10.6
2.2	0.2	97.6	5.2	—	94.8	30.1	2.6	67.3
...	...	...	57.8^i	0.3^i	41.9^i	45.4	−0.0	54.6
548.8	18.2	−467.0	69.5	9.5	21.0	85.6	8.6	5.8
...	...	...	119.5	12.2	−31.7	131.2	16.0	−47.2
100.5	−0.0	−0.5	103.2	1.6	−4.8	98.8	0.8	0.4
60.9	2.5	36.6	52.7	1.1	46.2	64.0	7.0	29.0
98.2	1.3	0.5	91.1	4.4	4.5	99.0	6.6	−5.6
42.0	0.5	57.5	−79.5	1.1	−21.6	57.1	1.6	41.3
58.2	0.7	41.1	87.6	5.3	7.1	77.5	10.0	12.5
33.1	2.1	64.8	^{i}82.8^f	—	^{i}17.2^f	39.8	6.5	53.7
26.5	0.0	73.5	55.2^f	9.0^f	35.8^f	40.9	4.5	54.6
49.7	0.8	49.5	39.1	2.5	58.4	78.8	1.2	20.0
76.7	4.5	18.8	97.9^i	1.4^i	0.7^i	88.2	5.2	6.6
56.0	1.0	43.0	66.3^i	—	33.7^i	66.1	0.8	33.1

The International Economy and Industrial Development

Sources: Based on United Nations, *Yearbook of Industrial Statistics*, Vol. I, various issues; *Commodity Trade Statistics*, various issues: and *Yearbook of International Trade Statistics*, various issues.

Notes: [a] Countries are arranged according to GNP *per capita* in 1975 at current US$.
[b] Only tobacco and textiles.
[c] Only wood, chemicals and chemical products, and non-ferrous metals.
[d] Only furniture.
[e] Excluding wood, chemicals, chemical products, petroleum refineries and products.
[f] Excluding furniture.
[g] Excluding petroleum refineries and products and non-ferrous metals.
[h] Only footwear.
[i] Excluding leather.
[j] Intermediate industries and capital goods and durables are combined.
[k] Excluding petroleum refineries and products, iron and steel, and non-ferrous metals.
[l] Excluding non-ferrous metals.
[m] Excluding clothing and footwear.
[n] Only clothing.
[o] Excluding iron and steel and non-ferrous metals.
[p] Excluding tobacco.
[q] Excluding chemical products.
[r] Excluding footwear.
[s] Excluding wood.
[t] Excluding clothing.
[u] Excluding wood and petroleum refineries and products.

Strategies for Trade and Industrialization in the Post-War Era

consumer goods a loose relationship with *per capita* GNP may be observed. The relative importance of domestic demand appears to decline at lower levels of *per capita* income. The figures for import substitution show an inverse relation; negative values are generally observed at higher levels of income and positive values are found at lower income levels. Apparently, among the more advanced countries further growth would depend on domestic demand and export promotion while, at lower levels, scope for import substitution still exists. The pattern is roughly similar for intermediate industries although, as indicated above, the figures for domestic demand generally dominate.

The figures for capital goods and consumer durables show a different 'growth structure'. Import substitution plays a more important role and is often the largest growth source, particularly for countries at the bottom of the income scale. Extreme cases are Cyprus, Guatemala, Ghana and Madagascar. These countries all have small domestic markets and, for this reason, the 'easy phase' of substitution is likely to be brief. Estimates of export expansion are generally very low, which may reflect both the policy bias inherent in the tariff structure of countries that had pursued an import substitution strategy and the growth pattern of 'late industries'.

As far as exports are concerned our preliminary estimates show that expansion in foreign demand is rarely important as a source of the output growth of capital goods or consumer durables. In manufacturing as a whole the ratio of exports to gross output does not generally exceed 6 per cent. For a majority of the twenty-eight countries in our sample the export-output ratio ranged from zero to 6 per cent.

Exports in this range may be important in earning foreign exchange. They may also be crucial to individual enterprises by contributing to capacity utilization or helping to overcome bottlenecks such as economies of scale. However, on average, the share of exports in domestic production does not suggest many instances of 'export-led' growth. Their role is better described as a supplementary one or, at best, that of a catalyst. Finally, a more significant feature of our estimates is the lack of a relationship between the level of development and the export of manufactures. Although the value of exports by Brazil, South Korea and Turkey

The International Economy and Industrial Development

far exceeds those of less advanced countries, their relative importance to the economies of El Salvador, Egypt, Jordan or Madagascar, etc. is of a similar or greater magnitude. This fact serves to qualify the general impression that exporting (particularly of manufactures) becomes significant only after a country has reached some threshold or minimum level of development.[37] Such is the case in terms of a country's share in world trade. However, the significance of exports for the domestic economy does not necessarily increase with development. This implies that supply constraints or problems of market access may be equally important to Jordan or Madagascar as they are to Brazil or Turkey.

The major conclusion to be derived from the analysis is that domestic demand stands in the forefront of the growth process. Although its significance is of less importance at lower levels of income, there are a few cases where the growth process is primarily based on trade expansion. This finding is somewhat paradoxical in view of the emphasis often given to trade-related strategies for industrialization. Our results would seem to point to the importance of policies aimed at spurring the growth of domestic demand. Import-restricting policies can shift demand from imports to domestic production although they may do little to increase consumer or investment demand for reasons discussed above. Export incentives may boost domestic demand by employment generation, increased intermediate demand, etc. although the existence of an export enclave would clearly do little to boost domestic demand. More direct policies for increasing employment, realizing a more equitable distribution of income, encouraging the intra-national diffusion of technology (as well as its international transfer), etc. may also deserve a higher priority.

2.4 Western trade strategies and their consequences for Third World industrialization

It has often been argued that many LDCs could have substantially expanded their export levels had the international environment been sufficiently conducive. Our own analysis in this chapter as well as in Chapter IV shows that the growth in world demand and the conditions prevalent in specific international markets were impor-

Strategies for Trade and Industrialization in the Post-War Era

tant determinants of export growth for manufacturing exports from LDCs. It has also been shown that the western countries were the Third World's main trading partners. The importance of western markets was particularly marked for the most successful LDC exporters—Malaysia, Singapore, South Korea and Taiwan. The West's trade policies in specific markets are likely to have a pronounced impact on LDC exports, particularly on the export performance of the most dynamic group of LDC exporters.

Basic changes that would eventually alter the international policy environment were already underway early in the twentieth century. By that time the United States had surpassed Britain as the world's leading economic power and trading nation. For nearly a century British predominance and initiative had been supreme in matters of world trade. The 1920s and 1930s were a period of uncertainty and confusion as Britain abandoned its global role for the Imperial Preference System. However, the United States was reluctant to accept the position of leadership which its industrial and trading prominence warranted. A number of chaotic years, complicated by the Great Depression, followed before the United States exerted its leadership in international policy.

The reciprocal trade act of the United States, originally designed to help overcome the consequence of the Great Depression, later became a cornerstone of that country's trade policy. The legal foundation for the programme which was later to emerge was the Reciprocal Trade Agreement Act of 1934. This programme was based on fundamental prepositions of classical economics. It endorsed the principle that more trade was preferable to less trade and that relatively unhindered trade would stimulate additional trade. Furthermore, the approach stipulated that all trading countries should be treated on an equal basis.[38] This line of reasoning eventually served as the model for negotiating the post-World War II framework for international trade relations.

Despite interruptions, the long-term pattern of structural change in world trade was clearly evident to both economists and policy makers prior to World War II. For example, between 1876–80 and 1913 total merchandise trade of western countries grew 40 per cent per decade and continued at this pace until 1953.[39] The comparable figures for manufactured exports were somewhat different; in the earlier period the rate was 36 per cent per decade but rose to 48 per cent per decade between 1913 and 1953.[40] Manufactures accounted for about one third of total trade of western countries in the late nineteenth century but, by 1950, the share was about one half.

It is well known that even prior to the existence of a co-ordinated western approach to international trade, individual countries frequently adapted their economic rhetoric to fit national interests. Britain's attempt to persuade its allies to reduce their tariffs on goods exported by Britain as a pre-condition for its last subsidies during the Napoleonic wars is but one example.[41] The competition between the United States and Germany for Latin American markets is another instance with destabilizing effects on the third party. In 1933, when the National Socialists came to power, Germany's trade with Latin America was still below its 1913 level. In the next five years the German share of Latin American imports rose to 16 per cent, reaching pre-World War I levels. With the outbreak of war, American interests in the region intensified through closer trade and financial relations in return for Latin American restraints on the prices of its primary exports and its political alliances with the Axis powers. 'Suddenly the United States found the means to assist national development projects such as a new steel works in Brazil, the National Development Corporation in Chile and highway construction in Mexico.'[42] During the war the Export-Import Bank's commitments (disbursed and undisbursed) totalled about $430 million but the Bank changed character immediately after the war. In 1946 almost one billion dollars was allocated to European borrowers compared to about $30 million to Latin America.[43]

Following World War II the United States emerged as the unquestioned world power in the spheres of industry, trade and finance and continued to pursue its reciprocal trade approach. The figures in Table II.3 indicate some of the favourable circumstances during the period when the United States began to assert its leadership in fashioning international industrial and trade policies. In 1948 the country accounted for over one half the net manufacturing output of the non-communist world, perhaps one third of the West's exports of manufactures and nearly one quarter of total exports. These unique circumstances suggest a compelling logic behind the country's approach to international policy in the trade sphere. Certainly, a strong coalition of liberal trade—even free trade—interests could be expected to emerge in such a dominant economy.

Table II.3 The United States' contribution to world industrial output and trade, various years

(percentages)[a]

Year	MVA	Total exports, f.o.b.	Exports of manufactures (SITC 5 to 8)
1938	37.7	14.5	...
1948	55.5	23.3	...
1953	54.3	21.0	23.7[b]
1958	46.9	18.5	23.1
1963	51.8	17.0	19.4

Sources: compiled from United Nations, *Growth of World Industry 1938–1953*, and subsequent issues; *Yearbook of International Trade*, various issues; *Monthly Bulletin of Statistics*, various issues; UNCTAD, *Handbook of International Trade and Development Statistics*, 1969; and IMF, *International Financial Statistics*, various issues.

Notes: [a] Percentages refer to the world less socialist countries.
[b] 1955.

Under these conditions American negotiators began to lay the groundwork for a world order that was to last for over two decades. Despite the economic content of the negotiations, the overriding objectives were political. They were: (i) to ensure, above all, that the economic interdependence of western countries was extended, primarily through expanded trade but also through increased flows of international investment, the transfer of technology and the spread of industrial capacity, and (ii) to integrate West Germany into European and world markets. In the case of Japan, the United States approach was somewhat different. There was no intention that the Japanese economy be re-integrated with other Asian economies as in Western Europe. Ironically, it was intended that the country become more dependent than before on foreign trade. United States policy was to provide unilateral trade concessions, admitting Japanese textiles and later steel, television sets, cameras, ships, etc. Behind a military shield provided by the United States, the Japanese were to build a self-sustaining economy with United States help.

Other western countries had no problem in accepting these political objectives. However, despite the economic pre-eminence of the United States, negotiations on specific issues were not always harmonious. One split arose from the fact that the United States sought to enforce free, non-discriminatory trade through a code-of-law approach. Three considerations led other countries to oppose total acceptance of the United States position. First, many found themselves compelled to continue existing trade restrictions. A wide range of motives explained this reluctance: overvalued currencies, massive unemployment, the retention of preferential trading arrangements such as the Imperial Preference System, etc.[44] Second, the United States' position made no allowance for the uncertainties associated with newly established and still tentative patterns of post-war trade, the Europeans' ambitions for self-sufficiency in agriculture and raw materials or their widely different rates of inflation. Third, the proposed institutional framework presumed enforcement of the substantive agreement or code of laws—a stance that other countries found difficult to accept.[45]

Discussions focused on two subject areas. The first was a proposed code of conduct on commercial policy which embraced the principle of non-discrimination. The second concerned the means to enforce a gradual reduction of trade barriers. In 1947 these objectives were accepted when the draft charter of the General Agreement on Tariffs and Trade (GATT) was drawn up, largely at the behest of the United States, and signed by twenty-three countries. This was a watershed in international trade relations. As one economist has noted, the Agreement led to a period in which government control over, and management of, international trade would increase greatly.[46]

The agreements reached in the late 1940s, notably the creation of GATT and the Bretton Woods Agreement, were part of a broader foreign policy concept. There was a general consensus that the political gains to be derived from expanded trade relations were more important than the economic gains although the latter were

Strategies for Trade and Industrialization in the Post-War Era

clearly recognized.[47] Tacitly, the resultant policy framework accepted the principle that national actions which influenced trade patterns were matters of *mutual* concern. This amounted to a departure from international trade relations prior to World War II when such policy matters were regarded as purely of *domestic* concern. In practice, the principle proved to have only a one-way application as the United States did not object when various countries continued to discriminate against its exports prior to the re-establishment of convertibility in 1958. Thus, the United States was unsuccessful in convincing its allies to accept non-discriminatory market access. Too many preferential trading arrangements persisted, established forms of protection were widely accepted in Europe and war-torn European industries pressed their governments for protection from United States competitors.[48]

From 1947 until the late 1960s this approach met with success according to several criteria. Trade among western countries thrived without wide-ranging disputes concerning market access, supplies of raw materials, trade wars or the creation of international cartels. As a result the trading environment was decidedly more liberal than during the interwar years when, for example, about 42 per cent of world trade was cartelized or subject to similar arrangements almost all of which were concerned with manufactures.[49]

During this period, the question of tariff reductions was the central theme of most international negotiations. These efforts emphasized—or at least experienced their greatest measure of success—in the field of manufactures rather than agriculture. The priority attached to manufacturing was due, in part, to the fact that revisions in the existing tariff structure held greater promise for increasing trade in this field. Moreover, the discussions of tariff cuts in agricultural trade were likely to be so difficult as to jeopardize the entire process.[50]

The post-war pattern of tariff cuts for trade in manufactures was actually a continuation of long-term trends. Data spanning the years 1902–62 show a steady decline in tariff levels in Europe, Japan and the United States.[51] The only break in the downward trend was in the inter-war year, 1925, when tariffs in European countries rose, resuming their decline in later years. Based on these figures we conclude that commercial policy trends for manufactures have long differed from those observed for agriculture and that the post-World War II period was not unique. In both the West and the Third World (see below) commercial policy trends were mainly policy reactions to deep-seated structural changes dating back to the early part of the twentieth century.

Few estimates of the extent to which tariff reductions actually contributed to trade expansion and industrial growth are available. Many economists, however, have tended to regard the wide-ranging reductions as an important stimulus. Nevertheless, available information shows only modest to negligible gains in income due to tariff liberalization. In most West European countries, estimates for 1955–62 suggest that the growth rates of national income were boosted by percentages between 0.02 and 0.16.[52]

Other forces were also at work encouraging trade in manufactures and their net impact may well have exceeded that of trade liberalization. One was the substantial fall in transport costs with the advent of supertankers, cheap air transport, new methods of bulk packaging and the completion of extensive motorway systems for overland transport between countries. Another was the growing standardization in the patterns of world consumption of various product categories. A third was the increasing importance of economies of scale as more powerful and more expensive machinery became available, thus rendering many producers more dependent upon export markets if they were to maintain efficient levels of operation.

From the LDCs' viewpoint, the western approach of development through trade left much to be desired. The American response to Third World appeals during this period came to be symbolized in the slogan 'trade, not aid', taken from a foreign policy study which argued that through tariff reductions and increased trade the costly burden of United States foreign aid could be reduced.[53] Hindsight suggests at least two logical reasons why the trade not aid approach would prove unsatisfactory to LDCs. First, political objectives were the West's major concern. During the Cold War the desire to see the emergence of a strong and unified Western Europe and Japan undercut the LDCs' hopes for expanded aid or expanded trade.

Second, the West's approach to tariff reductions on a reciprocal and most-favoured-nation (MFN)[54] basis encouraged intra-western trade. By definition, the tariff cuts which took place reflected concessions by one or several countries to producer interests in another country. However, in the bargaining process only western countries had the potential to make use of increased market access to consumers in other countries. Producers in these countries had little interest in acquiring greater access to relatively small markets in the Third World. In other words, negotiations served to stimulate trade between western countries that previously possessed a broad industrial base and to re-enforce an already expanding pattern of trade which partially excluded the Third World.

Basic self-interest had its effect on the pattern of tariff cuts negotiated during the trade expansion era. Numerous studies of the Kennedy Round, spanning the years 1964–7, suggest this tendency. First, duties on finished manufactures fell by larger margins than those on raw materials or semi-finished products (traditionally, Third World exports) with the result that effective protection of the former goods was probably reduced more than corresponding rates on the latter.[55] Second, the proportionate reduction in the average tariff for imports from all sources exceeded the average applied to imports from western countries.[56] The significant point here is that potential exporters in the West may have benefited from the pattern of tariff incidence in the post-Kennedy era *relative* to potential exporters elsewhere—specifically in the LDCs.

The significance of the policy trends for the Third World may be put in some perspective by briefly examining their dependence on the developed countries as potential markets. In 1955–9, western countries absorbed 64 per cent of the Third World's exports of manufactures. The percentage rose in the first half of the 1960s. Simultaneously, the LDCs' share in world trade (excluding socialist countries) declined from 6 per cent in 1955–9 to 5.7 in 1960–4.[57] Thus, their dependence on western markets increased although their participation in world trade stagnated. Placed in a long-term perspective, the LDCs' trade performance in the immediate post-war years amounted to a departure from earlier trends. The growth of their exports of manufactures exceeded corresponding rates for exports by the West throughout the period 1876–1953 although the converse was true for 1953–66.⁵⁸. Against this background the original slogan of 'trade, not aid' strikes an ironic note.

Originally, protectionist tendencies in the West owed much to the intensification of international rivalries. National differences of opinion mainly involved US-European relations but, in later years, also concerned Japan. Conflicting interests also emerged between various interest groups within national economies. These conflicts centred on the question of additional protection versus continued liberalization of trade. The positions taken by various producer interests and labour were greatly influenced by changing domestic comparative advantages relative to other sub-sectors in the domestic economy and to competitors abroad. Policy makers were also involved, either in response to pressures exerted by the interest groups or through their efforts to implement pre-determined policies in the face of domestic opposition.

With regard to multilateral disputes, the initial policy differences between the US and Western Europe have already been mentioned. The US was concerned with issues of security and strongly supported the objective that Europe play a leading role in the international economic system. In so doing, however, the country permitted its European trading partners to use their external policies to discriminate against US exports so long as domestic free trade interests prevailed over protectionist sentiments. For example, the special tariff preferences accorded many ex-colonies violated the MFN principle. Participating LDCs were granted preferential duty treatment by the EEC—a practice which worked against other competitors, particularly the US and Latin America. Exporters within the EEC also received 'reverse preferences' by participating countries and, again, US exporters may have suffered. One US response was to increase direct investment in Europe, thereby moving behind the tariff wall and minimizing the discriminatory impact of European policy.⁵⁹ It is significant that this investment was concentrated in manufacturing, in high technology industries. United States foreign investment in Europe became one transmission channel for the American priority on science-intensive industries, a trend with significant consequences for the pattern of structural change in both the West and the Third World.

Strategies for Trade and Industrialization in the Post-War Era

Eventually, European resistance to American inroads in key industries grew and the flow of foreign investment slowed. Simultaneously, organized labour in the US began to work aggressively to limit American foreign investment, arguing that the trend amounted to a practice of 'exporting American jobs'. The US policy response was the Foreign Direct Investment Program introduced in the early 1960s to limit the amount of foreign investment. These were not the only differences that characterized western policies. United States-Japan relations were also troublesome and the ability of American producers to side-step restrictions by foreign investment was more limited. Similarly, US-Canadian relations were sometimes tenuous as Canadian industry strove to become more competitive.[60]

Parallel to these international policy differences, conflicts at the national level (mainly couched in protectionist language) sporadically re-emerged. Protectionist pressures in the United States reappeared immediately after World War II as the economy shifted back to a peacetime orientation. Resistance continued throughout the 1950s and, as the Trade Agreement Act was frequently renewed during that decade, domestic interest groups obtained periodic concessions.[61] The calls for increasing protection grew, covering a widening range of manufactures. A short list of the items involved prior to 1967 includes cotton textiles and clothing, steel, window glass and woven carpet,[62] bicycles, thermometers, watches, shoes and stainless steel flatware.

The spread of US trade barriers served to strengthen the case of similar interest groups in other western countries. Protectionist interests, limited in their ability to raise tariffs due to previous international agreements, found a ready alternative in non-tariff barriers (NTBs), whose number mushroomed. The successor to the Long Term Arrangement on Cotton Textiles—the Multifibre Arrangement—is only one example. Similar measures have been proposed or implemented for steel. Among the proposals aired in 1978 were the Davignon Plan and the negotiations between the EEC, Japan and the United States, allegedly to plan a world steel agreement. Reference prices and mandatory minimum prices have been established for other products. Imports below the reference price are subject to anti-dumping rules with levies imposed to eliminate the price difference. Marketing agreements have been established for other products such as television sets and footwear. Import limitations normally allow for annual increases in quotas, although the levels attained in recent years would not be regained until the early 1980s. Such measures have encouraged similar demands for protectionist controls on electronic products, railroad equipment, bicycle tyres and tubes, copper and zinc.

Countries may also negotiate 'orderly marketing agreements' whereby the exporting country agrees to restrict the amount of its shipments to pre-determined levels. If these levels are exceeded, the importing country then imposes a quota on subsequent trade. The last alternative is similar to voluntary export restraints (VERs) and, together with VERs, was applicable to 3–5 per cent of world trade in 1975–7. In western economies, coverage varied widely, ranging from roughly 3 per cent of trade in steel products to over 50 per cent for textiles.[63]

Government aids to industry, often granted as a means of rationalizing the industrial structure, became common in the 1970s. These take the form of direct subsidies or preferential taxes and credit treatment, amounting to indirect protection to domestic industry by reducing production or sales costs. Many subsidies involve employment schemes which, although not specific to given branches, benefit labour-intensive activities that would have higher than average rates of unemployment.[64] Simultaneously, these are products in which the LDCs have an increasing interest.

All such policies are referred to here as 'neo-protectionism'. We distinguish between these policies and old protectionism which refers exclusively to trade-restricting and trade-expanding devices. Neo-protectionism is intended to have a much broader connotation, including intervention explicitly relating to foreign trade but not limited to this. In fact, the term embraces the totality of government interventions which affect trade. Given the growing significance of trade, and thus foreign demand, almost all forms of government intervention may eventually affect international trade relationships.

Most often, the justification for neo-protectionist measures has been that rapid import growth leads to politically unacceptable economic and social costs to the domestic firms and labour which are affected. Emphasis is on the need to forestall *rapid* adjustment that, so the argument implies, is more costly and disruptive than gradual adjustment. The justification represents a departure from the conventional arguments for protection. Accordingly, a new type of thinking has taken shape as underlying forces emerged which are of sufficient importance to coalesce producer interests, labour interests and government to act on behalf of *specific* industries. Neo-protectionism is not a policy response to problems of balance of payments or even employment.[65] It has become, instead, a tool of structural policy. While tariff barriers have been steadily reduced—most recently in the Tokyo Round—neo-protectionist measures have grown in significance and scope as domestic interests strive to reduce (or to prevent) the structural adjustments which a flood of new low cost imports would bring.[66]

Before going further it would be helpful to put current tariff and non-tariff policies in some perspective relative to more general trade-related policies. Although the protectionist debate has generated wide interest and concern, other policy elements have probably had a greater impact. Perhaps the most significant of these has been the unexpectedly volatile exchange rate changes occurring in the 1970s. The magnitude of exchange rate changes has dwarfed tariff reduction in the impact on trade and these changes are the most important contributors to the overall average level of 'quasi-protection' for tradeable goods. With frequent and substantial movements in exchange rates the 'competitiveness' of countries' exports fluctuates drastically over brief periods. An example is the rapid decline in the United States dollar relative to the mark and yen which, during seven months in 1977, altered by 6 and 11 per cent respectively. By comparison, the overall average tariff level on industrial products in 1973 was about 7 per cent in the United States and the EEC and slightly higher in Japan.[67] Other studies have re-affirmed the opinion that, after 1968, the internationally competitive position of certain western countries would have deteriorated at a considerably more rapid pace if exchange rate adjustments had not cushioned their effect. It is significant that labour-intensive industries were the main beneficiaries of devaluation among the countries in question.[68] This suggests that LDCs' exports are particularly vulnerable to such exchange rate adjustments.

The International Economy and Industrial Development

A comparison of the impact of tariff reductions and neo-protectionist measures is not practical given the complexities of such an exercise. It is possible that, to date, the net result of the post-war tariff rounds was to reduce the overall level of trade barriers. Nevertheless, trade barriers for specific industries have mushroomed as commercial policy became an instrument for regulating the pace of structural adjustment. The resultant biases apparently complement those attributed to devaluation. As one economist has clearly stated, '(Un)skilled–labour–intensity is everywhere the dominant characteristic of the protected sectors'.[69]

The impact of neo-protectionism on LDC trade can be seen from the following examples pertaining to Latin American exports. For 1051 export items with a total value exceeding $8 billion annually, the United States applied over 400 such measures, mainly quantitative restrictions or sanitary precautions. One hundred non-tariff measures were applied to 431 Latin American items exported to Japan valued at $3.6 billion, and 300 such measures were applied to 479 items imported by the EEC with an annual export value of $8 billion.[70] In 1977, NTBs occurred with the greatest frequency of incidence on trade in textiles and footwear—major exports of the LDCs.[71]

Thus, the emergence of neo-protectionism marks a turning point in the trade-industry relations of western economies. For over two decades these countries demonstrated a remarkable degree of adaptability regarding the composition of final production, the technologies employed, the links between industries and groups and the spread of industrial capacity. The reversal is, to a certain extent, a result of structural forces which are central to the theme of this book. In terms of the present discussion, the dramatic post-war growth of international trade in manufactures meant that the magnitude of international demand has taken on added importance relative to domestic demand. Two corollaries may be derived from this observation. First, the effectiveness of existing national policies to regulate macro-economic performance was reduced. New types of policies were desired as structural changes in the manufacturing sector became dependent upon international rather than national conditions. Second, each country's competitive position vis-à-vis its main trading partners has taken on added importance, prompting

Strategies for Trade and Industrialization in the Post-War Era

governments to directly intervene to alleviate structural problems rather than simply 'sending out signals' via the market. Consequently, industrial economies exhibit a reduced degree of structural flexibility. The growing number of instances where producers, workers and government find it in their common interest to limit the extent of structural change is the most obvious result of these trends.

At a more specific level we might inquire as to which industries have proven most reluctant to accept structural changes. First, it should be obvious that, invariably, the industries in question are contracting. Second, they are likely to be relatively large in terms of their capital investments and/or their employment forces. Although labour intensity is a frequent characteristic, capital investments are also jeopardized by structural change. Third, industries in the forefront of the neo-protectionist move are those which face their greatest competition from producers in other western countries.

Given the present and expected directions of structural change, it would be wrong to regard neo-protectionism as a cyclical or temporary phenomenon. Trade-related policies pertaining to contracting industrial branches will take on an increasingly defensive character similar in many ways to agricultural polices. Long-term structural changes will surely lead to further government intervention in manufacturing, to additional protectionism or to even more imaginative policies to retard the pace of structural change.

2.5 The consolidation of neo-protectionism —international consequences

A predominant theme emerging from the foregoing discussion is that the intensity of the neo-protectionist push depends to a great extent upon the pace and direction of structural change in the manufacturing sector. Elsewhere in this book a parallel is drawn between the present pattern of contraction in certain industrial branches and the historical long-term decline in the agricultural sector. There are several reasons why the pace and scope of contraction problems in manufacturing have accelerated. First, automation in manufacturing has proceeded at a rapid pace. Often governments strongly supported this trend, reflecting the growing importance they attach to maintaining their competitive position relative to that of trading partners.[72] Second, the modernization of various industrial branches has become more expensive, raising levels of indebtedness and reducing profits. At the same time abrupt rises in the costs of energy and raw materials have proven some long-term investments to be ill-timed and left producers committed to processes which were relatively inefficient with the new cost structure. Finally, a combination of structural forces such as changing patterns of consumption, trends in productivity and changing social values has led to slower growth in many industrial branches relative to the service sector.[73]

The figures in Table II.4 provide some idea of the scope and pace of changes in the manufacturing sectors of western countries. With few exceptions, the share of manufacturing output in GDP steadily declined between 1955 and 1975.[74] The drop was most pronounced in the United Kingdom, and clearly evident for Canada, France, Norway and the United States. In the newer industrialized countries (e.g. Italy and Japan) the share rose due to the post-war restructuring process in the West. Employment figures also show a downward trend although their movement has been more erratic than output—largely reflecting government employment policies and trade union resistance to job losses. Nevertheless, for most of the 'older industrialized countries' the share of manufacturing employment in the work force now ranges from 22 to 30 per cent. The figures bear out the fact that the relative decline in the manufacturing sector is a widespread characteristic in the West. Moreover, it occurred during a period of relatively high growth and has continued for several decades.

In terms of the individual industrial branches which make up the manufacturing sector, we can be sure that the 'contractive pressures' leading to neo-protectionism would have been greater than the net shifts in Table II.4 imply. This is so since we know that even in the late 1970s several industrial branches (e.g. electronics) continued to enjoy rapid growth in both output and employment. Furthermore, there are good reasons to expect that future growth patterns will lead to similar contractive trends in other countries where growth, to date, has been sufficient to avoid many contractive pressures.

Table II.4 Structural changes in manufacturing in selected western countries and years
(percentages)

	Share of MVA in GDP[1] (Producers' values at current prices)				Share of manufacturing employment in total civilian employment			
	1955	1965	1975	1977	1955	1965	1975	1977
Belgium	29	30	27	27	34	35	30	28
Canada	28	23	19	18	26	24	20	20
France	36[a]	35	27	27	27	28	28	27
Germany, West	41[a]	40	37	38	34[c]	38	36	36
Italy	26	29	30	32	23	29	33	28[f]
Japan	22[b]	32	29	28	18	24	26	25
Netherlands	31	32	27	26	30[d]	28	24	22
Norway	27	25	22	20	25	26	24	22
Sweden	32	26	28	24	34[e]	32	28	26
United Kingdom	37	30	25	25	40	35	31	30
United States	30[a]	29	23	24	26	25	22	22

Source: *Yearbook of National Accounts Statistics*, 1969, 1978, OECD, *Labour Force Statistics*—1954–64, 1956–67, 1967–76, 1966–77, 1967–78. For USA, 1965, 1975 and 1977 figures are derived from *ILO Yearbook*, 1974, 1978, 1979.

Notes: [a] GDP at market price.
   [b] Net domestic product at factor cost.
   [c] 1957, excluding West Berlin.
   [d] 1956.
   [e] 1961, includes mining, quarrying and manufacturing combined.
   [f] Figures for 1977 are not directly comparable with earlier years due to a revised definition of employment and a new industrial classification.

The foregoing analysis holds several implications for the character of neo-protectionism in the 1980s. First, a continuation (and, perhaps, an acceleration) of present structural trends will mean that in most countries manufacture's share of employment and output is likely to decline in the 1980s relative to other sectors. Eventually, these trends may alter the priorities which western countries give to new multilateral initiatives for trade liberalization and to further neo-protectionist efforts. For example, United States' sponsored initiatives for trade liberalization in manufactures will wane. Other countries—Germany and Japan—whose exports of manufactures continue to be of relative importance may retain their interest in freer trade. On the whole, however, trade liberalization efforts will take a lower priority due to (i) domestic pressures to reduce contraction and (ii) a relative decline in manufacturing as a contributor to employment and income generation. This type of reaction reflects the growing reluctance of western countries to rely upon the market to solve their adjustment problems.

A second possibility concerns the manner in which neo-protectionism may alter patterns of international investment. Increasingly, foreign investment has come to be a substitute for exports in several industrial branches. This tactic, of course, is not new. Earlier, many firms set up operations in LDCs in order to avoid the tariff barriers erected while import substitution was in vogue. In the present context, however, both investor and recipient are industrialized countries. The effect is to increase the 'coverage' of the tariff—i.e. the proportion of world output benefiting from the implicit subsidy—and, thus, the extent of resource misallocation.[75] Examples are numerous but motor cars, certain types of basic chemicals and household appliances are well publicized.[76]

Paradoxically, this trend should lead to a greater degree of international interdependence in those industrial branches which are now contracting. In the past, typical firms may have exported 5 to 10 per cent of their output without being closely concerned with conditions in the importing markets. In the future, an increasing number of firms will find themselves operating subsidiaries abroad or, conversely, becoming part of a foreign-based operation. Thus, they will have a direct interest in labour conditions, supply and distribution matters, financial conditions and industrial policy in the opposite country. We conclude that policy questions touching on foreign investment and the treatment of foreign earnings should take on added significance in policy formulation in the West.[77]

The consolidation of neo-protectionism in the 1980s will have consequences for expanding as well as contracting industries. Defensive policies for contracting industries have their counterpart in competitive policies for industries which Goran Ohlin has dubbed 'national champions'.[78] Both domestic and international circumstances point towards more aggressive forms of market intervention.

Strategies for Trade and Industrialization in the Post-War Era

Domestically, attempts to prevent or postpone contraction in one industry can hold up expansion elsewhere. Some compensatory efforts may be necessary to ensure that industries with real growth prospects are not too seriously handicapped when governments accede to neo-protectionist demands. Internationally, we have already stressed that the post-war growth of trade has led countries to attach greater importance to their competitive position relative to trading partners. There is some evidence that long-term gains in productivity through the application of additional capital investment have tended to decline.[79] The search for profitable investments has, therefore, become a matter of developing new systems of capital goods such as new types of machine tools and control systems.

These trends will spur competition between western countries, particularly in those advanced industries described as national champions. Automated capital equipment, basic electronic components, aerospace, computers, and nuclear energy are all examples. Countries make enormous commitments to these industries, buttressed by supporting military, R and D and procurement expenditures by governments and advances will have a widespread effect on many productive processes. As industrialized countries strive to maintain their technological independence in such fields, the magnitude and scope of the competitive efforts will grow with a significant impact on global patterns of investment, trade and industrial production.

2.6 Recent attempts at international reform

In the opinion of some observers the internationalisation of economic relations is inversely dependent upon the degree of equality in the distribution of power among nations. Thus, a completely open and integrated system requires a regulator or dominant national power. As we have shown, in the past this role was played by the US although, presently, international negotiations more closely approximate a system of collegial management. Before turning to other issues a brief look at two recent efforts at international reform—the Tokyo Round of Multilateral Trade Negotiations and the Brandt Report—is useful.

The International Economy and Industrial Development

In the wake of the 1973 oil crisis, the LDCs' hopes were mainly tied to the results of the Tokyo Round of GATT negotiations. They anticipated that these talks would lead to large-scale trade liberalization. The Tokyo Declaration of 14 September 1973 explicitly encouraged this impression, committing the talks to 'special and differential treatment' for the LDCs.[80] Yet when the Tokyo Round was concluded six years later almost all LDCs refused to sign the final documents and many expressed bitter disappointment with the results. Tariff cuts negotiated on products of interest to Third World countries were less than tariff reductions on western exports.[81] Tariff reductions on items covered by the Generalized Scheme of Preferences and on semi-manufactures were lower than the average level of tariff cuts negotiated. As the World Bank has noted, an important feature of the multilateral trade negotiation (MTN) agreements is that 'they largely exclude existing quantitative restrictions on textiles, clothing and agriculture'.[82]

Needless to say, LDCs are particularly concerned about the lack of progress on the reduction on non-tariff barriers (NTBs). A number of agreements on non-tariff barriers were concluded in the final stages of the Tokyo Round.[83] However, LDCs expressed particular concern about the inability to establish a code governing the application of trade safeguards. These safeguards, sanctioned explicitly by Article XIX of the GATT, permit contracting partners to apply 'emergency' measures to offset injurious effects of import expansion. Such measures are increasingly used to reduce imports from Brazil, Hong Kong, Mexico, South Korea and Taiwan. The LDCs' exports of textiles, footwear, steel and household electronic equipment, have been seriously affected by these measures. Safeguards are generally applied as a deliberate response to the exporting country's effort to restructure its production in accordance with its changing comparative advantage. Thus, the measures are an integral aspect of the industrialized countries' attempt to slow down the pace of restructuring.

In the Tokyo Round the LDCs argued for the establishment of a code on safeguards that would accord differential treatment to their exports. They maintained that stricter domestic inquiry criteria should apply to products that were of export interest to Third World countries and asked for a commitment from western countries to

Strategies for Trade and Industrialization in the Post-War Era

take concrete steps to restructure out of industrial branches where they had lost an international comparative advantage. None of these positions proved acceptable to the West and no code on safeguards could be included in the MTN agreements. Although negotiations continue, the prospects of achieving a significant breakthrough are not particularly bright. Meanwhile the status quo is maintained and LDCs continue to suffer from the application of a wide range of selective safeguards.

The inability to agree on a satisfactory code governing the application of safeguards has been described as 'certainly the major failure of the Tokyo Round negotiations'. The same observers go on to note that the failure to arrive at agreement on the safeguards issue in particular may mean that 'the evolving international trading system, in spite of the (other) gains achieved at the Tokyo Round negotiations, actually leaves less scope for export oriented growth and industrialization in the developing countries'.[84] All in all, the multilateral trade negotiations fell far short of the Third World's expectations. Much will depend on how signatories' obligations under the various codes will actually be carried out, but the general impression is that the negotiations provide no fresh impetus for LDCs to adapt their patterns of production and trade to changes in comparative advantages.

In the future, the LDCs may find it necessary to re-examine their trade strategies in light of several key structural trends. The ongoing process of structural change in western industry will continue to spur protectionist pressures as long as the current slow pace of growth persists. This trend is further complicated by the growing dispersion of industrial capacity among individual western countries (see Chapter III). As these countries' shares in world industrial production shift, their interests and abilities to influence international negotiations like the Tokyo Round are modified. Both conditions can limit widespread efforts at trade liberalization.

As later discussion will show, structural changes in the LDCs also promise to alter the approaches and alternative trade strategies available to them. These developments will lead to re-adjustments in relations between individual LDCs as well as necessitating fresh approaches with regard to the production and export of different industries in a given LDC. An appraisal of the potential consequ-

The International Economy and Industrial Development

ences of some of these structural changes requires a more detailed level of investigation which is provided in the following chapters. In devising more sophisticated trade strategies, two dangers are (i) that the significant role played by domestic demand in the growth process is obscured and (ii) that the importance of exports to the West (especially in view of present trends) is overemphasized at the expense of potential trade between LDCs. Without this perspective, essential objectives of growth such as basic needs and employment generation are lost in the pursuit of trade expansion, investment and advanced technologies.

With regard to the Brandt Report, a range of issues were addressed that are relevant to this discussion. It stresses that the process of structural adjustment and redeployment 'need not conflict with the long-term interests of the North if pursued in a way which avoids sudden disruptions and changes in trade flows'.[85] The danger is that the troubles of industrial countries are so much more easily, however fallaciously, attributed to the 'unfair' competition from 'low-wage' countries, rather than to their real causes, i.e. technical progress, 'horizontal' division of labour among industrial countries, changes in the structure of demand, etc. As noted elsewhere in this book, numerous empirical studies have confirmed the bogus practice of attributing these troubles to import competition from LDCs.

The types of structural shifts envisaged by the Brandt Report for the industrial countries are not described in any detail, except to note an emphasis on 'skill-intensive and technically advanced goods'. The movement into services is not considered by the Brandt Commission, although such a shift would be in line with changing structures of demand and production at high income levels, i.e. the 'Fourastié effect' as described by Tinbergen in his discussion of the Lima Target.[86]

The threatened spread of neo-protectionism is a central theme and the Report issues a passionate appeal for restraint here. It makes the valid point that the trend towards harsher restrictions hits imports from LDCs harder than those from industrialized countries—a GSP in reverse. The practice penalizes LDCs for adopting the very outward-looking development strategies that industrial countries and international agencies have impressed on them as preferable to inward-looking strategies. This appeal to the industrialized countries could have been elaborated by pointing out that the threat of restrictions, in itself, has a restrictive effect even if that threat is not carried out.

One could add that deflationist policies and restrictionist domestic policies also reduce import demand, and thus have the same effect as protectionist policies. The contractionary route to 'putting their own house in order' now followed by a number of industrial countries amounts to putting their house in order at the expense of LDCs. This fact in itself would create a case for compensatory international action.

While the Report finds grounds for optimism in the progress on codes of conduct for NTBs, government procurement procedures and other matters, it (like the LDCs) is critical of the 'clauses' of the safeguard system and openly sarcastic of voluntary export restraints and orderly marketing agreements. In contrast, the Report is cautious and non-committal as to whether any multilateral machinery designed to settle trade disputes arising from code of conduct agreements will be effectively used or sufficiently respected. Similarly, its recommendations as to the safeguard system are rather weak and non-specific. 'Safeguard measures must be internationally negotiated and should be taken only on the basis of established need. They should be non-discriminatory, of limited duration and subject to international surveillance'.[87] Technically, it could be claimed that the 'voluntary export restraints' and 'orderly marketing arrangements' meet these requirements. The promising idea of compensation—on the lines of proposals made, *inter alia*, by Jagdish Bhagwati[88]—is not taken up. By contrast, the idea of internationally agreed and monitored sectoral change[89] seems utopian in an age when countries jealously guard 'national sovereignty' over their own internal arrangement. Nothing is said about the possibility of sanctions against an offending country if the monitoring body finds that the country fails to comply with a commitment to make industrial adjustment. Compensation (in financial as well as commercial terms) seems much more the promising route. The Report repeatedly emphasizes the formidable difficulties in the way of internationally agreed adjustment and states that progress can only be made step by step.[90] All the more reason, one should have thought, to look more closely at alternative and complementary methods.

With regard to restructuring, Japan's policies are recommended as offering 'valuable lessons' to other industrial countries; but (as the Report implies) it can hardly be said that these policies have included efforts to liberalize and encourage imports. If all industrial countries had adopted strategies of restructuring for export promotion, that would hardly have helped the LDCs. In any case, it would be impossible for all industrial countries to achieve the export successes of Japan—one country's balance of payments surplus is another's deficit. In Japan's case, the export surpluses in manufactured goods based on successful restructuring were in effect largely recycled to OPEC in payment for oil imports.

On the question of fair labour standards, the recommendations correctly (although vaguely) make a distinction between conditions where wages are low because of poverty and thus in line with other incomes, and conditions where wages are held abnormally low in relation to other incomes, with exploitation, child labour, etc. But how in practice to distinguish between these two cases? Presumably some tests or rules are required along with an impartial determination and review. These steps would raise the sensitive issue of 'intervention in domestic affairs', but perhaps a simultaneous review of both industrial countries' adjustment policies and the LDCs' labour standards would be acceptable. But once again, this is looking considerably ahead; we are still a long way away from the level of international co-operation involved in such arrangements.

In conclusion, the Report clearly states the necessity of filling the gap in the Bretton Woods system left in 1947 when the Havana Charter for an International Trade Organization (ITO) failed to obtain ratification by the US Congress. This gap led to an unfortunate dichotomy between a 'rich man's club' (GATT) and a 'poor man's tribunal' (UNCTAD), with only minimum co-operation (mainly the International Trade Centre—ITC) with very limited functions and resources. Pending a new attempt at unification on the lines of the ITO, the Brandt Commission proposes a small co-ordinating body. With astounding optimism it declares that the creation of such a body 'should not be difficult', in clear disregard for the entrenched position of the two groups each embodied in 'their' organization. At this point, the limits of a 'conciliatory' or 'impartial' position as that of the Brandt Report become visible. The rationale for a new ITO or OTC (Organization for Trade Co-operation) remains as strong as it was in 1947 but one feels it can only come at the end of a long hard road after agreement on the substantive aspects of a reformed world trading system has been achieved. To say, as the Commission does, that 'the international community should work towards this objective' may be putting the cart before the horse.

Notes

[1] As discussed later in this chapter, the trade policies of the major protagonists in the World Wars were formulated to serve national political interests and had much to do with the LDCs' desire to minimize international trading links. This was particularly the case in Latin America.

[2] For a good analysis, see Irving Kravis, 'Trade as a handmaiden of growth: similarities between the nineteenth and twentieth centuries', *The Economic Journal*, December 1970, pp. 850–72. The impact of these international disruptions on Latin American economies is documented by Donald W. Baerresen, *et. al.*, *Latin American Trade Patterns*, Brookings Institute, Washington, 1965, Chapter II.

[3] The process has, occasionally, started with capital or intermediate goods which are needed in connection with agricultural or transportation activities. Examples include machetes, coffee hulling machines, trucks, fertilizers and spinning mills.

[4] ECLA, 'The growth and decline of import substitution in Brazil', *Economic Bulletin for Latin America*, Vol. IX, No. 1, March 1964, p. 6.

[5] Economists maintain that the home market bias could be avoided by providing a subsidy to production of all manufactures rather than a tariff. This policy would lead to a shift of resources out of agriculture and into both import-competing manufactures and the export of manufactures.

[6] These points are mentioned by I. Little, *et. al.*, *Industry and Trade in Some Developing Countries*, Oxford University Press, London, 1970, pp. 41–2.

[7] An extreme case may be that of Pakistan, where, on average, over two thirds of value added by industry was 'due to' protection in various forms. See Stephen R. Lewis and Stephen E. Gusinger, 'Measuring protection in a developing country: the case of Pakistan', *Journal of Political Economy*, Vol. 76, No. 6, 1968, p. 1191.

[8] Effective rates of protection were sometimes so high that value added by domestic industry, when evaluated at international rather than domestic prices, proved to be negative. Thus, the value of the industry's inputs at world prices exceeded its output at world prices and foreign exchange was therefore lost. The use of world prices in this connection is not free of controversy, however.

[9] In the case of Mexico the financial-industrial élite faced increased competition from transnationals whose move into domestic production had been spurred by protective

policies. This group played a significant role in developing the Mexican policy of expropriation as a response to foreign inroads. See D. Bennett, M. Blachman and K. Sharpe, 'Mexico and multinational corporations: an explanation of state action', in *Latin American and the World Economy*, Sage Publications, Beverly Hills, 1978, p. 271.

[10] These arguments are made by Albert O. Hirschman, 'The political economy of import substituting industrialization in Latin America', *The Quarterly Journal of Economics*, Vol. LXXXII, No. 1, 1968, p. 18.

[11] The availability of detailed SITC trade statistics at three-, four- and five-digit levels determined the choice of years. In 1968, twenty-eight countries were reported at sufficiently detailed levels.

[12] The individual country data upon which Table II.1 is based also revealed very few instances of successful import replacement in either capital goods or industrial supplies.

[13] The reference is to the definition of Hollis Chenery, 'Patterns of industrial growth', *American Economic Review*, Sept. 1960. For a discussion of differences in concepts and measures, see Padma Desai, 'Alternative measures of import substitution', *Oxford Economic Papers*, Nov. 1969, Vol. 21, pp. 312–24.

[14] An extreme example is the case of automobile production in Mexico. The imports of parts for the assembly of automobiles constituted, in one period, the largest single share of Mexico's total import bill—10 to 20 per cent of total imports between 1956 and 1959. See Secrétaria de Industria y Comercio, *Memoira de Labores*, Mexico, Talleres Graficos de la Nacion, 1959, Table 19.

[15] UNIDO, *Industrial Development Survey*, special issue for the second general conference, United Nations, New York, 1974, pp. 18–19.

[16] Hollis Chenery and Lance Taylor, 'Development patterns: among countries and over time', *Review of Economics and Statistics*, Vol. L, Nov. 1968, p. 412.

[17] Calculations were based on data in United Nations, *Growth of World Industry 1938–1961*. The countries included were Argentina, Brazil, Chile, Colombia, India, Korea, Mexico, Pakistan and Turkey. The figure is an unweighted average for the sample countries.

[18] Joel Bergsman, 'Industrial priorities in Brazil', in UNIDO *Industrial Priorities*, United Nations, New York, 1979, p. 18.

[19] This trend is well documented by G. K. Helleiner, 'Manufactured exports from less-developed countries and multinational firms', *Economic Journal*, March 1973, pp. 21–47.

[20] Y. Kurenkov, 'Scientific and technological progress and structural changes in world industrial production', paper presented at the Second International Conference on Industrial Economics, Székesfehérvar, Hungary, 5–9 Sept. 1978, p. 3.

[21] *Ibid.*, p. 15.

[22] Alfred Maizels, *Industrial Growth and World Trade, An Empirical Study of Trends in Production, Consumption and Trade in Manufactures from 1899–1959 with a Discussion of Probable Trends*, The National Institute of Economic and Social Research, Economic and Social Studies, XXI, Cambridge, 1963, p. 64.

[23] The figures cited in this paragraph were drawn from UNIDO, *World Industry Since 1960: Progress and Prospects*, United Nations, New York, 1979, Chapters 2, 3,

5 and 6.
[24] *Ibid.*, p. 177.
[25] United Nations, *Monthly Bulletin of Statistics*, various issues.
[26] In 1945 Latin America accounted for 42 per cent of all United States imports but, by 1975, this figure had dropped to 17 per cent. See Albert Fishlow, 'The mature neighbor policy', in *Latin America and World Economy, op. cit.*, p. 38.
[27] Gordon Connell-Smith, *The United States and Latin America*, Halsted Press, New York, 1974, p. 190.
[28] Latin Americans have pointed to the Common Agricultural Policy, the Common External Tariff and the preferential trade policies with associated countries as programmes which discriminate against Latin America relative to its competitors. See, for example, Albert von Gleich, 'The economic relations between Germany and Latin America and the significance of the European Community', in *Latin America and World Economy, op. cit.*, p. 111.
[29] Figures are cited in Bela Balassa, 'Export incentives and export performance in developing countries, a comparative analysis', *Weltwirtschaftliches Archiv*, Band 114, Heft 1, 1978, pp. 24–61.
[30] This impression is subscribed to by J. Donges, 'A comparative survey of industrialization policies in fifteen semi-industrialized countries', *Weltwirtschaftliches Archiv*, Band 112, Heft, 4, 1976, p. 655. For similar conclusions, see also, The World Bank, *The Philippines, Priorities and Prospects for Development*, The World Bank, Washington, D.C., 1976, pp. 216–18. B. Balassa, *Policy Reform in Developing Countries*, Pergamon Press, New York, 1977, pp. 34 and 75–7 makes the same point for Mexico and Chile.
[31] In Colombia and Brazil, for example, the number of state permits needed to arrange a foreign trade deal was reduced from 25–30 to 5–6, thereby decreasing decision-making delays. These moves coincided with the shift to an export oriented strategy.
[32] The method was originally proposed by Hollis Chenery, 'Patterns of industrial growth', *American Economic Review*, Vol. 50, No. 2, Sept. 1960, pp. 624–54, and H. Chenery, S. Shishido and T. Watanabe, 'The pattern of Japanese growth: 1914–1954', *Econometrica*, Vol. 30, No. 1, January 1962, pp. 98–139.
[33] See p. 45.
[34] In other words, proponents would include both the direct and indirect domestic production needed to replace imports. See S. A. Morley and G. W. Smith, 'On the measurement of import substitution', *American Economic Review*, Vol. LX, No. 4, pp. 728–35.
[35] G. Fane, 'Import substitution and export expansion: their measurement and an example of their application', *The Pakistan Development Review*, Vol. 11, No. 1, Spring 1971, pp. 1–17.
[36] See G. Fane, 'Consistent measures of import substitution', *Oxford Economic Papers*, Vol. 25, No. 2, July 1973, pp. 252–61.
[37] Various economists have stressed the relationship between *per capita* exports and *per capita* GNP. For example, the average country of ten million population will export $10 *per capita* at an income level of about $250 *per capita*. Hollis Chenery and Helen Hughes, 'Industrialization and trade trends', in *Prospects for Partnership*, ed.

The International Economy and Industrial Development
by Helen Hughes, John Hopkins Press, Baltimore, 1973, p. 4.

[38] Reciprocal trade was taken to mean that any tariff reduction granted by the United States would be matched by equivalent concessions from its trading partners.

[39] These and the following figures were taken from Kravis, *op. cit.*, p. 862.

[40] The predominance of manufactures in the growth of western countries' trade became even more pronounced in later years. For example, between 1953 and 1966 merchandise trade grew at 122 per cent per decade while manufactures expanded by 152 per cent. In our opinion, such a growth performance can hardly be attributed to the favourable international policies fashioned after World War II. More likely, it reflects the basic directions of structural change in western countries and policy makers were adroit in recognizing these trends when formulating their post-war politico-economic goals.

[41] Charles P. Kindleberger, 'Government, policies and changing shares in world trade', *American Economic Review, papers and proceedings*, Vol. 70, No. 2, 1980, p. 293.

[42] Albert Fishlow, 'The mature neighbor policy', in *Latin America and World Economy*, ed. by J. Grunwald, Sage Publications, London, 1978, p. 34.

[43] *Ibid.*, pp. 33–4.

[44] Detractors within the United States were also vociferous. The Department of Agriculture insisted on exemptions which would permit the United States to continue agricultural price supports in excess of world market prices. See Richard Gardner, *Sterling-Dollar Diplomacy*, Clarendon Press, Oxford, 1956, pp. 149–50.

[45] These considerations are discussed in more detail by Kenneth Dam, *The GATT, Law and International Organization*, University of Chicago Press, Chicago, 1970, Chapter II.

[46] Wilbur Moore, *International Trade Policy in Transition*, D. C. Heath and Company, Lexington, Mass., 1975, p. 13.

[47] Significantly, many of the economists' proposals at Bretton Woods were never fully implemented. Keynes had argued for the creation of an international trade organization to stabilize commodity prices, the establishment of a world central bank and a big world development authority. The first of these, in the form of the International Trade Organization, was never constituted due to disagreement regarding the extent of regulatory power. In fact, the United States itself failed to ratify the organization's charter. As for the other institutional ambitions, the IMF plays a partial role in the second case and the World Bank has a mandate—which is much smaller than originally intended—as a world development authority. The example illustrates the fact that failures to reach multilateral agreements on trade policy were due as much to overriding political issues in many countries as they were to differences of opinion between countries on purely economic grounds.

[48] The United States' failure to gain acceptance of several proposals supports the point made by Charles Kindleberger that unless a country can dictate the trade policies of its importers, government policies have a negligible effect on the competitive share of the country's exports. Kindleberger, *op. cit.*, p. 293.

[49] Bela Balassa, 'The new protectionism and the international economy', *Journal of World Trade Law*, Vol. 12, No. 5, 1978, p. 429.

[50] The problems were very basic. On the one hand, foreign trade and economic

policy justified market interventions intended to expand trade through co-operative national actions. On the other hand, agricultural policy demanded interventions intended to maintain or raise prices, an objective which was not compatible with that of expanded trade. The interests and motives of different groups of policy makers and producers were in direct conflict. For a good review of the subject during 1945–70, see William Diebold, *The United States and the Industrial World*, Praeger New York, 1972, Chapter 8.

[51] See Ian Little, *op. cit.*, pp. 162–3.

[52] Edward Denison, *Why Growth Rates Differ*, Brookings Institute, Washington, 1967, pp. 260–3. The estimates do not cover the later period of vigorous trade liberalization, however.

[53] Reference is to a Commission on Foreign Economic Policy, better known as the Randall Commission.

[54] The principle of most favoured nation meant that any concession granted by one country to another was automatically extended to all other countries even if they did not participate in the tariff negotiation. Thus, bilateral agreements had multilateral application.

[55] Because nominal rates on raw materials were already lower than those for materials, even equal percentage reductions would have lowered the margin of effective protection.

[56] See, for example, the pre- and post-Kennedy estimates for tariff averages in I. Little, *op. cit.*, p. 273.

[57] Figures are in constant prices of 1958. See UNIDO, *Industrial Development Survey*, Vol. I, United Nations, New York, 1969, p. 117.

[58] Kravis, *op. cit.*, p. 862.

[59] This practice was also encouraged by the overvaluation of the dollar relative to various European currencies.

[60] See, for example, R. M. Dunn, 'Canada and its economic discontents', *Foreign Affairs*, October 1973.

[61] Commercial policy legislation is rife with jargon which seldom conveys underlying meanings. A 'peril-point' clause was introduced requiring the United States Tariff Commission to determine in advance the minimum tariff which could be adopted 'without causing or threatening serious injury to domestic industry'. An 'escape clause' was incorporated giving the United States the right to alter previous tariff concessions if domestic producers experienced or were likely to experience serious injury. These types of clauses, in addition to qualifications on grounds of national security, were strengthened and broadened in the Trade Act of 1974.

[62] President Kennedy's use of the escape clause for these two rather insignificant items immediately after the Dillon Round sparked a major dispute with the EEC.

[63] Tracy Murray, Wilson Schmidt and Ingo Walter, 'Alternative forms of protection against market disruption', *Kyklos*, Vol. 31, p. 627.

[64] For example, West Germany provides 75 to 90 per cent of the difference between the full-time wage and wages earned by workers who are shifted to part-time work because of unfavourable business conditions. Weaker industries tend to benefit the most since they have proportionately more part-time workers. In 1977, about one half the benefits of the British Temporary Employment Subsidy Schemes went to the

textile, clothing and footwear branches. These proportions were still roughly the same in 1980 despite protests from the EEC.

[65] The imagined threat to employment in the West from expanded exports of the LDCs was, for several years, a subject of intense debate. Recent studies have concluded that employment in Western countries benefits in general from expanded trade with LDCs. See UNIDO, *World Industry, op. cit.*, pp. 20–1; UNIDO, 'The impact of trade with developing countries on employment in developed countries', Working Paper No. 3, 1979 and OECD, 'The impact of the newly industrialized countries', Paris, 1979.

[66] The macro-economic policy approaches of western countries were undergoing a slow evolution during the period 1945–70. As tariff barriers were reduced, their usefulness as a policy solution to short-term balance of payments and unemployment problems was eroded. Exchange rate adjustments became the predominant means of dealing with these problems in the 1970s. Thus, when trade restrictions were downgraded from a macro-policy tool, they became more useful in more specific instances, i.e. as a means of structural policy. The emergence of commercial policy as a means of structural adjustment has been persuasively posed by G. K. Helleiner, 'Structural aspects of third world trade: some trends and some prospects', *The Journal of Development Studies*, Vol. 15, 1979, pp. 70–87.

[67] This interpretation and the supporting data are provided by Helleiner, *ibid.*, p. 80.

[68] Interfutures, *Facing the Future: Mastering the Probable and Managing the Unpredictable*, OECD, Paris, 1979, p. 154.

[69] Helleiner, *op. cit.*, p. 80.

[70] Figures are based on Economic Commission for Latin America (ECLA), 'The resurgence of protectionism in the industrial countries' (E/CEPAL/1055) 1978, p. 5.

[71] A. Olechowski and G. Sampson, 'Current trade restrictions in the EEC, the United States and Japan', *Journal of World Trade Law*, May/June 1980, p. 231.

[72] Expenditures on automation can be substantial. For example, in the US purchases of fully and partially automated equipment and means of automation accounted for nearly 40 per cent of capital investment in manufacturing in 1976. See UNIDO, *World Industry, op. cit.*, p. 21.

[73] Goran Ohlin attributes manufacture's contraction problems to other reasons such as the slowdown in growth of population and the fact that agriculture is now too small to provide the 'reserve army' for expansion of manufacturing. See Ohlin 'Subsidies and other industrial aids', in *International Trade and Industrial Policies*, Steven J. Weinecke (ed.), MacMillan Press, London, 1978, p. 27. Rising rates of unemployment would seem to contradict these explanations, however.

[74] Output shares are expressed in current prices. The downward trend is not so pronounced when shares are calculated at constant prices. This divergence has been attributed to the fact that relative prices have tended to move against manufacturing. See C. J. F. Brown and T. D. Sheriff, 'De-industrialization: a background paper', in *De-industrialization*, Frank Blackaby (ed.), National Institute of Economic and Social Research, London, 1978, p. 239–40.

[75] Thus, as firms become more mobile internationally, resource distortions are magnified. See Melvyn B. Krauss, *The New Protectionism*, Basil Blackwell, Oxford, 1979, Chapter I.

Strategies for Trade and Industrialization in the Post-War Era

[76] It is significant that those branches where competition and growth is most vigorous—e.g. sophisticated electronics, aerospace—are not major participants in this process.

[77] Trends in recent years show an increasing interest on the part of western economies to discuss codes of conduct for TNEs, foreign investment practices, the international transfer of technology and even global investment funds. None of the questions was even open to discussion prior to 1975. Thus the willingness of governments to talk, if not yet act, may indicate some changes in priorities in these countries based on a re-evaluation of self-interests.

[78] Ohlin, *op. cit.*, p. 32.

[79] Interfutures, *op. cit.*, p. 349.

[80] General Agreement on Tariff and Trade, 'Declaration of Ministers, Tokyo, September 1973', in *Basic Instruments and Selected Documents*, 20 Supp., Geneva, 1974, p. 1.

[81] The World Bank has estimated that the simple average tariff cuts on LDC exports would be 2.5 per cent for industrial and 7 per cent for agricultural products. IBRD, *World Development Report, 1980*, Washington, 1980, p. 21.

[82] *Ibid.*

[83] Summarized in P. Ginman, T. Pugel and I. Walter, 'Mixed blessings for the third world in codes on non-tariff measures', *The World Economy*, Vol. 3, No. 2, 1981, pp. 217–34.

[84] Ginman, Pugel and Walter, *op. cit.*, pp. 230, 233.

[85] *North-South: A Programme for Survival*, the report of the Independent Commission on International Development Issues under the Chairmanship of Willy Brandt, Pan Books Ltd., London, 1980, p. 175.

[86] Jan Tinbergen, 'The target of twenty-five per cent for the Third World', *Industry and Development*, No. 3, edited by H. W. Singer, UNIDO (sales no. E.79.II.B.2), New York, 1979.

[87] *Ibid.*, p. 186.

[88] Jagdish Bhagwati, 'Industrial expansion in developing countries and implications for trade policies', *Industry and Development*, *op. cit.*, pp. 45–53.

[89] *North-South*, *op. cit.*, p. 181.

[90] *Ibid.*, p. 182.

Part II

Structural Relationships between Industry and Trade

Preface

Part I of this book examined the role of the external sector during the industrialization process in different societies, drawing on the experience of advanced countries in the nineteenth and early twentieth centuries and the LDCs after World War II. Comparatively little is known about the role and interaction of interest groups in formulating the Third World's strategies. This failure is partly due to the limited industrial experience (roughly three decades) of LDCs in applying strategies of import substitution or export promotion. As a first step in this learning process, Part II attempts to analyse in more detail some broad structural relationships between industry and trade. We are interested in how these structural forces influence industrial development in the Third World. Obviously, changes in the industrial structure of advanced countries have a significant impact on the Third World's development and must also be considered in this context.

A country's economic structure, measured, for example, by the contribution of primary, secondary and tertiary activities to GDP, typically undergoes a constant pattern of change. Simultaneously, the country's industrial structure, i.e. the composition of output within the manufacturing sector, will also reveal a similar pattern of change. These structural adjustments are partly a response to pressures resulting from technological advances, the accumulation of physical capital, the growth of a skilled labour force, changes in

The International Economy and Industrial Development

tastes, etc. As a result, the country's ability to efficiently carry out various types of industrial activities is altered over time giving rise to a restructuring process at both the national and international levels.

In recent years, the willingness of advanced societies to accept changes and to adapt their industrial structures accordingly has waned. Although adjustment pressures in industrialized countries may mount, labour and other resources no longer move smoothly from unprofitable, contracting activities to expanding ones. In LDCs the movement of resources into new industries often occurs at a comparatively rapid pace. One consequence is that the contraction of an industrial branch in one group of countries is often preceded by an expansion of production capacity in that branch in other countries. This distinction in timing can lead to international imbalances in product and factor markets and, in turn, to adjustment problems. Because the pattern of industrial growth is often similar in countries at comparable levels of development, the potential contraction or expansion of an industrial branch results in adjustment pressures common to several countries and further complicates the problem.

In today's world, a useful parallel may be drawn between certain contracting industrial branches and the historical long-term decline in the agricultural sector. The contraction, expressed both in terms of the sector's share in GDP and in employment, occurred as resources and manpower were shifted into manufacturing. These shifts (and the implicit costs involved) came to be handled through political means. The resultant social and political problems led to a network of policies that largely isolated agriculture from the market dicta which otherwise governed resource allocation. Although agriculture continues to decline, it does so at a reduced pace thanks to the generous range of protective measures and subsidies which governments accord to it.

Part II includes an extensive analysis of the changing pattern of production and trade in the West and the Third World. By examining different sets of industries and groups of countries, we are able to gain some insights which later prove useful for examining the interrelationships between the behaviour of various interest groups, the formulation of industrial policy and the pattern of structural change. These relationships can vary greatly depending

Preface

on the industrial branch. Part II concludes with a series of case studies intended to demonstrate the diverse set of considerations that affect the restructuring process.

Chapter III

Structural Changes in World Industry

Western and socialist countries have long dominated the industrial field. Prior to World War II their predominance was almost total. Although the period 1950–70 was the phase of most rapid industrial growth throughout the world, this pre-eminence continued; as late as 1977 the industrialized countries accounted for 92 per cent of world manufacturing value added.[1] The present chapter focuses on patterns of structural change in the manufacturing sectors of both the industrialized countries and the Third World. We begin by tracing the global spread of industry, starting from the industrial centre at the outset of the twentieth century. Growth patterns and changes in the industrial mix are singled out for particular attention. Patterns of industrial growth and structural transformation are then considered.

3.1 *The spread of world industry*

The global spread of industrial capacity is a comparatively recent phenomenon, roughly spanning the last three decades. During the first quarter of this century net manufacturing output was concentrated in ten countries that accounted for at least 95 per cent of the world's manufacturing value added (MVA). Estimates for subsequent years are given in Table III.1. They show that, prior to 1970, the predominance of the industrialized countries (both western and socialist) was unchallenged. However, among the industrialized countries, shifts in their relative shares of output and industrial capacity were considerable. Third World producers were mainly onlookers and not participants at this stage in the growth process.

The International Economy and Industrial Development

Table III.1. Estimated shares of world output in manufacturing by various country groupings, selected years

	1938	1948	1953	1963	1975
Western countries	61.0	72.2	72.0	64.8	64.5
of which:					
industrial centre[a]	...	...	65.8	51.8	44.5
recently industrialized[b]	...	...	3.9	7.8	13.9
other	...	...	2.3	5.2	6.1
Socialist countries	34.5	22.1	23.2	28.5	25.7
Third World	4.5	5.7	4.8	6.6	8.9
of which:					
NICs[c]	...	...	3.6	4.7	6.9

Source: United Nations, *Statistical Yearbook*, various issues; *Yearbook of Industrial Statistics*, various issues and UNIDO, *Industrial Development Survey*, various issues.

Notes: [a] 'The industrial centre' includes Belgium, Luxembourg, France, Italy, the Netherlands, Norway, Sweden, the United Kingdom, the United States and West Germany.

[b] Recently industrialized countries are: Greece, Ireland, Israel, Italy, Japan, Portugal and Spain.

[c] NICs are: Argentina, Brazil, Colombia, Hong Kong, India, Mexico, Panama, Puerto Rico, South Korea, Tunisia, Turkey and Yugoslavia.

During the 1970s, the latter countries did begin to claim larger shares of net manufacturing output and production capacity.

Table III.1 illustrates the major directions of these shifts. The socialist countries, the recently industrialized market economies and the newly industrializing countries (NICs) all gained at the relative expense of the established industrial centre. In turn, the comparative importance of individual countries in the industrial centre changed substantially. These shifts were instrumental in bringing about changes in the international policy environment. As the restructuring process continued, various industrialized countries (e.g. Japan, Switzerland, West Germany) acquired a greater relative influence in matters of trade, investment, technology and related industrial issues of an international character. Simultaneously, the ability of certain countries to influence or sway international industrial policy waned as their shares in world MVA declined.[2]

Structural Changes in World Industry

One consequence of the declining predominance of the United States (see Table II. 3) is that policy approaches must now be fashioned from a consensus between several decision-making groups often consisting of the European Economic Community (EEC), Japan and, sometimes, the Scandinavian and socialist countries. Clearly, no one position on a given subject prevails today in a fashion such as the American free trade position did following World War II. The rise in the number of large and relatively equal industrial powers has increased the degree of divisiveness among industrialized countries. Although relations between the United States and the Soviet Union have been the overriding divisive force, this trend is on the upswing among western countries, pitting the United States against the EEC or its individual members and drawing in Japan and the smaller developed countries. Confrontations among socialist countries, involving the USSR and China, Czechoslovakia and Poland, for example, have also occurred with growing frequency.

Industrial growth has also altered many relationships between the industrialized countries and the Third World. First, the overall growth of manufacturing activities has both facilitated and induced more trade (in primary goods as well as manufactures), accelerated the international transfer of technology and encouraged international movements of both labour and capital (especially foreign investment by transnationals). These economic links, although most obvious in the West, are of growing importance for all countries. Second, advances in related fields have had a similar result. The technological revolution in transport and communication has profoundly altered the ability to transfer goods, people and ideas to other countries. Third, new extraction technologies permitted the introduction of a wide variety of new goods which consumers in industrialized countries proved quite ready to absorb.

Each trend has prompted countries of the industrialized centre to reach out to the Third World in their search for new resources and markets. In so doing, their reliance on foreign suppliers (including those in LDCs) increased substantially after 1950. The LDCs, although not always willing participants, have seen their own relations with the industrialized countries expand as industrial progress continued. The West's predominant role in the economic

The International Economy and Industrial Development

links referred to above has further accentuated their importance for the Third World's industrial prospects. Moreover, the latter's growing familiarity with modern goods, technologies and new forms of organization facilitated this relationship.

The growing 'internationalism' of industry has affected national and international policy in complex ways due to different patterns of structural change in advanced countries and in the LDCs. A major policy objective of the West (cited in Chapter II) was the increased integration of the OECD economies through expanded trade and industrial growth. In the long term, these moves have led to a growing similarity in industrial structures of these countries. Similarity or homogeneity may, of course, be defined in a variety of ways. For present purposes one pertinent way of examining the phenomenon is in terms of changes in the branch distribution of net manufacturing output over time. Similarities in the composition of manufacturing output suggest roughly comparable factor requirements, technologies and structural bottlenecks. Under these conditions the industrial and trade policies of different countries are more likely to be loosely related, at least in their priorities and emphasises.

Prior to 1960 only very rough measures of structural change are available. Comparing structural changes in the 1960s with limited data for the first half of this century does lead to two generalizations. First, the pace of structural change, like the pace of industrial growth, was distinctly faster during the 1960s than in the previous fifty years. Second, statistical measures showed a steady increase in the similarity of the composition of output over time.[3]

Table III.2 provides more detailed information on output mix of selected western countries in the 1960s and 1970s. The weighted averages are best suited to represent the distribution of output in the group while the unweighted averages are more likely to reflect the output structure of a country chosen at random. Shifts in structure, according to both measures, were gradual between 1963 and 1975. In terms of the weighted measure the largest drop was in the share of iron and steel (1.2 per cent) while output of non-electrical machinery showed the largest increase (1.5 per cent). These figures also tell us something about directions of structural change. The traditional view is that a broadening industrial base is typically associated with a growing share of heavy industry in manufacturing output. This opinion is not necessarily confirmed, however, by the figures in Table III.2. The shares of several branches usually defined as light industry (e.g. ISIC 311/2, 313, 332, 342 and 356) actually rose. Others, identified as part of heavy industry (341, 351, 352, 362, 371, 372 and 384), showed a fall in their average shares.

Structural changes in western countries during the 1970s suggest two traits which may help to explain the possible contraction between recent experience and this 'rule of thumb'. First, the contraction in the shares of certain branches often depicted as 'early industries'[4] is approaching, or in some cases has reached, a limit. In the past, the declining shares of these branches were explained in terms of income elasticities of domestic demand (less than unity) and their reliance on relatively simple technologies. There are limits, however, to the extent of contraction in any branch. For political reasons, governments are not likely to permit the continued contraction of agriculture. Thus, they indirectly support agro-processing branches like food, beverages, tobacco and textiles. There are economic reasons, as well, to expect that contraction will be limited. The demand for necessities, although not serving as a long-term growth stimulus when manufacturing is expanding rapidly, will continue to be a significant component of aggregate demand particularly if the growth of income is slow.

Second, complementary trends in certain branches of heavy industry seem likely to re-enforce new patterns of structural change. The traditional view that rapid technological advances are associated with heavy industry or, in Chenery's terminology, 'late industries' (e.g. basic metals, printing and metal products) is no longer altogether true. Certainly, the pace of technological advance is rapid in electronics, specific types of machinery and capital goods. However, it has also led to substitution processes (e.g. aluminium, plastics and glass for steel) and to reductions of industrial inputs per unit of output.[5] Similarly, in several of these branches—iron and steel, non-ferrous metals, chemicals, petroleum refining and products of petroleum—interdependence has been accentuated with the effects of supply bottlenecks and flagging demand being rapidly transferred from one economy to another.

The structure of the manufacturing sector in LDCs is shown in

Table III.2 The structure of net manufacturing output in selected western countries,[a] 1963 and 1975 (percentages)

ISIC	Branch	1963		1975	
		Weighted share	Unweighted share (standard deviation)	Weighted share	Unweighted share (standard deviation)
311/2	Food products	9.5	12.0 (3.1)	9.6	10.9 (3.9)
313	Beverages	1.5	2.3 (1.0)	2.2	2.8 (1.1)
314	Tobacco	1.0	1.6 (1.5)	0.9	1.1 (0.8)
321	Textiles	4.7	7.4 (3.9)	4.3	6.0 (4.1)
322	Wearing apparel	3.4	4.3 (1.7)	2.8	4.4 (4.5)
323	Leather and fur products	0.4	0.6 (0.3)	0.4	0.6 (0.4)
324	Footwear	0.7	1.3 (0.8)	0.6	0.9 (0.6)
331	Wood and cork products	2.5	4.0 (1.6)	2.2	3.0 (1.6)
332	Furniture and fixtures, excluding metal	1.3	2.0 (0.8)	1.5	2.5 (1.4)
341	Paper	4.4	5.0 (4.0)	3.9	4.2 (3.0)
342	Printing and publishing	4.8	4.9 (1.9)	5.0	4.6 (1.7)
351	Industrial chemicals	5.2	3.6 (1.6)	5.1	4.2 (1.6)
352	Other chemicals	4.4	3.7 (1.0)	4.2	3.5 (1.2)
353	Petroleum refineries	1.5	1.7 (0.9)	2.1	1.6 (1.2)

Structural Changes in World Industry

354	Miscellaneous products of petroleum and coal	0.3	0.4 (0.2)	0.3	0.4 (0.3)
355	Rubber products	1.6	1.4 (0.6)	1.4	1.4 (0.7)
356	Plastic products	1.0	1.0 (0.5)	1.8	1.7 (0.5)
361	Pottery, china and earthenware	0.3	0.5 (0.5)	0.3	0.4 (0.3)
362	Glass	1.0	0.8 (0.2)	0.9	0.9 (0.3)
369	Other non-metallic mineral products	2.9	3.8 (0.8)	2.8	3.6 (1.1)
371	Iron and steel	6.6	5.0 (3.1)	5.4	4.8 (2.5)
372	Non-ferrous metals	2.1	1.7 (1.0)	1.8	1.9 (1.2)
381	Metal products, excluding machinery	6.9	6.9 (1.8)	7.0	7.9 (2.0)
382	Non-electrical machinery	9.7	8.1 (3.7)	11.2	8.0 (4.0)
383	Electrical machinery	8.1	5.8 (1.8)	8.1	7.2 (1.6)
384	Transport equipment	10.7	8.2 (2.3)	10.5	8.8 (2.7)
385	Professional and scientific equipment, photographic and optical goods	2.1	0.9 (0.7)	2.2	1.0 (0.8)
390	Other manufacturers	1.5	1.1 (0.4)	1.5	1.8 (1.7)

Source: United Nations, *Yearbook of Industrial Statistics*, various issues; and UNIDO, *World Industry in 1980*, New York, 1981, Chapter I, Table I.13, p. 53.

Note: [a] Countries with adequate statistical coverage in 1963 included: Australia, Canada, Denmark, Finland, Greece, Japan, South Africa, Spain, Sweden, the United States and Yugoslavia. Additional countries added in the 1975 averages were: Austria, Belgium, France, Israel, New Zealand, Norway, Portugal and the United Kingdom. Calculations were based on data in US dollars. For the weighting procedure, see UNIDO, *World Industry since 1960: Progress and Prospects*, pp. 69–71.

Table III.3. The structure of net manufacturing output in selected LDCs,[a] 1963 and 1975 (percentages)

ISIC	Branch	1963 Weighted share	1963 Unweighted share	1975[b] Weighted share	1975[b] Unweighted share
311/2	Food products	18.3	23.3	13.5 (12.7)	19.5 (18.8)
313	Beverages	4.4	7.1	3.4 (4.2)	5.4 (5.6)
314	Tobacco	3.2	4.1	2.9 (3.1)	4.7 (3.8)
321	Textiles	14.4	13.5	10.8 (10.5)	13.7 (11.6)
322	Wearing apparel	4.0	2.8	3.2 (3.0)	4.1 (2.5)
323	Leather and fur products	0.7	0.8	0.6 (0.6)	0.9 (0.7)
324	Footwear	1.4	1.3	1.0 (0.9)	1.6 (0.9)
331	Wood and cork products	2.4	2.4	2.2 (1.9)	2.9 (2.2)
332	Furniture and fixtures, excluding metal	0.9	1.2	1.2 (0.8)	1.4 (0.9)
341	Paper	2.4	2.4	2.3 (2.7)	2.0 (2.5)
342	Printing and publishing	2.6	3.2	2.4 (2.3)	2.4 (2.5)
351	Industrial chemicals	2.7	2.4	4.1 (5.3)	3.0 (3.9)
352	Other chemicals	5.5	5.0	5.8 (5.8)	4.9 (5.6)
353	Petroleum refineries	3.7	4.1	5.2 (6.1)	5.4 (6.8)
354	Miscellaneous products of petroleum and coal	0.2	0.2	0.7 (0.5)	0.5 (0.3)

Structural Changes in World Industry

355	Rubber products	2.9	2.6	1.9 (1.9)	1.8 (2.0)
356	Plastic products	0.6	0.7	1.6 (1.4)	1.4 (1.6)
361	Pottery, china and earthenware	0.7	0.3	0.7 (0.5)	0.4 (0.3)
362	Glass	0.8	0.8	0.9 (1.0)	0.7 (0.9)
369	Other non-metallic mineral products	3.5	4.0	3.5 (3.4)	4.0 (4.2)
371	Iron and steel	4.3	2.2	5.3 (5.7)	2.8 (3.5)
372	Non-ferrous metals	1.9	1.8	1.8 (2.2)	1.7 (1.9)
381	Metal products, excluding machinery	5.4	4.4	4.8 (5.2)	4.1 (4.5)
382	Non-electrical machinery	2.8	2.0	5.5 (4.6)	2.1 (2.6)
383	Electrical machinery	2.6	2.1	5.1 (4.8)	3.1 (3.7)
384	Transport equipment	5.2	4.0	7.6 (7.1)	3.6 (4.8)
385	Professional and scientific equipment, photographic and optical goods	0.3	0.2	0.5 (0.5)	0.4 (0.3)
390	Other manufactures	2.2	1.1	1.5 (1.4)	1.4 (1.0)

Source: Same as Table III.2. Table I.12, p. 52.

Notes: [a] Only a limited number of LDCs provided sufficient statistics adequately covering net manufacturing output at ISIC three-digit levels. The sample for 1963 included: Angola, Argentina, Chile, Colombia, Costa Rica, Ecuador, India, Indonesia, Kenya, Mexico, Morocco, Mozambique, Peru, Philippines, South Korea, Turkey, Uruguay and Venezuela. All data were in US dollars at current prices.
[b] The sample consisted of forty-three countries with complete coverage at ISIC three-digit level. Figures in parenthesis are coverages calculated for the identical country sample for which 1963 calculations were made.

Table III.3. The distribution of shares in the two years (1963 and 1975) is substantially different, a consequence of structural changes when the industrial base is incomplete. Here, the declining importance of various 'early industries'—food products, beverages and textiles—is obvious. Branches which increased their shares in net manufacturing output include industrial chemicals, petroleum refining, iron and steel, electrical and non-electrical machinery and transport equipment. In general, the magnitude of the shifts is greater than that found in western countries and more closely conforms to earlier notions regarding patterns of change. Our conclusion is that, unlike the pattern of structural shifts in western countries, those observed in the Third World continue to reflect the types of changes witnessed in the late 1950s and 1960s.

A similar exercise for socialist countries could not be carried out due both to data paucity and incomparability with other data sets.[6] The limited available information points to a pattern of specialization that is essentially different from structural changes in either western countries or in the Third World. The emphasis placed on the development of heavy industry has accentuated the relative importance of construction and engineering with relatively lower shares for other branches such as wood processing, paper, clothing, leather and food.

Admittedly, the foregoing comparison of structural changes in the output mix of western and Third World economies has yet to be thoroughly tested. Such an exercise would be extremely lengthy and severely hampered by a lack of appropriate data. The description does reflect a synthesis of opinion discussed in Chapters IV and V of this book. The interpretation offered would obviously hold different implications for the growth patterns of industrialized countries and LDCs. Specifically, we would expect that the structures of manufacturing output in western economies are becoming more homogeneous over time. It does not necessarily follow, however, that a similar trend would be experienced in LDCs.

The result of an empirical investigation comparing output structures is summarized in Table III.4. Output mix was defined in terms of the twenty-eight industrial branches considered above. The coefficients show a considerable similarity in the output mix of western countries. Equally important, this similarity has risen over

Structural Changes in World Industry

Table III.4. Kendall's coefficient of concordance between the rankings of industrial branches (value added) across countries, 1963, 1970 and 1975[a]

Sample group	Number of countries	1963	1970	1975
Western countries	11	0.787	0.812	0.830
		(36.948)[b]	(43.191)	(48.824)
LDCs	13	0.697	0.684	0.706
		(23.005)	(21.641)	(24.003)
Western countries	18	. . .	0.748	0.772
			(29.683)	(33.861)
LDCs	37	. . .	0.530	0.525
			(11.273)	(11.053)

Source: UNIDO, World Industry in 1980, Chapter I, Table I.12, p. 56.

Notes: [a] The definition of an adjusted coefficient of concordance (W') is given by the equation:

$$W' = \frac{[12(S-1)]}{k^2(n^3-n)+24}$$

where S is the sum of the squares of the durations of the total of the ranks obtained by each object from the average of these totals. The number of rankings are k and n is the number of objects in each ranking. See A. E. Maxwell, *Analysing Qualitative Data*, Methuen and Company, London, 1967, pp. 117–21.

[b] F values are given in parentheses. All coefficients are significant at 99 per cent.

time. An increase in the number of countries included in the sample (from eleven to eighteen) reduces Kendall's coefficient of concordance by only a marginal amount.[7] Comparing the coefficients for western economies with those for LDCs confirms that there is a distinct difference in output structures between the two groups.[8] Furthermore, there is no observable trend (upward or downward) in the homogeneity of the latter countries over time. The inclusion of additional LDCs reduces the coefficients considerably. Most likely, with more complete information, the differences in the coefficients of the two groups of countries would become even more marked.

Based on the foregoing analysis and results, there seem to be

The International Economy and Industrial Development

sufficient grounds to conclude that the structure of net manufacturing output in western economies has slowly but steadily become more homogeneous. Such a trend holds important implications for the pattern of trade in manufactures as well as trade and industrial policies. We can make no similarly definitive statement with regard to structural changes in LDCs, although the impression remains that, if anything, the output mixes of these countries are becoming more dissimilar over time.

The net effect of the global spread in capacity as well as changes in the branch structure of output may best be summarized by comparing the relative and absolute gaps in income and MVA *per capita* for different sets of countries. Other studies, comparing OECD countries and LDCs, have confirmed that the income gap has widened over time. While the significance of such measures is questionable when addressing issues of mass poverty, they are

Table III.5. Absolute and relative gaps in *per capita* GDP and MVA, 1960 and 1977

Country groups (number of countries)	Absolute gap (current US dollars)		Relative gap (percentages)	
	1960	1977	1960	1977
Low-income LDCs (72) with western economies (26):				
GDP *per capita*	1385	6242	7.3	5.1
MVA *per capita*	436	1724	3.2	3.0
High-income LDCs (21) with western economies (26):				
GDP *per capita*	1099	4845	26.4	26.4
MVA *per capita*	366	1398	18.8	21.3
Low-income LDCs (72) and high-income LDCs (21):				
GDP *per capita*	286	1398	27.4	19.5
MVA *per capita*	70	325	17.0	14.2

Source: Based on data from United Nations, *Yearbook of National Accounts*, various issues.

Note: Low-income LDCs were defined as those having a *per capita* GNP less than $1076 in 1975 at prices of that year.

Structural Changes in World Industry

extremely pertinent to discussions of the composition and cohesion of multilateral bargaining groups.[9]

Comparing *per capita* figures for western countries with those for two sub-groups of LDCs reveals some significant changes during 1960–77 (see Table III.5). As expected, the absolute gap widened substantially both for GDP and MVA. In terms of the relative gaps, the richer LDCs maintained or improved their position slightly compared to the western economies, while the poorer LDCs fell further behind by both measures. Furthermore, a similar pattern of divergence occurred within the Third World as the relative gap between low- and high-income countries widened.

3.2 Estimating the pattern of industrial growth

One means of gauging the differential impact of structural change on industrial growth in countries at different levels of development is to consider the distribution of their rates of growth over extended periods of time. Table III.6 summarizes the changing pattern for growth of MVA during the period 1960–77. Using the standard deviation of country growth rates as a measure of diversity, it is evident that the growth rates of manufacturing in LDCs were much more diverse than among industrialized countries. During the period of most rapid world growth (1960–72), the data show a tendency for high standard deviations to be inversely related to levels of income. In other words, differences in growth performance tended (roughly) to be more diverse among the poorer countries. The mean values and interquartile ranges show that, after 1969, the upper-middle- and high-income countries generally had the highest rates of growth. Quite likely, this would explain the fact that the LDCs' share in world MVA began to rise around 1969. This trend continued despite the fact that in the 1970s an appreciable number of Third World countries recorded negative rates of growth.[10]

These structural changes have been the subject of intensive investigation. During the era of rapid growth, many economists' thinking focused on the identification of uniformities in the development process. Simon Kuznets was one of the first to call attention to this possibility, concluding that 'the direct evidence on long-term trends in the industrial structure of national product is

Table III.6. The distribution of growth rates[a] of MVA (in 1975 prices) by income level and market orientation, 1960-77

County group (number of countries)	1963-66		1960-63		1966-69		1969-72		1972-75		1975-77	
	Standard deviation (mean)	Inter-quartile value	Standard deviation (mean)	Inter-quartile value	Standard deviation (mean)	Inter-quartile value	Standard deviation (mean)	Inter-quartile value	Standard deviation (mean)	Inter-quartile value	Standard deviation (mean)	Inter-quartile value
LDCs, by level of income:												
Low (30)	11.3 (9.1)	3.0/11.8	13.1 (9.2)	0.6/15.4	13.8 (11.3)	3.1/11.7	9.8 (5.7)	1.9/8.5	7.1 (5.2)	0.9/7.7	7.1 (3.0)	−0.4/6.0
Lower-Middle (22)	4.9 (8.3)	4.4/10.0	7.7 (9.7)	4.5/11.5	3.4 (7.8)	5.4/10.2	6.1 (5.2)	0.8/9.4	8.7 (3.3)	−1.2/7.3	12.1 (4.8)	−5.3/11.7
Middle (20)	7.7 (7.8)	1.4/11.4	6.8 (9.5)	4.3/13.9	5.9 (8.5)	5.1/9.3	7.9 (7.7)	5.3/12.0	7.0 (8.0)	5.5/11.3	9.1 (10.2)	3.7/12.5
Upper-Middle (11)	4.0 (7.2)	5.6/7.3	5.4 (7.0)	3.3/11.6	3.3 (8.8)	7.0/10.6	4.9 (9.2)	5.3/13.4	7.9 (2.6)	−3.9/6.4	10.1 (8.4)	−0.5/16.0
High (10)	3.6 (6.7)	4.8/8.9	4.5 (8.4)	4.2/10.5	5.7 (8.3)	3.6/10.5	11.7 (11.7)	6.4/15.4	9.9 (6.4)	−2.1/11.9	4.6 (9.1)	7.0/9.7
Western economies (26)	3.5 (6.3)	4.4/7.7	3.3 (7.5)	5.1/8.6	2.9 (7.3)	5.3/8.4	3.2 (5.7)	3.5/8.4	5.0 (2.8)	0.5/3.1	5.1 (4.5)	1.2/6.3
Socialist countries (8)	3.9 (9.2)	4.8/10.6	3.7 (9.5)	5.4/10.6	4.7 (11.4)	6.7/15.4	2.5 (9.2)	6.4/10.3	3.5 (9.6)	6.8/10.8	2.5 (7.2)	5.4/8.6

Source: Same as Table III.5.
Note: [a] Three-year averages were calculated for each country in each time period.

thus remarkably consistent with that provided by the association of international differences in industrial structure and in level of income'.[11] Kuznets' initial approach to the identification and measurement of development patterns was largely inductive. The subsequent proliferation of data, and the development of new techniques of analysis led to many refinements. The rationale behind models of structural change came to be an eclectic one, drawing upon development of theory in fields such as consumption, saving behaviour or industrial policy, along with other sources of empirical evidence (e.g. on population, labour force composition, rural-to-urban migration, etc.).

The basic hypothesis subjected to analysis is that as *per capita* income rises, industrialization occurs with a sufficient degree of uniformity across countries to produce consistent patterns of change in resource allocation, factor use and related phenomena.[12] This uniformity is attributed to similarities in underlying growth processes. For example, (i) the rate of capital accumulation (both physical and human) normally occurs at a pace exceeding growth of the labour force, (ii) the composition of domestic demand changes with rising *per capita* income and is typically characterized by a decline in the share of foodstuffs and a rise in the share of manufactures, (iii) most countries have access to similar technologies, capital inflows and international trade.[13] In turn, factors associated with different groups of countries—variations in social objectives and policy choices, in natural resource endowments or in country size, disparities in access to external capital and changes in the uniform factors over time—may lead to different growth patterns.[14]

It follows from the above that, prior to any empirical investigation of industrial growth, steps must be taken to account for the effects of 'group factors' that lead to diversities in growth patterns. Since group factors can result in significantly different patterns of structural change in different sets of countries, a single growth curve cannot accommodate the observed industrial circumstances in all countries. Accordingly, three types of group factors are singled out: natural resource endowment, market size and production orientation.

Although difficult to measure empirically, resource endowment plays both a direct and indirect role in determining the pattern of structural change. Direct effects are observed in the extent to which the availability of resources facilitates or constrains industrial growth. An indirect role is seen in the country's choice of industrial policies which are partially dependent on resource endowment. In exceptional cases where countries have an abundance of resources—Chile, Kuwait, Saudi Arabia or Zaire—endowment dictates policy choices to a large extent. Virtually all such countries have used their resources as an export base (whether as a raw material or processed export), which consequently affects pattern of trade and industrial production. As for market size, a variety of earlier studies has shown that this factor has a significant impact on patterns of structural change. The extent to which a country relies upon foreign trade is largely dependent upon market size. Countries with large domestic markets (e.g. Brazil) may easily achieve economies of scale in iron and steel, petrochemicals, etc. via domestic demand if they choose. Finally, the general policy orientation, loosely described here as the orientation of production towards agriculture or industry, can obviously influence both patterns of industrial production and trade.

In order to identify the significance of these group factors for the growth process, samples of homogeneous sub-groups of countries were first drawn. The construction of the samples relied upon statistical criteria and is described in the annex to this chapter. The following sub-groups were identified: large countries (L), small countries with modest resources (S1), small countries with ample resources and a primary orientation (S2P), and small countries with ample resources and an industrial orientation (S2I).

Another preparatory step was a decision as to precisely how structural changes in industry were to be defined. Here, the share of manufacturing (S_M)[15] in 'commodity GDP' was interpreted as describing this phenomenon and defined as follows:

$$S_M = V_M / Y_{NS} = V_M / (Y - V_S)$$

where V_M is value added in manufacturing, Y is GDP and V_S is value added in services.

The expression excludes the direct effects on the share of manufacturing which arises from the growth of services. The basis for this decision was the desire to distinguish conceptually between the process of industrialization, interpreted as a rise in the contribution of manufacturing to total production, and the growth of the service sector which would deserve a study of its own.

A final preparatory step was the choice of an estimating equation to represent the pattern of structural change across countries. Literature on the subject suggests several alternatives. One is a quadratic equation which entails the assumption that the sector's share in Y_{NS} increases at a declining rate. The other alternative is a logistic equation or S-shaped curve, implying that manufacture's share begins from a relatively low level, that its rate of growth accelerates over intermediate levels of *per capita* income and slows down once higher levels of income are achieved. Both hypothetical growth paths are illustrated in Figure 1.

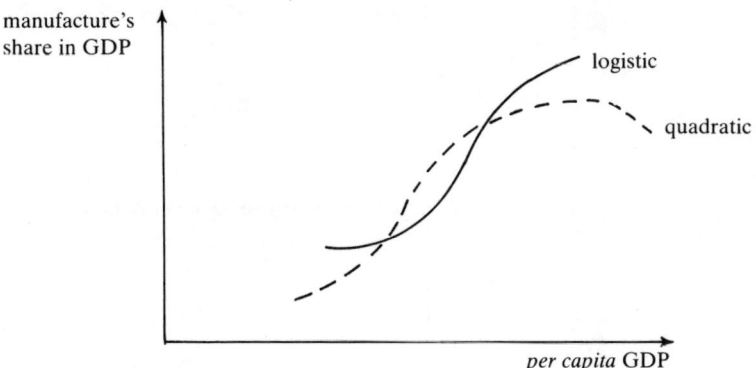

Fig. 1. Illustrative growth paths for manufacturing

Most current theoretical arguments suggest that an S-shaped curve best describes the long-term behaviour of MVA as a share of income.[16] Alternative quadratic patterns obtained by a split of the country sample according to income, together with the observed rotation of successive annual cross-section curves, support the conjecture of an underlying logistic curve.[17] The presumption that the dependent variable (see below) is near a lower asymptote at low levels of income and behaves symmetrically, approaching an upper asymptote as *per capita* GDP rises, also seems to be reasonable. Likewise, the hypothesis that the most pronounced structural

Table III.7. Estimated coefficients of logistic equation (2) for samples from four different country groups (annual pooled[a] cross section 1969–73 and 1974–77)

	Country group	Number of countries	Number of observations	Coefficient[d]				RMS_E[b]	$\bar{R}^{2c}$
				α	β	γ	δ		
A. 1969–73 constant prices of 1975	L	25	125	0.6732 (0.0228)	6.1305 (0.5860)	−0.9706 (0.0892)	−0.0967 (0.0621)	0.0627	0.89
	S1	33	165	1.0	5.9724 (0.4699)	−0.7799 (0.1757)	−0.1182 (0.0551)	0.0860	0.46
	S2P	15	75	0.7456 (0.1374)	7.9371 (1.1358)	−1.0326 (0.1941)	−0.0 (0.0701)	0.0793	0.81
	S2I	31	155	0.6160 (0.0195)	9.4455 (1.4338)	−1.5181 (0.2305)	−0.0 (0.0625)	0.0946	0.65
1969–73 current prices	L	25	125	0.7089 (0.0227)	6.0685 (0.4892)	−0.9330 (0.0739)	−0.1121 (0.0525)	0.0555	0.92
	S1	31	155	1.0000 (0.3899)	6.3130 (0.5282)	−0.8578 (0.1600)	−0.0761 (0.0536)	0.0837	0.56
	S2P	15	75	0.6552 (0.0606)	8.4509 (0.8836)	−1.1401 (0.1427)	−0.0216 (0.0549)	0.0565	0.89
	S2I	30	150	0.6453 (0.0239)	8.0969 (1.1781)	−1.2870 (0.1921)	−0.0237 (0.0502)	0.0832	0.71

B. 1974–77 constant prices of 1975	L	25	100	0.7080 (0.0388)	5.5454 (0.6047)	−0.8688 (0.0920)	−0.0764 (0.0660)	0.0637	0.89
	S1	33	132	1.0 (0.6177)	5.5865 (0.4701)	−0.7043 (0.1841)	−0.1346 (0.0614)	0.0877	0.47
	S2P	15	60	0.5909 (0.0596)	8.7585 (1.4412)	−1.2374 (0.2300)	−0.0 (0.0839)	0.0804	0.80
	S2I	31	124	0.6442 (0.0223)	9.2582 (1.4444)	−1.4578 (0.2262)	−0.0 (0.0698)	0.0939	0.69
1974–77 current prices	L	25	100	0.7014 (0.0284)	5.7779 (0.5903)	−0.8882 (0.0882)	−0.0999 (0.0640)	0.0605	0.90
	S1	32	127	1.0000 (0.6211)	5.3047 (0.4590)	−0.6769 (0.1815)	−0.0560 (0.0608)	0.0877	0.47
	S2P	15	60	0.5706 (0.0549)	9.0932 (1.5129)	−1.2894 (0.2392)	−0.0 (0.0880)	0.0807	0.80
	S2I	30	120	0.6501 (0.0233)	9.3534 (1.3956)	−1.4637 (0.2188)	−0.0 (0.0662)	0.0910	0.71

Source: Same as Table III.5.

Notes: [a] For country coverage, see UNIDO, *World Industry since 1960: Progress and Prospects*, New York, 1979, annex I.
[b] Root mean square for error.
[c] $\bar{R}^2$ is a proxy measure for the quality fit defined as: $\bar{R}^2 = 1 - RSS/SS$ where RSS is the residual sum of squares and SS is the total sum of squares (corrected).
[d] The asymptotic standard deviations of the parameters are given in parentheses.

change occurs at a medium-income range can be justified by empirical findings.

These considerations led to the formulation of the following logistic equation:

$$Sm = \frac{\alpha}{1 + \exp(\beta + \gamma \ln y + \delta \ln N)} = \frac{\alpha}{1 + e^\beta y^\gamma N^\delta}$$

where y is *per capita* GDP in dollars, N is population, α is a positive constant and γ and δ are negative.[18] Results of the exercise to fit the equation to the data for each of the four country groups are summarized in Table III.7. For comparative purposes, the table also shows the results for both 1969–73 and 1974–7.

A comparison of the estimations using current and constant price data shows only marginal differences in the two sets of equations. The root mean squares of error (RMS_E) are slightly lower for equations estimated in current prices. Similarly, the ratio of each estimated coefficient to its asymptomic standard deviation is generally higher for equations using current prices. Both results suggest that this set of data provides a slightly better fit. There are some differences in the shape of the corresponding curves for the two time periods. These are reflected by differences in the estimated coefficients (discussed below) which, for the most part, are marginal. Primarily for statistical reasons (although substantive justifications have also been offered[19]), we adopt the current price equations as the more informative set and limit subsequent discussion to these results.

Differences between the equations for the two periods are generally small but a comparison facilitates their interpretation. It is perhaps worth mentioning that these coefficients represent the extremes or outer limits of the growth path. However, changes in the coefficients imply shifts in the entire curve, including the applicable range within the extremes. The first coefficient, α, indicates the upper bound of the curve or the maximum share of industry in GDP. Changes in the coefficient were negligible with the exception of group S2P where the maximum height of the curve dropped perceptibly between 1969–73 and 1974–7. In terms of

Structural Changes in World Industry

structural changes, the phase of most rapid change (i.e. the income range around the point of inflextion) occurs earlier in the development process. The second coefficient, ß, represents a 'displacement parameter' or surface described by equation (2). The coefficient increased for small countries with abundant resources (S2P and S2I) but shifted in the opposite direction for the other two groups. The growth path attributed to S_M is inversely related to ß which indicates the timing of the 'industrial push' with reference to the level of *per capita* income. Thus, in comparison to 1969–73, industry was a slightly less dynamic force in the former two groups of countries during the mid–1970s.

The absolute values of the remaining two coefficients, γ and δ, represent upper bounds for the growth and size elasticities respectively.[20] Each of the estimates for δ took on smaller negative values in 1974–7. Thus, market size would be regarded as a marginally less important group factor in industrial development in the later period and the growth paths shifted leftward slightly. The effect of the growth elasticity, which is related to *per capita* income, is more important. Here, the upper bound (γ) took on larger negative values for small countries with ample resources (S2P and S2I) and moved in the opposite direction in the other cases.

The current price equations referred to in Table III.7 (part B) are pictured in Figure 2.[21] A comparison of the results shows the effects of the group factors and income on structural changes. In large countries S_M typically exceeds the corresponding shares of other groups at almost all income levels. Economists rightly attribute a natural advantage to large countries by virtue of their domestic market size. The opportunities for import substitution are simple and straightforward, particularly at lower levels of income. A broader range of industrial choice is also available to these countries than to their smaller counterparts. The benefits of economies of scale are also cited in the case of industries for which technologies require large production runs.

In addition to their economic advantages, the range of political alternatives which large countries can use to facilitate industrialization is significant. This point has been stressed elsewhere (see Chapter II), referring to industrialized countries where 'size' was interpreted in terms of the economy's relative contribution to world

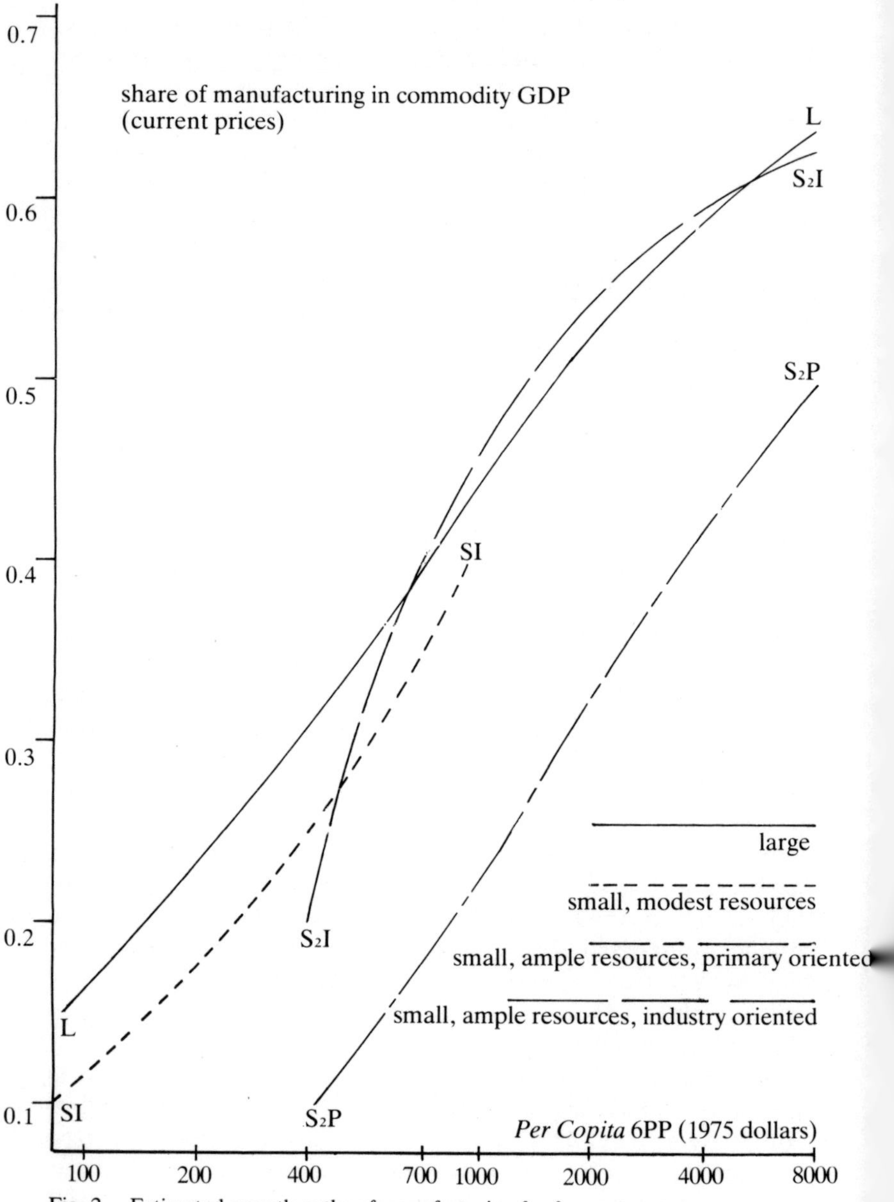

The International Economy and Industrial Development

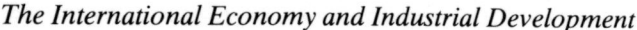

Fig. 2. Estimated growth paths of manufacturing for four country groups

Structural Changes in World Industry

trade or net industrial output. Their ability to influence bilateral or multilateral negotiations on industrial issues partly depends on their relative status as industrial and trading nations. Third World countries in this group (e.g. Argentina, Brazil, Egypt, India, Mexico, etc.) enjoy a range of independent international actions not available to smaller countries.[22] Such benefits are not so clearly ascribable to 'industrial strength', as in the case of the United States or West Germany, but depend as well on other factors derived from population size, or strategic considerations.[23]

In small countries, growth paths show considerable differences. S_M rises most rapidly for group S2I. Here the growth in domestic demand through income gains, often supplemented by an increase in exports of manufactures, facilitates these structural changes. The manner in which resource endowment affects industrial growth may also be seen by comparing the growth paths of small countries having modest resources with those of more generously endowed countries. In general, resource endowment affects the timing of industrialization in an opposite manner to that of market size. An abundance of natural resources leads to a greater emphasis on the agricultural rather than the manufacturing sector since the resource costs of exporting primary commodities are less. In contrast, small countries with modest resource endowments have little choice but to emphasize industry at an early point (e.g. $250 *per capita*) in the development process. Once intermediate income levels are attained, manufacturing accounts for a greater share of commodity GDP in countries with ample resources and an industrial orientation.

Comparing the two groups of small countries with abundant resources, industry's growth path varies widely depending on the country's production orientation (primary or manufacturing). Where policy orientation emphasizes the primary sector, the growth of manufacturing is decidedly slower than among countries with a manufacturing orientation. This gap between the two groups actually widens over the relevant range of *per capita* income ($400–$2000).

A final aspect of the results concerns the timing of structural changes. While the curves are approximate and represent only group averages, the growth paths do indicate the vicinity of *per capita* GDP where the rate of structural change is a maximum. Table III.8 shows the approximate values corresponding to the growth paths shown in Figure II. Large countries typically experience a phase of rapid structural change at an earlier stage of development than the other groups. They are followed by small countries having ample resources and an industrial orientation (S2I). Very few of the small countries with modest resources have yet to reach income levels corresponding to a rapid phase of manufacturing growth.

The impression that industrialization may be characterized by a phase of relatively rapid structural change, followed by a period of continued industrial expansion at a slackening pace, suggests several points relevant to the discussion in this chapter. First, such a phase was apparently experienced by several industrialized countries beginning sometime in the 1950s. It is not clear how long this phase endured but it is safe to conclude that, by the early 1970s, it

Table III.8. Income levels corresponding to maximum rates of structural change in industry

Country group	Per capita income
Large countries	430
Small countries	
with modest resources	...
with ample resources and oriented to primary production	1160
with ample resources and oriented to manufacturing	600

had been completed. Its impact, however, for trade in manufactures and industrial production was substantial. Second, several of the NICs (e.g. Brazil, Hong Kong, Mexico, South Korea and Yugoslavia) apparently entered a similar phase of rapid structural change in the 1970s. Again, there is a loose relationship between rapid structural change and the subsequent emergence of the country as a trading nation. Third, among the countries that now seemed poised to enter this phase of accelerated structural change are a number of small countries with ample resources and industrial orientation. If

Structural Changes in World Industry

they do, in fact, follow the 'typical' or 'normal' growth path, they might be expected to figure more prominently in world industry and trade by, say, the 1990s. The growth paths described here would be compatible with the points stressed in the preceding section regarding the growing heterogeneity among LDCs and the increasing similarity in industrial structures of western economies.

In conclusion, the structural changes described in this chapter alter national policies and, in the process, lead to a parallel set of changes in negotiation processes and in national bargaining power. Among western countries the situation today is multipolar. Although the economies of these countries are now closely interrelated, their policy approaches are probably less complementary than at any time in the past forty years.

The consequences of greater heterogeneity in the Third World require somewhat more description. The partial disintegration of the various voting blocks and pressure groups previously developed by the governments of these countries is likely for two reasons. First, several of the originally cohesive factors no longer exist. These include the goals of decolonization and independence that have largely been realized and the wish to avoid the East-West conflict through non-alignment, now jeopardized by the emergence of socialist LDCs.[24] The second reason, suggested by our analysis, is that the Third World is no longer a clearly recognized group defined essentially by the exclusion from the industrial centre. Increasingly, Third World countries face different industrial constraints and their self-interests dictate different positions on important economic issues. For example, oil-producing countries strive for higher oil prices while oil-importing countries seek lower prices. Leading exporters of manufactures, such as some NICs, want to restrain prices of internationally traded commodities while commodity producers look for ways of raising or at least stabilizing their prices. Ex-colonies seek to maintain preferential trading and financial relationships with their ex-colonists while other LDCs (e.g. Latin American countries) complain of discrimination.[25]

New political and economic alignments are likely to emerge from the restructuring process, altering relationships among industrialized countries, among LDCs and between the two groups. While these forces will not necessarily lead to the disintegration of the 'united fronts' that both sides have striven to maintain, they will, at the very least, alter the bargaining and negotiating process as it is known today. Either group of countries, to the extent that it maintains a flexible approach, may make use of the new situation to serve that group's interests.

Notes

[1] Calculated in 1970 US dollars. See, UNIDO, *World Industry Since 1960: Progress and Prospects*, New York, 1979, p. 33.

[2] The US share of world MVA dropped from 54 per cent in 1953 to 29 per cent in 1975 while the United Kingdom's share went from 10 to 5 per cent. Corresponding changes for France, West Germany and Japan were, respectively, 4 to 8 per cent, 7 to 12 per cent and 2 to ll per cent. Accordingly, each of the latter countries has taken on more significance as a source and final destination for trade, foreign investment and technological flows. Similarly, they have increased, or striven to increase, the extent to which they influence international policy and institutional reform.

[3] The results apply to a sample of ten West European countries between the period 1901 and 1968–70 and were as follows:

Period of comparison:	$\frac{1968-70}{1958-60}$	$\frac{1955}{1901}$	$\frac{1913}{1901}$	$\frac{1937}{1913}$	$\frac{1955}{1937}$
Similarity coefficient:	92.5	71	88	90	90

Figures were based on V. Paretti and C. Bloch, 'Industrial production in Western Europe and the United States 1901 to 1955', *Banca Nazionale del Lanaro Quarterly Review*, No. 39, 1956, and ECE, *Structure and Change in European Industry*, New York, 1977. For further discussion of the country coverage and method of estimate, see the latter publication, pp. 15–17.

[4] The term has been used by H. Chenery and L. Taylor, 'Development patterns: among countries and over time', *Review of Economies and Statistics*, Vol. 50, No. 4, 1968, p. 409.

[5] For example, in West Germany steel consumption per 1000 kg. of output dropped between 1970 and 1977 in various branches as follows: electrical machinery—412 kg. to 370 kg.; shipbuilding—873 kg. to 668 kg.; railing stock—883 kg. to 783 kg., UNIDO, *Picture for 1985 of the World Iron and Steel Industry*, ICIS, 141, June 1980, p. 18.

[6] Socialist countries do not compile data in terms of net manufacturing output. The use of net material product, where available, distorts the magnitude of structural changes.

[7] The coefficient determines the association between k sets of rankings and takes values between 0 and +1, the latter value indicating identical rank orders in all k sets ($k > 2$). Kendell's coefficient, unlike the Spearman rank correlation coefficient, can never be negative for the simple reason that there can never be complete

disagreement among more than two rankings. See A. E. Maxwell, *Analysing Qualitative Data,* Methuen and Co., London, 1961, pp. 114-20.

[8] The tendency for the structure of output to be more uniform over time was confirmed in one detailed study of ten West European countries in the 1960s. See ECE, *Structure and Change in European Industry*, New York, 1977, Chapter 1. A comparison of output structures in western countries and LDCs has also found considerable homogeneity among the former and heterogeneity among the latter countries. See UNIDO, *World Industry Since 1960, op. cit.*, p. 71.

[9] See, for example, David Morawitz, *Twenty-five Years of Economic Development: 1950 to 1975*, Johns Hopkins Press, Baltimore, 1977. Morawitz defines the absolute gap as the difference between *per capita* income in developed and developing countries. The relative gap is expressed in terms of the developing countries' *per capita* income as a percentage of the corresponding value in developed countries. Similar interpretations are used here. Morawitz points out the inapplicability of such measures for an analysis of poverty.

[10] The group's share in world MVA was 7 per cent in 1969 (at 1970 dollars), reaching 9 per cent by 1977. See UNIDO, *World Industry Since 1960, op. cit.*, p. 33.

[11] S. Kuznet's, 'Quantitative aspects of the economic growth of nations I, industrial distribution of national product and labour force', *Economic Development and Cultural Change*, July 1957, suppl., p. 17.

[12] A partial list of studies adopting this general type of approach to an analysis of structural change in manufacturing includes the following: *A Study of Industrial Growth*, United Nations publication (Sales No. 63.II.B.2); H. B. Chenery and L. Taylor, 'Development patterns: among countries and over time', *Review of Economics and Statistics*, Vol. 50, No. 4, 1968, pp. 391–415; *Sectoral Aspects of Long-term Economic Projections with Special Reference to Asia and the Far East*, Development Programming Techniques Series No. 6, ESCAP, Bangkok, 1967; H. B. Chenery and M. Syrquin, *Patterns of Development, 1950–1970*, Oxford University Press, London, 1975; UNCTAD 'The dimensions of the required restructuring of world manufacturing output and trade in order to reach the Lima target', (TD/185/supp. 1) April 1976 (mimeo) and UNIDO, *World Industry Since 1960, op cit.*

[13] See Hollis Chenery and Moises Syrquin, *op. cit.*, Chapter I.

[14] See Hollis Chenery, *Structural Change and Development Policy* published for the World Bank by Oxford University Press, New York, 1979, p. 6–7.

[15] Alternative expressions for this variable include the share of sectoral value added in GDP (Chenery and Syrquin, *op. cit.*), the log of sectoral value added (UNCTAD, *op. cit*) or the log of the above share (Chenery and Taylor, *op. cit.*).

[16] Chenery and Syrquin, *op. cit.*, p. 8, point out that, for industrialization, 'a logistic curve which describes a gradual transition from one limit to the other, illustrates the type of function needed for the analysis of these transitional processes'.

[17] M. Syrquin, 'The effect of sample composition on the estimation of development patterns', Staff Working Paper No. 204, World Bank, 1975, pp. 13–18.

[18] The geometric interpretation of these constants is as follows: α represents an upper bound for the share of manufacturing in commodity GDP (Y_{NS}); ß represents the displacement of the surface in three dimensional (S_m, lny, lnN) space; – α and

The International Economy and Industrial Development

—δ are the upper bounds of the income and size elasticities respectively. For further discussion, see the annex to this chapter.

[19] For example, Chenery and Taylor, *op cit.* used a constant price base. In a later work, Chenery and Syrquin, *op. cit*, argued that current prices are to be preferred since 'all behavioral discussions on the part of consumers, firms and the governments are based on current information about income, relative prices, and other pertinent data and not on the relative prices of an arbitrary earlier period.' p. 152.

[20] These elasticities show the percentage change in Sm for a one per cent change in income or population when the other variable is held constant. The two constants are only the upper bounds of the elasticities. The income elasticity can be shown to be:

$$\mathcal{E}_y(y, N) = \frac{\delta Sm}{Sm} \bigg/ \frac{\delta y}{y} = -\gamma \left[1 - \frac{1}{1+\exp[\beta+\gamma \ln y + \delta \ln N]} \right]$$

The size elasticity is

$$\mathcal{E}_N(y, N) = \frac{\delta Sm}{Sm} \bigg/ \frac{\delta N}{N} = -\delta \left[1 - \frac{1}{1+\exp[\beta+\gamma \ln y + \delta \ln N]} \right]$$

the evaluation of these results is discussed further in the annex to this chapter.

[21] The curves are plotted with population held constant at the average value for each country group.

[22] Akin L. Mabogunje makes the telling point that many LDCs lack both the guidance and the ability to alter their national circumstances when world conditions deteriorate for them vis-à-vis other countries. This point was also stressed in Chapter II with regard to Latin America which, during 1913–45, was the only developing region largely outside the colonist umbrella. Mabogunje goes on to argue that the concept of a nation, 'although not central to international trade theory, turns out to be one of its most important, if implicit, assumptions.' See 'International circumstances affecting the development and trade of developing countries', in *The International Allocation of Economic Activity*, ed. by Bertil Ohlin et. al, Macmillan Press, London, 1977, p. 434.

[23] China's relatively rapid emergence as a 'superpower' with little significance as an industrial or trading nation is an obvious example. The ability of other large countries to divert relatively scarce resources to politically significant projects such as nuclear defence has brought them a measure of international influence which richer, though smaller, countries could not attain.

[24] Afghanistan, Angola, Kampuchea, Laos, Mozambique and Viet Nam are examples. The future fole of countries like Iran and Zimbabwe is also unclear.

[25] The proliferations of special interest groups is one reflection of the growing differences in economic self-interest. Examples from United Nations fora are not only the least-developed countries, but the island and land-locked countries and the 'most seriously affected' countries. The African, Caribbean and Pacific (ACP) alignment, as outlined in Lomé II, is a good example of special arrangements

between Third World countries and the West. Sub-regional groups composed of like-minded LDCs abound.

Annex to Chapter III

(a) Stratification of the country sample

The first step in creating relatively homogeneous groups of countries was to express, in quantitative terms, those 'group factors' regarded as important to an analysis of industrial growth paths. The first of these, natural resource endowment, posed certain problems in selecting a quantitative criterion which was both sensitive to this factor and widely available. *Per capita* output of the primary sectors—agriculture, mining and quarrying—was eventually chosen as a proxy and defined as follows:

(1) $\quad V_P = V_A + V_I - V_M$
where V_A = value added in agriculture;
V_I = value added in total industry (mining, quarrying, manufacturing, electricity, gas and water);
V_M = value added in manufacturing.[1]

Primary *per capita* output was then derived for each country and for all years (1960–73) prior to the period of concern, 1974–7. An average value for the entire period was then calculated for each country.

The size of a country's domestic market is widely accepted as an important group factor. A country's pattern of trade and its general policy biases are influenced by the size of its internal market. Population size was adopted as the proxy for measuring the effects of this factor.

The third group factor to be accommodated in the analysis was a country's orientation of production (primary or manufacturing). As stressed in Chapters II and IV, different circumstances, including resource endowment and the interests of different groups of entrepreneurs (e.g. producers of consumer goods as opposed to producers of capital goods), limit policy options and influence the choice of strategy. The relative degree of industrialization, D, was taken as a proxy variable for a country's production orientation and defined as follows:

(2) $\quad \ln D = \ln V_M - \ln \hat{V}_M$
where $\hat{V}_M$ = the 'normal' level of MVA corresponding to levels of *per capita* income and population (see equation 3 below).

Biases arising from structural characteristics or development strategies were to some extent accounted for by this criterion.[3] Two principles were followed in the adoption of statistical procedures for creation of homogeneous sub-groups. First, each of the three criteria should be reflected in the resulting set of country groups. Second, subjective or arbitrary decisions should be kept to a minimum in so far as possible. The availability of quantitative criteria, coupled with the desire to avoid subjective decisions, led to the use of cluster analysis techniques for stratification.[4] Here, the alternative of sequential clustering of one-dimensional sets was adopted, following a step-wise procedure.[5] Apart from the use of cluster analysis, the step-by-step approach to the derivation of homogeneous sub-groups conforms to the treatment in other studies.

In the first step, population in 1970 was used, applying a hierarchical cluster algorithm for 139 countries. Similarity groups show a fairly compact cluster of 180 'small countries'. All countries excluded from this group were merged to form the group of large countries. The results of this step indicated that a 1970 mid-year population of approximately 20 million was a reasonable dividing line for size.[6]

The second step introduced resource endowment into the stratification process. Since resource endowment can be assumed to affect the production and trade patterns of small countries much more significantly than those of large countries, only the former set was considered. The results led to a group of thirty-five small countries described as having modest resource endowments. A remaining group of fifty countries with a higher level of resources endowment was retained for the final step in the stratification.[7] This step was concerned with production orientation defined in terms of net manufacturing output relative to income level and carried out with the help of a regression analysis. Accordingly, the 'normal' levels of manufacturing value added V_M were assumed to be determined by the relationship

(3) $\quad \ln \hat{V}_M = -4.146 + 1.328 \ln y + 1.131 \ln N$
where $\quad y =$ per capital GDP at constant prices, N is population and all terms are in natural logs.

A pooled set of observations pertaining to small countries with ample resources was used for the period 1969–73 of the present analysis. The results of this step distinguished between small countries with ample resources and a primary orientation (determined when the relative degree of industrialization, D, was < 1) and those with ample resources and an industrial orientation (D>1).[8]

(b) Estimating industrial growth paths

Two alternative functional forms, a logistic or a quadratic equation, are proposed in Chapter III to estimate the industrial growth path. A quadratic expression comparable to the logistic equation described in the text (Chapter III) may be stated as follows:

(4) $\quad S_M = \alpha + \beta_1 \ln y + \beta_2 (\ln y)^2 + \gamma_1 \ln N + \gamma_2 (\ln N)^2$

Such an expression is plausible since it implies a declining income elasticity of growth in manufacture's share of commodity GDP as income rises, as well as a declining size elasticity with a rising level of population.[9] The postulate of declining elasticities is supported by observation; the value of manufacture's share apparently begins to decline beyond a certain income level. Another attraction of equation (4) is simplicity in calculation; its parameters can be estimated by linear methods, a step which is not available to econometricians with the present cross-section application of a logistic curve.

However, there are two statistical drawbacks in the choice of equation (4). First, the interpretation of a polynomial equation as a linear one (a necessary assumption for linear estimation) contributes to a great deal of multicollinearity between the linear and the quadratic terms of the same independent variable. This circumstance is likely to violate one of the assumptions of the general linear model and to result in variances of the estimated co-efficients which are quite high while the corresponding t-values are small. Thus, the individual estimated coefficients could be quite uncertain, although the estimated relation as a whole could be of some use.

A second probable violation of the classical linear model concerns the specific sample design. The pooling of cross-section and time series can lead to both autocorrelation and heteroscedasticity of the disturbance term.[10] Variances and the standard error of estimate may both be underestimated by linear methods.[11] These statistical considerations, in addition to other desirable properties associated with the logistic[12] but not the quadratic curve, led us to discard equation (4) as the basis for estimating industrial growth paths.

For purposes of comparison with Table III.3, estimates using equation (4) were carried out for data in current prices and are shown here in Table A.III.1. The fit of the curves is fairly good as indicated by the coefficients of determination and the standard errors of estimate. With the exception of the quadratic term for population (γ^2), most coefficients are significantly different from zero.

Turning to the logistic semi-log equation, the reader of Chapter III will recall the following specification:

(5)
$$S_M = \frac{\alpha}{1 + \exp(\beta + \gamma \ln + \delta \ln N)} = \frac{\alpha}{1 + \exp(B + \gamma \ln y)}$$
where $B = \beta + \delta \ln N$

For purposes of estimation the principle of least-squares (LS) was preferred to the maximum-likelihood principle mainly due to computational concurrence. The statistical interpretation of such a non-linear would be extremely complex and is not considered; rather the discussion is confined to the exercise of fitting the logistic curve to the present data.[13]

(c) Interpreting the logistic pattern

Representation of an equation for a typical share-income curve is obtained by fixing population size at some value N_0 thereby fixing B at the same level B_0. A graph of the equation, shown in Figure A.1,

Table A.III.1. Estimated coefficients of quadratic equation (4) for samples from four different country groups (annual pooled cross-section for 1974–7)

Group	Number of countries	Number of observations	α	β_1	β_2	γ_1	γ_2	R^2	SEE
L	25	100	−1.1710 (0.2084)[b]	0.2941 (0.0498)	−0.0129 (0.0036)	−0.0913[a] (0.0693)	−0.0083[a] (0.0076)	0.90	0.0608
S1	32	127	2.0110 (0.2896)	−0.7377 (0.0984)	0.0714 (0.0083)	0.0698 (0.0227)	−0.0196[a] (0.0076)	0.64	0.0723
S2P	15	60	−1.4144 (0.5631)	0.3436 (0.1565)	−0.0132[a] (0.0107)	−0.0538 (0.0233)	0.0074 (0.0061)	0.83	0.0745
S2I	30	120	−3.0333 (0.5775)	0.8245 (0.1559)	−0.0463 (0.0104)	−0.0153[a] (0.0137)	0.0038[a] (0.0062)	0.71	0.0910

Notes: [a] Not significant at 5 per cent level.
[b] Standard deviations of parameter estimates are given in parentheses.

The International Economy and Industrial Development

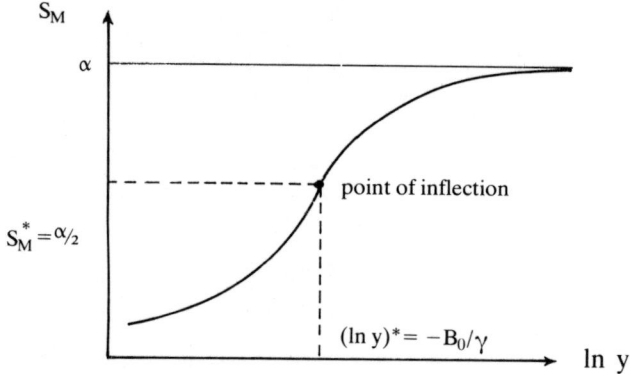

Fig. A.1. Graph of the logistic function of equation (5)

demonstrates several well-known geometric properties relevant to an interpretation of growth patterns. First, the range of the dependent variable $S_M = f(\ln Y)$ has lower and upper bounds ϕ and α. As $\ln y$ approaches minus infinity (the equivalent of income approaching zero) the share of manufacturing approaches zero asymptotically. Conversely, when $\ln y$ approaches plus infinity, S_M will approach α asymptotically. Finally, the point of inflection of the curve lies half-way between the two asymptotes and has co-ordinates $(\ln y)^* = -B_0/\gamma$ and $S_M^* = \alpha/2$.

The value of B_0 given in equation (5) determines the location of the curve without affecting its shape. An increase in population will lead to a decrease in B_0 owing to the negative sign of the coefficient δ, thereby shifting the curve in Figure A.1 to the left along the income axis. In other words, an increase in population would have a positive effect on the share as suggested by economic theory. Large countries are thought to attain a certain level of industrialization earlier—i.e. at lower income levels—than small countries.

Notes

[1] The inclusion of utilities in primary output is not conceptually desirable but was unavoidable since precise data were not uniformly available for many countries. Statistically, the defect is not serious for purposes of a cross-country comparison where V_P is expressed in *per capita* terms.

[2] This method was first employed by the United Nations, *A Study on Industrial Growth*

(Sales No. 63.II.B.2), p. 5.

[3] Other criteria were tested including *per capita* GDP, *per capita* primary exports and the share of primary exports in total exports. Each of these might allow for an economic interpretation. They were rejected because: (i) the limited availability of data resulted in the exclusion of many countries from the classification and (ii) the resultant groupings remained largely heterogeneous, most likely because the quantitative expressions used did not adquately represent the underlying theory. For a discussion of further tests of these and other criteria which were similarly rejected, see United Nations, *ibid.*

[4] This technique was suggested but was not employed by H.Chenery and M. Syrquin, *Patterns of Development, 1950–1970*, London, World Bank, 1975, p. 162.

[5] Preliminary testing revealed that when a hierarchical clustering algorithm was used and the desired number of sub-groups was not specified *a priori*, a step-wise procedure was preferred. See B. S. Duran and P. L. Odell, *Cluster Analysis, A Survey*, Berlin, Springer, 1974, p. 24.

[6] Chenery and Taylor, using population data for 1958, arrived at a similar dividing line of 15 million. See 'Development patterns: among countries and over time', *Review of Economics and Statistics*, Vol. 50, No. 4, 1968, p. 395.

[7] The reduction in the sample for this classification step was due to lack of data.

[8] A few intermediate cases—Algeria, Ireland, Jamaica, Malaysia and Mexico—were identified. Subsequent analysis, however proved to be insensitive to the placement of these borderline countries in one group or the other.

[9] The income elasticity for the quadratic semilog is given by
$$\varepsilon_y = (\beta_1 + 2\beta_2 \ln y)/S_M$$
The size elasticity is given by
$$\varepsilon_N = (\gamma_1 + 2\gamma_2 \ln N)S_M$$

[10] P. Balestra and M. Nerlove, 'Pooling cross-section and time series data in the estimation of a dynamic model: The demand for natural gas', *Econometrics*, Vol. 34, No. 3, 1966, pp. 585–612.

[11] A. S. Goldberger, *Econometric Theory*, Wiley and Sons, New York, 1964, p. 161.

[12] These desirable properties were mentioned in Chapter IV: (i) a symmetrical growth plan where the dependent variable approaches a lower asymptote with falling income levels and an upper asymptote with rising income, and (ii) the characteristic that the most pronounced structural change occurs at intermediate income levels.

[13] Estimating the coefficients for the non-linear case posed some statistical problems concerning numerical optimization. The use of a Gauss-Newton iterative procedure was employed to arrive at the LS estimates. See H. O. Hartley, 'The modified Gauss-Newton methods of fitting of non-linear regression functions by least squares', *Technometrics*, No. 3, 1961, pp. 269–80.

Chapter IV

Structural Changes in World Trade in Manufactures

In this chapter we compare the trade performance of the West with that of the Third World. The chapter begins with a brief summary of the long-term trends in world trade in manufactures, followed by an analysis of the internal and external factors determining export performance. The results of this analysis lead to an examination of the changing patterns of comparative advantage in the second section. The third section provides an evaluation of export-led industrialization as a source of growth for manufacturing. The chapter concludes by considering some of the more important consequences of export-led industrialization.

4.1 Determinants of export performance

The erratic growth of world exports in the nineteenth and twentieth centuries was instrumental in shaping economists' opinion of the role of trade in the growth process. During periods when trade expanded rapidly internal bottlenecks were regarded as a major constraint on growth. When trade slumped, an export pessimism emphasized issues of demand deficiency and dependency. A useful means of gauging the extent to which internal and external factors have influenced export performance is known as a constant market share (CMS) analysis.[1]

The analysis provides a method of allocating the actual increase in exports during a given period to different components. First, a part of export growth is attributed to the general increase in world exports or a 'world demand effect'. This component indicates what a country's export earnings would have been had they increased at a rate equal to the world average (i.e. if the country maintained its share in world exports during the period). Second, a market distribution effect recognizes the fact that the country's export performance depends on the market conditions of its major trading partners. The income elasticity of the same category may differ between consuming markets. Similarly, demand will not grow at the same rate in each importing region. A negative (positive) value would indicate that exports are largely directed to markets where demand is expanding at a relatively slow (rapid) pace. Third, a commodity composition effect represents a country's ability to concentrate on exports for which world demand is buoyant. A country's exports may consist largely of products for which foreign demand is growing very slowly. Here, negative values show that the country's exports are mainly products for which demand has stagnated or expanded at a relatively slow pace. Finally, the residual after deducting estimates from the actual value of exports is known as a competitiveness effect. The term represents the difference between actual growth and that which would have been realized if the country had maintained its share of exports of each product to each region under consideration. The country's willingness and ability to compete effectively with alternative sources of supply are relevant here. A positive (negative) value would indicate that the competitive ability, in terms of both price and non-price factors, improved (deteriorated).

The CMS model can be expressed in algebraic terms as follows:

$$\Sigma_i (X_{i.}^{(2)} - X_{i.}^{(1)}) \equiv r\Sigma_i X_{i.}^{(1)} + \Sigma_i (r_i - r) X_{i.}^{(1)} + \Sigma_i \Sigma_j (r_{ij} - r_i) X_{ij}^{(1)} + \Sigma_i \Sigma_j (X_{ij}^{(2)} - X_{ij}^{(1)} - r_{ij} X_{ij}^{(1)})$$

The superscripts (1) and (2) refer to the beginning and terminal years, 1966 and 1975, and terms are defined as follows:

X_{ij} = the country's earnings from the export of commodity i to market j;

$X_{i.}$ = $\Sigma_j X_{ij}$ = the total value of the country's exports of commodity i to the world;

r = the percentage increase in total world trade in manufactures between period (1) and (2),

r_i = percentage increase in world trade of industry i between period (1) and period (2);

r_{ij} = percentage increase in the world export of industry i to market j between period (1) and period (2).

The term on the left side of the equation shows the actual change in the country's exports during the period. The first term on the right represents that part of the export growth attributable to the general increase in world exports (the world demand effect). The second term measures the commodity composition effect and is a weighted sum of the value of exports by each of the various industries without differentiating between their destination. The third term, the market distribution effect, is a weighted sum of the value of each industry's exports going to each regional market. The weights here are the differences between the growth rate of a particular market for a particular product and the average growth rate for world exports of that industry. The last term is the residual representing the competitiveness effect.

The CMS approach is subject to several limitations which should be noted prior to an investigation of results. First, the model does not indicate any causal relationship. The approach is useful in decomposing export growth into its various components but provides no explanation for the behaviour of the various components. Second, the analysis requires the researcher to choose a standard or norm by which to judge export performance. World growth rates typically serve as the standard although there is no *a priori* reason why this measure would necessarily be the most appropriate one. Finally, the interpretation of the residual (the competitiveness effect) can be ambiguous. Competitiveness obviously depends on the country's export prices relative to those of its major competitors. However, the term could also reflect countries' differential abilities to fulfil export orders, differences in marketing systems and in the terms of finance for export sales.[2]

The data in Table IV.1 show the results of a CMS exercise for twelve important Third World exporters and five industrialized countries. Both groups of countries are ranked according to the actual increases in manufactured exports (SITC 5 to 8 less 688) between 1966 and 1976. World imports were divided into nine different markets for purposes of calculating the market composition effect. Among the four major trade categories, each three-digit SITC group was treated as an exporting industry or product category.[3]

For reasons examined in Chapter II, Asian countries—Korea, Hong Kong and Singapore—dominate the exports of LDCs,[4] accounting for almost two thirds of the total increase in exports by the LDCs shown in Table IV.I. Among the LDCs, miscellaneous manufactures (SITC 8) and basic manufactures (SITC 6) typically accounted for the largest export gains. Chemicals (SITC 5) accounted for only a small portion of the total increase, while exports of machinery and transport equipment (SITC 7) were modest relative to the other two categories. This pattern is clearly different from that of industrialized countries where export expansion was mainly in machinery and transport equipment. The industrialized countries' additional exports of other product categories were small in comparison.

These basic facts suggest that export success is dependent upon a largely distinct set of demand and supply constraints in the two groups of countries. Exports of the LDCs are more closely tied to the behaviour of consumer demand while the West's export successes are heavily dependent upon the derived demand for capital goods. Similarly, exports of industrial supplies or inputs are also dependent on derived demand. Trade in such products is not directly observable from the figures in Table IV.1 although other studies have shown that they account for a larger share of industrialized countries' exports than is the case for LDCs.[5]

An appreciation of the different types of demand conditions which influence export performance is important. Clearly, final consumers (i.e. mainly households) are the major beneficiaries of increased exports from the developing countries. They benefit by having access to a wider range of cheaper consumer goods than would otherwise be available. However, it is precisely this group which, to date, has lacked the cohesiveness and organization necessary to see their interests expressed through trade policy.

In contrast, the producers of consumer goods who typically compete with exports from LDCs—e.g. shoes, clothing, textiles, food products, etc.—have a long and effective record in lobbying for trade restraints. With regard to the West's exports, industry

Table IV.1. A constant market share analysis for major exporters of manufactures (SITC 5 to 8 less 688), 1966–76 ((percentages and US $ millions)

Country and product group	World demand effect	Market composition effect[a]	Product composition effect[b]	Competitiveness effect	Actual increase
		LDCs			
KOREA—Total	8.7	1.3	−0.8	90.8	6558.9
Chemicals	2.1	−0.0	0.8	97.8	115.0
Basic manufactures	10.7	−2.1	−0.3	91.7	2224.0
Machinery & transport	3.3	0.3	−0.4	96.9	1250.3
Misc. manufactures	8.2	4.6	−0.1	87.3	2969.6
HONG KONG—Total	66.7	−5.2	0.2	38.2	5500.1
Chemicals	90.4	−26.5	−4.6	40.8	38.0
Basic manufactures	98.9	−5.3	−20.6	27.0	648.1
Machinery & transport	46.8	−7.5	11.4	49.3	877.9
Misc. manufactures	66.6	−4.5	0.3	37.6	3936.2
SINGAPORE—Total	46.4	−15.0	−0.9	69.5	2581.4
Chemicals	74.6	−19.6	−12.0	57.1	202.0
Basic manufactures	87.1	3.8	−28.2	37.3	409.7
Machinery & transport	29.9	1.1	−10.7	79.7	1528.0
Misc. manufactures	47.3	−1.2	−15.8	69.8	441.6
INDIA—Total	132.2	−3.4	−45.3	16.6	2242.4
Chemicals	86.4	−0.1	−11.2	24.9	96.6
Basic manufactures	146.9	−8.1	−31.5	−7.3	1404.7
Machinery & transport	32.4	11.7	−0.7	56.5	287.9
Misc. manufactures	36.8	0.6	−0.6	63.3	453.1

Structural Changes in World Trade in Manufactures

BRAZIL—Total	21.6	-2.2	-1.2	81.7	2220.2
Chemicals	81.7	10.9	5.7	1.7	127.1
Basic manufactures	23.3	-5.4	1.0	81.1	791.6
Machinery & transport	16.0	-2.0	-1.2	87.2	922.3
Misc. manufactures	3.6	-0.4	0.0	96.8	1814.8
GREECE—Total	21.7	5.1	-3.5	76.7	1287.5
Chemicals	28.4	1.1	-1.2	91.3	119.6
Basic manufactures	20.2	5.6	-1.0	75.3	756.8
Machinery & transport	25.4	12.8	0.5	61.3	118.8
Misc. manufactures	10.6	2.5	-0.1	86.9	292.3
ARGENTINA—Total	43.6	-6.4	-6.0	68.7	875.0
Chemicals	167.3	-13.7	-43.1	-10.6	98.4
Basic manufactures	23.0	-6.8	3.2	80.6	306.1
Machinery & transport	23.4	-2.4	-1.1	80.6	385.5
Misc. manufactures	64.9	-14.1	-17.2	66.3	85.0
MEXICO—Total	133.5	-27.7	-25.5	19.7	860.1
Chemicals	135.0	-23.2	-15.5	3.6	188.2
Basic manufactures	185.3	-56.3	-13.8	-15.2	307.5
Machinery & transport	41.3	-1.2	0.3	59.6	227.1
Misc. manufactures	68.5	-13.9	-8.5	53.9	137.4
THAILAND—Total	52.6	-13.7	-33.0	94.0	567.9
Chemicals	15.4	-4.3	-0.8	89.8	12.1
Basic manufactures	60.0	-20.3	-33.6	93.9	373.8
Machinery & transport	5.0	0.1	0.5	94.5	59.6
Misc. manufactures	6.4	-1.1	0.2	94.5	122.4
PHILIPPINES—Total	38.8	-12.2	-3.6	77.0	472.1
Chemicals	51.6	-12.0	-0.1	60.5	21.9
Basic manufactures	49.5	-20.2	7.1	63.7	252.0
Machinery & transport	1.6	-0.3	0.4	98.4	19.9
Misc. manufactures	7.2	-0.5	-2.1	95.3	178.3

The International Economy and Industrial Development

Country and product groups	World demand effect	Market composition effect[a]	Product composition effect[b]	Competitiveness effect	Actual increase
TURKEY—Total	29.8	1.6	-18.2	86.8	445.3
Chemicals	32.0	-9.9	-0.3	78.2	40.4
Basic manufactures	33.3	2.5	-18.9	83.0	273.1
Machinery & transport	2.7	1.7	-0.3	96.0	21.6
Misc. manufactures	2.9	0.1	-0.5	97.5	110.2
COLOMBIA—Total	47.2	-8.7	-4.0	65.5	343.2
Chemicals	55.9	-17.4	-6.7	68.3	45.9
Basic manufactures	51.0	7.4	-10.4	52.0	177.7
Machinery & transport	15.3	-0.8	-1.6	25.9	38.7
Misc. manufactures	8.1	-0.5	-1.7	75.1	81.0
INDUSTRIALIZED COUNTRIES					
GERMANY, WEST—Total	97.1	3.4	3.9	-4.4	72484.3
Chemicals	95.7	5.6	1.3	-2.5	10076.0
Basic manufactures	84.6	5.8	6.0	3.6	16198.2
Machinery & transport	106.4	1.1	-1.0	-6.6	39078.1
Misc. manufactures	105.5	6.9	0.4	-12.8	7131.9
UNITED STATES—Total	129.7	-5.8	5.0	-28.8	56292.6
Chemicals	149.4	-16.7	9.9	-42.6	7146.1
Basic manufactures	136.3	-12.2	5.4	-29.6	7652.0
Machinery & transport	130.8	-2.1	-4.8	-24.0	36826.7
Misc. manufactures	162.2	-8.8	-8.6	-44.9	4667.9

Structural Changes in World Trade in Manufactures

JAPAN—Total	64.1	−5.0	3.7	37.1	53711.7
Chemicals	92.1	−11.6	4.8	14.7	2730.6
Basic manufactures	74.6	−8.4	2.7	31.1	14652.5
Machinery & transport	45.2	−0.9	7.3	48.4	31815.1
Misc. manufactures	128.5	−18.5	−0.7	9.3	4513.5
FRANCE—Total	90.1	5.1	0.0	4.8	34475.6
Chemicals	102.8	7.0	−3.6	−6.2	4394.4
Basic manufactures	102.3	5.7	6.3	−14.4	8496.2
Machinery & transport	74.9	5.3	0.2	19.7	17913.6
Misc. manufactures	109.8	0.2	0.0	−10.1	3671.3
UNITED KINGDOM—Total	178.1	0.6	−0.2	−78.4	26209.3
Chemicals	125.8	−3.3	−1.5	−21.1	4149.9
Basic manufactures	154.4	0.7	2.4	−57.6	6891.4
Machinery & transport	227.8	1.9	−6.3	123.4	11954.5
Misc. manufactures	137.1	0.3	−7.2	−30.2	3213.5

Source: Compiled from United Nations, *Commodity Trade Statistics*, Series D, various issues, and other United Nations publications.

Notes: [a] The analysis distinguished between the following importing markets: Western Europe, North America, Japan, other developed market economies, Africa, Latin America, Middle East, East Asia, and socialist countries of both Europe and Asia.
[b] Products were defined by using an SITC three-digit level of disaggregation. This led to a total of 101 product groups distributed as follows: chemicals—16; basic manufactures—49; machinery and transport equipment—18; miscellaneous manufactures—18. SITC 688 was excluded from the study.

itself is the major consumer and the policy environment differs accordingly. Although producers are effectively organized to lobby for market interventions of various forms, including protection, the self-interests of one group (e.g. an industry relying on imported capital goods or supplies) are often pitted against another (the domestic producer competing with these imports of the same product).[6]

Thus, export performance in the two groups of countries is subject not only to different demand conditions but also to different combinations of the domestic interests which exert an influence over the trade policy of industrialized countries. Bearing these distinctions in mind, we turn to an examination of the different effects which contribute to export performance. The first of these, the world demand effect, represents the overall growth in exports associated with a general rise in world demand. Here, the distinction between countries is clear cut. In the LDCs the growth attributable to this component was modest, accounting for more than one half the increase in exports of total manufactures in only three instances—Hong Kong, India and Mexico. In contrast, the world market effect was the predominant determinant of export gains in the West. The growth of world demand benefits those countries that are most extensively integrated into the world trading system. Thus, the present results—marginal significance in most LDCs and striking importance in the West and selected Asian exporters—are logical.

Like the growth of world demand, the composition of the markets to which a country exports may be regarded as an external condition contributing to export performance.[7] Among the LDCs, these estimates were usually negative, indicating that producers were not successful in redirecting their exports to the more rapidly growing markets. The industrialized countries benefited marginally by directing their exports to those markets (i.e. mainly other industrialized countries) where demand was expanding at a pace exceeding the world average.

Turning to the other components, product composition was not an important contributor to export performance for most Third World countries. These estimates were generally low (with the exceptions of India and Thailand) and often negative, a result which

Structural Changes in World Trade in Manufactures

suggests that countries have been unable, or have failed, to take full advantage of trade opportunities through export diversification. In the industrialized countries a marginal amount of diversification into more dynamic export products meant that the product composition effect was usually positive.[8]

The competitiveness effect which represents price and non-price factors was important in determining export performance. In many LDCs this was the major determinant of their export expansion. Exporters in the Third World proved to be relatively adept in improving their competitive position in both capital-intensive industries, such as machinery, and in labour-intensive ones like basic manufactures.

The estimates for industrialized countries provide a stark contrast with the above. With the exception of Japan, most estimates of the competitiveness effect were negative. Some of Japan's successes probably occurred at the expense of other industrialized countries whose exports directly compete with the Japanese. In any case, these results clearly suggest that, unlike the findings for the LDCs, internal factors operating on the supply side imposed some constraint or did not contribute greatly to the industrialized countries' export performance.

At the risk of some oversimplification, the first two of these components—the world market and the product composition effect—can be regarded as representing external factors related to foreign demand. The product composition and competitiveness effects are more closely associated with internal or supply-related circumstances. In these terms, export performances in the industrialized countries and the LDCs were again subject to distinctly different sets of factors. Internal factors related to the supply side made a significant positive contribution to export growth in the LDCs while external factors pertaining to the demand side were the major determinant in industrialized countries.

A variety of explanations for this result could be offered. The fact that many LDCs revamped their trade strategies in the mid-1960s (see Chapter II) is relevant. Prior to that time import substitution strategies were widely followed and resulted in substantial discrimination against exports.[9] Subsequently, many countries altered their strategy to give greater importance to exports and to reduce the policy bias against this sector. Korea and India (included in Table IV.1) are relevant examples. Korea's export orientation is well known while India has continued its import substitution strategy longer than most countries. Internal factors (mainly improved competitiveness) were overwhelmingly responsible for Korea's export gains. In India's case, exporters followed a more passive strategy by merely responding to increases in world demand. For many LDCs the internal adjustments taking place in 1966–76 were probably more substantial than would otherwise have been the case because of the switch from import substitution to export oriented strategies.

More specific determinants, in addition to policy initiatives in both the LDCs and the West, are obviously relevant here. Generally, these determinants may be lumped together under the rubric of comparative advantage. A CMS analysis, while providing a useful overview of changes in export performance, sheds little light on the magnitude or extent of changes in competitive ability among specifically identified industrial activities. The following section examines how patterns of comparative advantage are changing in both industrialized countries and LDCs.

4.2 *Estimating changes in comparative advantage*

An empirical investigation of comparative advantage is hampered by theoretical and conceptual problems. The theoretical determinants of comparative advantage are many and their interaction is complex. Even if this problem could be solved the researcher still faces the monumental task of estimating and comparing the results between different countries and different industries. As a result, most studies have resorted to a proxy measuring an industry's 'apparent' or 'revealed' trade performance which can serve as an indicator of revealed comparative advantage (RCA) in international trade.[10] The results have confirmed the general notion that LDCs tend to export goods requiring relatively large amounts of unskilled labour and/or raw materials while a complementary export composition is observed in industrialized countries. The present discussion has a slightly different focus. Inter-country differences in export performance (i.e. revealed comparative advantages) will

Structural Changes in World Trade in Manufactures

depend on differences in resource endowments, physical and human capital, technologies, etc. Insofar as the determinants of export performance change over time, comparative advantage would shift in a similar fashion.

In order to limit the study to a manageable scope, four country samples were selected for detailed study. The first includes six industrialized countries (ICs) representing an RCA pattern which, presumably, is the most advanced. The second sample consists of five recently developed countries (RDCs) that are thought to have an RCA pattern representing a less sophisticated export pattern. The third sample is composed of seven countries popularly known as the 'newly industrializing countries' (NICs). Conventional wisdom often singles out these countries as the most zealous exporters of manufactures. They have made strenuous efforts to acquire the technologies and develop the skilled labour necessary for this approach. The last sample is ten LDCs at an earlier phase of their industrial development and should indicate a more rudimentary export pattern. The country composition of each sample is indicated in the annex to this chapter.

In addition to the need to limit the country coverage of the study, two conceptual decisions were necessary. First, a precise definition for exports of manufactures was required.[11] Manufacturing is traditionally described in terms of production statistics (ISIC 300). Accordingly, exports of manufactures were defined here so that the coverage of trade roughly matched the range of activities commonly ascribed to production of the manufacturing sector. The interpretation led us to include the exports of resource-based industries with relatively little value added content that are usually omitted in studies concerned purely with trade aspects. This treatment seemed desirable since resource-based industries account for an important share of the Third World's exports and figure prominently in the structural changes these countries experience. A second conceptual matter was to give some precise meaning to the concept of an 'industry'. In order to account for the diversity in market conditions and production processes, a relatively specific definition was used which led to the identification of 134 different industries defined according to three- and four-digit SITC product categories.[12]

Finally, some proxy to represent an industry's comparative

advantage was required. Economists reason 'that "revealed" comparative advantage can be indicated by the trade performance of individual countries.'[13] This argument assumes that the pattern of trade reflects inter-country differences in relative costs as well as non-price factors such as quality differences, goodwill, servicing, etc. The first phase in such an investigation is usually the development of an index of export performance. The index employed here is a ratio between two shares. The numerator of the ratio represents an industry's share in a given country's exports of manufactures. The denominator is a share determined by exports of that industry from all countries divided by world exports of manufactures.[14] Thus, a value of 2.0 indicates that the industry's share in a given country's exports of manufactures is twice that of the corresponding world share. Export performances indices were computed for each of the 134 industries and twenty-eight countries in our sample using two-year averages for 1965–6 and 1975–6. Weighted averages of export performance for each of the four country samples may be found elsewhere.[15]

Our analysis begins by ranking industries according to their export performance indices. The degree of similarity between the rankings of each of the four country samples can then be appraised statistically. The results, based on each sample's weighted averages for seventy-nine industries,[16] are shown in Table IV.2. It is immediately obvious that the composition of the industrialized countries' exports differs markedly from that of the other groups. Moreover, this distinction is accentuated over time.

A second noteworthy point concerns the comparisons between the three remaining groups—the NICs, other LDCs and the recently developed countries. Some economists maintain that the composition of a country's exports changes in a sequential fashion as development proceeds. They argue that a country begins by exporting goods requiring simple production techniques and large amounts of cheap, unskilled labour. As the skilled labour force grows and wage rates rise, the country's comparative advantages are thought to shift into new product lines whose production requirements are more in line with these factor combinations. This interpretation, closely associated with Balassa, pictures countries moving along a scale of comparative advantage. Asian countries are

Structural Changes in World Trade in Manufactures

Table IV.2. Spearman rank correlation coefficients in export performance indices of seventy-nine industries, 1966–7 and 1975–6[a]

Pairings	1966–7	1975–6
NICs—ICs	−0.271*	−0.349*
NICS—other LDCs	0.596	0.597
NICs—RDCs	0.431	0.517
LDCs—RDCs	0.512	0.717
ICs—RDCs	−0.247*	−0.275*
ICs—other LDCs	−0.245*	−0.306*

Source: Compiled from United Nations, *Commodity Trade Statistics*, Series D, various issues, and other United Nations publications.

Notes: [a] Calculations were based on two-year averages for exports and imports. For a definition of the export performance index, see note 14.
An asterisk indicates statistical significance at the 5 per cent level. All other values are significant at the 1 per cent level.

often used as an example. A case in point is Japan whose comparative advantage has shifted towards capital-intensive exports and away from goods requiring unskilled or even skilled labour. In turn, countries with adequate supplies of human capital (e.g. Korea) may take the place of Japan in exporting the original products. Countries at lower levels of industrialization may supplant previous suppliers in the export of unskilled labour-intensive products.[17]

The results in Table IV.2 provide no support for this interpretation, however. The correlation of export performance in the RDCs, NICs and other LDCs shows a composition that is similar and became more so over time. The only divergent trend was in the comparison of the industrialized countries with each of the other groups. Rather than supporting a 'stage interpretation' of comparative advantage, the results, in fact, suggest a dependency relationship between the industrialized countries on the one hand and other exporters on the other. The 'dependency' theorists[18] have argued that industrialization induced through export-led development strategies or through the initiatives of transnational corporations does not lead to a fundamental restructuring of host economies. Frank cites the case of the Latin American economies which

143

experienced an accelerated pace of industrialization in the first four decades of the twentieth century, but failed to develop into mature capitalist economies.[19] A pre-capitalist mode of production continued to dominate the agrarian sector and external capital remained of crucial importance in sustaining industrialization. Many of the countries classified as RDCs (Greece, Israel, Portugal, Spain and Yugoslavia) have strong links with foreign capital. An appreciation of the importance of foreign capital is one reason why three of these countries aspire to full membership in the EEC. Israel also is well aware of the importance—both political and economic—of its dependence on US capital. There are, then, some grounds to describe the industrial development of these countries as 'dependent industrialization'.

Our finding that the list of leading export industries in RDCs bears a closer relationship to that of Colombia, Egypt, India, the Philippines, Thailand, etc. than to countries like France or the UK suggests that industry in the peripheral European economies poses no serious competitive threat to the 'industrialized centre'. This characteristic contrasts markedly with German industrialization in the nineteenth century, the Japanese experience in the twentieth century and the impact of these structural changes on the UK and US positions in international markets. To some extent metropolitan capital has successfully integrated the industrial expansion of the industrial centre and the peripheral countries according to a division of labour which sustains (and does not erode) existing differences in the structure of international industry.

Western industries that have attained a substantial degree of export success face no serious threat from competitors in other parts of the world. Instead, any competitive threat to these producers comes from potential exporters in other western countries. The composition of world trade patterns, however, does pit the interests of high performance exporters outside the West against 'poor performance' industries in these countries.

The foregoing information provides an overview of export performance in a large part of the manufacturing sector but tells us little about the export performance of specific industries. Here, the efforts of trade economists to broaden and extend the original Heckscher-Ohlin (i.e. factor proportions) model are a useful guide.

The original emphasis on labour and capital endowments as the major determinants of comparative advantage was modified by introducing human capital, R and D inputs, and technological transfer.[20]

Much of this reasoning can be found in the literature dealing with the product cycle. The original view, while accepting the factor proportions explanation for trade in 'old' products, introduced the idea that some products pass through a 'cycle' from new to old. The production of new products requires large amounts of skilled labour in the form of scientists, engineers, professional managers and skilled craftsmen. Once these new products enter the market, they experience a phase of rapid growth and the production process is simplified, meaning that lesser amounts of skilled labour or R and D are required. Producers then require relatively large inputs of unskilled labour and capital and the product is regarded as 'mature'. Thus, in addition to distinguishing between industries according to whether they require relatively large amounts of unskilled labour or capital, new and mature industries may also be denoted.

An alternative interpretation of the product cycle distinguishes between industries according to their rates of product development. This version treats product development as a form of competition whereby firms attempt to gain new markets by introducing, at established prices, products substantially different from the available ones.[21] The development of new technologies (and associated skilled labour requirements) are not stressed in this version. Instead, it is the rate of product turnover which serves to distinguish between an industry producing relatively 'standardized' products and one producing 'unstandardized' products.

Thus, the two interpretations focus on somewhat different sets of products. Transistor radios, semi-conductors and electronic calculators are examples of products which have passed through a cycle from new to mature products.[22] The footwear industry provides an example appropriate to the second version of the product cycle. Here, style changes are frequent (i.e. meaning a high rate of product turnover) and certain production processes such as injection moulding are relatively new.[23] Such products, although unstandardized, are not necessarily skill-intensive in their early stages.

Table IV.3 Average increases in export performance indices by country sample and by product characteristics, 1966–7 to 1975–6[a] (percentages)

Type of industry		Industrialized countries	Recently developed countries	NICs	Other LDCs
All manufactures		13.8	67.1	91.4	156.4
Resource-based		98.0	18.9	8.1	84.8
Mature industries	labour-intensive	−7.0	25.7	103.2	292.5
	capital-intensive	5.9	265.3	177.4	94.6
	total	−2.7	101.0	117.5	258.4
New industries	labour-intensive	−3.8	58.5	156.0	209.9
	capital-intensive	−7.1	63.1	91.5	268.5
	total	−2.1	70.6	152.1	220.9

Structural Changes in World Trade in Manufactures

Standardized industries	labour-intensive	−5.0	30.4	115.9	311.9
	capital-intensive	−4.0	129.0	140.0	216.8
	total	−2.9	53.1	121.2	298.7
Unstandardized industries	labour-intensive	−2.2	44.8	161.8	59.2
	capital-intensive	6.6	297.7	169.2	50.6
	total	−1.4	172.3	167.7	91.4

Sources: Data were compiled from United Nations, *Commodity Trade Statistics*, Series D, various issues. For the classification of industries, see UNIDO, *World Industry in 1980*, New York, 1981, pp. 103–8.

Note: [a] Industries' increases of EP-ratios are weighted by 1975–6 average values of exports. Only 'established' industries which contributed more than 0.1 per cent to the exports of manufactures in 1975–6 were included in the respective weighted averages.

The International Economy and Industrial Development

The literature on the product cycle does contain certain ambiguities which pose problems of interpretation. First, the distinction between a technology gap hypothesis and a product cycle hypothesis is not always clear. Some writers have viewed the product cycle as a passing disequilibrium, implying that the gap eventually disappears, while others (e.g. Finger) see the gap as more or less permanent equilibrium. Obviously, the two interpretations have distinctly different predictive implications.

Second, various interpretations of the product cycle come dangerously close to being *ex post* statements of exceptions to the factor proportions theory. As such, their operational significance can be considerably weakened. The approaches described above represent different versions of the product cycle theory which, based on the work of Hirsch and Vernon in the first instance and Finger in the second, represent the two schools of thought on the subject.

Both interpretations were drawn upon in order to gain further insights into countries' export performance and their underlying comparative advantages. Accordingly, most industries which were not resource-based (a total of seventy-nine) were classified as mature or new industries or as standardized or unstandardized industries. The classifications drew upon earlier work by S. Hirsch, H. Lary, G. Hufbauer and J. M. Finger and are described in further detail elsewhere.[24]

Sample averages showing changes in export performance indices between 1966–7 and 1975–6 are given in Table IV.3. Changes in the indices applying to all manufactures are inversely related to the degree of industrialization. This is expected given the larger initial export base of the more advanced countries. Much more surprising is the role of exports. Improvements in the industrialized countries' export performance are almost totally due to the gains made by resource-based industries. Increases of a comparable magnitude (84.8 per cent) are found only among those LDCs at the lower end of the development spectrum. Many of these industries are closely related to the agricultural or mining sectors and export products with little industrial processing. Moreover, international trade in most of the products—fish, sugar, coffee, cocoa, tea, rubber, petroleum products, rubber—is highly concentrated in the hands of a few transnationals. Finger persuasively argues that the power of these firms is even more pervasive than their small number would suggest, often dominating the entire market for particular commodities thanks to their superior information and control.[25] The predominance of oligopolistic conditions means that excessive margins and quasi-rents are factors which could help to explain the export performance of resource-based industries in western countries.

The basis for comparative advantage, as well as firm structure, also makes resource-based industries unique from other lines of manufacturing. Various factors such as the availability of skilled labour and the cost of capital or labour have little or no impact on a country's ability to compete internationally unless domestic resources are available. Furthermore, the technology is largely concentrated among the relevant TNCs. For all these reasons, western countries are likely to retain their comparative advantages in resource-based industries. The significance of these exports is, in fact, likely to grow for industrialized economies. Non-resource-based industries generally experienced a deterioration in export performance between 1966 and 1976 while other countries' gains were much more widespread.

These results carry our previous findings one step further. We have observed that the industrialized countries' export performance in 'traditionally defined' manufactures[26] was largely due to external rather than internal factors (see Table IV.1). The major external factor was the network of intra-OECD trade, carefully built up and encouraged during the 1950s and 1960s. Although the scope of internal adjustments or structural change among these countries was significant in 1966–76, the results were seldom a response to outside competitive pressure and did not lead to improvements in export performance. Export performance in the more traditionally defined fields of manufacturing seems to depend on forces which are not accurately reflected in terms of competitive ability or performance.

Again, the distinctions among the other country samples are not great. In NICs and other LDCs, improved export performance is not uniquely dependent on the availability of either capital or labour. Somewhat more marked differences related to the product cycle results. The LDCs show a slight bias in favour of mature industries rather than new products and in favour of standardized rather than unstandardized products. An opposite tendency may be claimed for export performance in the NICs. The major distinction between the two country samples concerns the group of unstandardized industries. Here, the other LDCs' export gains were meagre compared to other industry groups or to the corresponding figures for NICs. The ability of producers to keep abreast of foreign marketing development and changes in taste is important when exports are distinguished by product turnover. Exporters in LDCs may be handicapped relative to those in recently developed countries or NICs. Alternatively, these producers may be less inclined to engage in forms of export competition based mainly on product differentiation or product development.

Lastly, the RDCs showed a preference for expanding capital-intensive rather than labour-intensive exports. This characteristic is most apparent in the case of mature industries where the RDCs' emphasis on capital-intensive exports contrasts with the NICs' reliance on labour-intensive exports. Exporters in these two sets of countries probably benefited from better market information (important for exporting unstandardized products with high rates of product development) in the first instance and TNC assembly operations (mainly mature industries) intended mainly for export in the second instance.

The scope of these improvements in export performance can more clearly be seen through an examination of revealed comparative advantage (RCA). The measure used here combines export performance indices in the two periods to reflect the extent and direction of change.[27] An industry was denoted as having a 'marked' revealed comparative advantage if (i) its RCA exceeded a 'normal' level of 100 by at least 50 per cent, and (ii) the industry's ratio of net exports (exports minus imports) to total trade (exports plus imports) was not less than the corresponding ratio for all manufactures. The second condition serves to exclude those industries with a relatively large excess of imports over exports for the given country sample. The results of this exercise are summarized in Table IV.4.

Here, the importance of labour-intensive exports becomes clear.

Structural Changes in World Trade in Manufactures

Table IV.4. Exports with a marked RCA as a share of exports of manufactures, 1966–7 and 1975–6
(percentages and number of industries)

Product category		RDCs	NICs	Other LDCs
Mature industries	labour-intensive	21.0 (19)	32.5 (19)	22.6 (17)
	capital-intensive	7.7 (5)	1.8 (3)	1.7 (2)
	total	28.7 (24)	34.3 (22)	24.6 (20)
New industries	labour-intensive	4.3 (5)	5.3 (6)	0.6 (2)
	capital-intensive	0.6 (2)	0.1 (1)	0.4 (1)
	total	6.8 (9)	5.4 (7)	1.0 (3)
Standardized industries (low rates of product development)	labour-intensive	22.3 (20)	34.6 (19)	20.3 (16)
	capital-intensive	3.1 (4)	0.7 (2)	1.5 (2)
	total	25.8 (25)	35.3 (21)	21.8 (18)
Unstandardized industries (high rates of product development)	labour-intensive	2.9 (4)	3.2 (6)	2.9 (3)
	capital-intensive	5.2 (3)	1.2 (2)	0.6 (1)
	total	8.1 (7)	4.4 (8)	3.8 (5)

Source: United Nations, *Commodity Trade Statistics*, Series D, various issues; UNIDO, *World Industry in 1980*, New York, 1981, p. 77.

Even in those cases where countries recorded large gains in their exports of capital-intensive products (e.g. the RDCs' exports of mature, capital-intensive manufactures), the significance of these strides was not great by international standards. Similarly, progress was largely restricted to mature rather than to new industries and to standardized rather than unstandardized ones.

The foregoing results lead us to place emphasis on a distinction between industrialized countries and others rather than stressing a graduated scale of exporters according to their level of development. Moreover, the opinion that dramatic changes in comparative advantage, largely taking place in the Third World, are generating considerable pressure for the industrialized economies may be partly attributed to the fact that recent structural changes did little in the way of creating durable or lasting export advantages.[28] The gains of Third World exporters are largely confined to labour-intensive products despite progress in industries where other types of inputs or production characteristics predominate. The following section addresses the extent to which these exports actually contributed to the growth process in the Third World.

4.3 The contribution of exports to growth

The interrelationship between exports and growth has again come to occupy the attention of economists. In part, renewed interest may be traced back to the link between analysis and trade performance discussed in Chapter II. This issue is of valid interest in any case, since a growth objective is frequently tied to an emphasis on exports.

Several earlier studies have supported the hypothesis that the rapid growth of exports accelerates growth of an economy. A smaller number of studies has reached similar conclusions when the investigation was limited to the manufacturing sector.[29] The data in Table IV.5 relate growth by type of industry to growth of all exports of manufactures. The results are largely consistent with those shown in Table IV.4. Those industries with a 'marked RCA' provide the main export impetus in the manufacturing sector. Apparently, resource-based exports are not a particularly important contributor to the growth of exports except for the LDCs. Among Third World

Table IV.5. Contribution to the growth of manufactured exports (1966–7 and 1975–6) by country group

$$\triangle X_i^j / \triangle X_i^m \text{ (percentage)}^a$$

Type of industry	Industrialized countries	Recently developed countries	NICs	Other LDCs
Resource-based	15.4	26.5	28.6	55.7
Mature industries				
labour-intensive	11.2	24.4	38.5	25.4
capital-intensive	12.9	13.3	6.5	6.6
total	38.8	43.1	47.8	33.7
New industries				
labour-intensive	32.5	21.6	18.9	5.9
capital-intensive	4.2	2.5	1.9	2.1
total	44.4	29.1	23.1	9.8
Standardized industries				
labour-intensive	6.0	41.8	52.4	28.3
capital-intensive	39.2	6.0	3.4	4.8
total	51.5	50.3	57.4	34.1
Unstandardized industries				
labour-intensive	4.6	4.2	5.0	3.1
capital-intensive	10.9	9.8	5.1	3.9
total	30.9	20.1	13.1	9.1

Source: United Nations, *Commodity Trade Statistics*, Series D, various issues; UNIDO, *World Industry in 1980*, New York, 1981, p. 81.

Note: [a] $\triangle$ designates the difference between the 1975–6 and 1966–7 levels of exports; i stands for a country group; j refers to a given industry; and m stands for total manufactures. Because certain industries were not classified by type, totals do not sum to 100.

producers labour-intensive exports—specifically those associated with mature and standardized industries—predominate. Thus, these products are important both in terms of their present contribution to export growth and in terms of their future potential given present patterns of change in RCAs.

These impressions relate the growth of exports by various industries to that of manufactured exports. However, the studies referred to above are concerned with the relationship between export growth and the growth of national income (GDP). The latter

Table IV.6 Spearman rank correlation coefficients between exports and output growth in LDCs[a], 1968–74

		Wood products	Textiles	Clothing	Footwear	Furniture
1.	Export growth and growth of value added	0.504 (0.029)	0.170 (0.249)	0.150 (0.297)	0.182 (0.258)	−0.418 (0.102)
2.	Export growth and growth of output net of exports	0.271 (0.165)	0.005 (0.492)	−0.332 (0.114)	−0.364 (0.092)	−0.536 (0.047)
3.	Incremental export-output ratios and growth of value added	−0.371 (0.087)	0.259 (0.149)	0.179 (0.263)	0.357 (0.096)	−0.655 (0.017)
4.	Incremental export-output ratios and growth of output net of exports	−0.496 (0.031)	−0.513 (0.013)	−0.561 (0.016)	−0.025 (0.465)	−0.609 (0.026)

5.	Increments in export-output ratios and growth of value added	−0.157 (0.288)	0.397 (0.051)	−0.125 (0.329)	−0.029 (0.460)	−0.736 (0.006)
6.	Increments in export-output ratios and growth of output net of exports	−0.379 (0.082)	−0.288 (0.122)	−0.854 (0.001)	−0.521 (0.024)	−0.782 (0.003)

Source: annex to Chapter IV.

Notes: Levels of significance are in parentheses. Precise values were available for small samples (e.g. furniture with eleven observations) taken from E. L. Lehmann and H. J. M. d'Abrera, *Nonparametrics, Statistical Methods Based on Ranks*, Holden-Day Inc., San Francisco, 1975, p. 433. Other significance levels were approximated by use of a t-distribution function.

[a] All growth rates are compound annual rates. Incremental export-output ratios were defined as $\Delta X/\Delta G = (X_2 - X_1)/(G_2 - G_1)$ where X refers to exports and G is gross output. Increments in export-output ratios were annual averages defined as $\Delta(X/G)/t = (X_2/G_2 - X_1/G_1)/(t_2 - t_1)$ where t_1 is the beginning year. Output net of exports is G−x. All data for value added and gross output were converted to US dollars using IMF exchange rates.

view is, of course, much more meaningful for a discussion of development. Accordingly, the following discussion addresses export performance in terms of its income-generating attributes. In doing so, we restrict our attention to five labour-intensive industries since the preceding investigations have shown such exports to be of immediate and future significance. The industries chosen are textiles, clothing, footwear, wood products and furniture.

An investigation of this sort required additional statistical analysis prior to testing. First, Third World countries for which data were available were included. Second, a concordance matching domestic production with the corresponding exports was needed.[30] Each industry's exports, gross output and value added were compiled for 1968–74.[31] That period was selected for reasons of data availability and the desire to reflect the LDCs' policy re-orientation towards export promotion.

The appropriate criteria for testing the export-growth relationship have been the subject of recent discussions in the literature. Earlier studies had correlated the growth of exports with the growth of national product. The former, however, is a component of the latter and a positive correlation between the two is almost inevitable. Apparently, the correct correlation tests of the hypothesis are between the export and the non-export components of output.[32] A second point is that the growth rates of exports are not reliable indicators when countries begin from a low base[33] Accordingly, six sets of correlation coefficients are calculated for each of the five industries. The coefficients relate either incremental export-output ratios or increments in the export-output ratio to the appropriate rates of growth.

The best measure of growth is open to choice when attention is restricted to a specific industry. More general investigations used GNP or the share of manufacturing in GNP as growth measures. Both are value added concepts and are not strictly consistent with data for exports which are recorded in terms of their gross value.[34] Here, two alternative concepts of growth at the industry level, gross output net of exports and value added, are tested. The former is statistically compatible with export data while the latter coincides with the growth process as understood by economists and planners.

The results of a Spearman rank correlation are given in Table

Structural Changes in World Trade in Manufactures

IV.6. The correlation between the growth rates of exports and those of value added or gross output net of exports shows few cases of statistical significance and no distinct pattern in the sign of the coefficients. A clearer pattern emerges from the coefficients involving either the incremental export-output ratio or increments of the export-output ratio. When these ratios are correlated with the growth rate of value added, six of the ten coefficients are negative although levels of statistical significance are not high. When the export measures are correlated with the growth of output net of exports, all coefficients have a negative sign. Furthermore, seven of the ten are statistically significant at 95 per cent levels of confidence or higher. The conclusion seems to be that the relationship between growth of exports and growth of income among labour-intensive industries is, at best, very weak and, perhaps, even negative.

Exports of labour-intensive manufactures are influenced by the behaviour of international demand and supply considerations in the LDCs themselves, or a combination of both elements. Thus, a search for plausible explanations for this result may begin from a CMS analysis for these products. In this case we are concerned with the industrialized countries' imports of labour-intensive manufactures from the LDCs. The results, shown in Table IV.7, indicate that external factors are more important among labour-intensive exports than was the case for total manufactures (see Table IV.1).

Table IV.7 A constant market share analysis of the LDCs' labour-intensive exports, 1967–8 to 1973–4
(percentages and US $ millions)

Effect	
World market	59.6
Product composition	0.5
Market composition	−1.7
Competitiveness	41.6
Actual increase in LDCs' exports	$7,275.6

Source: United Nations, *Commodity Trade Statistics, Series D*, United Nations, New York, various issues.

Note: The growth rate of OECD imports of labour-intensive manufactures from the world was used as the norm in this exercise. For country coverage, see the annex to this chapter.

The International Economy and Industrial Development

Since export performance is influenced by both foreign and domestic considerations, explanations for the weak relationship between the growth of exports and output can conceivably involve economic and policy consequences in either field. Turning first to the external factors, foreign demand for the labour-intensive exports of LDCs has steadily grown. Third World countries have enjoyed considerable economic advantages in the production of these goods relative to foreign competitors. Since the mid-1960s, wage and exchange rate trends in western countries have also worked in favour of the LDCs. Consequently, their penetration of western markets, often through the displacement of other suppliers, continued at a brisk pace during the period 1968–74. Thus, casual observation suggests that the growth of foreign demand for labour-intensive products probably matched or even outstripped the growth of domestic demand in the LDCs themselves.[35] These circumstances increase the likelihood of a positive export-growth relationship and the failure to observe such a result cannot be easily attributed to external economic conditions.

Regarding internal effects, systematic changes in comparative advantage and in the LDCs' industrial structure shed some light on the export-growth relationship. In three industries—textiles, clothing and footwear—comparative advantage was found to be negatively correlated with *per capita* value added.[36] Further evidence may be found in studies of structural change. Cross-country studies show a similarity in the development patterns of specific industries according to their growth elasticities (i.e. the percentage change in value added given a one per cent change in total income). One of the first studies of structural change described certain industries as early leaders that 'exhaust their potential for import substitution and export growth at fairly low levels' of *per capita* income.[37] That study and others have associated each of the five labour-intensive industries with a similar type of growth behaviour.[38] A likely corollary is that the growth impetus of additional exports will also be diminished at later stages of development.

The commercial policy practices of LDCs and the western countries are another aspect which can affect the export-growth relationship, although generalizations are extremely difficult for specific industrial branches. Differences in demand elasticities, the existence of externalities, divergences of social and private returns and, most important, political considerations all contribute to the diversity. Export incentives and rates of effective protection vary widely among product lines, among manufacturing branches and among countries. One comprehensive study of effective protection led only to the limited generalization that consumption goods (which include the five industries examined here) are usually more highly protected than intermediate or capital goods. The study went on to single out 'cloth, clothing, shoes, leather goods and furniture' as labour-intensive products which are sometimes highly protected.[39] Intuitively, a policy bias favouring production for domestic markets over exports can be expected for the industries considered here since import substitution practices usually began in the consumer goods sector and would be most firmly entrenched there. Similarly, rates of effective protection have tended to rise with the stages of fabrication. Many individual products of interest are final goods and effective rates could often exceed the levels accorded to semi-finished manufactures, industrial intermediates and supplies.

Although producers in LDCs have probably seen a decline in overall protection as well as a reduction in its variability, the extent of resource misallocation is reduced only in so far as the domestic market is concerned. Exports of manufactures are still discriminated against since they are sold at world market prices while material inputs are sold at some premium above world prices. On these, admittedly impressionistic, grounds it is probable that commercial policy biases in the Third World have contributed to the failure of export expansion to spur growth in labour-intensive industries.

Among the commercial policies of western countries, neo-protectionist measures are of interest. Although precise information is again not available, rough estimates indicate the scope and relative burden of such measures. Data for 1968 suggest that these measures were, even at that time, of considerable significance for Third World exports. Almost 21 per cent of the LDCs' exports of all manufactures and semi-manufactures to the West were subject to non-tariff barriers in that year. In comparison, LDCs supplied only

The International Economy and Industrial Development

16.5 per cent of the industrialized countries' imports of these goods. Thus, NTBs were somewhat more frequently applied to imports from LDCs than to imports from elsewhere. Further analysis has also indicated several reasons why potential exporters in LDCs would have greater difficulties in coping with a given NTB than do their competitors in industrialized countries.[40]

Detailed studies reveal that NTBs are much more conspicuous among the LDCs' exports of labour-intensive industries than they are for other exports. For example, in a study of industrialized countries' imports of 82 specific manufactured items, NTBs were applied on approximately 22 per cent ($9 billion) of those products supplied by LDCs in 1970. Only twenty-one of the items were produced by the textile (excluding cotton textiles), clothing or footwear industries.[41] However, this sub-group accounted for 87 per cent of the imports from LDCs which were subject to NTBs. Additional information on cotton textiles indicates a similar situation. In 1975 industrialized countries imported $2.3 billion of these goods from the LDCs of which 91 per cent were covered by the Multifibre Arrangement.[42]

Both tariffs and NTBs are significant restraints on market access and, with their reduction or removal, trade expansion would be considerable. However, the complaint of limited market access, though legitimate, does not shed any light on the apparent failure of exports to stimulate growth in the five industries studied. Despite these trade barriers the LDCs' exports of labour-intensive manufactures have steadily risen. The manner in which the commercial policies of western countries have influenced the composition of the LDCs' exports—and, consequently, their industrial structure—is more relevant to the present discussion.

The growth of the LDCs' exports of labour-intensive manufactures has been heavily concentrated in very narrow product lines. This characteristic applies both to established export lines and to those which have grown rapidly.[43] Quite likely, commercial policies in the West have encouraged this extreme pattern of export concentration within each industry. Perhaps the best examples are textiles and clothing. In the early 1970s, market penetration (in terms of imports from the world) of specific product categories was slowed or even halted, demonstrating the effectiveness of the

West's trade barriers.[44] At the same time, producers in LDCs proved to be both adept and flexible by specializing, increasingly, in narrow product lines where the danger that restrictions would be imposed, or at least enforced, was not substantial. One result has been that exporters in LDCs have concentrated on narrow product lines of clothing rather than, say, textile fabrics since there is a higher value added for each 'square yard equivalent' of the quotas.[45]

The continued spread of neo-protectionism can contribute to forms of monopoly behaviour in the Third World that limit the growth benefits of export expansion. For example, voluntary export restraints, orderly marketing arrangements, the Multifibre Arrangement, etc., in addition to various pernicious effects, offer established producers in LDCs the assurance of continuing markets and (supposedly) expanding quotas. These arrangements can lead to cartelization and monopoly practices. Thus, they may not be so onerous for the exporting firms as they are for the LDC involved.

Evidence of monopoly behaviour on the part of exporters in LDCs is largely inferential. There are indications that export licences are bought and sold at positive prices in LDCs which are subject to trade restrictions.[46] Furthermore, in most countries there are relatively few firms exporting a particular product and *de facto* monopolization can be observed. United States officials have reportedly acknowledged such practices in the case of voluntary export restraints pertaining to the textile agreement.[47] The number of cases registered by the GATT Committee on Anti-Dumping Practices in 1970–5 also provides relevant insights. Data show a clear rise in the frequency of investigations opened against Third World producers. Partial evidence suggests that monopoly positions may prevail in the domestic markets of these countries. Due to a combination of monopoly conditions and redundant tariffs, price discrimination in the home market and dumping practices are employed in certain semi-industrialized countries.[48] This has occurred despite the fact that Third World producers are competitive at world prices.

Studies of neo-protectionist measures reveal other instances where monopoly behaviour could result in market solutions that are not compatible with a maximation of the growth benefits of exports.

The International Economy and Industrial Development

One example is where import quotas or voluntary export restraints cover two or more products in a single category. If monopoly conditions pertain, there will be an incentive to allocate export licences in a manner which will maximize joint profits. It has been shown that, in these circumstances, a shift away from exporting a high profit-per-unit product toward the low profit-per-unit product is consistent with monopoly.[49]

The analysis provides us with at least a partial answer to one of the questions posed earlier in this chapter. Economists have often maintained that the rapid growth of exports accelerates growth of an economy. The approach is thought to encourage the rapid diffusion of technological advances and increase the availability of foreign exchange. Exporting enables firms to benefit from economies of scale or improve rates of capacity utilization which they might not otherwise have done. Learning-by-doing effects, which may influence managerial, marketing and related functions, as well as labour productivity and other 'catch-up' processes are also thought to work to the benefit of exporters. In general, supporters maintain that a relatively open market enables an LDC to find its areas of comparative advantage and to avoid high-cost, inefficient activities.

The failure to find a stronger relationship between export expansion and growth in the present case is attributed to two basic conditions: (i) the consequences of a network of extensive trade barriers in both the West and the LDCs; and (ii) systematic changes in comparative advantage and the growth characteristics of labour-intensive industries on the one hand and rising levels of *per capita* income on the other. As a result, the Third World's exports of labour-intensive products have been increasingly concentrated in narrow product lines which are not among those industries with the greatest growth potential.

With regard to commercial policies, interest in tariffs and NTBs usually focuses on the issue of market access in the case of western countries or biases in favour of a sector (industry rather than agriculture) or a market (domestic rather than export) in the case of the LDCs. However, where protectionism and trade barriers are prevalent, an industry's structure may be altered substantially. Studies of the extent of structural change associated with the removal

Structural Changes in World Trade in Manufactures

of trade barriers give an approximate idea of the magnitudes involved.[50] Industrial restructuring would entail considerable resource and factor shifts. The preservation of various depressed industries (notably several of the labour-intensive industries analysed here) is achieved largely through protectionist devices. These industries would experience the largest relative reduction in size.

Roughly symmetrical shifts could be expected in the maufacturing sectors of those LDCs which export a large share of their production. Here, too, the impact on the industrial structure of labour-intensive industries would probably be accentuated. This symmetry would not extend to the question of who bears the transitory costs, however. In the West it is generally assumed that governments would provide adjustment assistance to the production factors moving out of depressed industries. In the LDCs (except, perhaps, for Hong Kong, Korea and Singapore) the industries themselves would have to bear expansion costs incurred in the transition.

The emergence of neo-protectionist measures, coupled with the slow erosion of tariff levels in the Kennedy and Tokyo rounds, raises another side of the commercial policy question. These trends amount to a further reduction in the role of the market as NTBs replace tariffs as the dominant policy mechanism. Growing evidence of monopolistic behaviour among exporters in LDCs is not surprising in these circumstances. The fact that patterns of export and production in labour-intensive industries have steadily become more concentrated and less diversified only serves to facilitate this change in market structure.

As industrialization has continued, internal circumstances with a bearing on the export-growth relationship have changed. In relative terms, the comparative advantage of labour-intensive industries will decrease as *per capita* income rises. A decline in the growth elasticities of these industries has also been noted. Changes in the commercial policies of these countries have not kept abreast of these structural changes. In this instance, growing monopoly strength of exporters can eventually pose a threat to ability of these countries to adjust their commercial policies to new internal conditions. The twin observations that: (i) industrialists in LDCs achieve political influence by virtue of being exporters, and (ii) only a cohesive and influential industrial class is apt to reorient the sector from import substitution to export promotion are useful to recall.[51]

The results and explanations offered here amount to an appeal for caution in the formulation of trade policy and the establishment of export targets. If export-oriented policies are evoked as a means of fostering growth (rather than procuring foreign exchange or increasing employment), a broad perspective is required. First, the weak empirical relationship between exports and growth noted here contrast with the stronger results noted in economy or sector-wide studies. Labour-intensive industries are mainly processors of agricultural inputs and have close links with the primary sector. The benefits of export expansion may operate through these links and, if so, policies to encourage growth via exports should take this fact into account. Second, existing trade policy in both the South and the North has led to an increase in the extent of monopoly power among exporters in the former countries. Supplementary policy adjustments may be required of LDCs if monopoly behaviour is not to erode the growth benefits accruing from export expansion. Finally, history provides ample evidence of cases where the export-growth relationship has broken down. Increased exports, in fact, may slow growth by diverting attention from the necessity to develop new industries or to adapt to new technological conditions.[52] Given the policy emphasis of some LDCs on export expansion, the danger of ignoring such issues is a real one.

Notes

[1] See Edward Leamer and Robert Stern, *Quantitative International Economics*, Allyn and Bacon, Boston, 1970, p. 171.

[2] For further discussions, see Leamer and Stern, *ibid.*, Chapter 9 and Ranadev Banerji, 'The export performance of less developed countries: A constant market share analysis', *Weltwirtschaftliches Archiv*, Band 110, 1974, pp. 445–57.

[3] The choice of a definition for industries will alter the results since the elasticity of substitution between competing industries will vary. In the present study industries were defined to be SITC divisions at the three-digit level of disaggregation. A related study reached the conclusion that the three-digit definition most closely

corresponds to a conventional concept of an industry when defined as a set of producers competing in the production of the same set of commodities. See H. G. Grubel and P. J. Lloyd, *Intra-industry Trade; The Theory and Measurement of International Trade in Differentiated Products*, Macmillan Press, London, 1975, p. 5 and Chapter 4.

[4] See Chapter II. The Asian predominance is underestimated by UN data which exclude Taiwan whose export performance would probably match that of Hong Kong and Singapore.

[5] In 1974, over 53 per cent of the West's exports of manufactures were industrial inputs compared to 34 per cent for LDCs. The corresponding figures for capital goods were 20 per cent and 2 per cent respectively. See UNIDO, *World Industry Since 1960*, op. cit., p. 166.

[6] For example, the interests of automobile producers may be served by large amounts of duty-free imports of steel although this conflicts with the self-interests of domestic steel producers. Similarly, domestic firms producing synthetic clothing can benefit by importing man-made fibres at low prices but domestic chemical firms would often lobby to prevent such trade.

[7] Logically, a country can be expected to have some control over the markets to which it exports, shifting its efforts from slower growing to faster growing markets. In practice, however, many Third World countries have retained the same set of trading partners, throughout their industrialization process. Institutional, political, cultural and neo-colonial relationships may have more to do with a country's trading partners than does policy. Thus, for LDCs the contribution of the market composition effect may be regarded as largely subject to external rather than internal conditions. For a discusssion of long-term trade patterns which supports these observations, see Charles P. Kindelberger, 'Government policies and changing shares in world trade', *The American Economic Review, papers and proceedings*, Vol. 70, No. 2, May 1980, pp. 293–8.

[8] The UK was a notable exception to this trend.

[9] For further discussion, see Chapter II.

[10] One of the more prolific writers on this subject has been Bela Balassa, 'Trade liberalization and revealed comparative advantage', *Manchester School*, Vol 33, May 1965, pp. 99–123; 'Revealed comparative advantage revisited: an analysis of relative export shares of the industrial countries, 1953–1971', *Manchester School*, Vol. 45, December 1977, p. 327–44; 'The changing pattern of comparative advantage in manufactured goods', *The Review of Economics and Statistics*, Vol. LXI, May 1975, pp. 259–66 and 'A stages approach to comparative advantage', paper presented to the Fifth World Congress of the International Economic Association, 29 August 1977, Tokyo. Other relevant studies are referred to elsewhere in this section.

[11] This decision is not so mundane as it might first appear. At least six alternative definitions can be found in the literature and the resultant estimates of volume, value or rates of growth vary in an unrelated manner. See V. Prakesh, 'Measuring Industrial Exports: A Comparative Statistical Study of Variations Arising from Differences of Definition', World Bank Staff Working Paper No. 225, February 1976.

The International Economy and Industrial Development

[12] In trade studies, the most common definition of an industry is a three-digit SITC category. See, for example, Bela Balassa, *op. cit.*, 1965, p. 104. This practice, with the addition of several four-digit categories, was adopted here. For an empirical investigation of this point, see Herbert Grubel and P. J. Lloyd, *op. cit.*

[13] B. Balassa, *op. cit.*, 1965, p. 103.

[14] The export performance index (EP) is defined as follows:

$$EP_{ij} = \frac{X_i^j}{X_i^m} \bigg/ \frac{X_.^j}{X_.^m}$$

where: i = country
j = industry
m = total manufactures
· = world total
X = value of respective export flow

See B. Balassa, *op. cit.*, 1965, p. 106.

[15] For a summary of results, see UNIDO, *World Industry in 1980*, New York, 1981, Chapter II. The export performance indices (EP_{gj}) for each sample is obtained as a weighted average for each industry where each country's value of total trade (exports plus imports) were taken as weights:

$$EP_{gj} = \sum_{i=1}^{G} (X+M)_{ij} \, EP_{ij} \bigg/ \sum_{i=1}^{G} (X+M)_{ij}$$

where g refers to one of the four country samples, G is the number of countries in the sample and other notation is as shown in note 14. The actual export performance indices used in these calculations may be found in UNIDO, *op. cit.*, chapter II, annex.

[16] Resource-based industries were excluded from this particular test since their export performances are largely dependent on countries' resource endowments and not upon the determinants of comparative advantage described elsewhere in this chapter. The aggregate export share of resource-based industries is of interest and will be discussed later.

[17] For an elaboration, see Balassa, *op. cit.*, 1977.

[18] See, for example, A. G. Frank, *Dependant Accumulation*, Macmillan Press, London, 1979, and Samir Amin, *Accumulation on a World Scale*, Harvester Press, Brighton, 1974.

[19] A. G. Frank, *Capitalism and Underdevelopment in Latin America*, Monthly Review Press, New York, 1969.

[20] There are different shades of interpretation; some economists have treated technology as a capital augmenting factor and have stressed the need to distinguish between physical and human capital. Others have explicitly introduced technological change into their analysis, treating comparative advantage as a consequence of the interaction between product characteristics and resouce endowments. An example of the first approach is Hal. B. Lary. *Imports of Manufactures from Less Developed Countries*, National Bureau of Economic Research, New York, 1968. For an example of the second approach, see Roger W. Klein, 'A dynamic theory of comparative advantage', *The American Economic Review*, Vol. LXIII, 1973, p.

173–87.

[21] See J. M. Finger. 'A new view of the product cycle theory', *Weltwirtschaftliches Archiv*, Band III, 1975, pp. 79–99.

[22] Electronic calculators made from discrete components were first produced in the US in 1962, but soon spread to Japan. Costs steadily dropped as the number of components were reduced and assembly operations were simplified. Several such assembly operations (i.e. only a part of the production process) eventually relocated in LDCs. For a study of electronic calculators, see Badiul Alam Majumdar, 'Innovations and international trade: an industry study of dynamic competitive advantage', *Kyklos*, Vol. 37, Fass. 3, pp. 559–69. A study of assembly operations in LDCs is found in G. K. Helleiner, 'Manufactured exports from less developed countries and multinational firms', *Economic Journal*, March 1973, pp. 21–47.

[23] Finger, *op. cit.*, p. 83.

[24] For a detailed description of the classification along with the methods used, see UNIDO, *World Industry in 1980*, Chapter II.

[25] G. K. Helleiner, *International Economic Disorder*, Macmillan Press, London, 1980, Chapter II. Helleiner cites most of the commodities mentioned here as examples of markets where high concentration is typical.

[26] The reader should recall that the CMS analysis used an SITC definition of trade which excludes most resource-based exports. For a list of those industries excluded by the traditional definition, see the annex to this chapter.

[27] In order to obtain a simple indicator for both the most recent competitive position of an industry and for its trend in comparative advantage over the sampled time period, the following RCA-index was used (see B. Balassa, *loc. cit.*, 1965, pp. 106):

$$RCA_{ij} = \tfrac{1}{2} \; EP_{ij}^{1} \left[1 + \frac{EP_{ij}^{1}}{EP_{ij}^{0}} \right] \times 100$$

where EP stands for the export performance ratio, i for a country group, j for an industry, and the superscripts 0 and 1 indicate averages for the years 1966–7 and 1975–6 respectively.

[28] As shown in Chapter V, export performance in several leading industries—petrochemicals, steel, electronic products—is partly based on artificial and, perhaps, transient advantages such as cheap energy and feedstock costs, dumping practices resulting from obsolete and/or excess capacity or the ability to fragment the production process.

[29] Examples include R. Emery, 'The relation of exports and economic growth', *Kyklos*, 1967, Vol. 20, pp. 470–86; Kravis, *op. cit.*; M. Michaely, 'Exports and growth, an empirical investigation', *Journal of Development Economics*, Vol. 4, 1977, pp. 49–53, B. Balassa, 'Exports and growth, further evidence', *Journal of Development Economics*, Vol. 5, 1978, pp. 181–9 and B. Balassa, 'Export incentives and export performance in developing countries: a comparative analysis', *Weltwirtschaftliches Archiv*, Band 114, 1978, pp. 24–61.

[30] Production is classified according to the ISIC, rev. 2, while exports are denoted by the SITC rev. 1. The following concordance (ISIC–SITC) was used: wood products (331–63), textiles (321–65), clothing (322–84), footwear (324–851),

furniture and fixtures (332–821). Definitions were based on those used by T. K. Morrison, *Manufactured Exports from Developing Countries*, Praeger Publishers, New York, 1976.

[31] One-year shifts in the period were sometimes necessary for increased country coverage.

[32] See Michaely, *op. cit.*, and, particularly, Peter S. Heller and Richard C. Porter, 'Exports and growth, an empirical re-investigation', *Journal of Development Economics*, Vol. 5, 1978, pp. 191–3.

[33] See B. Balassa, 'Exports incentives', *op cit.*, p. 34–5.

[34] Balassa, 'Exports and growth', *op. cit.*, p. 183, notes this inconsistency. The gross value of domestic production is nowhere available for an economy and, for the manufacturing sector, is not available from national accounts.

[35] For additional evidence of the dramatic growth in the LDCs' exports of labour-intensive products, see UNCTAD, 'Improving the Capability of the Developing Countries to Supply Exports of Manufactures and Semi-Manufactures', TD/B/C.2/1978, 1977.

[36] S. Hirsch, 'Capital or technology? confronting the neo-factor proportions and neo-technology accounts of international trade', *Weltwirtschaftliches Archiv*, Band 110, 1974, p. 544. The wood products branch is characterized by a heavy dependence on local natural resources while changes in the comparative advantage of the furniture branch are not related to *per capita* value added.

[37] Hollis B. Chenery and Lance Taylor, 'Development patterns: among countries and over time', *The Review of Economics and Statistics*, Vol. L, No. 4, 1968, p. 409.

[38] Recent studies have not retained the distinction between early, intermediate and late industries. Taking the growth elasticity of total manufacturing as a benchmark, an impression of early or slow growth industries may be formed. Accordingly, one study of both western countries and LDCs found low-growth elasticities for textiles, clothing and footwear (United Nations, *A Study of Industrial Growth*, New York, 1963). A UNIDO study, *Industrial Development Survey*, Vol. V, United Nations, New York, 1973, p. 142–43, found low growth elasticities for textiles, footwear, wood products and furniture in both set of countries. An UNCTAD study, 'The Dimensions of the Required Restructuring of World Manufacturing Output and Trade in Order to Reach the Lima Target', TD/185/Supp. 1, 1976, p. 3, indicated that textiles, clothing, and footwear are early industries, while the elasticity for wood products only slightly exceeded the corresponding value for total manufacturing. A UNIDO study, *World Industry since 1960: Progress and Prospects*; special issue of the Industrial Development Survey for the Third General Conference of UNIDO, United Nations, New York, 1979, Chapter III, attributed similar growth characteristics to textiles, footwear and wood products. Other authors have identified textiles and leather goods, including footwear, as early industries. H. B. Chenery and Helen Hughes, 'Industrialization and trade trends: some issues for the 1970s', in *Prospects for Partnership*, edited by Helen Hughes, Johns Hopkins Press, Baltimore, 1972, Tables 1 and 3. In West European countries, textiles, clothing and footwear were found to be 'slow growth' industries in the period 1958–70 while wood products and furniture were characterized as 'average growth' industries. See Economic Commission for Europe, *Structure and*

Change in European Industry, United Nations, New York, 1977, p. 32.

[39] I. Little, et. al., *Industry and Trade in Some Developing Countries*, published for the development centre of OECD by Oxford Press, London, 1970, p. 187.

[40] For data and additional discussion, see Ingo Walter, 'Nontariff barriers and the export performance of developing countries', *The American Economic Review*, Vol. LXI, No. 2, 1971, pp. 195–205.

[41] The study, UNCTAD, 'Liberalization of Non-Tariff Barriers', TD/B/C.2/115/Rev. 1, 1974, excluded wood products, furniture and cotton textiles covered by the Arrangement Regarding International Trade in Textiles.

[42] UNCTAD, 'Improving Access to Markets, International Trade in Textiles and Developing Countries', TD/B/C.2/192, 1978.

[43] Evidence is found in a detailed study of trade among 423 individual products. Using as a selection criterion the growth rate of the West's imports in 1967–75, trade in thirty-two product lines grew exceptionally fast. In 1975 the West's imports from the LDCs were $4.03 billion. Seven of these narrowly identified items were produced by labour-intensive industries and accounted for over 81 per cent of the LDCs' total share. See UNCTAD, 'Improving the Capability of the Developing Countries to Supply Exports of Manufactures and Semi-Manufactures', TD/B/C.2/1978, 1977, p. 6. By comparison, the value of these seven exports was almost equal to the West's imports of all manufactures from the LDCs in 1967 and amounted to over 16 per cent of that trade in 1975.

[44] For the US, market penetration ratios (imports as a percentage of imports plus production) demonstrate this trend. Figures for 1971–5 show that, following the strict enforcement of trade restrictions, the ratios dropped substantially below values in the beginning year. Furthermore, during the subsequent four years penetration ratios never attained values recorded in 1971 for the following products: knit fabrics, cotton sheets, woven shirts and dresses, pyjamas and nightwear, underwear and hosiery (US Department of Commerce, *Cotton, Wool and Man-made Fiber Textiles and Apparel: U.S. Production, Imports and Import/Production Ratios*, Washington, 1976).

[45] Anomalies in production patterns abound. Data for 1974 on *per capita* production in physical units can be used as an illustration. For example, the production of woven cotton fabrics in Argentina, Egypt, India, Israel, Spain and Yugoslavia was one to 3.5 times the level of the UK. Similar comparisons emerge for many items such as footwear, certain types of underwear and trousers, shirts, veneer sheets, etc.

[46] Export licences for cotton textiles can sometimes sell at 15-20 per cent of the products' export value. Where the number of producers is relatively small, this could indicate a 'monopoly' premium. See A. McKay, 'Textile quota trade making millionaires', *Journal of Commerce*, October 1977.

[47] Tracy Murray, Wilson Schmidt and Ingo Walter, 'Alternative forms of protection against market disruption', *Kyklos*, Vol. 31, Fasc. 4, 1978, p. 633.

[48] See A. Tovias, 'The outcome of closer economic links with the EEC for LDCs' exports previously dumped in world markets', *Oxford Economic Papers*, Vol. 31, No. 1, 1979, pp. 121–32. These conditions also explain why the LDCs have argued that their domestic prices are not a reasonable measure of the 'normal value' of a

The International Economy and Industrial Development

product and should not be used for price comparisons to prove the existence of dumping. See GATT, *Basic Instruments and Special Documents*, supplement no. 22, 1976.

[49] Murray, *op. cit.*, p. 634.

[50] Baldwin and Mutti estimate that, in only five industries, the adjustment costs from tariff removal (excluding quantitative restrictions) would have been $284–578 million for the US in 1969. Such costs, of course, are transitory and are much less than the benefits of freer trade. See 'Policy issues in adjustment assistance: The United States', in *Prospects for Partnership*, Helen Hughes (ed.), Johns Hopkins University Press, Baltimore, 1973, p. 161.

[51] Albert O. Hirschman, 'The political economy of import substituting industrialization in Latin America', *Quarterly Journal of Economics*, Vol. LXXXII, No. 1, 1968, pp. 11 and 28.

[52] Kindelberger offers the example of the UK in the nineteenth century. The export emphasis on iron and steel rails, galvanized iron roofing, cotton textiles, etc. led to a failure to develop new industries such as, electricity and chemicals or to adopt new processes in old industries such as steelmaking. See Charles P. Kindelberger, 'The ageing economy', *Weltwirtschaftliches Archiv*, Band 114, 1979, p. 410.

Annex to Chapter IV

Table A.IV.1. Composition of four country samples used in estimating comparative advantage

Industrialized countries	Recently developed countries
France	Greece
Germany	Israel
	Portugal
Japan	Spain
United Kingdom	Yugoslavia
United States	
Newly industrializing countries	Other LDCs
Argentina	Cameroon
Brazil	Colombia
Hong Kong	Egypt
Korea	India
Mexico	Ivory Coast
Singapore	Nicaragua
Turkey	Philippines
	Sri Lanka
	Thailand
	Tunisia

Structural Changes in World Trade in Manufactures

Table A.IV.2. Country samples used in the computation of Spearman rank correlation coefficients for exports and growth

	Wood products	Textiles	Clothing	Footwear	Furniture
Brazil	x	x	x		x
Colombia	x	x	x	x	x
Cyprus	x		x	x	
Ecuador		x			
Egypt			x	x	
Greece	x	x	x	x	x
India	x	x		x	
Iraq		x		x	
Jamaica		x	x		
Jordan		x	x	x	
Kenya	x	x		x	
Korea, Rep. of	x	x	x	x	x
Madagascar		x	x[a]		
Malta				x	x
Mexico[b]	x	x	x	x	x
Nigeria	x				
Panama		x			
Philippines	x	x	x	x	x
Singapore	x		x	x	x
Spain	x	x	x	x	x
Tanzania, U.R.		x			
Tunisia	x	x	x		x
Turkey	x	x	x		
Yugoslavia[c]	x			x	x

Sources: United Nations, *Yearbook of Industrial Statistics*, Vol. I, various issues; *Yearbook of International Trade*, various issues; *Commodity Trade Statistics, Series D*, various issues; OECD, *Foreign Trade Statistics, Series C*, 1974; national industrial censuses, national publications of trade statistics.

Notes: [a] Gross output was not separately reported in the terminal year. The figure was estimated using values for previous years and value added for 1974.

[b] Reported United Nations data represent slightly less than one half the manufacturing sector's total activity. The extent to which activities were not reported was estimated using census data for 1965 and 1970. These results were used to 'blow-up' reported UN data, thereby accounting for the incomplete coverage.

[c] Gross output for 1969 was estimated by applying the gross output value added ratio for 1970 to the figure for value added in 1969.

Chapter V

Policies and Prospects for Industrial Development in the Third World

Chapters III and IV have sketched the major changes taking place in the structure of world industrial production and trade. We now take up the consequences of these changes—the policy modifications they will induce, the new alignments between interest groups that are intended to accelerate or retard the pace of restructuring and the desired responses from policy makers that (in our view) are required to maximize the development impact of world industrial progress. This chapter addresses developments in four major industries—steel, chemicals and petrochemicals, food processing and textiles—that have the potential of rapid growth in the Third World. The analysis describes the international market structure of the branches, identifies forces accelerating and retarding the process of restructuring and assesses the consequences of an expansion of these branches for development. We attempt to show that industrial development in the Third World means protracted interaction between a wide range of economic decision-makers with divergent policy objectives. A reconciliation of the strategies of these actors—and hence a convergence of their long-term objectives—requires a careful study of the circumstances and opportunities that shape their objectives. A case study approach was adopted here as the most useful means of illustrating industry-specific characteristics and their possible consequences for international industrial restructuring.

5.1 Iron and steel

(a) Structural change and market conditions

Iron and steel is an industry long regarded as synonymous with industrialization. Like other basic industries, steel production spread rapidly among most developed countries. Table V.1 shows that until the late nineteenth century Britain was the world's leading iron and steel producing nation. After 1900 the US emerged as the world leader and retained this position until the early 1970s when it was overtaken by the Soviet Union, which remains the world leader in iron and steel production today. It has ample resources for expanding output and has generally escaped the slump which has beset the steel industry in the West since the mid-1970s. The USSR's production is geared to meet domestic demand and its steel imports are generally balanced by the level of its exports of iron and steel plant and engineering equipment.

Between 1960 and the mid-1970s output of iron and steel expanded at rates fluctuating around 6 per cent per annum. In 1974 world consumption of crude steel reached a high of 709 million metric tons. Consumption actually decreased in three later years (1975, 1977 and 1980) and generally moved erratically.[1] Thus,

Table V.1. Iron and steel production in industrialized countries, 1870–1975

	Production as percentage of total world output				
Year	EEC[a]	UK	USA	Japan	USSR
1870	30.0	37.4	16.2	—	2.7
1900	26.3	17.5	35.2	—	6.2
1920	20.3	13.4	59.8	1.1	5.1
1950	16.5	8.0	47.1	2.5	14.2
1960	21.0	7.1	26.4	6.4	18.8
1965	18.7	6.0	26.7	9.0	19.8
1970	18.9	4.9	21.1	16.1	20.0
1975	16.9	5.2	17.6	16.5	22.8

Source: UNIDO, *The World Iron and Steel Industry*, ICIS.89, 1978, p. 42.

Note: [a] EEC = Belgium, France, West Germany, Italy, Netherlands and Luxembourg.

The International Economy and Industrial Development

recent years have been bleak, particularly in western countries, as the steel industry struggled to come to terms with its newfound maturity.

Three sets of forces have contributed to the slump in western countries. First, patterns of consumption have been altered largely through various forms of technical progress that have reduced steel requirements per unit of output.[2] For example, new materials, such as aluminium, plastics, highly resistant glass, etc., have replaced steel in many traditional usages. The introduction of higher quality steels, such as light alloys, led to a reduction in the quantity of steel required per unit of final product. Second, technical progress in steelmaking, such as continuous casting,[3] and improvement in rolling and finishing, also reduced the steelmakers' requirements of crude steel per unit of finished steel. Finally, steel consumers have begun to economize on the quantity of steel required. An example is the design of lighter bodies and engines by car makers.

Another explanation for the declining growth of the steel industry is found in the changing composition of manufacturing output as economic growth proceeds. For many years modernization was closely identified with the widening use of steel as an industrial input. Steel contributed to the transformation of surface fleets, the creation of railways, and the development of powerful and long-lasting machines. Today, the major growth industries (telecommunications, space and computers) are not intensive users of steel. Steel is no longer a growth industry but is dependent on the strength of demand in other branches which themselves are losing ground relative to overall economic activity.

Parallel with its new maturity, the steel industry has witnessed continued modifications in production processes favouring greater economies of scale and increased product differentiation. While economies of scale have encouraged longer production runs, the growing variety of product characteristics demanded by steel users has led to increased product specialization. Both trends prompted producers to place a greater emphasis on exports because firms now tend to specialize in selected products which they produce in great quantities.

The growth of world trade in steel products has consistently exceeded that of world steel production. Differences between the two rates of growth actually widened during the 1970s despite the general slowdown in industrial activity.[4] In 1950 exports accounted for nearly 11 per cent of world steel production. Their share rose steadily, exceeding 24 per cent in 1977.[5] The importance of trade has been accentuated by the growing variety of product characteristics demanded by steel users[6] coupled with a move towards greater specialization which limits the number of products each producer supplies. Favourable circumstances such as reduced transport costs may have also contributed to trade. Finally, the rapid growth of steel consumption in some LDCs has given an added boost to the exports of established producers in the West although this condition cannot be regarded as lasting.

The general slowdown in steel consumption conceals important differences between various product groups and among various areas of the world. An outstanding feature is the shift to high-quality steels at the expense of ordinary steels. In Japan, consumption of high-grade and specialty steels in 1978 was 23 per cent above the 1973 level while consumption of ordinary steels had declined 15 per cent.[7] Specialty steels enable manufacturers to reduce the weight and vulnerability of corrosion of their products. These products are able to withstand very low temperatures (e.g. transportation of hydrocarbon in arctic regions or the haulage of liquified gas) and very high pressures (as in the chemical industry). It is significant that, in 1980, Japan expected to overtake the United States as the world's largest steel producer behind the USSR.

Different growth experiences in various countries and regions are also due to the fact that a falling steel intensity, i.e. a stagnation or decrease of steel usage per unit of national output, is primarily applicable to the more industrialized economies. Observers note that beyond a certain level of development, corresponding roughly to 'industrial maturity' (or when *per capita* income reaches $2500 at 1963 prices), steel consumption tends to have a declining share in overall economic activity and in the country's expenditure pattern.[8] As development continues, the service sector's share in GDP rises at the expense of the production of material goods, while investment gives way to consumption in the expenditure of national income. Since services and consumption are less steel-intensive than material goods and investment (especially non-residential private investment), steel's share in output and income declines.

As noted above, this type of shift has been more pronounced in western countries that face problems of contraction and the redeployment of resources away from steel. Some, such as Japan, have coped rather well and have largely succeeded in moving capital and expertise out of declining product areas and in achieving high levels of specialization. Others have sought refuge in protectionist policies that deliberately seek to slow down the pace of structural adjustment. These policies have been forged on the basis of an expanding consensus on objectives and strategies between western governments, producers and labour unions representing the interests of the steel work force. An understanding of the policy-related negotiations is helpful since it provides important insights into the more general political issues of neo-protectionism.

(b)   Neo-protectionism in the steel industry

Although there is a general spreading of neo-protectionist' policies in Western Europe and North America, the strength of the coalition between producers, labour and government varies among countries. Furthermore, the strategies of the major producing regions—EEC, Japan and the US—reflect other motives too complex to adequately fit a single label. The nature of growth in the 1970s intensified competition and a defensive rivalry between the three groups. The figures in Table V.2 show substantial long-term shifts in various groups' share of world steel exports. The relative changes in the position of both the US and Japan are dramatic. EEC producers made some gains in the 1970s after losing a large portion of their export market. Other countries that recently acquired substantial new steel capacity have yet to make an impact on the pattern of world trade due to the domestic orientation of their production.

Trends in import penetration have been in an opposite direction. In 1960, imports accounted for 4 per cent of apparent consumption in the US, rising to over 17 per cent by 1978. The corresponding figures for the EEC were 21 per cent in 1960, reaching 45 per cent by 1978. Domestic demand for steel grew more rapidly in the EEC than in the US, however, which provided European producers with some respite. The share of imports in the Japanese market was

Table V.2. Distribution of world iron and steel exports
(in million metric tonnes of raw steel equivalent)

Exporter	Exports as percentage of aggregate world exports		
	1955	1970	1974
United States	18.7	10.0	5.8
Japan	8.9	27.3	34.9
EEC	54.0	30.9	36.7
Socialist countries	12.9	21.0	13.0
Others	5.5	10.8	9.6

Source: International Iron and Steel Institute, Committee on Economic Studies, *Projection '90*, Brussels, 1980.

consistently less than 2 per cent during 1960–78.[9]

Thus, it is not surprising that the most vehement neo-protectionist attitudes are found today in the US. Policy positions are more muted in the EEC while, to date, the Japanese position remains unique. In the first two instances the neo-protectionist response was ostensibly intended to improve the position of domestic interests vis-à-vis competitors in other industrialized countries. However, in view of the pending entry of new producers (including LDCs) on the international scene, these policies are increasingly focusing on steel production and exports in the developing world.

Among the neo-protectionist measures invoked perhaps the most significant is the US trigger price mechanism which, beginning in 1978, set a minimum price for imports based on 'constructed costs' from Japanese data. Using this benchmark, which was periodically updated, anti-dumping investigations could be instigated when imports sold below reference prices. Protectionist pressures continued to mount after 1978, largely due to price dumping by European steelmakers which in some instances (e.g. the British Steel Corporation) observers conceded to be 'grossly unfair pricing'.[10] One concession was to shift responsibility for defending the trigger price from the US Treasury, which was a reluctant enforcer, to the Commerce Department. Steel producers, however, pressed for a two-tier system—one based on Japanese costs, the

The International Economy and Industrial Development

other on European. The proposal, which was not accepted, would have led to massive duties on European producers since their costs were higher than the Japanese while landed US prices were sometimes lower. Subsequent pressure from the industry eventually resulted in a higher trigger price in September 1980. Throughout this period the US steel lobby proved itself to be an adept and powerful group, working closely with the so-called 'Steel Caucus' in Congress and professional lobbyists said to be 120 strong.[11]

The ebb and flow of US protectionist interest holds some instructive clues for potential exporters in LDCs. Government has been reluctant to endorse the protectionist drive for two reasons. First, concern for wider trade relations with the EEC was apparent; retaliation against US exports of chemicals and textiles was feared. Second, and equally important, officials were anxious not to prevent cheap foreign steel from becoming available to the country's motor car manufacturers who were under serious competitive pressure from Japanese imports. Both concerns suggest interesting possibilities. The increasing frequency of government-to-government negotiations on trade questions was noted in Chapter II. In the future, governments of LDCs may find they can exert some leverage in protectionist issues through the strength of their own importing markets. Alternatively, they may find 'friends in the court' by aligning themselves with other industries whose self-interest would be served through cheaper imports.

A second approach, widely known as the Davignon Plan, constituted the EEC response to problems in the steel industry. The main feature of the plan is that it seeks to reconstruct the European steel cartels of the 1920s and 1930s. Voluntary discipline was imposed, administered by an official cartel, Eurofer. Anti-dumping duties were fixed and import quotas were negotiated with suppliers of 85 per cent of the EEC's steel imports.[12] In return for this suspension of competition, producers were supposed to rationalize their plants and reduce surplus capacity. The short-term impact was appraised as follows: 'Thanks to the Davignon Plan, imports have been frozen at 10 per cent of the EEC market and prices have been boosted by 21–30 per cent since 1977.'[13]

European producers were concerned with their excess capacity, mainly a result of massive investment programmes begun in the early 1970s. To a large extent, however, both European and American producers were slow to react to technical change during a particularly crucial period when steel demand began to level out. As a result, the problem of overcapacity was to some extent a misnomer. Many steel works were neither really useful nor had effective capacity. However, neo-protectionist policies made no distinction between domestic technological backwardness and 'cyclical' capacity.

Japan's approach to its structural problems in the steel industry is in marked contrast to those of the EEC and the US. The overt threat of overcapacity—which we have argued is really a problem of technical obsolescence—was blunted by producers' rapid shift into continuous casting. As a result, Japan's output of steel products quickly recovered from the post-1974 slump although output of crude steel was still below earlier levels.

The Japanese approach to foreign investment and the transfer of know-how has been more outward-looking than that of its competitors—just as in the case of exports. Many Third World producers are now coming on stream with plants designed and built by the Japanese. Recent Japanese-Mexican negotiations have concerned extensive participation in the large-scale expansion of Mexican steel works, construction of a casting and forging plant and a steel mill. This participation, which would involve substantial Japanese credits, is now described as a 'national project'. Mexico, in return, would make a long-term commitment to supply crude oil. Whether or not this particular negotiation is finalized, it illustrates the outward orientation of the Japanese steel industry.

(c) The steel industry in the Third World

Mexico, of course, is not the only LDC with an ambitious programme of steel expansion. In 1978 the six largest steel producers (in millions of tons) were: Brazil (12.1); India (10.1); Mexico (6.7); South Korea (5.0); Argentina (2.8); and Turkey (2.2). Together these countries supplied 79 per cent of the steel produced in the Third World. Brazil, apart from being the largest producer, was also one of the fastest growing, expanding at a rate of 12.7 per cent per year during the period 1974–8. This pace was surpassed by South Korea with a yearly rate of 30 per cent for the same period.

When examined in terms of their domestic steel requirements, there is a sharp contrast between two sub-groups of LDCs. In one group, the newly industrializing countries (NICs), steel consumption has expanded vigorously in recent years. The NICs share two characteristics: fairly rapid increases in *per capita* income rising from very low to intermediate levels, and a development strategy which emphasizes rapid industrialization. The NICs have seen substantial and rapid changes in their patterns of domestic consumption and production, particularly related to construction and the development of basic infrastructure, capital goods requirements and consumer durables. These sorts of structural changes spur the demand for steel to be used in the production of such goods. Furthermore, several NICs (e.g. Brazil and South Korea) have begun to export steel-intensive products such as automobiles. The apparent consumption of steel is further increased by these indirect steel exports.

In the second group of LDCs, which is by far the more numerous, *per capita* steel consumption has stagnated. The manufacturing sector in these countries still consists mainly of traditional industrial activities. They are too poor to invest a large portion of their income and, at the same time, consume significant quantities of durables per inhabitant.

In the longer term both groups are likely to accord a high priority to the need for a steel complex. Steel is a basic industry the development of which opens the way for large-scale industrialization. Moreover, heavy industries with large production units and elaborate organizational structures provide a means for nascent state bureaucracies to assume control of the national economy and to appropriate a portion of the economic surplus. In countries with abundant mineral resources heavy industries seem to provide the only route for national economic integration and for assuming effective control over the terms of resource extraction and utilization.

Governments of LDCs have become major investors in steel facilities. Even when foreign collaboration has been sought, it has not usually involved a private sector enterprise. Such collaboration is by no means uncommon in Latin American countries—particularly Brazil and Mexico—and may assume increased significance for the oil rich Middle Eastern countries. TNCs are unlikely to take major initiatives in this regard, however. Most of the programmes of redeployment to Third World countries announced during the early 1970s by US and European corporations were hastily abandoned as the steel crisis deepened. Our review of neo-protectionism has also shown that the increased participation of producer groups in national policy making renders it unlikely that TNCs will be a major force for international industrial restructuring.

Other characteristics can also make iron and steel a possible choice for countries at an intermediate level of development. For production of bulk steels, technology is relatively easily available. To some extent large modern plants can offset the lack of an experienced labour force. As steelmaking uses relatively few workers (4000 to 6000 workers per million tons produced), training of manpower is not an unmanageable task for countries which have a good basic educational system and a relatively large population[14] Small countries, however, may encounter considerable obstacles if they want to undertake basic steelmaking.

Regardless of the growth path, a critical minimum level of production must be reached due to scale economies, particularly with respect to rolling mills. Direct reduction (DR) is one technology which can be considered by small countries having extensive hydro-carbon resources. Although this alternative still faces a number of difficulties, its possibilities and applications with regard to reducing agents and the range of ores used may be extended in the future. Another alternative is non-integrated, simple rolling mills and small semi-integrated plants using ultra high-power electric furnaces. At present, these are usually specialized plants producing a narrow range of products (concrete reinforcing rods, merchant products) but the range could be enlarged to include flat products. A third alternative would be in the direction of small (100 to 200 thousand tons) integrated iron and steel units following the classical route.

A general obstacle that may be encountered by Third World countries is that prompt procurement of spare parts and quick repair work are vital for the functioning of a steel plant.[15] Transportation facilities for bulk products and for heavy machinery (for instance, 300 tons) must be available from the very beginning of plant construction. Shelter for 15,000 workers and their families must be provided in the case of a moderately sized plant. Notwithstanding these and other difficulties, production is rising in LDCs and is expected to continue to do so.

UNIDO has estimated the expected 1985 crude steel capacity of LDCs as follows:

Country or region	Million tons
Africa	11.2
China	45.0
Other Asia	50.0
North Korea	6.5
Other centrally planned economies of Asia (excluding China and North Korea)	0.5
Latin America	58.0
Middle East	10.7
Total	181.9

China and the LDCs together would supply 16.5 per cent of world capacity in 1985.[16] From six to ten Third World countries will have capacities for production of capital goods for the iron and steel industry (and also more or less highly developed design and engineering capabilities), eleven or twelve countries will have high-grade and special steels production capacities, seventeen will have flat product capacities; twenty-one will have integrated steel mills, twenty-eight are expected to have DR installations and almost fifty will be producing crude steel.[17]

Even if these forecasts are met by 1985, the Third World will probably have to import approximately 60 million tons.[18] This imbalance may be partly attributed to the cancellation of several projects launched on the initiative of European, Japanese or US firms when world demand was buoyant but later abandoned or postponed as the downswing occured.[19] Declining profits and larger investment in programmes designed for protecting the home market reduced the finances available to producers in the West.[20] Most of the projects planned for LDCs were intended to produce for the export market. However, these markets were most severely hit.

Given the general deterioration of growth prospects, restructuring trends in steel are being increasingly resisted through the defensive policies of traditional producers. However, steel remains an important activity for continued industrialization for both the NICs and other developing countries at a similar stage of development. Although defensive policies may distort the otherwise efficient redistribution of capacity, they cannot in the long run deny the growth impetus of steel production in LDCs. A greater degree of structural flexibility in the Third World would, however, mean that western producers rationalize their existing capacity while moving downstream into specialty steels and steel-using activities where they are more competitive. Without such flexibility, continued growth in LDCs means that the problem of excess (and sometimes obsolete) capacity in industrialized countries will not only persist but will widen in scope.

5.2   Chemicals and petrochemicals

(a)   Structural changes and market conditions

In western countries chemicals were consistently the fastest growing industrial branch from the late 1950s until the late 1960s. Output grew at rates almost double those for total manufacturing.[21] The industry's development has had a substantial impact upon consumption patterns of both industry and households, on investment, on research and development (R and D) and trade. The employment impact is less pronounced.

The extent of structural change implied by this growth performance required a substantial reallocation of resources, particularly investment capital and R and D, during the industry's development phase. Figures for West Germany and the UK show that, for 1959–70, cumulative investment in chemicals was 19 to 20 per cent of the total for manufacturing.[22] The US probably recorded an even larger share in the 1960s.

As for R and D, data for OECD countries show that over 20 per cent of the qualified scientists and engineers working in the manufacturing sector were employed by the chemical industry. In these terms chemicals were surpassed only by electronics.[23] Much of the R and D effort, as well as the capital investment by the

The International Economy and Industrial Development

developed countries, was channelled into petrochemicals. This led to basic changes which serve to distinguish between the chemical industry of the 1960s and that of the 1970s.

World production of the main petrochemicals rose from 3 million tons in 1950 to 71 million tons by 1974.[24] Today, these products represent about 60 per cent of the chemicals produced. In reality, their influence on the industry is even more pervasive. Not only do they directly provide a wide range of synthetic products, they are also crucial inputs used in combination with inorganic chemicals.[25]

This massive expansion effort, encouraged by most western governments and supplemented by natural structural forces, transformed the industry. Chemicals outgrew their initial 'supplier role' and entered a second 'product' phase largely dominated by petrochemicals. The nature and composition of resource flows (capital investment and R and D) changed as the industry's product phase took shape. Data for the period 1970–5 indicate that nominal investment in the West remained stable at about 11–12 per cent of total investment in manufacturing. One consequence was that real investment (at constant prices) fell in many countries for most of this period. In the socialist countries levels of investment were generally higher than in the West, although a downward trend was also noted.[26] In any case, the proportion of investment in manufacturing which was devoted to the chemical industry in developed countries was definitely below that achieved in the 1960s.

The pattern of R and D expenditures and its emphasis also changed in the first half of the 1970s. First, increased competition for available funds, including government support and industrial aids, probably contributed to the fact that chemicals dropped behind both electronics and aerospace in expenditures on R and D. Second, the directions of research altered, with greater emphasis being put on improving existing production processes and on applied rather than pure research. Third, product oriented research also increased, particularly in pharmaceuticals. For example, in the United Kingdom that sub-group, along with synthetic rubber, resins, plastics, paints and varnishes, absorbed almost one half the chemical industry's R and D expenditures in 1975.[27] Finally, advances in pure research seemed to slow down. The development of new molecular combinations for plastics and fibres became more problematic. Only the more difficult molecular chains were left to develop and the prospect of high returns on R and D expenditures faded.

This brief summary suggests that, in the industrialized countries, chemicals were going through a transition in the 1960s and 1970s. The emergence and dramatic growth of petrochemicals altered the industry's growth pattern. By the early 1970s, however, even this sub-sector was beginning to show some signs of maturity. The onset of 'middle age' for the chemical industry has been accelerated by rising energy costs in western countries. Some analysts have held that price trends for feedstocks and oil singularly forced the slowdown in world growth during the 1970s. There are sound reasons to relate the two trends since over 90 per cent of organic chemicals are derived from oil and gas feedstocks.[28]

The years prior to the energy crisis (1960–7) were an era of rapid growth throughout the West. Production of chemicals slowed somewhat in 1967–3 for reasons unrelated to the energy question. Growth in later years, 1973–9, declined significantly and rising energy costs were certainly a contributing factor. The drop in growth rates was most significant in energy-poor Europe. The fall among producers in socialist countries, though noticeable, was only moderate.

The initial impact of energy costs was twofold, operating directly via higher energy prices and indirectly through more expensive raw materials and intermediates.[29] The impact on production costs varied widely among western countries. Most governments exercised some control over energy prices (and still do). In the US, for example, price controls on gas have been relaxed more slowly than those for oil. Since that country's chemical industry relies mainly on gas, its feedstocks cost over 30 per cent less than those of European producers. The price of landed American products in Europe was said to be 10 to 20 per cent lower as a result.[30]

Today's petrochemical producers can be more accurately described as 'feedstock-intensive' rather than as 'capital-intensive'. In those countries with a relatively well established chemical industry, this branch often requires more than one sixth of the total commercial energy purchased by the manufacturing sector. Its share generally rose between 1963–4 and 1975–6. The highest share was recorded by Japan where chemicals consumed about one quarter of the manufacturing sector's energy requirements in the mid-1970s.[31] The relative 'feedstock intensity' implies that economies of scale, realized by building larger plants, will not necessarily lead to substantial cost advantages.[32] It is, therefore, likely that the emphasis placed on applied rather than pure research will continue to grow as firms search for ways of reducing raw material and feedstock costs. Viewed in this way adjustments in energy markets seemed to re-enforce, and greatly accelerate, changes in the direction of R and D expenditure.

The energy question is also directly related to another factor mentioned above—the spread of production capacity to the LDCs. The traditional view has been that market proximity was the major determinant of the location of chemical production capacity. However, the rising importance of feedstocks has led some observers to conclude that it will eventually be the determining factor for the location of new production centres (specifically for petrochemicals). With variable costs (mainly feedstocks and fuel) determining up to three fourths of production costs, the significance of low-cost inputs becomes crucial.[33] Such trends may eventually favour production in LDCs.

(b) Neo-protectionism in the chemical industry

Government involvement in the chemical and petrochemical industry of western countries has assumed increased importance since the early 1970s. Initially, government action was largely inspired for environmental reasons but is now becoming much broader in scope. The entry of new state-owned producers is the most obvious sign of a new 'politically oriented' era and reflects the industry's growing maturity. Today, the impetus for the closer relationship between the government and the chemical industry is an outgrowth of the restructuring process. The approach evolving in various developed countries cannot, unambiguously, be described as predominantly 'defensive' in nature. This is due to two factors. First, the industry is very diverse and heterogeneous, as circumstances vary widely among the different types of producers and product groups. Second, the policy of different countries and/or the approach of their leading chemical producers differs from country to country.

In Europe, analysts see over-capacity as a major problem which will influence the industry's development through the early 1980s. They attribute the problem to over-investment in the mid-1970s, sparked by an 'artificial boom' in demand in 1973–4 after a wave of supply shortages. A good example of the consequences is polypropylene. In 1973 there were twelve EEC producers with a capacity of 600,000 tonnes per annum. Only five years later, sixteen producers existed with a total capacity three times the level of 1973.[34] The general problem of over-capacity has led to occasional charges of dumping as firms attempt to maintain rates of capacity utilization by exporting marginal production to neighbouring countries at cut-rate prices. This brought calls for a European cartel although a more effective solution would be to restrain investment.[35]

Concern with international trade questions has been evident for a relatively long time. At the centre of the current debate on trade policy is the question of imports of low-cost chemicals into the EEC, particularly from the US. As indicated earlier, some observers contend that American producers enjoy significant cost advantages derived from their access to cheap feedstocks and energy used in chemical plants.[36] The policy is seen as a hidden subsidy due to the very gradual relaxation of price controls on internal gas and oil prices in the US. The response from the European chemical producers to date has been selected appeals to the EEC Commission to provide additional protection and prevent possible 'dumping'.[37]

It is not clear that US cost advantages in this branch are artificial. There may well be structural reasons—fewer/large producers operating in a large, homogeneous market where economies of scale are significant—that contribute to the lower costs of imports. Moreover, protectionism in the chemical industry may raise prospects of potential trade reprisals in other areas like steel and textiles. In view of these complications, one recently proposed compromise is to seek an 'industry restraint deal' which would limit further cheap imports whether they involve dumping or not.

The effects of defensive trade policies may also spill over into other fields. Investment patterns have been influenced as firms sought to 'move behind' the wall of import restrictions by investing in the markets of their major trading partners. Firms in countries with hard currencies have also lost some of their competitive edge relative to producers in countries with soft currencies. This circumstance, which is a result of exchange rate policies, has led the former group of chemical producers to invest in countries with soft currencies.[38]

Thus, there appears to be a general trend (by both European and North American firms) to invest in the US. This may reflect investors' opinion that the rapid growth of European chemical markets in the 1960s and 1970s will slow down in the 1980s. This investment commitment has tempered the attitude of several European countries on the question of new protectionist measures. Those countries with the largest foreign investments in the American market are not inclined to take steps which might start a trade war.

The spread of industrial capacity through more vigorous investment programmes in Austria, Greece, Norway, Portugal, Spain, Turkey and an equal number of socialist countries will further alter trade patterns. Established exporters may lose part of their foreign markets as a result, and eventually face additional competition from these newer producers in their own home markets. The emergence of new potential export bases (including, in the future, some LDCs) is an added reason for the probable move of established producers into finer chemicals with higher value added content—fields where their technological lead would provide them with a tangible competitive edge.[39]

In contrast to the EEC and the US, evidence from Japan suggests a different strategy which, if realized, has important implications for several LDCs. Within that country present trends point towards some reduction in the number of petrochemical firms. Simultaneously, there is a shift towards products of higher quality and greater value added content rather than bulk chemicals. This 'rationalization' can be attributed to (i) the shortage and rising cost of feedstocks and (ii) competition from other chemical exporters (mainly firms in the US and Europe but also South Korea) in Asian markets. Rationalization of the

Policies and Prospects for Industrial Development in the Third World

domestic chemical industry represents only one side of this strategy. Equally important is the country's active participation in joint ventures with LDCs. The relatively high costs of pollution control and the desire for access to capacity located in countries where feedstock costs are less than costs of Japan's imports of oil and naphtha are the considerations spurring the industry's internationalization.

Partial information is available for a more detailed examination of Japan's approach. First, with regard to the rationalization process, Japan was perhaps harder hit by the rise in feedstock costs than many other western countries. In 1970 the proportion of raw material costs in total production costs of its petrochemical firms averaged 64 per cent; by 1975 the figure had risen to 84 per cent.[40] Not only did this hamper Japanese firms' ability to compete for Asian export markets, but it spurred a move towards self-sufficiency in LDCs who had experienced shortages and rising prices of their imports of intermediates, resins and synthetic fibres.

Some observers also argued that pricing policy decisions in other areas artificially boosted feedstock costs. The production of naphtha, kerosene, fuel oil, petrol and other products all result from cracking the same barrel of crude oil. The desire to maintain low costs for rural household heating (mainly relying on kerosene) and power generation (fuel oil) meant that the price of some other product would have to be raised. Consequently, the cost of feedstock rose by greater amounts than the adjustment in energy prices.

The new emphasis on joint ventures results from the decision to relocate production to the sources of supply of the raw materials. Joint ventures with Saudi Arabia, Singapore and South Korea are only a few examples. Much of the production (ethylene, polyethylene and other derivatives) is earmarked for export to Asia, particularly to Japan.

(c) The chemical industry and the Third World

New petrochemical production capacity in LDCs should increase considerably by 1985 with over twenty plants in operation in Iraq, Kuwait, Mexico, Qatar, Saudi Arabia and some other LDCs. Obviously, growth prospects are best in countries with ample feedstock supplies. Chemical producers in other Third World countries may be called upon to make substantial adjustments due to the rise in energy prices. In India, for example, the basic price in naphtha was said to rise by 145 per cent in the year ending August 1980. Accordingly, the prices of resins and compounds rose 30–40 per cent.

The prospects of energy-rich LDCs are based on the availability of relatively cheap feedstocks. Originally, most observers held that cheap gas feedstocks would be of most importance in the production of ammonia, fertilizers and ethylene but that developing countries would encounter difficulties in more sophisticated products (e.g. plastics, polymers and fibres) due to high transport and operating costs.

Two key factors have decisively influenced the relationship between producers in Europe and in the Asian Middle East between 1974 and 1979. First, the price of European feedstock (naphtha) rose substantially.[41] Second, much cheaper financial terms—including export finance and other soft loans—became available. Both factors worked to the benefit of potential producers in the Third World. However, relative construction costs have also changed: a chemical plant built in the Middle East in 1979 cost two thirds more than one built in Europe, rather than one fifth more as in 1974.

The recent approach of several major western oil firms suggests the possibility of similar tactics by LDC governments. In 1976 about 13 per cent of the world's leading oil companies' investment went into petrochemicals.[42] The oil firms' movement into the production of basic petrochemicals and plastics is explained by the simple fact that it is a profitable way of selling oil, particularly as these firms become more and more processors of oil rather than actual producers. One reason for the oil firms' ability to make inroads into chemicals is that they already control the basic facilities to produce the base petrochemicals needed for polyethylene and styrene. The fact that they have access to a variety of feedstocks is also helpful. Thus, when prices rise for one feedstock, e.g. naphtha, they can easily shift to another, say, gasoil. In the longer term a similar principle might find applicability among chemical firms in energy-abundant LDCs—

provided that the necessary technology is available. Some European companies believe themselves threatened by the expansion of the Middle Eastern petrochemical industry which is expected to have a significant impact on world production levels by the end of the 1980s.

Many of the new production units are being set up as joint ventures between Western TNCs and Middle Eastern Governments. Iraq, Kuwait, Qatar and Saudi Arabia have concluded a series of investment and technology transfer agreements with Japanese, American and German companies on the establishment of petrochemical plants.[43] Although Japan has made the most effective penetration, the European transnationals—particularly Shell and the German companies—also have a significant stake. Their spokesmen have taken care to play down the supposed threat of a Middle East petrochemical invasion.[44] If the expansion of that region's petrochemical industry is pioneered by joint ventures involving European transnationals, they will attempt to moderate its impact upon the European market in order to protect their own commercial interests. There are suggestions, however, that some transnationals may 'trade off' losses in the chemical and petrochemical sector for guaranteed access to supplies of crude.[45]

Other experts believe that LDCs—including Middle Eastern producers—have the greatest comparative cost advantage in products close to natural gas—such as ammonia, methanol and ethylene.[46] They foresee a clear division of labour between Third World producers specializing in these base chemicals and Western transnationals concentrating on high-quality speciality products. Such a 'division of labour' may also imply a 'division of markets' with Middle Eastern exports being directed mainly towards South-East Asian Markets.

Mexcio, and to a lesser extent Brazil, may soon present the same type of problems for North American producers that the Middle East now poses for Europe. Mexico has a more developed techno-industrial infrastructure and a higher level of technological capability than the Middle Eastern oil exporters. Although joint ventures are encouraged, PEMEX—the state petroleum and petro-chemical enterprise—is clearly in command and has demonstrated its ability to effectively co-ordinate production and marketing strategies and to benefit from international opportunities. A consensus of US-Mexican views on the organization of regional trade in petroleum and petrochemicals may not be easy, particularly when energy and feedstock costs rise in North America and over-capacity in the production of important base chemicals is exposed. Clearly, Latin American oil exporters are beginning to develop a comprehensive regional economic strategy. The recent decision of Venezuela and Mexico to provide cheap oil to non-oil-exporting Latin American countries points in this direction.

Reasons for the West's uneasiness about the spread of industrial capacity—particularly to the Middle East—are fairly obvious. The chemical industry is inextricably interconnected with the oil business and, hence to politics. The Arab OPEC members have used oil as a political weapon during the 1973 war and are explicity committed to doing so again if other means of achieving a Palestine 'settlement' fail. Some regimes in the Middle East are presently unstable and threatened with intermittent civil wars. Thus, the temptation to take drastic external measures in order to build a national consensus for the preservation of the State is ever present. If the Iranian revolution should spread to neighbouring countries, political and economic confrontation with the West may become inevitable. In such a scenario an international division of labour with the West specializing in quality chemicals and the Third World producing commodities closely linked to natural gas and feedstocks may never become operational. Third World producers would have to gear their production and marketing strategies to domestic markets and growth would be curtailed.

If, on the other hand, existing patterns of economic and political associations between the West and the Third World are maintained, the expansion of the industry in the Middle East need pose no threat to Europe. It is perhaps inevitable that Europe will gradually abandon the illusion that the chemical industry is merely suffering from a cyclical recession and that short-term *ad hoc* subsidization and protectionist policies can restore it to its former health. When this is realized, long-term structural adjustments will occur as production and trade structures are modified to reflect the change in the pattern of international comparative costs. Thus,

Policies and Prospects for Industrial Development in the Third World

transnationals may attempt to capture much of 'the gains from trade' by increasing the proportion of *intra-firm* trade within the chemical industry. The extent to which they succeed will depend in many cases on the policies and performance of the public industrial enterprises in the LDCs who are the main domestic investors in the chemical industry.

The impact of increased production in the chemical industry on the level of development of a typical Third World country is likely to be complex. Increased resources may have a positive impact on levels of national consumption and foreign exchange earnings but the chemical industry has relatively little potential for enhancing employment levels. Thus, UNIDO estimates that by 1985 manpower requirements in the petrochemical sector of Third World countries will be only 21 per cent of total world employment in this industry.[47] This proportion is only slightly above the Third World's share in the production of most base chemicals and end products. There is some evidence to suggest, therefore, that factor intensity in the Third World in this sector is not significantly different from in the West—an observation that does not augur well for the income distribution impact of a large-scale expansion of the chemical industry in LDCs.

Although the main contribution of the chemical industry in LDCs is likely to be increased export earnings, its expansion can also play a part in indirectly stimulating employment and increasing the earnings of relatively lower income groups. We have seen that much of the output of the chemical industry is used by other industrial branches. A development programme which consciously aims at integrating the expansion of the chemicals industry with industries such as fertilizers or pharmaceuticals can go a long way in ensuring that a number of development objectives are simultaneously served. If expansion of chemical production stimulates the domestic fertilizer industry, this is likely to have a pronounced impact on agricultural productivity on employment levels and the distribution of income within the country. Similarly, if expansion of the chemical industry leads to an increase in the supply and a reduction in the price of medicines, then the growth of the chemical industry can be an indirect means for improving the quality of life of a large proportion of the population. A number of other examples can be

The International Economy and Industrial Development

cited to show that the expansion of chemical production in the Third World can be integrated within a broad industrialization strategy that is capable of efficiently utilizing resource potential and of facilitating industrial restructuring in accordance with changing comparative advantage.

5.3 Textiles
(a) Structural change and market conditions

Compared to others, the textile industry has a long international history. For the LDCs, the industry's initial appeal was based on its (i) simple technological requirements, (ii) the reliance on local raw materials (e.g. cotton and jute), (iii) relatively modest capital requirements, and most important, (iv) the predominantly labour-intensive nature of the production process.

These characteristics suggest that textiles will continue to be an industry with considerable growth potential for LDCs. While this view is certainly applicable, the textile industry does not offer the growth potential of some other industries due to specific structural features. For instance, income elasticities of domestic demand are usually less than unit,[48] and the potential for import substitution is rapidly exhausted. Long-term changes in demand and fashion trends have dictated that garments become lighter in weight, meaning that the amount of fibres used has declined. Rising wage rates have also penalized textiles relative to capital-intensive industries.

Prior to 1973, growth in western countries was roughly 4 per cent per annum. Much of the growth impetus was due to the production of synthetics which was particularly hard hit by the rise in energy prices. The movement of textile capacity away from industrialized countries to the Third World continued even after the slowdown. Western Europe and Japan, where production has stagnated or even declined, were the main losers. Only in North America did production continue to grow, albeit at a slow pace. The figures in Table V.3 give a rough idea of the global shifts in net output during the 1970s. They show a significant shift away from western countries to both socialist countries and LDCs in a brief period.

Indicative of the mature status of the industry, sluggish growth of

Policies and Prospects for Industrial Development in the Third World

demand has been a persistent constraint for western producers. In the Third World, inequalities in the distribution of income have restricted the growth of demand to rates below those in the West.[49] These circumstances meant Third World producers had little choice but to put a high priority on exports. Thus, their share of world MVA is not representative of their role in world trade.

Table V.3 Distribution of world MVA in textiles
(percentages in 1975 dollars)

Year	Western countries	Socialist countries	LDCs
1970	61.4	23.8	14.8
1975	55.4	27.8	16.8
1978[a]	54.3	28.8	16.9

Source: UNIDO, *World Industry in 1980*, New York, 1981, Table I.3, p. 35.
Note: [a] preliminary estimates.

Throughout the post-war period observers tended to evaluate the industry's progress along North-South lines, ignoring the fact that the bulk of industrial capacity was located in socialist and OECD countries. This tendency reflected producers' preoccupation with the potential threat of competitors in the labour-abundant LDCs. Thus, trends in factor usage have attracted considerable attention. Writing in 1965, the OECD Special Committee on Textiles described cotton as 'increasingly becoming a capital-intensive industry with investments easily amounting to $20,000 per workplace.'[50] Western producers began to press for protection by emphasizing the prospect that textiles were being converted into a highly capital-intensive industry. Commercial policy issues were invoked by reversing the infant-industry argument. Despite the claims, textile production continued to be relatively labour-intensive. This fact is not surprising, given the massive capital inflows to other industries (energy, aerospace, capital goods, etc.) and the demand constraints mentioned above. These conditions were not conducive to large investments or outlays for R and D.

Western producers did make labour-saving advances throughout the 1960s and continued at a slower pace in the 1970s. Resultant productivity increases were the major explanation for the job displacements which occurred. For example, between 1973 and 1978, improvements in productivity accounted for 80 per cent of the job losses in the US. Corresponding figures for Japan and the EEC were 74 and 59 per cent respectively.[51] Ironically, job losses in the textile industry were mainly attributed to imports from LDCs.

In addition to their labour-saving objective, western producers stressed product development. Like other mature industries the emphasis was on creating new products and upgrading existing ones. Success with either variant brought a market-creating effect and opportunities for firms to move out of fields where price competition was prevalent and into product lines where success depends on other factors. The structure of firms in western countries reflected the emphasis on product development and fashion. This orientation favoured firms of a moderate or small size that, compared to larger firms, had the flexibility to exploit such an approach. Similarly, where emphasis was on high quality products, small rather than large-scale enterprises proved best able to compete.

Midway through the slowdown of the 1970s both western governments and producers became increasingly occupied with the need to rationalize the industry. Although there are certain strategic differences among individual countries, their basic structural problems were similar and the theme was a common one. The motivations for rationalization varied in their intensity, being greater in the US than in Europe (see below). In 1977 European spindle capacity actually rose by 3.1 per cent, masking declines in the Netherlands (51 per cent), in the UK (38 per cent), West Germany (33 per cent) and elsewhere.[52] Downward trends were noted in North America.

Today, the average textile plant in Europe remains only one tenth of the size of the US average. This pattern has made it difficult to justify the installation of expensive, modern equipment. EEC investment in textiles has lagged far behind the rest of manufacturing—by 40 per cent in Britain, 63 in Belgium and 27 in France.[53] Only in the capital-intensive production of synthetic fibres (where thirteen producers dominate the EEC's industry) has rationalization made really significant headway.

The fall in Western production capacity accelerated after 1973 although most of these moves were the result of decisions by individual firms rather than part of a broader strategy. Differences in the production costs of western textile producers compared to those of Third World competitors explain these moves. In 1977, for example, the range in labour costs between the most expensive and cheapest producer was thirtyfold. In Belgium labour costs were $8 per hour, compared to $4 in the US, $3 in the UK, $0.45 in South Korea and $0.28 in Pakistan.[54] While currency movements and inflation have somewhat altered the relationships, the wide range remains indicative of the cost advantage of the LDCs.

Efforts at product development have paralleled the rationalization drive. Examples include the upgrading of key materials (linen) and improving the apprearances of garments including knitwear. Advances in these fields help to offset the cost advantages of Third World competitors. Many European producers also favour additional steps such as the sharing of research results among participants and ample fundings by the EEC.[55] Given these circumstances, trade is an important source of industrial growth, influencing both the pattern of structural change and the development strategies of the actors. These aspects are taken up below.

(b) Neo-protectionism and the textile industry

Global shifts in textile capacity meant that trade expanded at a fairly rapid pace for an industry which, otherwise, grew slowly. World exports rose from $23 billion in 1973 to over $40 billion in 1978, equivalent to an annual growth rate of 15.1 per cent.[56] The pattern of trade underwent only modest changes; more than one half of world exports consisted of trade between western countries. The LDCs were only secondary suppliers accounting for roughly 14 per cent of OECD imports throughout the 1970s. In contrast, buyers in the LDCs absorbed about 20 per cent of the West's exports of textile products.

The constancy of western trade patterns, despite changes in international competitive ability, may be attributed to the broad policy objective to integrate the industrial sectors of western countries during the 1950s and 1960s and to the results of the Multifibre Arrangement (MFA) discussed below. Given the large

The International Economy and Industrial Development

portion of world trade between western countries, the fact that protectionist forces were preoccupied with imports from LDCs seems peculiar. There are several explanations, however. First, the LDCs' competitive threat differed from that existing among producers in the West. Exporters in LDCs competed in terms of price rather than product differentiation or fashion. Moreover, their effective price levels are substantially below those prevailing in western countries. Second, due to the nature of the prevailing technology, a disproportionate share of world trade in textiles consists of either mature, standardized products or products that will reach that state. Such industries are most vulnerable to aggressive competition based on price advantages since, to date, they have not succeeded in achieving the necessary rates of product development and product turnover which would alleviate the import pressure. Third, the average skill level of textile industries in OECD countries is 20–50 per cent below that for all industry.[57] Thus, the expense of labour retraining and the degree of occupational maturity pose special problems.

These conditions, coupled with the emphasis LDCs attached to textiles, meant the industry became an early battleground for neo-protectionist forces. While programmes for product development, rationalization, etc. were primarily on producer-government initiatives, trade unions were vigorous and co-operative participants in the neo-protectionist push. Initially, the protectionists' appeal amounted to an infant-industry argument to restrain imports, while the industry was converted from a labour-intensive to a capital-intensive one (see above). Soon, however, protectionists came to emphasize losses in jobs and production capacity, attributing them to cheap imports.

The US was in the forefront of the protectionist drive in the early 1960s, employing bilateral quotas to limit exports of cotton textiles although other items entered free. US trading partners responded by increasing their exports of unrestricted textiles. Subsequently, producer and labour interests in the US intensified their efforts to reduce the flow of textile imports. Government officials maintained 'close liaison' through the Management-Labour Textile Advisory Committee.[58] These initiatives spread to the EEC and Canada, eventually leading to the Long-Term Cotton Textile Arrangement.

Policies and Prospects for Industrial Development in the Third World

Despite the efforts of domestic producers, US imports continued to grow. In 1971 the US took further steps to limit textile imports through bilateral agreements with major suppliers including Hong Kong, Japan, South Korea and Taiwan. Prior to that action, imports of textiles—particularly of man-made fibres—had steadily risen. Once the bilateral agreements took effect, the growth of imports of man-made fibres was stifled and their market share declined to less than 10 per cent.[59] Simultaneously, imports shifted from man-made fibres to cotton textile products, presumably because of the cost advantages enjoyed by various Asian suppliers.

Eventually, the Long-Term Cotton Textiles Arrangement was replaced by the Multifibre Arrangement (MFA) which had a wider product application. The first MFA was concluded in December 1973 and, after negotiation, renewed for 1978–82. Negotiations for a third four-year term for 1982–6 took place in 1981. The MFA is unique, being the only North-South agreement for the regulation of trade. Its key elements are (i) a limit of 6 per cent on the annual growth of the West's textile imports from the LDCs and (ii) a provision for bilateral negotiation where 'market disruption' has occurred.[60]

Under the present MFA, the US is reported to have twenty-one bilateral agreements with suppliers covering 107 product categories.[61] As in Europe, the Government is under pressure to modify its stance in the next MFA round by eliminating the present agreement's guaranteed 6 per cent per annum rate of growth in imports. Lobbyists argue that growth should be limited to the increase in the size of the domestic market which, in the US has been 1–2 per cent in recent years.

EEC countries were slower to negotiate their own bilateral deals and imports filled the gap between demand and supply in 1974–5. A more protectionist stance was later adopted. In 1977–8 the EEC concluded bilateral agreements with twenty-three countries, including twelve in Asia, devised special arrangements for six Mediterranean countries with which it has preferential trade agreements and unilaterally regulated imports from Taiwan and socialist countries. In 1979 a total of forty agreements, covering 127 categories of textile products were in force.[62]

The European textile lobby has gained in strength, partly because its efforts were reinforced by those of big chemical producers whose investment in synthetic fibres was vulnerable to the imports of textiles and clothing from LDCs. In the US, changing circumstances have also strengthened the textile lobby. Because the industry is the biggest employer of women, blacks, hispanics and other minorities, Congress has become more sympathetic to its protectionist cause. A new industry-Government partnership has been forged since 1978 which suggests that the two sides will work closely together during the next MFA talks.[63]

The Japanese instance offers a marked contrast to neo-protectionist gains in the West. To date, Japanese textile markets remain relatively free of trade restraints despite the pleas of domestic textiles and garment producers for import quotas. Most likely, the Government's reluctance reflects the importance of Japanese exports of yarn, fabric and particularly synthetic fibres to neighbouring countries. This behaviour is largely a reflection of the country's regional development strategy for textiles as discussed below.

(c) The textile industry in the Third World

In many Asian countries the industry became the catalyst for an industrial push in the 1950s. In part, this was because the region's massive labour force and abundant raw material (e.g. jute) closely matched the industry's requirement. The Japanese approach which, in the immediate post-war era focused on textiles, helped to set an example for its Asian neighbours. Moreover, the industry was developed as an export oriented one. In addition to its appeal in terms on input characteristics, foreign demand in the immediate post-war period seemed almost infinite and textiles' potential for earning foreign exchange was thought to be good.

The structure of textile firms in Third World countries differs from that in the West due to the former's emphasis on the mass production of cheap goods for export. In Korea, for example, almost 50 per cent of textile production was attributable to fifteen large companies or groups in 1979.[64] In that country and elsewhere the emphasis on cheap exports led to a considerable degree of vertical integration from raw materials to yarn and fabrics.

The development with perhaps the greatest impact on the textile industry was the rapid introduction of synthetic fibre production in both the LDCs and the industrialized countries. Synthetic fibres first appeared on the market in 1938 when oil cost less than $10 per barrel. Producers enjoyed an era of rapid growth from the mid-1950s until the mid-1960s, replacing natural fibres in many uses and providing the impetus for a wide range of new final products. Firms in the Third World were quick to follow the move into synthetics. Importing petroleum-based synthetic fibres appeared to be an attractive alternative to the production of natural fibres (mainly cotton and silk) which were produced using comparatively inefficient, traditional methods. Thus, rather than attempting to become self-sufficient in raw material supplies, many Third World producers opted to concentrate on synthetic fibre production. Meanwhile, the governments of LDCs preferred to build petrochemical processing plants rather than encourage cotton production with its attendant dangers of climatic disasters and volatile world prices.

The experience in Asian countries again provides an instructive example of interrelationships between foreign investment, technology transfer and market structure. The introduction of synthetic fibre-making capacity in Hong Kong, South Korea, Taiwan and the ASEAN countries was largely a part of the marketing strategy of two big Japanese fibre-producers, Teijin and Toray. These operations retain their oligopolistic structure today.[65] In related operations (e.g. spinning and weaving) competitive structures emerged through joint ventures, the transfer of control to local firms and the emergence of local producers. The resultant pattern of trade in synthetic fibres was remarkably different from that of natural textiles. By the mid-1970s only South Korea and Taiwan had begun exporting; other Asian countries continued to be net importers of synthetic fibre while Japan remained a net exporter.

By the time of the first oil crisis much of the world's textile industry was dependent on synthetic fibres. The increase in the prices of petroleum-based raw materials had two major consequences. First, the industry's import bills soared and firms' share of value added in gross output was reduced proportionately. Second, the rise in materials costs dramatically reduced the competitive advantage of textile producers in the Third World. Labour costs fell

The International Economy and Industrial Development

as a proportion of total manufacturing costs from roughly 50 per cent to less than 20 per cent.

The abrupt shift in the costs on textile production posed problems for all producers. However, Third World producers and their governments were slowest to respond by reverting to natural fibres, an alternative not readily available to most western countries. Most textile firms could not afford the investments to reverse this trend while their governments were deterred by the long-term investment in agriculture necessary to bring raw material production up to levels which would support natural fibre production. Paradoxically, cotton production experienced a modest revival in some industrialized countries while natural fibres continued to lose ground to synthetics in LDCs.

Perhaps more than most industries, the textile industry in the Third World is interrelated with the strategies of Western products and, hence, the neo-protectionist drive. Thus, LDCs' prospects cannot be evaluated in isolation from developments in the West. In the US, textile producers were quietly altering their basic approaches during the 1970s. Previously, firms adopted a singularly inward orientation which was feasible due to a large domestic market protected by higher tariffs than other western countries. The effects of rising wage costs were minimized by shifting plants from the north-east to the south where the labour force was largely non-unionized.

More recently, the enforcement of stringent government regulations on workers' health, coupled with spreading unionization, forced firms to quickly modernize—a step which producers had largely avoided in the past thanks to the MFA and the domestic circumstances cited above. A large portion of old, inefficient capacity was scrapped. In 1974–80 firms imported more than $2 billion worth of spinning and winding machines, air-jet looms, etc.[66] In 1978-9 alone the three leading manufacturers of textile machinery reported an increase in orders of 80–300 per cent—all placed by American firms.[67] At the same time, the fall in the dollar exchange rate, the artificial advantage of cheap feedstocks and the export opportunities due to MFA restrictions on Third World producers led to a new outward orientation among US textile firms.[68]

In the past, the US textile industry accounted for 20 per cent of world production but only 9 per cent of all exports. In 1979 modernization and the new export orientation began to show results as exports jumped 45 per cent. Roughly one fifth of these exports went to LDCs like Hong Kong and Mexico where low-wage workers sew American fabric into apparel for re-export to western countries, including the US. This tactic, known to textile producers as 'outward processing', and to economists as fragmentation of the production process, is more widespread in the US than elsewhere. United States tariff practices encourage the procedure by allowing firms to export materials and re-import the finished product at duties which apply only to the value added and materials supplied by foreign processors. A more important element in explaining the growing popularity of outward processing, however, is the ability of American firms to pressure US suppliers of garments (e.g. Hong Kong and Korea) to use more American textiles. The large American market for imported clothing makes this a formidable threat.

The recent modernization cum export drive has led to other changes with significance for the industry's future. Product strategies in the US have increasingly come to focus on a narrow range of items, e.g. denim or corduroy, in order to achieve higher productivity and maintain quality. Similarly, producers of synthetics often opt for only one or two high-technology fibres.[69] The adjustment in strategy has implications for the rationalization process in the US. Already the share of output of the top largest fifteen companies has risen from 25 to 40 per cent. Analysts expect that the number of firms (presently 7000) will be reduced by one third in the 1980s.[70]

The consequences of these trends for producers in LDCs are important. Both the structure and the orientation of American textile firms have come to resemble those in LDCs. The emphasis on exports, mass production techniques, large-scale firms and cost reducing measures distinguish American producers from their competitors in other advanced countries. It is significant that producers in LDCs like Thailand are fearful that firms in the US, South Korea and Taiwan may dump their excess production and appeal for adequate government support.[71]

An increase in the industry's exports destined for outward

processing may eventually stir interest in freer trade in much the same way as occurred for US producers of electronic products: TVs, radios. However, this would provide no relief for existing textile producers in LDCs (although clothing manufacturers might benefit). As in western countries, textile producers in LDCs look to the clothing industry as their main market and the consequences in terms of excess capacity and lost jobs would be substantial if American producers should successfully replace them. The long-standing reluctance of American firms to engage in joint ventures and interrelated expansion as followed by the Japanese (see below) is a result of the traditional US approach—high tariff barriers and an inward orientation. The international investment patterns and their consequences are longer-lasting than attitudes towards export and the result could increase friction between textile producers in the US and the LDCs.

A more sophisticated response to adjustment pressures concerns both European and US producers and amounts to an attempt to alter the structure of consuming markets. Presently, the clothing industry may absorb 50 per cent or more of the textile industry's production. Other users are the housing and construction industry (25–35 per cent) and industrial and technical branches, particularly transport and health. Consequently, the demand for textiles is mainly dependent upon the market for clothing, an industry which has its own problems associating with flagging demand and competition from imports. Moreover, long-term trends in productivity in textiles have outstripped the pace of technical progress in clothing,[72] contributing to an imbalance between the suppliers and their major markets.

Current government-industry initiatives are apparently aimed at reducing the textile industry's link with clothing. Thus, the earlier theme of product development has taken on a new and wider dimension. Specific examples of advances which would alter this dependence are protective wear for military and police forces, a new lightweight fibre to be used in inner panels of aircraft to reduce fuel consumption, a more durable nylon to replace plastics for use in aircraft, long-lasting nylon tyres and heat-resistant fibres to replace asbestos products. Although there is no confirming evidence, such a re-ordering in the demand pattern may easily provide textile producers with a built-in protection from imports. Closer links between textile suppliers and users in technical branches (transport, health, military, etc.) which are largely state-run could eventually lead to trade restraints in the form of state purchasing practices, health and safety regulations, etc. which decidedly favour domestic producers.

In Europe, producers are likely to retain their predominantly defensive orientation largely because the EEC has been slow to develop any co-ordinated strategy. Rationalization programmes have been plagued by disputes over the desirability of a 'crisis cartel' for synthetics, low rates of investment to modernize and only tentative efforts at pooling R and D efforts and programmes for outward processing.[73] The inability to co-ordinate strategies and policies is partly due to the varying degrees of lobbying power and orientation of government, producers and labour in different countries. It is further complicated by the fact that new EEC entrants—Greece, Portugal and Spain—may drastically alter the degree of internal competition faced by existing producers.

The hopes of European interests are, therefore, pinned on a renegotiated MFA which includes quotas on US exports and the demand that the US lower its tariffs on Third World textiles. Such an approach promises little relief for existing or potential textile exporters in the latter countries in view of the foregoing description of the neo-protectionist successes in that country. An additional danger is that the new US export drive may simply be diverted from the EEC to Japan and neighbouring countries, reversing the direction of previous forms of trade diversion.

Finally, Japan's approach offers a sharp contrast with the above. The textile industry has been officially described as 'structurally depressed'. The Ministry of International Trade and Industry has been charged with overseeing the planned contraction of textiles. Government programmes include specialization in limited product lines, the formation of cartels, scrapping excess facilities and, most important, the provision of finance for the needed moves. Under the guidance of the Industrial Structures Council—a group unique to Japan—these programmes will continue into the 1980s.

Direct foreign investments and joint ventures have meant the complementarities between Japanese textile producers and those in neighbouring countries are further advanced than in the case of the US. Information exchanges, management practices and production technologies all reflect the textile network which, though fragile, has emerged. A more extensive network may emerge as large Japanese retailers by-pass existing channels and import directly and as large firms relocate abroad rather than subcontracting to smaller Japanese firms. These trends should eventually lead to a rise in Japanese imports from LDCs (still not large) although much will depend on the behaviour of US firms and the results of the next MFA.

In the longer term the salient constraint remains the slow growth of textile consumption in the LDCs themselves. Inequalities in the distribution of income in LDCs have long restricted the growth of home demand to rates below those in the West. Until this basic constraint is removed, the future of Third World producers will be subject to the whims of neo-protectionism in the West.

The importance of the textile industry for most LDCs remains unchanged. It employs almost a quarter of their manufacturing labour force and this proportion has remained constant during 1965–75.[74] In the poorer Third World countries, textiles' share on manufacturing employment is likely to be considerably higher. Moreover, textiles have played an integrative role in linking agricultural and manufacturing development over a long historical period. They produce 'basic needs' commodities and use inputs often produced by the poorest section of a typical Third World country's population. There is thus a strong case for according some priority to the accelerated development of the textile industry in many LDCs.

5.4 Food processing

(a) Structural changes and market conditions

Food processing consists of two clearly delineated sub-sectors: producers of basic foodstuffs (staples and/or other food items for mass consumption) and producers of luxury food products (various types of fruit, vegetables, seafood, poultry and all the associated processing facilities). The division between the two sub-sectors is distinguishable in the application of national policy, by their respective trade orientations, in their pattern of growth and demand and by the relative importance of each in LDCs and western countries.

In the case of basic foodstuffs, national objectives are to attain or preserve a measure of self-sufficiency. Western countries usually interpret this objective in terms of national security while LDCs often describe it as a part of a programme of basic needs or self-reliance. Notably, the former countries have been much more successful in realizing their objective and treat the possibility of exporting basic foodstuffs as a secondary priority. For the West, exports provide an outlet for surplus production (which results from excessive subsidies to agriculture) or a political tool in the case of world shortages. Priorities are not necessarily the same in LDCs. The production of luxury food products often receives a high priority, being regarded as a logical corollary of export oriented industrialization. In countries that are hard pressed for foreign exchange, exporting luxury foods may receive a higher priority than basic needs or employment generation. Thus, either or both sub-sectors may occupy planners' attention in LDCs depending upon whether they stress basic needs and/or employment generation of exports and foreign exchange earnings.

Growth characteristics and demand patterns also distinguish between the two sub-sectors. Typically, the growth of net output in food processing has lagged behind that of other industries. Today, western countries still account for roughly two thirds of world MVA although their share is slowly declining. The shares of socialist countries stabilized after 1975 while the LDCs have continued to make steady and significant gains.[75]

At the global level, one of the industry's most significant features is the low rate of increase in *per capita* availability of several important food products (e.g. meat products, wheat, refined sugar, etc.). Much of world production of these and many other food items is concentrated among a very few countries—Argentina, Brazil, China, the USSR and the US. This near-monopoly situation led to the intrusion of politics into food production as countries tried to use their economic predominance to serve foreign policy goals.

In the case of basic foodstuffs, the growth of net output has typically lagged behind that of other industrial branches. One explanation is that the demand for food products tends to be income inelastic. As real income rises, the proportion of household expenditures devoted to food declines. This is particularly true in western countries.[76] The industry also faces a supply constraint; expansion is limited by land availability. Again, this condition is primarily applicable to the western countries where the cost of land has risen most rapidly and its availability is limited at any price. The industry is often squeezed between sharply rising raw material prices and operating costs on one hand and price controls (and occasionally price-cutting wars) on the other.

This description, however, is mainly applicable to basic foodstuffs. The production (and export) of luxury foods grew phenomenally in the 1970s. Mainly as a result of this trend, the LDCs' share of world MVA rose during these years. Furthermore, demand is often income elastic, increasing more rapidly than income. There are also constant changes in the types of luxury foods demanded. Convenience foods, foreign foods and health foods are examples. Firms that anticipate these shifts (due to demographic and social factors) can find profitable market niches. Obviously, western producers or TNCs based in these countries enjoy a considerable advantage in this respect over producers in LDCs.

Because of national policy objectives described above, the luxury food industry is more prone to be footloose or to relocate abroad than are producers of basic foodstuffs. During the 1970s this process of relocation was dramatic. Western production centres like Hawaii quickly lost importance to sites in LDCs like Indonesia, Mexico, the Philippines or Thailand. Today, luxury food exports account for about one quarter of the Third World's total production of processed foods[77]—another reflection of the importance accorded exports rather than basic needs or employment. The relocation process was mainly a response to cost conditions cited above. The processing facilities for chilling, cutting, packing and wrapping naturally followed. In some cases rising labour costs also contributed to the move. Poultry processing, which includes manual deboning, is an example. Although both sub-sectors are dominated by the TNC, it is the luxury food producers operating in LDCs which reflect a single-minded export orientation.

The move to LDCs found ready supporters there. Governments

in search of foreign exchange welcomed new producers in non-traditional sectors like luxury foods that were likely to have an export orientation. The industry was also attractive to local entrepreneurs who, having succeeded in industry or commerce, were looking for new ventures. Commercial agriculture was lucrative, especially with the proliferation of government incentives which were harder to secure in more mature industries. Moreover, it was only the urban-based businessman who had sufficient capital and the know-how required for joint ventures with TNCs for marketing purposes. Organizations such as producers' co-operatives and state enterprises are still not significant in this field.

This description leads us to conclude that for purposes of discussing international investment, trade or the spread of production facilities in the food processing industry, the role of the TNC is paramount. According to one study, the industry's leading TNCs number around 175 of which one half are based in the US.[78] Some, like Unilever and Nestlé, have long corporate histories and almost all are highly diversified enterprises that produce a wide range of food and non-food products. For example, Cargill Corporation, International Telephone and Telegraph and Standard Oil all have large investments in food processing.

The industry's structure, being dominated by TNCs, is highly monopolistic. The concentration of firms has been spurred by the growth of mergers, particularly in the United States and in West Germany where for the period 1955–69 mergers in the food industry exceeded those in all other industrial branches.[79]

International expansion is another important feature of TNC policy. Among the 170 largest food manufacturing firms the total number of subsidiaries established in western countries was 827, compared to 655 in LDCs. Notably, however, the largest firms (those with an annual turnover of $5 billion) had eighty-six subsidiaries in the LDCs and only forty-eight in the West.[80] In comparison, the degree of global vertical integration in food processing is far greater than in basic commodities like rubber, cocoa or palm oil. Fewer intermediaries in the industry—from production to final retail marketing—mean greater profit margins and more opportunities for transfer pricing.

The International Economy and Industrial Development

The industry's TNCs have been influenced by the policies of their home governments. These tend to vary because of the differences in objective conditions among the western countries. North America is a net food surplus economy, Japan a major deficit one and the EEC and the socialist countries have been aiming at self-sufficiency. In the US many policy instruments such as investment guarantees, tax relief, aid programmes and trade concessions are designed to facilitate foreign investment with a heavy emphasis on luxury food items. The Japanese Government on the other hand encourages investment in the food industry to ensure supplies for home markets, to diversify sources and reduce commodity prices. It has been estimated that Japanese firms control foreign capital worth over $500 million in the food related industries.

The relationship between western governments and transnationals in the food processing industry has been an important determinant of trade policies and policies affecting foreign investment formulated by these countries. We turn to an assessment of these policies in the next section.

(b) Neo-protectionism in food processing

The distinction between basic foodstuffs and luxury food products is again applicable to a discussion of neo-protection. With regard to basic foodstuffs, the now familiar approaches described in preceding case studies apply. Space does not permit a detailed examination of all trade restrictions but a brief summary of the three major markets, the EEC, Japan and the United States is worthwhile. Imports into the EEC face numerous and complex NTBs as well as variable levies. Few items are permitted preferential entry under the Generalized System of Preferences (GSP) or Tokyo Round concessions. Meats are subject to levies of 15–20 per cent while preparations of meat enter at considerably higher rates.[81] Furthermore, most imports are subject to licensing, health, packaging and labelling regulations. In Japan, the tariffs on imports of live animals and meat are not high but are often 25 per cent for prepared and preserved meats and are buttressed by a variety of health and sanitary regulations and discretionary licensing.

The US has often relied on import quotas while maintaining

Policies and Prospects for Industrial Development in the Third World

relatively low tariff rates. Cattle, for example are subject to a 16 per cent *ad valorem* rate plus a variable levy. Sheep are subject to a 15 per cent duty while beef imports encounter a 20 per cent levy. Levies on processed and tanned meats are often significantly higher. The US Meat Import Act of 1964 established import quotas that go into effect if imports exceed a pre-determined amount.[82] The US maintained agreements with thirteen meat exporting countries in 1977.

The recent Tokyo Round of Trade Negotiations resulted in some reductions of tariffs on food manufactures but, in general, the changes were not great.[83] Two multilateral arrangements were agreed upon, however, one for bovine meat and the other for dairy products. Under the Arrangement regarding Bovine Meat, which covers beef, veal and live cattle and aims at trade expansion, liberalization and stabilization, an International Meat Council was established to allow consultation among trading countries. The International Dairy Arrangement aims at stabilization through the setting of minimum prices by an International Dairy Product Council.

Neo-protectionist intentions in the case of luxury food items are entirely distinct from those described above. (The reader should recall that the definition of neo-protectionism given in Chapter II refers to any government interventions that affect trade.) The common approach of western countries has been to facilitate the production and export of luxury food items by LDCs in a variety of ways. The boom in Asian exports to Japan and to the West provides an illustration. Hawaii was for many years the world's leading supplier of tropical fruit (fresh, canned, sliced, etc.). However, in the 1970s it was supplanted by the Philippines and Thailand as leading exporters of many items. Beginning from no base, exports of bananas from the Philippines rose, on average, 225 fold per year in 1965–75; Thailand's exports of canned seafood increased 11.5 times (to US $50 million) in 1975–9 and its exports of frozen fruit and poultry rose 3.3 fold annually in the same period.[84] Despite such rapid growth—which is not atypical—no mounting neo-protectionist movement was incurred. This response is in marked contrast to the protectionist surges observed in the case of steel or textiles.

Complementary steps were also taken to develop the agricultural infrastructure, with international and national assistance, to make export agribusiness commercially feasible. Japanese and American firms like Dole, Del Monte, United Brands and Sumitomo Shoji have taken the lead in this move. An explanation for the lack of protectionist initiatives is the almost complete domination of marketing, distribution and other activities by the TNCs. In this respect, western policies on luxury foods are similar to those on consumer electronics (e.g. television, radios, semi-conductors). Not surprisingly, the TNCs are predominant in off-shore assembly, processing, etc. in this industry as well.

Exports of luxury foods promise to grow in response to the demand of affluent Japanese and, to a lesser extent, European and American tastes. As they do, governments of LDCs will be faced with two important issues: (a) their relations with TNCs operating in this field and (b) the priorities to be accorded to the production of basic foodstuffs and/or the export of luxury foods.

(c) Food processing industries and the Third World

Food processing industries in LDCs have a strong link with agriculture but only weak interindustry relationships with other parts of the manufacturing sector. This is so because value added by food processing represents only 25–30 per cent of the products' final value, the remainder being supplied by the agricultural sector. Despite the low value per unit of output, food processing accounted for almost 20 per cent of MVA in the Third World in the mid-1970s.[85] Food processing industries are also of great significance for employment. For example, in 1970, 50 per cent of the manufacturing labour force in the LDCs was employed in the food industries. Thus, policy decisions regarding this industry can be extremely important in a country's future development and the crucial trade-off between manufacturing and agriculture often hangs in the balance.

For countries at early stages of development food processing is largely in the hands of domestic firms. TNCs may become involved in food processing activities through product sales to local processors and distributors. This is particularly true for the markets of most meat, dairy, grain and oil based consumer products.[86]

Policies and Prospects for Industrial Development in the Third World

Alternatively, TNCs may begin production of processed foods after negotiating the establishment of subsidiaries and the sale of licences. Initially, these units are usually oriented towards the domestic market. It is expected that the diversity of food products directly produced in the LDCs will increase over time. Many food processing TNCs have taken advantage of import substituting policies to establish subsidiaries in the LDCs.

The ability of TNCs to develop integrated commodity/processing systems varies widely according to the product. In the case of meat products, for example, only eight major TNCs have operations in LDCs. Similarly, there is limited involvement of TNCs in grain-based products like crackers, biscuits, macaroni, etc. These products are usually manufactured by small-scale domestic firms. Traditionally, fruit canning and processing were in the hands of private firms in LDCs although this ownership pattern is changing with the new interest in exporting luxury foods.

More extensive involvement of TNCs can be noted in the poultry industry where highly integrated international distribution networks exist for production and processing. Likewise, TNCs producing formular animal feed have integrated their operations with poultry processing and have expanded into LDCs. Processed fish products are produced on a large scale by India, Indonesia, Mexico, Peru, South Korea, Thailand, Viet Nam and the West Indies. There is a pronounced trend in favour of exporting these products and a number of TNCs are involved. Finally, about thirteen TNCs are engaged in the processing and distribution of oilseeds produced in the Third World.[87]

Generally, the TNC's involvement in food processing in LDCs is growing. Some of these firms operate their own estates rather than buying from local suppliers. Most Third World governments, however, are increasingly wary of foreign control over natural resources and many TNCs have changed their procurement and investment strategies. Quite often TNCs have followed a strategy of reducing their investment exposure while retaining a strong and dominant marketing position. The strategy's attraction is that it does not tie the firm to fixed investments such as land. When the resource is exhausted—which can be due to overintensive cultivation or chemical saturation of the soil—the TNC can easily

The International Economy and Industrial Development

relocate. The key to control of the industry appears to be direct ownership of processing and marketing facilities and not necessarily the land itself as Third World governments often presume.

Major expansion of the industry, particularly if luxury food items and exports are envisaged, must involve co-operation between LDCs and transnationals. Even if the host country can produce these products domestically, the TNCs exercise effective control over international distribution and marketing channels and are in a position to deny market access. They are also in a position to develop complex relations with domestic suppliers and retailers which gives them control over prices in a very wide area. The dominance of the TNCs in the food processing markets may create serious problems for LDCs that lack the resources and expertise to develop effective bargaining capacity vis-à-vis giants such as Unilever and Mitsubishi.

In general, TNCs seek to retain control of decisions regarding technology, location and finance in order to integrate the policy of the subsidiary within the overall corporate strategy of optimizing sales and revenue. Host governments and local entrepreneurs may seek to make these decisions the subject of negotiations and to limit the managerial autonomy of the TNC. This requires effective monitoring of the activities of the TNC by authorities in the LDC. Indeed, it is only on the basis of fairly accurate knowledge about motives and modes of operations that understanding can be developed and an element of complementarity be introduced into the policies of governments and TNCs.

There are dangers, however, in a government's decision to encourage the development of food processing in collaboration with a TNC. For example, the capital provided by the firm for its operations in the LDC is likely to be a relatively small proportion of resultant sales. In comparison, repayment obligations to TNCs are often higher than those for governmental loans. TNCs may displace local plants that generate employment on a far higher level. The share of wages in many of these operations is notoriously low, often accounting for less than 5 per cent of the price of the agricultural product. Similarly, the expected contribution to foreign exchange earnings may be offset by the TNCs' ability to conceal resource flows through transfer pricing. In food processing industries, transfer pricing occurs mainly through intra-firm transactions for capital goods and intra-economy financial transactions—particularly loan and banking arrangements. A quantitative assessment of the extent of intra-firm transactions is not available. Nor is information available on participation by these firms in market sharing arrangements that may restrict exports of food products from LDCs. However, given the high level of diversification that is characteristic of TNCs and the significant level of horizontal and vertical integration they often achieve, the level of intra-firm transactions and market sharing arrangements is thought to be relatively high.

Investment by TNCs in the food processing industries may also be a source of inappropriate production technology. Technological innovation of a labour (or land) saving type has not been as rapid in this industrial branch as in other sectors—notably agriculture.[88] Little technical change has occurred in meat processing and canning, malt beverage production, baking and fruit and vegetable drying. The technologies can be easily adapted by domestic producers in LDCs and the TNC's main advantages are in packaging, marketing and quality control, not in production.[89] Thus, technological acquisition and assurances of market access can be treated separately by LDCs, meaning that there are important gains to be made by 'breaking open the package' offered by TNCs. Domestic technological adaptations are likely to have a greater 'learning by doing' impact than technological procurement through 'TNC package' process and can be more employment generating,[90] although the impact on the pattern of income distribution is not clear.

Expansion of the food processing industries must be based upon a clear understanding of the decision's consequences for meeting the basic needs of the population. If the product in which specialization is sought has little nutritional content, or if it is meant primarily for export (e.g. a luxury food), specialization can impose a cost on the production of agricultural commodities necessary for basic consumption. It may pull investment resources away from this latter group of products and inflate their price. Since the lowest income groups devote a relatively high proportion of their income to the consumption of basic foodstuffs, they will be seriously affected. Moreover, food processing, if pioneered by TNCs, is likely to have an impact on consumption patterns and tastes which may substitute low nutritional content products such as breakfast food, canned milk, soft beverages for cheaper natural products of higher nutritional value.

The host government's ability to circumvent some of these drawbacks depends upon (among other things) the balance between the organizational and management capabilities of the TNCs and the governments. Food TNCs have flexible management structures and efficient information systems due to the accelerated movement towards merger acquisitions in these markets. Overall management responsibility is firmly centred at headquarters and, according to some authors, branch plant management has restricted access to the TNCs' top organizational hierarchy. Countries with weak administrative structures may find the TNC's grasp of tax management and marketing practices overwhelming. The TNC usually has an incentive in making domestic market organization as effective as possible. They initiate market information systems and build networks for distribution of their production. Having consolidated its own position within the domestic market, the firm may shift from aggressive to market maintenance tactics.

To summarize, the extent to which food processing can serve as a focus for an industrialization strategy is limited by a number of factors. As we have seen, expansion is often restricted by TNC domination of major international markets and by the protectionist policies on western countries—such as the East European and EEC countries—intent on preserving agricultural self-sufficiency. Nevertheless, these industries are potentially highly labour-intensive, they have strong links with the agricultural sector and their production technology can easily be adapted in most poor countries. It is an area in which the relatively small—perhaps co-operatively managed—enterprise has an important role to play. There is a need for governments to encourage domestic private initiative in this field and to orient activities towards the production of high nutritional value products for domestic consumption. As far as export initiatives are concerned, progress can be made on two fronts. First, TNCs may be persuaded to reduce barriers to entry in specific markets through a process of protracted negotiations in which LDCs consciously seek to pool their administrative and technical expertise within the context of regional co-operation

Policies and Prospects for Industrial Development in the Third World

agreements and free trade areas. Such arrangements can be used to negotiate trade liberalization programmes with western countries—notably the EEC—and then pressure can be brought to bear for desired adjustment of TNC attitudes in line with the policies of their home governments. Secondly, LDCs should methodically attempt to establish links with consumer interest groups in the West, and press for greater access to the markets of the rich countries.

Notes

[1] Producers did not restrict their capacity expansion during this period, apparently anticipating only a brief downswing. Until 1974 the world's steel industry operated at over 90 per cent of effective capacity. Afterwards, utilization rates plummeted to less than 60 per cent. See Interfutures, *Facing the Future: Mastering the Probable and Managing the Unpredictable* OECD, Paris, 1979, p. 369.

[2] A comparison of steel inputs per unit of output in kilograms in West Germany in 1970 and 1977 showed the following percentage reductions per 1000 kilograms of finished product: electrical machinery, 10 per cent; shipbuilding, 23 per cent; rolling stock, 9 per cent; nuts, bolts and similar products, 11 per cent. Similar trends were noted in the case of Japan. See UNIDO, *Picture for 1985 of the World Iron and Steel Industry*, ICIS. 161, June 1980, p. 18.

[3] This process changes molten steel directly into slabs and billets, bypassing the ingot stage.

[4] Trade in steel products grew at 9.3 per cent per annum in 1968–74 while production expanded at a rate of 5.0 per cent. The corresponding figures for 1975–7 were 5.7 and 2.1 per cent respectively. See International Iron and Steel Institute, *World Steel in Figures, 1979*, pp. 13–14.

[5] *Ibid.*, p. 14.

[6] According to one report, in a group of thirty large steelmakers more than 300 new products were introduced between 1978 and 1980. *Financial Times*, 22 May 1980.

[7] UNIDO, *op. cit.*, p. 18.

[8] International Iron and Steel Institute (IISI), *Steel Intensity and GNP Structure*, IISI Committee on Economic Studies, Brussels, 1974.

[9] Figures are based on the Economic Commission for Europe, *The Steel Market in 1978*; the *Annual Bulletin of Steel Statistics for Europe and Long-Term Prospects for Steel Consumption until 1985*.

[10] *Financial Times*, 21 August 1980 and *The Economist*, 13 September 1980.

[11] Ingo Walter and Kent A. Jones, 'Industrial adjustment to competitive shocks: a tale of three industries', paper submitted to the international symposium on industrial policies for the '80s, Madrid, 5–9 May 1980, p. 25.

[12] Minimum price controls were originally included but dropped in later versions of the plan. See *The Economist*, 2 August 1980.

[13] *The Economist*, 24 November 1979.

The International Economy and Industrial Development

[14] However, blast furnace operation requires considerable labour skills since the metallurgical reactions occurring in it cannot be predicted completely.

[15] See, M. Osaki, *Basic ideas and practices of co-operation for establishing integrated steelworks in developing countries*, in IISI, Report of Proceedings, Eleventh Annual Conference, Rome, 10–12 October 1977, pp. 65–79.

[16] See, UNIDO, *op. cit.*, pp. 11–14.

[17] *Ibid.*, annex 1.

[18] *Ibid.*, p. 22.

[19] See UNIDO, *The World Iron and Steel Industry*, ICIS, 89, 20 November 1978, pp. 50–1.

[20] The early 1970s had witnessed massive investment programmes to cope with ecological regulations, expand capacity and reduce the share of coke in the cost structure. But the rise in petrol prices upset the traditional cost structure. Investment had been aimed at replacing coke by petrol, then the cheap factor, and suddenly petrol became more expensive than coke. Thus several firms were caught unawares when the recession began.

[21] Calculations were in constant prices. See ECE, *Structure and Change in European Industry* (Sales no. E.77.II.E.3), especially Table 1.2.

[22] The original data were at constant prices and included petroleum and coal products in chemicals. See *op. cit.*, p. 44.

[23] The distribution is similar if based on expenditures rather than number of researchers. See OECD, *A Study of Resources Devoted to R and D in OECD Member Countries in 1943/1964*, Statistical Tables and Notes, Paris, 1968, and *International Survey of the Resources Devoted to R and D in 1967 by OECD Member Countries*, Statistical Tables and Notes, Vol. 1, Paris, 1970.

[24] Production dropped somewhat in later years. The petrochemicals included here are plastics, synthetic fibres, synthetic rubbers and detergents. See UNIDO, *First World-Wide Study on the Petrochemical Industry: 1975–2000*, ICIS.83, December 1978, p. 20.

[25] For example, polyvinyl chloride is derived from inorganic chloride (60 per cent) and ethylene (40 per cent), a petrochemical building block.

[26] See ECE, *Market Trends for Chemical Products 1970–1975 and Prospects for 1980*, Vol. 1 (Sales no. E. 78.II.E.14), p. 8.

[27] *Ibid.*, p. 10.

[28] Over 95 per cent of ammonia, one of the most important inorganic chemicals, is also derived from these feedstocks.

[29] Between mid-1973 and mid-1974, the prices of raw materials (e.g. naphtha) rose 300–400 per cent; intermediates such as ethylene and propylene increased 100–200 per cent; plastics such as polypropylene and polyethylene rose 50–100 per cent; while finished products (bags, film, moldings, etc.) rose 35–50 per cent. See Economic Commission for Europe, *Annual Review of the Chemical Industry*, CHEM/8, December 1974, p. 2.

[30] *The Economist*, 10 May 1980, p. 13. These cost relationships are constantly changing. The recent (1978) rise in the price of naphtha penalized European producers more than the United States producers who rely on natural gas for fuel and raw materials. By 1980 the cost of feedstock for the latter producers was 40 per cent

Policies and Prospects for Industrial Development in the Third World

cheaper than naphtha.

[31] Significantly, the Japanese Government is reported to have singled out the petrochemicals industry for restructuring. Chemical firms in that country are concentrating on diversification away from energy-intensive processes and on joint ventures with developing countries. See *The Economist*, 3 May 1980, p. 83.

[32] An extreme example is one Japanese firm which estimated that in 1980 raw material accounted for 90 per cent of its costs for production of methanol.

[33] Figures are for 1977 and refer to ethylene, a basic building block. The comparable share of variable costs in production costs was 44 per cent in 1974. See *The Economist*, 7 April 1979, p. 18.

[34] *The Economist*, Chemical Survey, 7 April 1979, p. 13.

[35] Rising feedstock costs will make dumping a less attractive alternative as variable rather than fixed costs become more significant.

[36] For example, in the fourth quarter of 1980, the United States price of naphtha was said to be $50–$70 per tonne less than the European price. In the case of ethane the gap was $100 per tonne. The American decision to do away with all price controls on oil and on natural gas could eliminate, or substantially narrow, any cost advantages.

[37] At present, as many as eighteen dumping complaints are reportedly being prepared by European chemical producers. This would amount to almost one half the number of cases normally dealt with by the Commission in a year on behalf of all manufacturing. See *Financial Times*, 24 June 1980.

[38] For example, chemical groups in West Germany have argued that their labour costs in 1979 were roughly 28 per cent higher than those in the United States. Hourly costs were $13.20 compared with $10.32 in the United States. This gap was partially due to the behaviour of the two currencies' rates of exchange. (Calculations here were based on an average exchange rate of DM 1.83 per dollar in 1979.)

[39] Examples of these speciality chemicals are agrochemicals, pharmaceuticals and specialized plastics.

[40] Rising feedstock prices were not the only factor, however. The rising value of the yen made imported naphtha much more expensive. By the late 1970s the domestic price of naphtha was as much as 9000 yen per kilolitre above the European price. See *Far Eastern Economic Review*, 18 April 1980, p. 46.

[41] The estimates assumed a price of $250 per ton. By August 1980 the European contract price was $325 per ton, down slightly from an early summer price of $350.

[42] *The Economist*, Chemical Survey, 7 April 1979, p. 24.

[43] *The Economist*, 9 April 1979, p. 20.

[44] See the opinion of a senior Shell executive reported in the *Financial Times*, 29 July 1980.

[45] *Financial Times*, 29 July 1980.

[46] *The Economist*, 7 April 1979, p. 22.

[47] UNIDO, *First World-Wide Study . . .*, op. cit., p. 249.

[48] Chenery and Taylor, *op. cit.*, p. 409. However, for synthetic fibre-using products, the income elasticity of demand is fairly high.

[49] During 1964–74, *per capita* consumption of textiles rose by 19 per cent compared to a 21 per cent increase in OECD countries. Interfutures, *op. cit.*, p. 262.

[50] Special committee on textiles, *Modern Cotton Industry—A Capital-Intensive*

Industry, published by the Organization for Economic Co-operation and Development, Paris, 1965, p. 95.

[51] Wilhelm Kurth, 'Textiles and clothing: a national and international issue', paper submitted to the international symposium on industrial policies for the '80s, Madrid, 5–9 May 1980 p. 6.

[52] Figures are based on data from the International Textile Manufactures Federation in *Financial Times*, 23 May 1980. Similar trends were noted for looms used in weaving.

[53] *The Economist*, 6 December 1980.

[54] Figures were based on a study by Werner consultants, as cited in *The Economist*, 6 December 1980.

[55] *Financial Times*, 6 October 1980.

[56] United Nations, *Monthly Bulletin of Statistics*, May 1979 and May 1980.

[57] OECD Industry Committee, *Labour and Skill Intensity of Industrial Activities*, OECD, Paris, 1979, pp. 24–5.

[58] The 'close industry-government relationship' was sharply criticized as 'a dangerously intimate industry role in the administration of this major international program' in a 1966 report of Congressman Curtis. He raised the 'troublesome question . . . whether it is the policy of the US cotton textile industry that the US Government has for the last five years been implementing, rather than a policy representative of the national interest.' Hal Lary, *Imports from Less Developed Countries*, Colombia University Press, New York, 1968, p. 125.

[59] D. B. Keesing, 'World trade and output of manufactures: structural trends and developing countries' imports', Washington D.C., World Bank, February 1978 (mimeo.) p. 58.

[60] The phrase 'market disruption' has never been clearly defined, however.

[61] *Financial Times*, 29 May 1980.

[62] *Far Eastern Economic Review*, 4 April 1980.

[63] Notably, in 1979 the informal textile caucus managed to pass a bill excluding textiles from the US offer in the GATT multilateral trade negotiations although the bill was later vetoed.

[64] *Far Eastern Economic Review*, 4 April 1980.

[65] Ippei Yamazawa, 'Long range prospect for trade and industrial co-operation in East and Southeast Asia', paper submitted to the international symposium on industrial policies for the '80s, Madrid, 5–9 May 1980, p. 8.

[66] *Fortune*, 5 May 1980.

[67] *Far Eastern Economic Review*, 4 April 1980.

[68] Traditionally, US firms turned to exports only when there was a slump in domestic demand and retreated when demand at home picked up. Thus, until recently, few maintained overseas sales offices. They exported through agents and engaged in few, if any, joint ventures.

[69] Dupont, for example, plans to concentrate on only one super-strong fibre, Kevlar, for use in bullet-proof vests, strong ropes and concrete reinforcement. Monsanto plans to focus all R and D on a single synthetic now under development.

[70] *The Economist*, 6 December 1980.

[71] *Far Eastern Economic Review*, 28 March 1980.

[72] Kurth, *op. cit.*, p. 5.
[73] *The Economist*, 6 December 1980.
[74] UNIDO, *World Industry in 1980*, New York, 1981, Table I.7, p. 43.
[75] *Ibid.*, pp. 160–1.
[76] For example, in the United Kingdom the proportion of household expenditure on food dropped from 2 per cent in 1977 to 1.8 per cent in 1980, representing part of a steady long-term decline.
[77] *Far Eastern Economic Review*, 11 July 1980.
[78] United Nations Centre on Transnational Corporations (UNCTC), *Transnational Corporations in Food and Beverage Processing*, ST/CTC/19, New York, 1980, pp. 217–78.
[79] Evidence for the US is found in 'Structure of Food Marketing', National Commission on Food Marketing, Technical Study, Washington D.C., June 1966. For West Germany, see K. Georg and A. Selberston, 'The causes and effects of mergers', in *Markets, Corporate Behavior and the State*, A. Jacquereen and H. W. de Jong (eds.), The Hague, 1976, p. 129.
[80] United Nations Centre on Transnational Corporations (UNCTC), *op. cit.*, pp. 217–78.
[81] UNIDO, *World Industry in 1980*, p. 172. Preparations of beef enter at a rate of 26 per cent, excepting a 17 per cent rate applied to GSP recipients.
[82] James H. Cassing, 'Alternatives to protectionism', in *Western Economies in Transition*, edited by Irving Leveson and Jimmy W. Wheeler, Croom Helm, London, 1980, p. 409.
[83] See General Agreement on Trade and Tariffs, Document MTN/27, 11 April 1979.
[84] *Far Eastern Economic Review*, 11 July 1980.
[85] UNIDO, *World Industry in 1980*, p. 159.
[86] *Ibid.*, p. 165.
[87] *Loc. cit.*
[88] W. S. Greig, 'The changing technological base in food processing', in Greig (ed.) *The Economics of Food Processing*, Westport, 1971, pp. 152–204.
[89] T. Horst, *At Home Abroad*, Bullinger, Cambridge, Mass., 1974, p. 56.
[90] TNC food processing operations are generally capital-intensive. See E. Peter, 'Agro businesses in underdeveloped agriculture', *Economic and Political Weekly*, Delhi, 17 July 1976, pp. 1065–80.

Part III

Agents for Industrialization in the Negotiating Process

Preface

Preceding chapters have addressed the restructuring process from various perspectives: (i) in terms of the interest groups that are instrumental in the choice of a development strategy, (ii) in terms of the global dispersion of industrial capacity for the manufacturing sector as a whole, and (iii) in terms of unique conditions prevailing in specific industrial branches. Two types of economic actors or decision-makers have come to play an increasingly important role regardless of the perspective chosen to examine the restructuring process.

One of these actors is the transnational corporation (TNC) whose role in the restructuring process has steadily grown. The interaction between domestic interest groups (in both the West and the LDCs) and TNCs has become more extensive and elaborate as these firms have expanded their international role. TNCs have proven themselves increasingly capable of achieving high levels of vertical and horizontal integration across a wide range of production and marketing activities. While the TNCs' role in the restructuring process is generally acknowledged if not fully appreciated, a second phenomenon—the emergence of the public manufacturing enterprise—has been less obvious. Trends in industrial organization have led to a gradual overlapping of activities in the public and private sectors, diluting the 'public' and 'private' character of a given industrial enterprise. The fusion of functions and responsibilities of

Preface

public and private enterprises is evident in both contracting and expanding industrial branches. Both groups increasingly rely on state agencies to create the conditions necessary for their survival or expansion. Simultaneously, governments are becoming more dependent on the performance of these enterprises to achieve national objectives written into their political programmes.

More than ever before, pricing and production decisions are arrived at, not with the help of Adam Smith's 'invisible hand', but through the interaction of corporate strategists, government planners and managers in the public sector. Elaborate networks for institutionalizing these relationships have been constructed, and protracted negotiation and bargaining have become regular features of policy formulation and modification in both the West and the Third World. Such networks, we believe, will eventually constitute an integral part of the restructuring process in the Third World.

Chapter VI

The Transnational Corporation as an Agent for Industrialization

The importance of the transnational corporation (TNC) as an agent of international economic restructuring is generally recognized in the voluminous and rapidly growing literature.[1] In this chapter we identify some salient features of TNC investment and financing policy, and compare these policies with those of domestic investors in order to assess the role they can play in the industrialization of the Third World.

It is important to stress at the outset that an analysis of TNC operations cannot be carried out within a narrowly defined economic framework. TNCs have demonstrated a remarkable capacity to integrate diverse economic structures. They have bridged the distance between economic and social systems with avowedly opposing objectives. They span widely distanced markets and have evolved organizational structures possessed of a surprisingly high degree of adaptability and flexibility. In short, TNCs are among the most dynamic agents of change in the post-war world.

This does not mean that TNCs are omnipotent. The past twenty-five years have revealed many important weaknesses and vulnerabilities. Of particular significance is the evolving relationship between TNCs and national state bureaucracies. A central feature of the international socio-economic system in the late twentieth century is the growing interdependence of its leading political and economic decision-makers. Governments and TNCs are becoming increasingly conscious of the fact that they cannot 'will each other out of existence' and that they are participants in a protracted bargaining process from which exit of either party is not practicable. An appreciation of each other's potential, policies and objectives can be a basis for meaningful dialogue. TNC investment in LDCs can contribute significantly towards industrial restructuring in accordance with changing comparative advantages. TNCs can channel finance away from contracting industrial branches in the West and to expanding ones in the Third World. They can also contribute towards an expansion of these branches by investing a large proportion of their profits. TNCs may, however, invest in industrial branches that do not reflect the comparative advantages of the host country, thereby limiting their development impact. It is, therefore, appropriate to begin this chapter by identifying the factors which induce a TNC to invest in the Third World.

6.1 TNC objectives and Third World industrialization

Why do TNCs invest in the industries of Third World countries? Neo-classical theory has identified cost factors as being among the most important determinants of industrial location and relocation. Thus, the extent to which governments of LDCs reduce input costs of specific industries should be a significant indicator of the degree to which relocation takes place and growth is spurred. Evidence that a deliberate policy of cost reduction has induced industrial growth acceleration can be cited for some LDCs—notably Brazil and Mexico.[2] The government's ability to alter cost structures depends on a large number of complex factors. First, one must estimate the relative importance of different inputs to the industrial cost structure and then estimate the extent to which it is in the power of LDC governments to reduce these costs. Second, much will also depend on the elasticity of substitution that exists within given production structures on the one hand, and the extent to which the industrial demand for a specific input is price elastic on the other. Third, if an industrial activity—notably in the food and mineral processing branches—is integrated within a larger production complex, a reduction in the input prices of one product may not outweigh other considerations that determine the level of investment and the industrial location of the units producing this product. Fourth, the decision to reduce the input price of a particular industrial branch may be contested by actors interested in maintaining its present location or its present level of production. These actors are suppliers of inputs for TNCs or LDC governments. Either or both may reduce the price of inputs for a particular production process thereby inducing the TNC to alter its input composition, its output mix or to change its industrial strategy.

Thus, industrial relocation is not simply a response to differentials in input prices (even if we include indirect inputs in a producing process like communication networks, worker welfare facilities and other infrastructural developments that are necessarily implied in any major programme of industrial growth). Since the early 1960s, studies in the theory of the growth of the firm[3] have argued that managerial behaviour is much too complex to be adequately explained by the conventional theory of production. These studies stressed the existence of a mutiplicity of managerial goals, arguing that in markets characterized by imperfect competition, management possesses significant scope for exercising discretion. Management may be content with a 'satisfying' profit level and choose an objective of maximizing growth—as measured by sales or net assets—since the latter is a more important determinant of the power of the management élite and the security it enjoys. This interpretation of managerial behaviour would suggest that market characteristics and the structure of industrial enterprises are important determinants of the level and distribution of investment within specific industrial branches. Thus, a host of studies has found that a firm's ability to respond to technological changes and to accept new processes of production and management were related to the size of the firm, its market share and the rate of growth of the industrial branch as well as management's perception of cost and profit opportunities.[4] Baldwin and Childs have argued that industries in which a few firms predominate are slow to adapt to technological change—the smaller firms would wait for the dominant firms' reaction to the technological innovation possibilities.[5]

Firm behaviour may also modify long-run investment opportunities in response to cost reduction. Davidson's study of innovation in the United States shows that, after taking account of changes in factor costs, firms concentrate their R and D expenditures on those inputs that have most recently become relatively expensive. The resulting innovations ensure that the cost of these inputs is reduced and a comparative cost advantage is created in product lines that are relatively intensive in their use of factors that were originally considered as scarce.[6] This practice offsets, to some extent, any tendency to redeploy resources to branches where input costs have been reduced.

We see, therefore, that when considering the consequences of redeployment and restructuring for specific industrial fields, possible cost reductions and technological innovation on the one hand are closely interrelated with organizational structures and market structures on the other. Among the latter group of factors account must be taken of a host of interrelated circumstances. Investment levels and the impact of this investment upon the economy of the LDC will be affected by the form of ownership of the leading enterprises in the industrial branch. The extent to which foreign capital and technology is required for expansion is an important determinant of the impact of a given level of investment in a particular industrial branch. Moreover, foreign capital, technology and access to foreign export markets can be combined in a variety of ways each involving a qualitatively different mix of costs and benefits. Thus, industrial branches may be categorized as those in which public sector participation is dominant, those which rely mainly upon private sector initiatives in LDCs and those where expansion requires collaboration with TNCs. This latter group may again be subdivided into: (a) industries in which TNCs operate through the establishment of subsidiaries; (b) industries in which they enter into joint ventures with Third World public or private entrepreneurs; and (c) industries in which foreign capital and technology can be obtained largely through licensing and contracting arrangements. The type of TNC involvement in specific industrial branches is partly determined by the industry's foreign capital, technology and information requirements. In general, the greater these requirements, the greater the likelihood that the TNC will exercise effective control over units located in LDCs.[7] Similarly, the form of TNC collaboration may also limit the access to foreign markets.

Different industrial branches have different potential for permitting LDC governments to combine direct investment, joint venture and licensing agreements. In some instances 'breaking open the

The Transnational Corporation as an Agent for Industrialization

package'—i.e. combining joint ventures and licensing arrangements with the operation of TNC subsidiaries—may imply significant gains.[8] Different equity and control structures also have different implications for technology choice. TNCs and large public sector corporations may exhibit a preference for capital-intensive technologies,[9] a bias with significant implications for income distribution and the development of a skilled labour force. Moreover, the extent to which technologies adopted in one industry 'spill over' to others depends on the backward and forward linkages of that industry and the rest of the economy. Technological diffusion is also influenced by the terms on which acquisition was negotiated in the first instance. In general, the wider the diffusion of technology in the industrialized world, the less costly is its acquisition (separate from ownership) for the LDCs.

The diffusion of technology varies widely among industries. In the pharmaceutical industry, as far as patented drugs are concerned, scientific information may be specific to individual firms. In the aluminium industry scientific information may be available to all the firms and, in the case of cement plants, technological information is widely available to experts and technicians outside the industry. Thus, the cost of acquiring technical know-how diverges significantly.

Another set of factors to be considered when assessing the economic impact of investments by TNCs pertains to the structural characteristics of international markets. For many mineral and manufactured exports there are powerful restrictions on market access. The cost of acquiring a distribution channel may be considerable. The need to evaluate international marketing conditions in different industries raises the possibility of co-operation between LDC governments. Such co-operation clearly played an important role in allowing the OPEC countries to obtain unprecedented benefits from increasing the price of oil since 1973. Attempts at organizing other producer cartels have generally failed to produce the desired results, however.[10] In many oligopolistic markets the possibility of co-operation among LDCs or between TNCs and LDCs to improve their ability to control price and output conditions remains a tangible one.

The organizational and decision-making structures of TNCs are also important determinants of the impact of investment expansion where these firms are significantly involved. The central headquarters office plays a supervisory and co-ordinating role in all TNCs[11]—indeed the dominance of headquarters over branch offices distinguishes a TNC from an international holding company. The extent of centralization varies considerably, however, and branches and affiliates may have a substantial degree of autonomy. The degree of centralization may be determined by the original motivation for international expansion. Dunning distinguishes three patterns of TNC developments: (a) those designed to secure supplies of raw material—so-called 'backward vertical operations', (b) those designed to protect or secure markets—'forward vertical operations', and (c) horizontal operations within an industrial branch.[12] The extent of centralization may reflect these original concerns and motivations. 'Product based' multinationals—i.e. those that delineate authority and responsibility in terms of production and distribution of specific products—are also more decentralized and permit greater autonomy to their subsidiaries than area-based TNCs.

In the next section we present a review of the existing evidence on the impact of TNC investment on industrial restructuring in the Third World. This contribution can be assessed by identifying the impact of TNC investment on growth, on the utilization of resources and on the level of exports of the host economies. The greater the long-term impact of TNC investment on growth, the greater the likelihood that it acts as stimulant to investment reallocation in accordance with changing production opportunities. Similarly, if TNC investment generates significant levels of employment it will contribute to a more effective utilization of resources in the LDCs that are labour-abundant economies. Finally, if TNCs can be an effective instrument for increasing access to world manufacturing. markets, LDCs can be encouraged to take advantage of their changing international competitive position and industrial restructuring will be in accordance with changes in comparative costs. The next section evaluates the evidence on the contribution that TNC investment has made to the expansion of industrial production, capital formation and employment and the access that LDCs have acquired in international markets for a diverse range of industrial products.

6.2 The developmental impact of investment by TNCs

(a) Impact on growth

Conventional economic analysis regards foreign investment as a positive contributant to income growth in the host country provided: (i) there is unemployment of labour and shortage of capital; (ii) the elasticity of substitution between domestic saving and foreign capital is high and growth is constrained by foreign exchange scarcity; (iii) foreign capital is allocated 'efficiently'.

Any beneficial income effect may, of course, be partially offset by a decline in the host country's terms of trade due to a (possible) rise in the productivity of the export sector and a (probable) increase in foreign exchange spending to service foreign capital. In general, there is a strong presumption that the inflow of foreign capital is beneficial to host countries. Borrowing is usually presumed to take place under competitive conditions and governments are seen as sufficiently powerful to offset monopolistic tendencies. Externalities are generally held to be beneficial. Extensive work has been done within this analytical framework by many authors although the models developed are highly abstract. Their empirical applications[13] require a large range of simplifying assumptions, making an evaluation of real-world problems very difficult. Externalities, market characteristics and interaction of economic and socio-political factors cannot be adequately taken into account.

Some studies, broadly within the neo-classical tradition, lead to empirical results that are at variance with the traditional view that foreign investment has a positive impact on the growth of the host economy. Researchers have found a negative association between the inflow of foreign resources and domestic saving. It is argued that frequently the degree of TNC penetration (defined as the ratio of capital stock controlled by TNCs to the total capital stock of the host country) is negatively associated with the subsequent pace of income growth in the host country. This relationship is described as 'particularly strong for less developed countries with a large modernized sector'.[14] In other words, the higher the level of TNC involvement in an LDC in a given year, the less probable that the country will achieve high rates of growth in subsequent years. This empirical finding lends support to the 'decapitalization thesis'.

The International Economy and Industrial Development

According to this, TNC operations reduce the supply of funds available for investment, transferring resources out of the host economy by repatriating declared profits or by over-pricing production inputs. This drain of investment resources leads to an inevitable reduction in subsequent growth. The possible negative relationship between TNC penetration and growth in the host country has also been explained in terms of its impact on the domestic industrial structure. In particular, if it can be shown that an extensive TNC presence is associated with high levels of industrial concentration that contribute to income inequalities and a rapid depletion of investment funds in agriculture, then the possibility of a 'saturation point' for TNC involvement seems plausible. In such a case domestic demand fails to rise sufficiently, import substitution possibilities become increasingly difficult and foreign trade opportunities are limited by protectionist policies of trading partners and the reluctance of TNC subsidiaries to encroach upon the markets of sister companies. Hence, profit rates fall, investment levels are reduced and the high growth rates associated with high levels of domestic and foreign investment do not pertain.

In view of these possibilities it is important to assess the impact of TNC investment on the industrial structure of the host LDCs. If TNCs absorb a disproportionately high share of investment resources, then policy measures are called for to constrain the firms' ability to transfer domestic investment resources on the one hand, and to make the domestic deployment of these resources more attractive on the other. The former objective can be achieved most effectively by reducing concentration and increasing competition within the manufacturing sector.

Evidence on levels of concentration in LDCs is sparse. In Latin America, industries with the highest levels of concentration are tobacco, rubber, basic metals and rubber manufacture. Some studies have investigated the relationship between TNC penetration and concentration. They found that TNCs predominate in industrial branches with the highest levels of concentration in Brazil, Mexico and some Central American countries.[15] However, there is little systematic evidence on the impact of TNC policies on levels of concentration within specific industrial branches in LDCs. It is sometimes argued that TNCs have a strong preference to enter new markets through mergers or takeovers—particularly in the 'low' technology industries.[16] However, excessively high levels of concentration in specific industrial branches may be due to factors that have little to do with prevailing ownership forms. For example, economies of scale or production technologies may lead to wider differences in concentration levels of different industrial branches than do marketing or financial policies. If TNCs adopt technologies that are more capital-intensive than those of comparable domestic enterprises, then the degree of firm concentration is likely to be pronounced. Evidence on this count is mixed, however, as will be shown in the next sub-section.

The possibility that TNCs may reduce the volume of funds available for investment in host countries can be countered by increasing linkages between domestic firms and transnational corporations. Little systematic research has been devoted to an assessment of the impact of TNC operations on the performance of domestic enterprises. However, there is some evidence of increased subcontracting in India and a clear tendency to increase locally purchased components. This implies greater autonomy for domestic subsidiaries. Imports as a proportion of total components have been declining. They represented 62.5 per cent of automotive manufacturing output in 1956, but declined to less than 4 per cent by 1969.[17] In Morocco and Peru the share of procurement from local firms to in-house manufacturing content was considerably lower than in India. This may be due to differences in levels of industrial development and in government policy. In India the Government has followed a policy of encouraging the local manufacture of components and local procurement. Moreover, Indian policies, particularly through their licensing procedures, have made it expensive for TNC subsidiaries to move into the manufacture of components and have encouraged small enterprises instead. Local procurement has also been stimulated by the Indian Government's emphasis on import substitution. Studies have often stressed that a main determinant of linkage creation is host government policy. Measures focusing on the specifics of the process of the creation of linkages seem to be more effective if they are implemented in the framework of a broad industrialization strategy, where actions related to the stimulation of TNC linkages are guided by the dynamic comparative advantages of the host country.[18]

In conclusion, government policy can modify the impact of TNC investment on the LDC economy in many ways by reducing levels of industrial concentration and increasing the domestic linkages of foreign investment. If successful, these policies can increase the attractiveness of the domestic economy to foreign investors by ensuring a high growth of domestic demand. Sustaining this growth, however, requires that investment be concentrated in industrial branches with international comparative advantages, the development of which requires an optimum utilization of productive resources.

(b) Impact on employment

Since most LDCs are labour-abundant economies, sustained growth implies a substantial long-term expansion in employment. Estimates of total direct employment provided by TNCs—admittedly subject to a large margin of error—range from 13 to 30 million.[19] Even if the most liberal estimates are accepted, the proportion of total global employment accounted for by TNCs is only 1.3 per cent. In terms of industrial employment, TNCs contribute approximately 4.8 per cent of the job total.[20] In the Third World, TNCs are credited with the creation of between 2 to 4 million jobs (representing 0.3 per cent of total employment and 2 per cent of total industrial employment).[21] These figures show that employment generation by TNCs is mainly concentrated in western countries.

Among certain LDCs, however—Brazil, Mexico, Peru, Singapore and South Korea—employment in TNCs is a significant proportion of total industrial employment. In some instances TNCs accounted for one fifth of a country's total industrial employment in the mid-1970s. Generally employment generation by these firms seems to be concentrated in the manufacturing sector although the investment of TNCs is fairly evenly spread between manufacturing and the extractive industries.

In Mexico and South Korea, TNCs account for a large proportion of direct employment in heavy industries such as chemicals, petrochemicals, electrical machinery and metal products. In Peru, which is at an earlier stage of industrial development, direct employment generation by TNCs is also significant in consumer goods industries such as beverages and tobacco.

Depending on the extent of backward and forward linkages, TNCs are also capable of generating significant indirect employment. This is relatively limited in the extractive industries, but in manufacturing it may be substantial. For South Korea, estimates of the indirect employment effects have been substantial; investment by TNCs generated a total of 102,000 jobs through backward linkages with domestic producers.[22] However, the indirect employment effects attributed to TNCs are likely to be of less significance than those of domestic manufacturers since the former firms are larger net importers of both raw material and capital than are local firms.[23] Moreover, the output mix of TNC subsidiaries may not be particularly suitable for generating high employment in some LDCs. Although there is no firm evidence to support the opinion, many observers suggest that subsidiaries providing the domestic market emphasize the production of 'luxury' goods destined for consumption by the higher income groups.[24] Because luxury goods are relatively capital-intensive, their production generates relatively less employment.

The investor's choice of technique is another important determinant of the investment-employment relationship. Stewart has argued that technologies imported into the Third World are fairly rigid[25] and the production function methodologies employed to estimate substitution elasticities in the LDCs are based on unrealistic assumptions yielding overestimates.[26] Technologies employed by TNCs are likely to be relatively rigid since they tend to predominate in modern, complex industries with continuous production processes. The rigidity is also enhanced by increased vertical integration between the units of a TNC family. In general the literature suggests that technological adaptations by TNCs are modest.[27] Evidence regarding the difference in factor intensity between TNC affiliates and local firms is mixed. A number of studies[28] fail to find any significant difference in the factor intensities of local and foreign firms operating in LDCs. Other studies have found that foreign firms use more capital-intensive technologies than local ones.[29] Clearly no general statement can be made on the relative difference between TNCs and local firms, as far as their ability to adapt technology to local conditions is concerned. However, there are circumstances in which TNC subsidiaries have been induced to deploy relatively labour-intensive technologies in various Asian and Latin American countries.

(c) Impact on exports

In most LDCs an export oriented industrialization strategy cannot be effectively pursued without co-operation from TNCs, primarily for reasons of limited market access. Clearly, any redistribution of global industrial capacity in line with international patterns of comparative advantage requires TNC support. Market barriers and protectionist policies can effectively frustrate this pattern of international specialization. It is essential, therefore, to explore the potential of the TNC as an instrument for overcoming protectionism.

TNCs have rapidly increased their level of international involvement during the past decade. The United Nations Commission on Transnational Corporations has estimated that over the period 1971–6 the foreign subsidiaries of 251 TNCs grew 25 per cent faster than the parent companies. A large proportion of exports of western countries is conducted by transnationals and there is some evidence that this proportion may be increasing.[30]

The expanded role of TNCs in the export sector of western countries has led many researchers to assume that they have also played an important role in the articulation of the export-led growth strategy adopted by some newly industrializing economies. In the past, foreign firms played a dominant role in the organization of international trade in primary commodities and it was thought that they would adapt with relative ease to the LDCs' drive to expand manufactured exports. A small number of countries—Argentina, Brazil, Colombia, Hong Kong, India, Malaysia, Mexico, Pakistan, Singapore and South Korea—currently account for about 60 per cent of the Third World's manufactured exports. Six—Brazil, Hong Kong, India, Mexico, Singapore and South Korea—account for approximately 57 per cent of the stock of direct foreign investment in the non-OPEC developing world.[31] In many of these countries TNC subsidiaries provide over 20 per cent of manufactured exports. However, the three rapidly industrializing East Asian economies—Hong Kong, Singapore and South Korea—are not included within this group. The share of US TNCs in total manufactured exports from LDCs fell from 10 per cent in 1966 to 8.7 in 1974. This share has declined in all major regions of the Third World, even in Latin America where US subsidiaries have traditionally been important sources of exports.

Two aspects of the TNCs' trade have taken on added importance over the past decade. First, intra-firm trade has expanded tremendously. Estimates for the early 1970s indicate that 50 per cent of US exports are of this type. Corresponding percentages for Canada, Sweden and the United Kingdom are 60, 29 and 39 respectively. Second, tariff provisions for off-share assembly have encouraged the rapid growth of international subcontracting. United States imports under tariff items 807.00 and 806.30 have grown rapidly. In 1966 their gross value represented 1.6 per cent of the LDCs' manufactured exports to the US. By 1974 this figure had risen to over 7 per cent. Five LDCs accounted for 85 per cent of imports permitted under tariff items 807.00 and 806.30 to the US, however.

What are the factors that influence a transnational's decision to expand exports? Lall has attempted to answer this question for US transnationals. He hypothesizes that the decision whether to invest in a foreign market or to export to it will be influenced by the extent to which monopolistic advantages enjoyed by TNCs are internationally transferable. The smaller the potential transferability of these monopolistic advantages in a particular product line, the greater the inducement to export.[32] Lall finds that non-transferable advantages (technological intensity[33] and the possession of skill advantages—generally regarded as factors with low transfer capacity internationally) are closely related with export growth.[34]

Assessing the export orientation of TNC subsidiaries is an important first step in determining their impact on the industrialization process in LDCs. Export oriented affiliates operating in the Third World are unlikely to create domestic linkages because they are concerned primarily with transferring complex technologies to LDCs in order to serve established world markets. Such 'border' industries—the electronic industrial complexes of Mexico and Singapore, for example—create very few domestic linkages in

LDCs. They rarely use locally available components. Thus, Kionig found that the Mexican economy, despite its fairly advanced level of industrial development compared to the other LDCs, could not supply its border industries even with one per cent of their input requirements in 1975.[35] Domestic linkages are also likely to be limited in the case of export oriented TNC subsidiaries that transfer only a (labour-intensive) part of the production process to an LDC. Once again the electronic industry is a good example. Here, 'the rapidly changing technology, the demanding specifications and requirements of cost minimization reduce the scope for domestic linkages to practically nothing.'[36]

Significant domestic linkages can be created by firms that switch from import substitution to export oriented policies. These TNC affiliates generally operate standardized mature technologies. They have usually been located in LDCs for a relatively long period and have developed strong linkages with local markets and domestic suppliers. In some industries, such as textiles, footwear and leather manufacturing, relatively small foreign firms, many of them based in other Third World countries (e.g. Hong Kong and India) are quite common. They are likely to be as labour-intensive as their local counterparts.

Governments must continuously aim for a strategy that attracts TNC investment to those industrial branches where the country has a potential international comparative advantage. They must seek an understanding with TNCs in order to overcome protectionist barriers. These barriers are increasingly taking the form of administrative controls and are often least restrictive in the case of intra-firm trade. Such an understanding can induce TNCs to reduce non-tariff barriers—particularly in restrictive business practices—that are sometimes imposed at a heavy cost to developing countries.[37] Similarly, co-operation can lead to an improved access to technological resources and marketing and distributive networks.

On the whole, the contribution of TNCs to industrial restructuring in LDCs can perhaps be described as modest. The long-run impact of TNC investment on domestic production and domestic investment has been shown to be negative, particularly in LDCs that have a large modernized sector. TNCs frequently have a

The Transnational Corporation as an Agent for Industrialization

technology of production that is 'rigid' and generates little employment within the host economies. They have not played a major role in the export expansion drives of the rapidly industrializing South-East Asian countries. The review does suggest, however, that there are a number of ways in which the TNCs can be induced to reorient their investment strategies so as to increase their developmental impact. Domestic linkages can be fostered by promoting local subcontracting. Technological flexibility can be encouraged by changing work patterns and facilitating the use of lower quality inputs. An export orientation may be stimulated by emphasizing the establishment of joint ventures between TNCs and leading domestic exporters. Many other such policies may be suggested. Governments in the Third World must base their policies on a realistic assessment of the TNC's corporate strategies and objectives. The next section consists of an empirical investigation of the determinants of TNC investment and growth. The results will allow us to estimate the costs of this investment—in terms of its impact on industrial concentration and on the level of resource transfer from the host economy—and will be a basis for suggesting policies which modifyTNC corporate strategy and make it an instrument for achieving industrial restructuring.

6.3 Policies of transnational corporations: an empirical investigation

This section attempts to answer two questions: (1) What are the main determinants of the growth of TNCs and of their investment behaviour? and (2) What are the main determinants of their profitability?

These questions have been widely studied theoretically and empirically, within the context of the theory of the growth of the firm and the theory of investment. There is a wide range of explanations and findings about the behaviour of firms with respect to their investment and financing behaviour. Foreign investors have also been extensively studied in this context, but in the words of a recent study 'there is still a large grey area of semi-ignorance, illuminated only by fragmentary and scattered evidence from small samples or else provided on a highly aggregated basis'.[38] The size of the sample taken here is also small, but it is hoped that some of the issues discussed may provide insight into aspects of TNC policies that are useful in developing a realistic assessment of their impact on industrialization in LDCs.

This study relies mainly on data gathered from balance sheets and profit and loss statements of individual companies collected for the United Kingdom and India. Standardized 'Analyses of Accounts' were available for India. For the UK documents were procured directly from the companies themselves. Company accounts are, of course, subject to wide margins of errors and are not a wholly satisfactory criterion for evaluating performance (particularly when many of the costs are determined on the basis of transactions internal to the firm and its affiliates). Moreover, the estimates are generally based on accounting conventions that do not adequately represent the impact of inflation on the valuation of fixed assets. There are many important errors of omission particularly in the Appropriation of Income Statement. Items such as wages and purchases of raw material are often absent and the 'Sources and Uses of Funds' statements omit 'book' transactions, i.e. transactions internal to the company, such as scrip issues, revaluation of fixed assets and the conversion of debenture stock to ordinary or preference shares. Obviously, these omissions are important when one is considering consolidated statements. Subsidiary accounts could not be procured in the case of the UK companies and the necessary adjustments could not be made.

Thus, our data are subject to many shortcomings and limitations. However, the existence of a broadly similar framework of presentation and similar company objectives (most companies seek to maximize profits or growth and a preference for either objective does not lead to significant differences in business strategy[39]) ensures that there is a basic consistency in these figures. It can be predicted that, generally speaking, fixed assets will be undervalued in balance sheet statements. 'It is considered almost criminal to over value and prudent to undervalue'.[40] Accounting conventions remain fairly stable over time and across continents.

The present sample was drawn from two sources. The first set was thirty British manufacturing firms selected from the list of British firms in *Fortune's* analysis of the 500 largest industrial companies outside the US. Balance sheets and income statements could not be procured for about 46 per cent of UK manufacturing enterprises included in Fortune's list. For the thirty firms included in our study, consolidated accounts and financial statements were collected for the period 1975–9. The second set of information consisted of forty-six Indian manufacturing subsidiaries that existed over the period 1966–71 and were judged to be affiliates or subsidiaries of TNCs by the Indian Government.

In terms of the value of net assets, the British firms in the sample accounted for approximately 38 per cent of the net assets of the listed manufacturing companies recorded by the United Kingdom Business Monitor for the years 1975–77.[41] In terms of sales the companies included in the study accounted for 53 per cent of sales by the sixty-five largest manufacturing companies in the UK.

The extent of overseas involvement of these firms could not be ascertained with accuracy. However, there are grounds for believing that foreign investment in LDCs by the group of companies included in this study was significant. Over the period 1975–8,[42] investment by British firms in the manufacturing sector of LDCs constituted about 22 per cent of their total overseas manufacturing investment.[43] In the early 1970s 19 per cent of the stock of British foreign manufacturing investment was in LDCs (as compared to 17 per cent for the US and 28 per cent for West Germany).[44] Moreover, over the period 1975–8 foreign manufacturing investment by British firms grew at an annual rate of 39 per cent. Morgan has estimated that for the years 1975 and 1976 British foreign manufacturing investment constituted 4 per cent of gross domestic fixed capital formation and 24 per cent of domestic manufacturing investment. In terms of the first ratio, the UK is clearly leading both Japan and West Germany.[45] For a group of large British companies the same study reports that overseas production constituted 34.7 per cent of the group's output[46] and was equivalent to 215 per cent of their exports from the home country.[47]

The 'multinationalization' of British big business proceeded rapidly during the period 1950–70.[48] The number of firms with more than six foreign subsidiaries increased from 20 per cent of the total number of British firms to over 50 per cent. 'Effectively all the top 100 British manufacturing companies by the early 1970s were

The International Economy and Industrial Development

multinational in operation.'[49]

It was possible to gather data on the number and location of the subsidiaries and affiliates of nineteen companies in our sample. Table VI.1 gives the distribution of these subsidiaries. The sample mean for the total number of subsidiaries was 125.6; the sample mean for LDC subsidiaries was 24.8. As expected, the number of subsidiaries in LDCs is positively associated with the total number of subsidiaries. The firms included in the sample were located in eight industries. However, three industries—food, metal products and chemicals—contained two thirds of the respondents. The largest number was in the food manufacturing industries (nine). It is, of course, difficult to classify respondent TNCs into industrial groups. Most span a number of industrial branches and actively seek vertical integration of their production structures.

Table VI.1. Distribution of subsidiaries and affiliates of companies in the UK sample

Number of subsidiaries	Number of firms	Number of subsidiaries in LDCs	Number of firms
Below 20	0	0	2
20–49	5	1–5	4
50–99	4	6–20	5
100–199	4	21–50	5
≥200	6	> 50	3

As far as the Indian data are concerned, net sales of these companies were about 19 per cent of the net sales of the 300 largest Indian public corporations. In the absence of a proper scientific sample design it is not possible to assess the 'representativeness' of this sample. But it is clear that these firms acount for a significant proportion of foreign manufacturing investment and that their policies are likely to be of considerable importance in determining the overall impact of TNC investment on the Indian economy. The firms are located in the chemical, petrochemical, machinery, electrical machinery, food, metal manufacturing and transport equipment industrial branches. The largest group is in the chemical industry.

The Transnational Corporation as an Agent for Industrialization

The subsequent analysis concentrates on analysing the relationship between financial estimates of growth, size, profitability and investment for the TNCs and affiliates included in our sample. An attempt will be made to study the impact of TNC growth on the level of industrial concentration, and to identify factors influencing investment growth and profitability. If it can be shown that TNC investment leads to increased industrial concentration or that the domestic economic environment does not determine investment behaviour, it can be concluded that the growth of TNCs in host LDCs is a hindrance to 'efficient' industrial restructuring. The first question addressed is the relationship between size and growth of firms' assets. This investigation is useful for studying the impact of TNC growth on industrial concentration in the host economy.

(a) Growth and size

The literature on the theory of the growth of the firm is of post-World War II vintage.[50] This theory breaks with its neo-classical progenitor and treats growth as a strategic choice available to management which may, in certain circumstances, prefer a strategy which emphasizes growth maximization rather than profit maximization. The two major themes that emerge from this literature seem to be the relationship between growth and size of the firm on the one hand, and growth and the level of profitability on the other.

The former question has been addressed mainly through investigations focused on testing 'The Law of Proportionate Effect' (Gibrat's Law). This law has aroused a great deal of interest because it can easily be verified by fairly simple analytical methods. It states that the probability of the firm growing at any (given) rate is independent of the initial size of the firm. Hence the 'Law' implies that there is no 'optimal' size of the firm.[51] Neither assertion is generally supported by the modern theory of the growth of the firm. Penrose argues that firms of medium size tend to grow faster than smaller or very large firms while Marris maintains that, in general, a firm's 'willingness to grow' beyond a certain size may be reduced because of the nature of the association between growth and profitability.[52] Investigators have tried to determine which of these situations hold in the real world.

The 'Law' also implies that the rate of growth of a firm in one period does not influence its rate of growth in a subsequent period. The 'Law' further hypothesizes that there is an inherent tendency towards increasing concentration (for if large and small firms grow at the same rates, the large firms will tend to get larger over time).

In order to test the Law of Proportionate Effect for the sample of companies in this study, the following linear regression models were applied to the data:[53]

$$G = a + bS + \varepsilon$$
$$\log G = a + b \log S + \varepsilon$$

where G is the difference in the net assets of the firm at the beginning and end of the period under study measured as a ratio of the net assets at the beginning of the period, and S is the net assets of the firm at the beginning of the period.

These models were tested in order to ascertain whether the growth rates varied in some regular way with the size indicator. The equations were tested separately for the British and Indian data. Neither the regression coefficient nor the coefficient of determination was found to be significantly different from zero at a 5 per cent level in either equation. This implies that no simple linear or log linear relationship exists between size and growth for the firms in the sample. The findings do not, of course, conclusively establish that the 'Law' operates—growth may have a non-linear relationship with initial size.

In the case of the British sample the number of firms is too few to divide into different size classes and test for a significance of difference in the means and standard deviations of growth rates in different size classes. In the case of India, Table VI.2 shows that there is some form of variation of average growth with firm size. Using the Welch Aspin test[54] (which does not assume equal variance of growth rates) it was found that the mean growth rates of size classes I and IV, II and IV, and III and I were significantly different. Therefore, a tentative conclusion is that a systematic, though weak, association exists between size and growth. Larger firms tend to grow more slowly than the rleatively smaller TNCs.

Differences in the standard deviation of the different size classes were also tested.[55] Once again it was clear that the larger subsidiaries enjoyed a more even growth performance than the smaller ones. Although their average growth rates are significantly lower than those of relatively smaller firms, the larger subsidiaries demonstrated relative stability. In the case of the UK an earlier study by Singh and Whittington found that for a sample of over 200 firms there was a clear association between initial size and growth rate dispersion during the period 1948–60, although no difference in the growth of firms of different sizes was observed. However, for the period 1954–60 firms in the largest size class had an average growth rate that was (statistically) significantly greater than that of most other size classes.[56]

In order to test for the relationship between initial firm size and the variability of growth, the following regression model was applied to the UK and Indian data:

$$sG = a + bS + \varepsilon$$

where sG is the standard deviation of the growth of individual firms over the specified time period in the two country samples. For the UK firms a significant (negative) regression estimate was obtained and the value of R^2 was 0.30. Thus, some evidence exists that size is negatively associated with the dispersion of growth over time. Larger firms tend to grow more steadily than smaller ones. In the case of the Indian data the regression coefficient was again negative but not significantly different from zero and the value of the coefficient of determination was very small. Thus, no relationship between size and the variation of growth could be discerned for the Indian subsidiaries.

The validity of the Law of Proportionate Effect has also been tested by studying the relationship between the logarithms of firm sizes at the beginning and end of a time period. In the regression equation

$$\log S_{t+1} = a + b \log S_t + \varepsilon$$

a value of unity for b implies that all firms, irrespective of size, grow at the same rate of proportionate growth.[57] This equation was estimated for the British and Indian sample of companies. The estimate for b for the British sample was 0.997, not significantly different from unity. The result contrasts with Singh and Whittington's findings of a positive relationship between growth and opening size,[58] but supports Hart's evidence of the validity of the Law of Proportionate Effect for a sample of British firms.[59] For India the

The International Economy and Industrial Development

Table VI.2. Average rates of growth of firms in different size classes: India

Size class	Mean growth rate	Standard deviation	Number of firms
I. (less than Rs 5 million)	115.75	134.80	15
II. (between Rs 5 and 10 million)	57.41	61.01	10
III. (between Rs 10 and 20 million)	33.76	39.16	12
IV. (above Rs 20 million)	30.79	39.82	9

value for the regression coefficient was 0.89, significantly different from zero and below unity. This implies that the smaller TNC subsidiaries were growing at a more rapid rate than the larger ones and that the gap between them was closing. The value of the coefficient of determination for the Indian sample, however, was only 0.46 (as compared to 0.91 for the UK firms), and there is some doubt about the extent to which the estimated equation correctly represents the distribution of the Indian growth rates. In general the result is not strong enough to lead to a conclusive rejection of the possibility of the operation of the Law of Proportionate Effect.

Notably, the present results do not contradict the evidence on increasing concentration presented by Prais for the UK.[60] He found that the share of the top 100 manufacturing companies increased from about 20 per cent of net output in 1950 to almost 50 per cent by 1970.[61] Our results for the UK firms are broadly consistent with the operation of the Law of Proportionate Effect, and the Law has often been interpreted as implying increased industrial concentration. This is so, however, only if the Law operates in what has been described as a 'strong form'.[62] If, as Kalecki argues, the probability of growing by a given proportion declines with the size of the firm,[63] the operation of the Law need not imply increasing concentration over time. In any case, the small number of firms in our sample makes it impossible to reach definite conclusions about the impact of TNC growth on levels of industrial concentration in Britain. In the case of Indian firms on the other hand, neither of the major propositions derived from the Law of Proportionate Effect—that (1) average growth rates and (2) their dispersion will be similar for different size classes—is supported by this analysis. We have found that growth declines systematically with opening size; smaller firms grow more rapidly. This finding might provide some support to the 'decapitalization' thesis according to which, after the 'saturation' point, growth in TNC investment tends to fall off. There is thus some evidence that the growth of TNC subsidiaries has been a factor in reducing overall industrial concentration in India.

Industrial concentration may be studied from both a static and a dynamic point of view. The former would involve the use of an index of concentration which would measure the predominance of the largest firms in the economy over a time period. The dynamic approach, on the other hand, examines the way in which firms in the industrial sector have changed size classes as a result of growth. A 'transition matrix' has been built to study the internal mobility of firms in the Indian sample.

Table VI.3 shows, for example, that 20 per cent of the firms in the smallest size class at the beginning of the period remained in the

Table VI.3. Transition matrix for measuring Indian subsidiaries' internal mobility

Opening size	Closing size (percentages)			
	Lowest	Second lowest	Second highest	Highest
I. (lower than Rs 5 million)	20	50	10	20
II. (between Rs 5 and 10 million)	0	46.6	40	13.4
III. (between Rs 10 and 20 million)	0	14.3	71.4	14.3
IV. (above Rs 20 million)				100

	Proportion of total firms changing classes by (percentages)			
− 1	0	+ 1	+ 2	+ 3
2.10	60.82	23.91	6.52	4.34

same size class at the end of the period. On the other hand, 50 per cent went up by one size class. Among firms in class III at the beginning of the period, 71 per cent remained in that class while an equal proportion (14 per cent) moved up or down by one size class. The results are known to be downward biased since construction of the matrices does not permit firms in the largest opening size class (IV) to move up. For example, the top three firms in class IV had 'closing sizes' over 25 per cent in excess of their opening sizes. If these firms are to be moved to a 'highest plus one' size class, twenty-one of the forty-six firms in the sample (i.e. 45.6 per cent)[64] would have gone up by one size class or more. Thus, although the majority of the firms were found to remain in their original size class, the possibilities of 'switching' are considerable and there is likely to be a significant impact of growth rate differentials on the levels of industrial concentration.

The finding that levels of industrial concentration are quite likely to be affected by differential growth performances in the case of India, is also confirmed by a Spearman rank correlation analysis. The value of the coefficient for firms ranked by 'opening' and 'closing' size was 0.927 for UK firms, but only 0.629 for Indian. Lower values of the coefficient imply greater relative mobility of firms. Thus, whereas mobility was relatively high among the group of Indian subsidiaries, it was virtually non-existent for the United Kingdom TNCs. For the UK sample the estimates of mobility are significantly lower than similar estimates for national industry produced by Singh and Whittington. Their estimates for surviving registered (i.e. large) British firms for a twelve-year period range between 0.69 and 0.72, and for a six-year period from 0.771 to 0.873.[65]

The low level of internal mobility of United Kingdom TNCs relative to national firms once again points to the existence of a positive impact of the growth of the former group of firms on the level of industrial concentration. Growth of TNCs cannot be regarded as a factor stimulating 'efficient' industrial restructuring in Britain. On the other hand the growth of TNC subsidiaries in India did not retard such restructuring in as much as it did not have a pronounced impact on the level of industrial concentration in that country.

The Transnational Corporation as an Agent for Industrialization

(b) Growth and profitability

Conventional theory expects that no equilibrium relationship between growth and profitability exists. In such a circumstance all firms will have achieved their optimum size and ceased to grow. If equilibrium does not exist the relationship between growth and profitability will be determined by the causes of disequilibrium and the speed with which firms adjust to their equilibrium position.[66] The theory treats a firm's growth as dependent on (a) its ability to grow and (b) its willingness to grow. Profitability clearly adds to a firm's potential for growth and, therefore, in an expanding economy we expect a positive association between these two variables. A firm's willingness to grow, on the other hand, is likely to be related to its level of profitability in a more complicated manner.

As far as subsidiaries are concerned there may be a tendency to transfer profits from the host country to the home country, or to other host countries. Hence, the observed association between profits and growth may be a weak one within a given national sample. The 'willingness to grow' may also depend on demand and labour conditions in a wide range of industries that TNCs seek to integrate. Furthermore, these firms are likely to be predominantly 'management controlled' rather than 'owner controlled', weakening the relationship between growth and profitability. Some authors also argue that the former type of firm maximizes growth subject to a 'profit satisfying' constraint. Beyond a certain point these firms consciously sacrifice higher profits for higher growth.[67]

The following equations were estimated for the firms in the sample:

$$\text{Growth} = a + b \text{ Profitability Index} + \varepsilon$$
$$\text{Growth} = a + b \log \text{ Profitability} + \varepsilon$$
$$\log \text{ Growth} + a + b \log \text{ Profitability} + \varepsilon^{68}$$

Profitability indices were (1) rate of return on net assets; (2) net profit to sales; (3) net profits to equity assets. There was a total of six estimates. The 'best' estimates are produced in Table VI.4. For the UK a significant positive relationship between levels of profitability and growth is discerned. For both samples, however, the value of

The International Economy and Industrial Development

the coefficient of regression is very small. It is clear that a simple linear relationship between profitability and growth does not obtain for the firms in the samples. The low value of the coefficient of determination may be accounted for by a significant specification error in the regression models. This may be due to heteroscedasticity in the variance of the distribution of the errors in the models and/or the fact that the relationship between growth and profitability was not linear. Some evidence of differences in the relationship between growth and profitability at different growth rates has been estimated.[69] However, the time constraint prevented a search for the most appropriate polynomial to depict this relationship. This search was also not undertaken because of the difficulty in putting an economic interpretation on statistical estimates employing polynomial functions.

Table VI.4 Impact of growth on profitability

Name of independent variable	United Kingdom		India	
	Value of b	Value of R^2	Value of b	Value of R^2
Log rate of return on net assets	2.265	0.27		
Net profit to net assets			2.61ˣ	0.12ˣ

Note: x = significantly different from zero at a 5 per cent confidence level.

These equations (as shown above) were also estimated for fifty of the largest Indian domestic manufacturing enterprises over the same period. There is a marked difference between Indian subsidiaries and Indian national firms in this respect. The double log models provided the best fit with R^2 ranging from 0.48 to 0.51. In three of the four cases the regression coefficient was highly significant. There is, therefore, some justification for arguing that Indian subsidiaries were either growth maximizing firms and not dependent on high profit rates for growth, or these firms did not utilize their profits for domestic expansion. For about 46 per cent of the subsidiaries the rate of growth of net profits exceeded the rate of growth of net assets. It can be argued that there was a significant proportion of subsidiaries that did not employ a large proportion of earnings for domestic expansion.

The UK results are broadly in correspondence with Singh and Whittington's estimates of the relationship between profitability and growth for large firms.[70] Their estimates of the coefficient of determination for the period 1954–60 range from 0.10 to 0.29.[71] They found that there were differences in the relationship between profitability and growth among large and small firms within their sample. In the majority of the cases Singh and Whittington obtained a higher value of R^2 for a smaller firm sample than for the larger firms.[72] This implies that changes in levels of profitability explain a larger proportion of the variation of growth among smaller firms than in a larger firm sample. Our own relatively modest estimates for R^2 and for the regression coefficient suggest that TNCs in the UK are less dependent on short- and medium-term profitability. Profitability is a longer-term constraint on these firms than on the relatively smaller firms which constitute the majority in the Singh-Whittington sample. It is not possible, however, to establish the extent to which the TNCs in the present sample are 'profit satisfying' entities and deliberately 'sacrifice' profits for maximizing growth on the basis of the preceding analysis. The lack of association between growth and profitability, however, provides no evidence of rising industrial concentration—the firms with the highest ability to grow (as measured by the profitability indices) do not exhibit a growth performance different from the others in the sample.

The growth process is not explained by levels of profitability for the firms in our sample. Theory predicts that, in such cases, variables measuring the level of capacity utilization explain growth patterns more adequately. These theories, however, take a more restricted view of the growth process than that implied by the definition used so far in this study. They are concerned with analysing changes in the level of a firm's investment—defined as changes in fixed assets—over a period of time. The next section uses the theoretical framework developed by these theories to examine the investment behaviour of the TNCs and subsidiaries in the present sample.

(c) Determinants of investment

A theory of investment behaviour concerns itself with an explanation of the factors that induce a firm to increase its demand for capital equipment and the factors which influence the availability of funds. Investment theory aims at integrating both demand and supply factors in its explanation of changes in captial expenditure.

Capacity utilization theories of investment have predicted that changes in capital stock are strictly proportional to the (positive) rate of change in output. It is held that investment is proportional to the difference between desired capital stock and the existing capital stock at the beginning of the period. The desired capital stock is predicted on the assumption that the current level of sales will continue into the future. This approach assumes that investment varies with output and sales. Capacity utilization models have been developed by the use of complex distribution lags and a consideration of irreversibilities. However, the basic framework and format have remained largely unchanged.

The main alternative to the capacity utilization theories are profit theories. These may broadly be divided into (a) those that hold that investment depends on present profit rates as a reflection of future profits, and (b) those that postulate a linear relationship between profits and sales and hence consider the profit theories to be a form of the capacity utilization interpretation.

The investment behaviour of the firms in the present sample has been analysed by fitting a number of simple, single-equation regression models to the data. The major drawback of the models is the inability to experiment with a number of distributed lag systems which may allow a better specification of the relationship between investment and the independent variables included in the model. Moreover it was not possible to take asset appreciation or other price changes into consideration.

The specification of the investment models is along conventional, generally accepted lines.[73] The best fit is provided by the model
$$FA_t - FA_{t-1} = a + b_1 (FA_t) + b_2 (S/FA)_t + b_3 (S)_t$$
for the Indian firms and[74]

The Transnational Corporation as an Agent for Industrialization

$$FA_t - FA_{t1} = a + b_1 \left(\frac{S_t}{(S/FA)\,FAt} \right) + b_2 \left(\frac{S_{t-i}}{(S/FA)\,FA_{t-1}} \right)$$

for the UK TNCs[75] where FA = Fixed Assets, and S = Sales.

Table VI.5 summarizes the results of an exercise in which a number of accelerator, profit and combined models was fitted to the British and Indian data. For UK firms, capacity utilization models generally provide results superior to those obtained for the other two alternatives. In the case of the Indian data high (and relatively similar) values of R^2 are obtained by all three types of investment models, but very few profit coefficients are statistically significant.

Table VI.5. Investment behaviour of TNCs and subsidiaries

	United Kingdom	India
Highest R^2 for capacity utilization models	0.99	0.86
Highest R^2 for profit models	0.78	0.84
Highest R^2 for 'combined' models	0.81	0.80
Number of significant sales coefficients	12	23
Number of significant capital stock coefficients	12	31
Number of significant capital intensity coefficients	24	32
Number of significant profit coefficients	0	4

The results for the Indian subsidiary sample differ from the studies of national firms. Although capacity utilization variables have been shown to be associated with growth in capital stock,[76] financial variables are also important determinants of the investment decision. For 1962–70 Krishnamurty and Sastry have analysed the behaviour of about 360 Indian firms in a number of industries. They conclude that: 'In the capital goods sector the cross section results suggest the importance of financial variables [but] the accelerator estimates do not seem to have any impact at all.'[77] The few significant profit coefficients estimated for subsidiaries in the present study suggest that domestic demand conditions are more important determinants of their investment decisions and medium-term profitability less important determinants than is the case with the national Indian firms. It is important to note that the present estimates of R^2 are invariably higher than those of Krishnamurty and Sastry.[78] This may in part be accounted for by differences in model specifications.

The better performance of the capacity utilization models for the UK TNCs also calls for some comment. It has been argued that, in periods of economic expansion, capacity utilization variables are more likely to be important determinants of the decisions to invest than profit variables. In periods of recession, external borrowing becomes difficult and the ability of a firm to make profits becomes an important determinant of its ability to expand its capital stock.[79]

The years 1975–9 can hardly be described as a period of industrial expansion in Britain. It is interesting to note that during this period the decline in profit rates was not an important constraint on the investment plans of the large TNCs included in this study. Clearly their investment schedules were based on longer-term planning perspectives. They could mobilize resources to maintain investment levels and demand conditions were important in determining investment levels.

On the basis of the foregoing analysis, it is possible to state that systematic variations in the growth process of TNCs in Britain and subsidiaries in India have been identified. However, we have failed to discern any systematic association between profit estimators and other variables. In the next section an attempt will be made to identify the determinants of profitability.

(d) Determinants of profitability

The theory of the growth of the firm emphasizes the relationship between profits and the size of the firm. If a positive relationship can be established, or if the dispersion of profits can be shown to decline systematically with size, then it can be argued that higher profits provide an incentive for growth. If there is no systematic variation of profits with size, profitability will not provide an incentive for expansion.

Regression analysis was employed to estimate the relationship between size and profitability. The following regression models were used:

$$P = a + bS + \varepsilon;$$
$$P = a + b \log S + \varepsilon;$$
$$\log P = a + b \log S + \varepsilon;[80]$$

where P = (a) rates of return on net assets;
(b) post tax rate of return on equity losses;
(c) post tax profits to net sales;
S = opening size of the firm.

Table VI.6 summarizes the results and shows that the relationship between profits and size is very weak.

Table VI.6. Profitability and size: the regression analysis

	Average value of R^2	Number of significant regression coefficients
UK sample	0.042 (0.11 highest)	0
Indian sample	0.038 (0.08 highest)	2 (both negative)

A comparison of these results with those for national firms reveals diverse trends. For India the regression coefficient of net profits to net assets on opening size was statistically significant and negative for a sample of fifty national firms. The coefficient of determination, however, was only 0.10. So far as UK national firms are concerned, figures are not available for the same period for which this investigation was undertaken. For an earlier twelve-year period Singh and Whittington found no systematic association between size and average profitability, although they found that larger firms had less variable profit performances.[81]

Whittington's study of the relationship between size and profitability for a sample of over 700 companies that existed throughout the period 1960–74 found that average profitability is largely independent of firm size but such relationship as there is tends to be negative. . . . It is clear that profit does not on the average provide an incentive for larger firms to grow at a relatively high rate. Equally, it does not provide them with the means for greater growth in terms of a high level of profit. . . . There does appear to be some reward in the form of greater stability of the rate of return through time (however).[82]

We investigated the relationship between size and profit variability by estimating the equation:
$$S = a + bO$$
where S is the standard deviation from average values of different profitability indicators and O is opening size of individual firms.

In the case of the UK data no relationship could be discerned. The value of the regression coefficients was negative but not significantly different from zero. For the Indian firms a significant negative relationship is evident. Larger subsidiaries clearly have less variation in their profits over time. These results are similar to estimates for Indian national firms. The overall conclusion must, therefore, be that size is not a prime determinant of profitability of firms in our sample. This is not a distinguishing characteristic of transnational enterprises and their subsidiaries. National firms did not exhibit marked association between size and profitability either.

Following other researchers, an attempt was also made to relate profitability to financing patterns.[83] For the Indian data there is evidence of significant positive association with both total liquidity and levels of profit retention. The value of R^2 is 0.64. In India there is also significant positive association between profitability and divided payments. The results for the UK sample indicate a weak positive association between profitability and indicators measuring retention (the R^2 is only 0.17). There is also a relatively strong association between profitability and divided payments indicating the relative importance of equity resources. No significant association appears between profitability and measures of external financing. This is not unexpected in a period generally characterized by a trend towards relative industrial stagnation.

The general conclusion is that conventional analysis is not a particularly adequate tool for explaining differences in levels of profitability of subsidiaries and of transnationals. These results are not at variance with those of other researchers.[84] On the other hand, a number of studies of corporate profitability of domestic Indian firms has shown a significant association between profitability indicators and financing variables. Thus, conventional theory does seem to provide an adequate framework for an analysis of profitability variations among national firms in India.

Finally, an attempt was made to determine the persistency of profits. If a firm enjoys monopoly power or possesses superior management resources it could be expected that it would remain relatively more profitable over a period of time. The persistency of profitability was estimated by the equation

$$P_t = a + bP_{t-1} + \varepsilon$$

where t is the last year of the period, and t−1 the first year and P represents different indicators measuring pre- and post-tax profitability. These equations were fitted to the Indian and UK samples. For the Indian data all regression cocfficients are positive and highly significant. However, the average value of R^2 was only 0.201. For the UK sample, the average value of the coefficient of determination is as high as 0.87 and, once again, all regression coefficients are positive and highly significant. Further, the value of Spearman's rank correlation coefficient for firms ranked by the profitability indices in the first and last years of the period under study was 0.763 for the UK sample and 0.422 for the Indian subsidiaries. It is clear, therefore, that while persistency of profits was relatively high for the UK TNCs, it was moderate for the Indian subsidiaries. The Spearman coefficient for the fifty largest Indian national manufacturing firms ranked by profitability in the first and last years of the same period was 0.399—not significantly different from the estimates for Indian subsidiaries. On the other hand, the correlation for TNCs in the UK was significantly higher than Singh and Whittington's estimates for 364 British manufacturing firms over a twelve-year period.[85] It appears that there is a distinction in the persistence of profitability in the UK and Indian samples. In neither case, however, has the preceding analysis been particularly successful in revealing the major determinants of inter-firm variations in profitability.

The lack of an association between profitability and what are generally regarded as its financial and economic 'determinants' may

The International Economy and Industrial Development

partially be explained by the practice of transfer pricing in TNCs. Transfer pricing is associated with the extent of intra-firm trade. This, in turn, is affected by technology, the divisibility of the production process and the need for after-sales servicing.[86] The potential for and incidence of transfer pricing is highest in product areas characterized by high levels of specialization. It is also associated with economies of scale and significant levels of international integration of production structures. Industries that operate 'high' (i.e. R and D-intensive) production processes, use firm-specific products and closely co-ordinate production and marketing are usually dominated by TNCs that 'maximize the profitability of possessing special monopolistic advantages by internalizing trade.'[87]

Intra-firm trade—and hence the potential for transfer pricing—is greatest in the technology-intensive industries such as office machines, plastics, transport equipment, etc. Textiles and apparel have what is described as 'an intermediate level of intra-firm trade' attributable mainly to their highly integrated marketing structures. Industrial branches with low levels of intra-firm trade are characterized by the existence of standardized products, a widely diffused technology and a relatively loose international marketing structure. These include metals, non-metallic minerals and industrial chemicals. In general it may be argued that the more widely traded and less specific is a product, the smaller the likely difference between 'arms length' and transfer prices. Regarding these industries, governments of LDCs need not be unduly perturbed. In others, such as pharmaceuticals with highly specific products, differences between arms length and intra-firm prices have been found to be very extensive.[88] In such cases it is important to identify factors inducing a TNC to increase this difference and also to take countervailing measures in the interests of the host and home economies.

Neo-classical price theory does not adequately explain the practice of transfer pricing among transnationals. The theory is concerned with the behaviour of buyers and sellers, both seeking to maximize profits, while the aim of intra-firm transactions is to maximize profits over the whole spectrum of activities within the TNC system. Important incentives for transfer pricing are the existence of international differences in tax and tariff rates, the

The Transnational Corporation as an Agent for Industrialization

operation of multiple exchange rate systems (which apply relatively costly exchange rates to profit transmissions) and limits imposed on the legal remittance of profits from host to home countries. Transfer prices may also be used by subsidiaries to increase the parent company's share of profits or to appreciate the value of the capital equipment that has been provided by way of equity participation. Obviously, these policies may be at the cost of local shareholders. Local and foreign equity holders may, however, collude and use transfer pricing as a means for foreign accumulation of funds.

There is no *a priori* reason to expect that transfer pricing will always be to the detriment of the host country. The present study finds no association between declared profits and what are usually recognized as variables determining inter-firm profitability for the UK TNCs. Many 'home' countries—notably the United States—have enacted measures to control transfer pricing.[89] However, many analysts have held that 'the cards are in fact stacked heavily against the LDCs'.[90] Tax rates tend to be higher, import duties on intermediate inputs are relatively low, quantitative restrictions on repatriation of profits are in force, and the socio-economic environment is vulnerable to external and internal destabilizing pressures. It is therefore important that LDCs pay some attention to the task of developing a consistent policy on dealing with problems of transfer pricing.

6.4 Conclusions

The present chapter has used conventional economic analysis to study the investment behaviour of transnationals and of their subsidiaries located in LDCs. It concentrated on an analysis of investment patterns. The main findings may be summarized as follows:

(1) Growth measured in terms of (net) fixed and current assets is weakly associated with size in the 'transnational' and the 'subsidiary' samples. This implies that there is some evidence to support the 'saturation' thesis (which holds that foreign investment falls off after a certain level of foreign participation has been achieved). No evidence has been found to substantiate the claim that TNC

investment contributes to increased industrial concentration in India. The result suggests that measures aimed at limiting industrial concentration apply with equal efficacy to subsidiaries and local firms.

(2) Variations in levels of investment were best explained by the 'accelerator' theory which employed sales and capacity utilization variables. This result was clearly evident for the sample of transnationals and the Indian subsidiaries. The closer association between investment and the capacity utilization variables suggests that the economic conditions in host economies are likely to be important determinants of the level of TNC investment. In growing economies with a high level of capacity utilization, such investment is likely to expand rapidly. However, since TNCs and their subsidiaries appear to be less constrained by the availability of finance, government tax concessions and liberal treatment of TNCs (in terms of permission to retain monopoly control of markets and thus ensure the continued existence of artificially high levels of profits) are not useful to attract foreign investment, particularly in the long run.

The finding that TNC investment is related to the rate of output growth and to the level of market stability (it is this second factor that induces high levels of capacity utilization) leads to the expectation that TNCs can be persuaded, through a process of protracted negotiations, to accept lower levels of short-run profitability in order to overcome structural bottlenecks in specific industrial branches of LDCs. The relatively industrialized LDCs with potentially large domestic markets are advantageously placed to persuade TNCs to develop a longer-term perspective and to share the costs of industrial consolidation and rationalization. This is evident from the present analysis of the investment behaviour of Indian subsidiaries. For smaller LDCs having limited domestic markets, opportunities in this field hold modest prospects. However, domestic market size is by no means necessarily limited by the rate of growth of domestic income and population. Regional economic co-operation (within the ASEAN or CACM framework, for example) may be an important determinant of market size in a wide range of industrial branches. In this instance, 'collective bargaining' with the TNCs may be an effective means of enhancing the development impact of foreign investment.

(3) The analysis failed to show any systematic association between inter-firm variations in profitability and growth, size or the financial variables that were examined. This is not an entirely unexpected result. Since the mid-1970s a number of authors have opined that TNCs have considerable ability to transfer profits between home and host countries. If this is true, then declared profits may not be an accurate index of actual profitability. Hence, the relationship between balance sheet estimates of rates of return and other variables may be obscured. Given the nature of the data available, a lack of association between profitability estimates and estimates of financing and investment behaviour may be explained partially by the existence of some elements of transfer pricing. Moreover, the fact that this lack of relationship is found in both the TNC sample and in the sample of subsidiaries suggests that transfer pricing was not confined to transactions from host to home countries. Such practices may occur in the opposite direction, particularly if the home country experiences economic difficulties and the subsidiaries of the TNC are located in healthy and rapidly growing economies.

In general there is considerable scope for both a modification and a reappraisal of TNCs' policies. Despite the rapid growth of literature in this field a detailed enquiry concerning the determinants of TNC behaviour as industrial investors is still required. The limited evidence presented in this chapter clearly points to the fact that socio-economic conditions prevalent in host economies are one important determinant of TNC investment. Policies facilitating the location of TNC investment in industrial branches in which host economies have a dynamic comparative advantage are likely to be of benefit to the transnationals as well as to the recipient countries. These are the industries with the brightest medium- and long-term growth prospects. Co-operation between TNCs and LDCs can ensure that the costs and benefits of the expansion of these branches are equitably shared and the expansion of TNC investment contributes towards international industrial restructuring. However, Third World governments have not been particularly successful in attracting TNC investment to these industrial branches. This is in sharp contrast to the experience of the 1950s and 1960s when import substituting policies induced a large volume of TNC investment in

The International Economy and Industrial Development

the Third World. Our analysis suggests that increasing opportunities for capacity utilization should accelerate TNC investment within export oriented branches as well and that such an acceleration need not contribute to increased industrial concentration and thus frustrate the potential for 'efficient' industrial restructuring. Nevertheless, the experience of some South-East Asian countries indicates that TNCs are reluctant to encourage LDC export expansion as long as such expansion is likely to erode markets of their own subsidiaries. Their interest in export expansion remains largely confined to industrial branches in which the production process can be geographically split up—such as off share assembly plants. It has been argued that the developmental impact of such investment is minimal. It is essential, therefore, that the possibilities of expanding TNC investments in industrial branches, the development of which facilitates an efficient utilization of the resources of the Third World, be explored. Clearly, increasing the TNCs' contribution to export expansion in LDCs requires a drastic reduction of protectionist barriers in relevant international markets. The recently concluded Tokyo Round negotiations have shown that governments are particularly reluctant to endorse a large-scale dismantling of these barriers in the 1980s. It is appropriate, therefore to suggest that involving TNCs in multilateral negotiations may be a means for linking international trade and investment issues in a way which permits the gradual restructuring of economic relationships in a diverse range of industrial branches. These negotiations can pave the way for developing inter-industrial linkages of a global scale and can contribute to a clearer perception of the long- and medium-term gains of trade liberalization. Moreover, the growing economic co-operation among LDCs at a regional level can also provide a focus for involving TNCs in investment and trade negotiations and stimulating their interest in the development of 'integrative' industries. In this respect co-operation between TNCs and public manufacturing enterprises may be of particular importance. This is recognized by many Middle Eastern governments who are actively seeking to establish joint export ventures with the world's leading TNCs in the petrochemical industry.

The next chapter addresses the question of the potential for

The Transnational Corporation as an Agent for Industrialization

co-operation between TNCs and public manufacturing enterprises as a means for facilitating industrial restructuring in accordance with changing comparative advantages of LDCs.

Notes

[1] For a comprehensive survey, see S. Lall, 'Transnationals and domestic enterprises: a survey', *Oxford Economic Papers*, 1978, pp. 217–48.

[2] R. F. Newfarmer and S. W. Mueller, *Multinational Corporations in Brazil and Mexico*, United States Senate Sub-Committee on TNCs, Washington D.C., 1975.

[3] Pioneered by Edith Penrose, *The Theory of the Growth of the Firm*, Oxford University Press, London, 1958, this became a major growth area in economics in the 1960s. Other important works include P. Cyert and S. March, *A Behavioural Theory of the Firm*, Prentice Hall, New York, 1933; R. Marris, *The Economic Theory of Managerial Capitalism*, Cambridge University Press, London, 1964; D. Williamson, 'Managerial Discretion and Business Behaviour', *American Economic Review*, 1963, pp. 1032–57; and A. Singh and T. Whittington, *Growth Profitability and Valuation*, Cambridge University Press, London, 1968.

[4] R. Nabseth and G. Grey (eds), *The Diffusion of New Industrial Processes in International Study*, Harvard University Press, Cambridge, Mass., 1974.

[5] G. Baldwin and W. Childs, 'The past record and prospects in research and development', *Southern Economic Journal*, 1969, pp. 18–24.

[6] W. H. Davidson, 'Factor endowment, innovation and international trade theory', *Kyklos*, 1979, pp. 764–74.

[7] L. Stopford and L. Wells, *Managing the Multinational Enterprise*, Harvard University Press, Cambridge, Mass., 1973, document the difference in information flow from partners to subsidiaries and joint ventures.

[8] See S. Lall, 'Transfer pricing by multinational manufacturing firms', *Oxford Economic Papers*, August 1973, pp. 173–95.

[9] D. Morawetz, Employment implications of industrialization in LDCs', *Economic Journal*, 1974, pp. 491–542.

[10] I. Haque, 'Producers' alliances among LDCs', *Journal of World Trade Law*, 1973, pp. 511–26.

[11] C. Tugenhadt, *The Multinationals*, Penguin, Hardmondsworth, 1971, p. 31.

[12] J. Dunning, *International Investment*, Penguin, Harmondsworth, 1972, p. 112.

[13] H. Brems, 'A growth model of international direct investment', *American Economic Review*, 1970, pp. 320–31; E. L. Bacha, 'Foreign capital inflow and the output growth rate of the recipient country, *Journal of Developing Studies*, 1974, pp. 374–81; R. E. Baldwin, 'International trade in inputs and outputs', *American Economic Review*, 1970, pp. 430–4; J. Chipman, 'International trade with capital mobility', in J. Bhagwati *et al.*, *Trade Balance of Payment and Growth*, North Holland, Amsterdam, 1977, pp. 93–161.

[14] V. Bornischer, 'Multinational corporations and economic growth', *Journal of Development Economics*, June 1980, pp. 191–210.

[15] See R. S. Newfarmer and S. W. Mueller, *op. cit*, pp. 62 and 185 and L. Wilmore, Direct foreign investment in Central American manufacturing', *World Development*, 1976, pp. 490–578.

[16] S. Lall and P. Streeten, *Foreign Investment, Transnationals and Developing Countries*, Macmillan, London, 1977, pp. 220–1.

[17] United Nations Centre on Transnational Corporations, *Transnational Corporation Linkages in Developing Countries*, New York, 1980, p. 41 (mimeo).

[18] *Ibid.*, p. 58.

[19] UNCTC, *The Employment Impact of Transnational Corporations*, New York, 1980, p. VII (mimeo).

[20] Figures are for the late 1970s (mainly 1978). The second estimate assumes that all TNC direct employment is in the industrial sector. UNCTC *ibid.*, p. XI, and IBRD *World Development Report 1980*, Washington D.C., 1980, pp. 110–11, 146–7.

[21] These estimates exclude China, Cuba, Mongolia and North Korea but include Viet Nam.

[22] S. H. Jo, *The Impact of Multinationals on Employment, South Korea*, ILO/WEP No. 12, Geneva, 1976.

[23] G. L. Reuber, *Private Foreign Investment in Development*, Oxford University Press, London, 1973, pp. 151–4.

[24] On this, see S. Hymer, 'The efficiency (contradictions) of multinational corporations', *American Economic Review Papers and Proceedings*, May 1970, pp. 441–8.

[25] F. Steward, 'Technology and employment in LDCs', *World Development*, March 1974, pp. 17–46.

[26] See e.g. H. Pack, 'Capital-labour substitution; a microeconomic approach', *Oxford Economic Papers*, 1974, pp. 388–404.

[27] Reuber (1973) *op. cit.*, p. 126, Stewart (1974) *op. cit.*, p. 23 and J. Baranson, *Manufacturing Problems in India: The Cummins Diesel Experiment*, Syracuse University Press, New York, 1967, pp. 73–99.

[28] B. Cohen, *Multinational Firms and Asian Exports*, Yale University Press, New Haven, 1975, pp. 123–8 and R. H. Mason, 'Some observations on the choice of technology by multi-national firms in developing countries', *Review of Economics and Statistics*, 1973, pp. 349–55; J. Reidel, 'The nature and determinants of export oriented direct foreign investment: Taiwan', *Weltwirtschaftliches Archiv*, 1975, pp. 505–28; S. Lall and P. Streeten, *Foreign Investment, Transnational and Developing Countries*, Macmillan, London, 1977, pp. 99–130.

[29] These studies include C. Vaitsos, 'Employment problems and TNCs in developing countries', ILO/WEP, Geneva, Paper No. 11, 1976; S. H. Jo, 'The impact of multinational firms on employment and incomes: South Korea', ILO/WEP, Geneva, Paper No. 12, 1976; N. Agarwal, 'Factor proportions in foreign and domestic firms in Indian manufacturing', *Economic Journal*, 1976, pp. 367–79.

[30] United Nations Centre on Transnational Corporations, *Transnational Corporation Linkages, op. cit.*, p. 43.

[31] D. Nayyar, 'TNCs and manufactured exports from poor countries', *Economic Journal*, Vol. 88, March 1978, pp. 61–3.

[32] The hypothesis is constructed from a survey of literature in the areas of industrial economics, trade theory and the theory of the growth of the firm. See S. Lall,

'Monopolistic advantages and foreign investment by US manufacturing industry', *Oxford Economic Papers*, July 1980, pp. 102–24.

33 As distinct from capital intensity.

34 S. Lall, *op. cit.*, p. 123.

35 W. Kionig, 'Towards an evaluation of international subcontracting activities in developing countries', Economic Commission for Latin America, Santiago, 1975 (mimeographed).

36 S. Lall, 'Transnationals and domestic enterprise, a survey', *Oxford Economic Papers*, 1978, pp. 217–48.

37 A. J. Yeats, 'Monopoly power, barriers to competition and the patterns of price differentials in international trade', *Journal of Development Economics*, Volume 5, No. 2, 1978, for example, estimates that small countries pay more for imported capital equipment than do larger ones.

38 S. Lall and P. Streeten, *op. cit*, p. 98.

39 See. R. Larner, *Management Control and the Large Corporation*, Johns Hopkins University Press, New York, 1970; P. Holl, 'Effect of control type on the performance of the firm in the U.K.', *Journal of Industrial Economics*, June 1975, pp. 257–71.

40 Singh and Whittington, *op. cit.*, (1968), p. 221.

41 *H.M.S.O. Business Monitor*, MA3, HMSO London, 1980, Table 7, pp. 32–3.

42 The latest year for which data are available.

43 *H.M.S.O. Business Monitor* MA4, 1978, p. 12

44 A. Morgan, 'Foreign manufacturing by U.K. firms', in F. Blackaby *Deindustrialization*, Heinemann, National Institute of Economic and Social Research, London, 1978, p. 79.

45 *Ibid.*, p. 85.

46 *Ibid.*, p. 86.

47 This figure is taken from Holland's comment on Morgan's paper (p. 95).

48 For a detailed discussion, see D. Channon, *The Strategy and Structure of British Enterprise*, Macmillan, London, 1973.

49 S. Holland, *Comment* on Morgan, *op. cit.*, p. 96.

50 The major writings in this area are those of Edith Penrose; *The Theory of the Growth of the Firm*, Oxford University Press, London, 1959; R. L. Marris, *Economic Theory of Managerial Capitalism*, Cambridge University Press, London, 1964; Myron Gordon, *The Investment, Financing and Valuation of the Corporation*, Irwin, Illinois, 1962; O. Williamson, *The Economics of Discretionary Behaviour: Managerial Objectives in a Theory of the Firm*, John Wiley, Englewood Cliffs, N.J., 1964; and J. Steindl, *Random Processes and the Growth of the Firm*, Allen and Unwin, London 1965; P. Hart and S. Prais, 'The analysis of business concentration: a statistical approach", *Journal of the Royal Statistical Society*, series A, 1956, pp. 150–81; T. Barna, *Investment and Growth Policies in British Industrial Firms*, Cambridge University Press, London 1962; H. Simon and G. Bonini, 'The size distribution of business firms', *American Economic Review*, September 1958, pp. 607–17; S. Hymer and B. Pashigan, 'Firm size and the rate of growth', *The Journal of Political Economy*, December 1962, pp. 556–69; and E. Mansfield, 'Entry, Gibrat's Law, innovation and the growth of firms', *American Economic Review*,

The International Economy and Industrial Development

December 1962, pp. 1023-51; A. Singh, *Takeovers*, Cambridge University Press, London, 1971; G. Whittington, *Prediction and Profitability*, Cambridge University Press, London, 1971; J. Palmer, 'The profit variability effect of the managerial enterprise', *Western Economic Journal*, 1973, pp. 73-89; E. Kuh, *Capital Stock Growth: A Microeconomic Approach*, North Holland, Amsterdam, 1963; A. Singh and G. Whittington. *Growth Profitability and Valuation*, Cambridge University Press, London, 1968.

[51] Gibrat's Law implies that the technology and market demand will not generate an optimal size of a 'typical' firm. But this may not necessarily imply that individual firms within an industry do not have optimum induced sizes.

[52] Marris, *op. cit.*, p. 63.

[53] These specifications are generally used in empirical studies of Gibrat's Law. See Singh and Whittington *op. cit.*, p. 113.

[54] A. C. Alpin and B. C. Welch, 'Tables for use in comparison whose accuracy involves two variances', *Biometrika*, 1949, pp. 290-6.

[55] The standard F test for testing significance of difference in variance was used.

[56] Singh and Whittington, *op. cit.*, p. 80.

[57] This is a restricted version of the Law that implies that the frequency distribution of opening size and closing size represents a log normal surface.

[58] Singh and Whittington, *op. cit.*, pp. 63-5.

[59] P. E. Hart, 'The size and growth of firms', *Economica*, 1962, pp. 134-47.

[60] J. Prais, 'A new look at the growth of industrial concentration', *Oxford Economic Papers*, July 1974, pp. 78-85.

[61] J. Prais, *op. cit.*, p. 83.

[62] Singh and Whittington, *op. cit.*, p. 73.

[63] M. Kalecki, 'On the Gibrat distribution', *Econometrica*, 1945, pp. 71-83.

[64] According to Table VI.8 this proportion is 34.78 per cent.

[65] Although Kendall's k (not Spearman's s) is estimated, Singh and Whittington note 'the same pattern of relative mobility is observed when Spearman's s is computed as where Kendall's k is used.' Singh and Whittington, *op. cit.*, p. 102.

[66] R. Marris, *Economic Theory of Managerial Capitalism*, Cambridge University Press, London, 1964, Chapter 2.

[67] R. Marris, *op. cit*, Chapter 2.

[68] For specification of these models, see Singh and Whittington, *op. cit.*, pp. 150-1.

[69] But not reproduced.

[70] Singh and Whittington, *op. cit.*, pp. 162-8.

[71] Higher values are estimated for an earlier period.

[72] Singh and Whittington, *op. cit*, pp. 154-7 and 163.

[73] They are primarily based on Kuh's work. E. Kuh, *Capital Stock Growth: A Microeconomic Approach*, North Holland, Amsterdam, 1963.

[74] Four such models were estimated; average value of the coefficient of determination was 0.85.

[75] Four such models were estimated; average value of R^2 was 0.96.

[76] K. Krishnamurty and D. N. Sastry, *Investment Accelerator and Financial Factor*, Institute of Economic Growth, Delhi, 1973, p. 29.

[77] D. N. Sastry, *Investment Behaviour in the Capital Goods Industry*, Institute of

Economic Growth, Delhi, 1973, p. 19.
[78] Krishnamurty and Sastry, *op. cit.*, p. 41.
[79] M. Meyer and E. H. Kuh, *The Investment Decision*, Harvard University Press, Cambridge, Mass., 1957, pp. 116–36.
[80] The specification of these models is given in Singh and Whittington, *op. cit.*, pp. 120–4.
[81] *Ibid.*, p. 73.
[82] G. Whittington, 'The profitability and size of UK companies', *Journal of Industrial Economics*, June 1980, p. 350.
[83] Lall and Streeten, *op. cit.*, pp. 123–9. Due to lack of data, advertising expenditure and indicators measuring barriers to entry could not be included in this analysis.
[84] Lall and Streeten, *op. cit.*, pp. 124–7.
[85] Singh and Whittington, *op. cit.*, p. 123.
[86] S. Lall, *The Multinational Corporation*, Macmillan, London, 1980, p. 106.
[87] *Ibid.*, p. 139.
[88] C. Vaitsos, *Intercountry Income Distribution and Transnationals*, Oxford University Press, London, 1974.
[89] See M. C. Duess, *Tax Allocations and International Business*, The Conference Board, New York, 1972.
[90] S. Lall, *op. cit.*, p. 117.

Chapter VII

The Public Manufacturing Enterprise as an Agent for Industrialization

In the previous chapter we identified the major determinants of the investment and growth policies of the TNCs and evaluated their contribution to industrial restructuring. We saw that TNCs can be induced to adopt policies that facilitate the restructuring process in accordance with an LDC's changing comparative advantages, provided that the Government succeeds in fostering a healthy economic environment and strengthening inter-sectoral linkages.

In this chapter we examine the policies of public manufacturing enterprises (PMEs) and attempt to assess their potential as agents of industrial restructuring in the Third World. The literature on PMEs is of more recent vintage than the TNC studies and, as a consequence, does not have the same depth and breadth of vision. However, the rapid growth of PMEs in LDCs has prompted some economists to raise questions that are of relevance to our study. We begin by assessing the relative importance of PMEs in the Third World, discuss the motives for public manufacturing investment and analyse the policies of PMEs in India. The possibility that these policies can be modified to increase the impact of PME investment on Indian industry is considered. Finally, we discuss the problems and prospects of co-operation between TNCs and PMEs and evaluate the extent to which such co-operation can facilitate industrial restructuring in accordance with changing comparative advantages.

The Public Manufacturing Enterprise

7.1 Growth of public manufacturing enterprises in LDCs

Public manufacturing enterprises have grown rapidly over the last two decades in both socialist and market oriented LDCs. According to Malcolm Gillis,

> only in a very small number of natural resource exporting nations have the multinationals loomed larger in terms of investment shares, generation of value added, employment or foreign exchange. By whatever standard employed, state-owned enterprises now play a more critical role in the development process of a greater number of developing countries than do multinationals and [their] relative importance is likely to grow in the future.[1]

All those firms based in LDCs and included in Fortune's 1979 list of the 500 largest industrial enterprises outside the United States were PMEs.[2] In many countries—such as Brazil, Indonesia, Mexico and South Korea—PMEs are among the largest industrial producers. State-owned enterprises account for over 75 per cent of non-agricultural investment in Bangladesh, Bolivia and Mexico. In India and Turkey their share is over 50 per cent. Even in Taiwan where a policy of limiting PME expansion has been in operation for over a decade, the share of state enterprises in total investment is in the range of 30 per cent. The share of PMEs in industrial value added is high in countries as diverse as Bangladesh, Egypt, India, Nepal, Sri Lanka and Turkey. PMEs have successfully undertaken import substitution and export expansion programmes in a wide range of industrial branches, including steel making (in India, Indonesia and South Korea), petrochemicals (in Brazil, Mexico and Venezuela), shipbuilding and textiles. Thus, there is increasing scope for both co-operation and competition between TNCs and public manufacturing firms in many international markets.

During the 1970s PMEs, along with other state trading concerns, emerged as important borrowers in international credit markets.

> Flows of external commercial debt contracted by such firms rose by nearly 35 per cent over the period 1976–1978. Growth in external borrowing by state-owned enterprises based in LDCs was particularly

The International Economy and Industrial Development

marked in the Euro-currency market where recorded new loan commitments reached an estimated $12.2 billion in 1978. This amounted to nearly one third of total LDC commercial borrowings for all purposes and fully one eighth of total international borrowing of all types by all debtors, including firms and governments from industrial countries.[3]

The emergence of PMEs in the late twentieth century is attributable to a continued centralization of technological power and an increasing separation of ownership from control in most growing economies. The public and private sectors of economic national systems are interlocked in a network of relationships that are both complementary and competitive. In the nineteenth century economic theory placed a great deal of emphasis on the pioneering role of a national bourgeois class as the main agent of industrial development. Our review of British and German industrialization has shown that this emphasis was by no means misplaced and that the existence of an innovating entrepreneurial group willing to take substantial risks was a crucial factor in the industrial development of both these countries. In France, Germany, and Japan, public economic policy and PMEs played a vital role in sustaining private sector initiatives.

Today, in LDCs the national bourgeoisie plays a less conspicuous role as innovator and organizer. It usually acts in concord with the public sector or with transnational enterprises. Even in countries like Brazil and Pakistan, which have remained committed to a 'free enterprise' economic philosophy for a considerable time, the role of public enterprises as industrial investors and price setters has grown rapidly. In part this is due to the fact that rapid international integration of most commodity and factor markets has made it impossible for nascent national capitalist groups to influence levels and terms of transactions unilaterally. The transnational corporation has proved a powerful instrument of market domination. National capitalist groups of the Third World have found that state support is vitally important for growth and survival, particularly in oligopolistic markets.

This rapid growth of PMEs has induced some economists to analyse the impact of PME investment on the development of the Third World. A review of this type of work helps to clarify the motives of the PME management as organizers of production and to assess the extent to which PME policies can be modified to accelerate industrial restructuring in the Third World.

7.2 The public manufacturing enterprise as an agent of industrialization

Economic theory—in both its neo-classical and neo-Marxist variants—does not provide a wholly adequate frame of reference for analysing the impact of PME policies on Third World industrial structure. Neo-classical work on public enterprises is focused on problems of 'efficient' investment allocation and pricing.[4] This does not involve a refusal to recognize the multiplicity of objectives served by public enterprises,[5] but it is generally held that an aggregation of these objectives makes economic sense only if government intervention aims at correcting the divergencies between marginal social value and marginal social cost. Neo-classical appraisal of government intervention is thus firmly rooted in welfare theory and is concerned primarily with the 'optimum' provision of public goods and with an analysis of government intervention in the natural monopolies.[6] This theoretical perspective necessitates that public ownership of manufacturing enterprises be regarded as one of a number of instruments that can be employed to attain, at most, a second-best welfare optimum where the net gains from the removal of the initial divergence between marginal social value and marginal social cost are offset by the loss caused by the creation of some other divergence.[7] Investment in public industrial enterprises is justified if it maximizes social welfare— where 'social welfare' is taken to be a function of the consumption level of the citizens of a country over time and where the social value of commodities is measured in terms of 'border' prices. Non-traded goods are also valued with reference to international price structures and accounting prices of factors of production are evaluated in terms of uncommitted public income valued in terms of foreign exchange as well.[8]

The limitations of such an approach have been addressed by several authors.[9] The approach assumes that the individual's attempt to maximize his own welfare provides the economist with a knowledge of correct social preferences. It is these preferences that 'ought' to be fulfilled and the optimization of social welfare would be achieved through their fulfilment.[10] The formulation of these preferences is not regarded as an appropriate area for economic analysis; nor does economic analysis attempt to assess the extent to which the fulfilment of different preferences will increase social welfare. This liberal philosophy—and its implied theory of the state and of the role of government in society—provides an inadequate point of departure for evaluating a development strategy that emphasizes basic needs, self-reliance, or the creation of a better pattern of income distribution. Any of these strategies may be regarded as 'economically irrational' since their pursuit can lead to a pattern of investment that is 'sub-optimal' in welfare terms because it does not maximize the flow of consumption over a given time.

This flow of consumption is measured with reference to world market prices in the Little-Mirlees model. These prices are taken to represent the country's opportunity cost of obtaining any given product. However, as Lall and Streeten have pointed out, 'the relative values of these products represent the demand patterns and preferences of the developed countries and the technological and marketing patterns of the large oligopolists which dominate production there.'[11] Since price formation in oligopolistic markets is heavily influenced by bargaining processes, there is a strong temptation to use policy mechanisms to exert pressure and influence price formulation.

Equally important, the process of establishing preferences in LDCs is affected by international economic forces. By sheer force of circumstances the governments of LDCs are compelled to modify the impact of these forces on the pattern of resource allocation in the national economy. This desire to modify individual preferences, and to make them conform to the government's own perception of the country's social needs, lies at the root of most attempts at economic intervention by Third World governments.[12] Analysis of PME policies and performance within the neo-classical framework does not, however, take account of this factor.

Marxist and neo-Marxist authors have also placed considerable stress on an economic analysis of public sector enterprises. Seizing control of the 'the commanding heights of the economy' is a basic tenet of orthodox Marxism. To Marx himself 'private property is the product, the result, the necessary consequence of alienated labour'.[13] Capitalism does not emerge as a distinct socio-historical epoch 'with the mere circulation of money and commodities. It can spring into life only when the owner of the means of production and subsistence meets in the market with the free labourer selling his labour power.'[14] In such a society, alienation is a direct consequence of the existence of private appropriation by the capitalists of the products of the labour process. Hence, it was possible for Marx and Engels to write: 'The theory of the communists may be summed up in the single sentence: Abolition of private property.'[15] This abolition is to be achieved by 'the political supremacy [of] the proletariat [which] will wrest by degrees all capital from the bourgeoisie, to centralize all instruments of production in the hands of the State, i.e. of the proletariat organized as the ruling class and to increase the total of productive forces as rapidly as possible.'[16]

Marxist parties have, on coming into power, usually undertaken comprehensive nationalization programmes particularly within the industrialized sector. But has this led to the 'centralization of instruments of production in the hands of the proletariat organized as the ruling class'? In other words, do public sector enterprises in socialist countries constitute a property form that is organically distinct from the private firm? Marxist analysts have not given a clear answer to this question. Some, such as Rahman Sobhan (following Michael Kalecki), have contrasted public enterprise in socialist and non-socialist countries by stressing their quantitative differences in operation performance. Sobhan writes:

> Where the role of public enterprise has been stabilized in a supportive role to the national bourgeoisie its operational performance may improve. . . , [however] in a bourgeois dominated regime an overly successful public sector encourages the workers of these enterprises and even its managerial cadres to seek a more dominant role at the expense of the private sector . . . [thus] the established and aspirant bourgeois tend to develop a vested interest in the failure or poor performance of public enterprise.[17]

On the other hand, according to Sobhan, 'in a regime of the masses public enterprise becomes a primary engine for generating surpluses'.[18] Other Marxists argue that nationalization leads to an abolition of commodity production,[19] and to an eventual termination of the system of wage labour and of the realization of surplus product in the form of surplus value.[20]

While it is difficult to accept that a public enterprise system, by the mere fact of its superior productivity would be sufficient to transform property relations within society, it seems plausible to argue that if nationalization leads to the abolition of the exchange economy it would indeed amount to a fundamental revision of 'the sanctioned behavioural relations among men that arises from the existence of things and pertain to their use'.[21] The desirability of such a revision concerns the field of social ethics and we do not pursue it in this book. We believe that, as a matter of fact, nationalization does not lead to the suspension of commodity production, the abolition of wage labour or the termination of the realization of surplus product in the form of surplus value in any known historical social formation.[22]

Substantial evidence can be cited in support of the view that the public sector enterprise belongs to the same genre of property forms as the private corporation. A hierarchic managerial élite exercises executive authority in both organizations. Moreover, there are no substantive differences in the nature of the relationship between the managers of Soviet enterprises and the State which legally owns them on the one hand, and the relationship between 'capitalist' managers and private stockholders on the other. The Soviet manager, like his capitalist counterpart, is in a position to 'use the firm's resources to increase his personal satisfaction at the expense of the Government's objectives'.[23] The relationship between Soviet managers and the Government has been studied by Zaleski,[24] who finds considerable and expanding scope for policy making and implementation for managerial groups within the Soviet industrial system. Within this system the workers do not exercise any ownership rights over state property directly and thus there is little reason to expect that their position would reflect any element of control or management authority. Soviet workers are wage labourers and public industrial enterprises do not seek to transfer executive powers from the managerial boards to the shop floor.

In Yugoslavia, on the other hand, many attempts have been made to institutionalize 'self management'. The workers in public enter-

The Public Manufacturing Enterprise

prises have been given limited ownership rights over surpluses (minus taxes) generated by these firms.[25] However, it cannot realistically be claimed that the workers manage the firms themselves.[26] The management structure of Yugoslav firms consists of a number of tiers. At the bottom are the workers who send delegates to a Council consisting of between fifteen to 120 members.[27] This Council then elects a Collective Executive Organ. This body is described as the 'executive organ of the Workers Council'.[28] But there also exists a 'Business Managerial Organ' which 'prepares and executes the decisions of the Workers Council as well as of the Executive Organ'.[29] This Business Management Organ is headed by a Director who 'is responsible for the execution of legal regulations'.[30]

A review of the organizational structure of Yugoslav enterprises makes it clear why 'informal group managerial circles and administrative teams have emerged [whose] usurpation of power in some organizations of associated labour[31] was not a rare exception',[32] and why 'technocratic and bureaucratic tendencies and various other forms of usurping the rights of workers [have] often encouraged statist and bureaucratic ideas and activities'.[33] Workers are particularly disadvantaged vis-à-vis the managerial élite. In the absence of market valuation of the future consequences of current management policies, there is no ready measure of management efficiency.[34] Yugoslav workers have demonstrated their understanding of the real essence of 'self management' by consistently preferring investment in saving accounts to investment in the firm they supposedly manage.[35] The relative scarcity of retained earnings means Yugoslav firms have high debt equity ratios. Many are faced with chronic liquidity shortages and the economy has been suffering from high levels of inflation and unemployment for quite some time.[36] These problems contribute to the annual outflow of Yugoslav workers to Austria, Germany and Switzerland—another indicator of the Yugoslav proletariat's own evaluation of the consequences of worker 'self management'.

The Yugoslav model of public enterprise management is not likely to be widely adopted in LDCs for a host of social, political and economic reasons. Political regimes in the Third World, like other governing élites, are not primarily interested in suspending commodity production, abolishing wage labour or eliminating the realization of surplus product in the form of surplus value. Instead, they are concerned with augmenting their own bargaining power—within the national economy and within international markets—and in re-ordering preferences in accordance with the priorities of their development strategies. In the past, public industrial enterprises have played a crucial role in Germany, Japan and the USSR in achieving these objectives.[37]

Public industrial investment in LDCs is, in our opinion, primarily an instrument to modify existing preferences and influence terms on which commodities and factors are made available to national producers. It is not primarily intended to maximize consumption flows over a given time, nor does it have an objective of transcending capitalism. A concern with preference re-ordering and enhancing national bargaining power can influence the process of industrial restructuring. The impact of investment induced by these motives—i.e. PME investment—on industrial restructuring can be positive if such investment spurs growth in industrial branches in which the LDC is developing a comparative advantage, if it contributes towards an expansion of employment or if it induces significant growth in exports. On the other hand, PME investment can retard industrial restructuring if it accentuates monopolistic tendencies within the economy, if it favours capital-intensive projects or if its expansion reduces the LDC's ability to seize existing international opportunities.

In the next section we will analyse the policies of PMEs operating in India. The main concern will be with identifying the determinants of PME investment and with comparing the investment behaviour of PMEs and TNCs within the Indian manufacturing sector. This will allow us to draw some tentative conclusions about the potential of PMEs and TNCs as agents of industrial restructuring in accordance with India's changing comparative advantages.

7.3 Policies of Indian public manufacturing enterprises: an empirical study

The most important limitation of the present study is that data gathered on PMEs relate to a different time period from the data on

The Public Manufacturing Enterprise

TNCs used in Chapter VI. Standardized accounts of Indian public sector firms were available from 1972/73 to 1978/79. The difference in period imposes severe restrictions on the direct comparability of the results. Despite this limitation the analysis reveals some underlying trends in the behaviour of TNCs and public manufacturing firms that allow us to identify possibilites of co-operation (and also of conflict) between these two groups of firms.

Data were taken from the volumes published by the Ministry of Finance, Government of India, over the period 1972/73–1978/79.[38] Firms selected satisfied both the following criteria:
(1) They continued to exist over the entire six-year period.
(2) They belonged to one of the following industrial branches:
   (a) iron and steel
   (b) chemicals and pharmaceuticals
   (c) medium and light engineering
   (d) transport equipment
   (e) food manufacturing and leather processing firms included in the 'agro-based' industrial branch
   (f) petroleum.[39]

In the absence of a proper sample design it is, of course, impossible to correctly gauge the 'representativeness' of this sample. The fifty-two firms in the sample account for about 72 per cent of the total assets of Indian manufacturing public sector enterprises.[40] Clearly the sample includes the largest PMEs in India and an analysis of the data can provide useful insights into the policies procured by the Indian public manufacturing sector.

We begin by focusing on the possible relationship between growth of PMEs and their size. Although in India some key manufacturing sectors are reserved for the public sector, a single enterprise does not span an entire industrial branch. Complete monopoly does not exist and is approached only in the iron and steel industry which is limited to two PMEs.[41] It is relevant, therefore, to determine whether or not concentration has been increasing as a consequence of PME growth. Economic theory generally holds that an increase in industrial concentration will have consequences for both industrial policies and the performance of firms in these markets. Moreover, if it can be shown that concentration within the public sector increased over time, it can be argued that the growth of the PMEs was a factor inhibiting industrial restructuring. Increased concentration may 'distort' the price structure and thus create obstacles in the path of an 'efficient' allocation of resources which reflects true changes in industrial cost structures within the country.

We examined the relationship between size and growth by once again testing for the existence of the Law of Proportionate Effect. The results, where OS refers to opening size, were as follows:

$$\text{Growth} = 3.920 - 0.000044 \text{ OS} \qquad R^2 = 0.007$$
$$(2.46) \ (-0.61)$$
$$\log \text{Growth} = 1.047 - 0.288 \log \text{OS} \qquad R^2 = 0.179$$
$$(3.57) \ (-3.31)$$

Neither the regression coefficient nor the coefficient of determination is significantly different from zero in the linear model. In the logarithmic equation both these coefficients are significantly different from zero (at a 5 per cent confidence limit). However, the value of the coefficient of determination is extremely low. Thus, only a weak association is found between size and growth. Table VII.1 provides further information on growth performance according to firm size in 1972. The average rate of growth was lower for the larger size classes. (This is partly a statistical phenomenon because higher rates of growth occur when beginning from a small base.) The standard deviations show that the growth performance of firms within a given class were more comparable for larger enterprises than for smaller ones. It is evident that some form of association between growth and size exists although the foregoing equations do not provide a clear specification of this relationship.

An alternative version of the 'law of Proportionate Effect' was tested by examining the relationship between the opening size (S_t) and closing size (S_{t+1}) of the PMEs in our sample. The estimated equation was:

$$\log S_{t+1} = 1.083 + 0.797 \log S_t \qquad R^2 = 0.813$$
$$(3.76) \ (14.78)$$

The value of the coefficient is less than one. Statistically, the coefficient was significantly different from unity and the results explain a considerable portion of the variance. Thus, the equation implies that the smaller PMEs were growing at a faster rate than larger ones and that the level of industrial concentration must have

The Public Manufacturing Enterprise

Table VII.1. Relationship between opening size and growth for fifty Indian PMEs, 1972–9[a]

Opening size[b]	Average growth	Standard deviation	Number of firms
I. <10 million rupees	2.94	2.56	20
II. 10 to 20 million rupees	2.56	2.04	7
III. 20 to 40 million rupees	0.79	0.46	7
IV. Over 40 million rupees	0.97	0.60	16

Notes: [a] Information was available for a total of fifty-two firms. Two firms with extreme growth values have been excluded.
[b] Class size, in millions of rupees, was defined in terms of net assets.

declined. This impression is strengthened when we look at the information given in Table VII.2 which is a transition matrix showing the percentage of firms that remained in the same size class or changed size classes during the period studied. For example, among firms of the smallest size, 42.8 per cent remained in that class at the end of the period. Over 28 per cent expanded equivalent to one size class; another 19 per cent grew by two size classes and 9.5 per cent increased by three size classes. Consequently, slightly more than one half of the original firms (i.e. 57.2 per cent) moved out of the smallest size class. In comparison, among firms in class II at the beginning of the period, almost 86 per cent expanded by at least one class during the same period.

The results in Table VII.2 are biased downward because they do not allow for increases in the size of the largest firms during the period studied. Eight firms in largest class more than doubled their net assets in 1972–9. If these firms are moved up to a 'highest plus one' size class, the proportion of all firms not changing class size would be 49.1 per cent compared to the 63.6 per cent reported in the Table. This result would indicate a significant degree of internal mobility among the PMEs. Notably, mobility is greatest among the smaller firms. Again, the results provide indirect evidence that the growth of PMEs has had a modest negative impact on industrial concentration in the Indian manufacturing sector.

Table VII.2. Transition matrix for measuring firms' mobility: Indian PMEs, 1972–9

Opening size class		Closing size class			
		I	II	III	IV
		(percentages)			
I.	<10 million rupees	42.8	28.5	19.0	9.5
II.	10 to 20 million rupees	0	14.2	71.4	14.2
III.	20 to 40 million rupees		0	87.5	12.5
IV.	Over 40 million rupees				100.0

Proportion of total firms changing class by:

−1 size class	0 size class	+1	+2	−3
	63.6	23.0	9.6	3.8

Changes in industrial concentration may also be studied by analysing the relationship between growth and profitability. Following the methodology of Chapter VI, the relationship between growth and profitability was examined using single equation models. The 'best' estimates are given by the equation:

$$\text{Growth} = 7.927 + 0.397 \log \text{RREAS} \qquad R^2 = 0.132$$
$$(1.59) \quad (2.56)$$

where RREAS = rate of return on equity assets. This was the only instance where the regression coefficient was significantly different from zero.[42] There were no results where the value of the coefficient of determination exceeded 0.13. Consequently, the relationship between growth and profitability is thought to be weak.

When these results are compared to those in Chapter VI, important similarities become evident. The analysis of the TNC subsidiaries also revealed a weak (although statistically significant) negative relationship between growth and size on the one hand, and an equally weak positive association between growth and profitability on the other. This leads us to the conclusion that neither group of firms has grown in a fashion that accentuates existing levels of industrial concentration. Moreover, profitability has not been an important constraint or impetus for accelerating investment. As noted earlier, profits are strongly associated with growth in our sample of domestic private Indian manufacturing enterprises. Thus, significant differences in the determinants of the investment behaviour of PMEs and private firms in India seem likely.

The investment behaviour of PMEs in the sample was examined in terms of the capacity utilization, profit and 'combined' models.[43] In all, thirteen different equations were tested with best results given by the following

$$FA_t - FA_{t-1} = a + b_1 (FA_t) + b_2 (\overline{S}/\overline{FA}) + b_3 (S_{t-1})$$

where FA = fixed assets; S = sales and a bar indicates an average taken from period t-1 to period t.

These equations were fitted to annual cross-section data for the period 1973/74–1978/79. The salient results are summarized in Table VII.3. The capacity utilization equations provide a better estimate of variations in inter-firm investment rates, while the profit coefficients are rarely significant. The results are at variance with Krishnamurti and Sastri's findings for the Indian private corporate sector,[44] but are similar to our study of the investment behaviour among Indian subsidiaries. Apparently short-term profitability is not a determinant of investment behaviour for PMEs or TNCs as is the case for national private sector manufacturing enterprises.

In both PMEs and TNC subsidiaries demand considerations play an important role. Their investment is in response to domestic market conditions and short-run profitability is not a binding constraint on their ability to take advantage of buoyant demand. There are likely to be significant differences in the sources of finance available in PMEs on the one hand and TNC subsidiaries on the

Table VII.3. Investment behaviour of Indian PMEs: a summary of regression results

'Capacity utilization' models, highest R^2	0.97
'Profit' models, highest R^2	0.61
Combined models (containing both capacity utilization and profit indicators as independent variables, highest R^2	0.82
Sales coefficients (percentage of significant coefficients in total)	57%
Capital stock coefficient (percentage of significant coefficients in total)	84%
Capital intensity coefficient (percentage of significant coefficients in total)	35%
Profit coefficients (percentage of significant coefficients in total)	17%

other, but the preceding analysis suggests that both groups mobilize resources in response to changing demand conditions. This means that within the context of the Indian socio-political environment both PMEs and TNC subsidiaries may legitimately be viewed as 'economic' actors. Political pressures limit the ability of PMEs to pursue 'economic' objectives. Similarly, the need to achieve vertical integration over a wide range of internationally dispersed activities limits subsidiaries' ability to pursue profit or growth maximization in the host country.

Although these constraints did not prevent domestic market conditions from influencing investment decision in the case of India, there may be many LDCs (many 'intermediate regimes' in Kalecki's terminology) where such a relationship does not obtain for either PMEs or TNC subsidiaries. For example, in Thailand it has been found that the investment behaviour of the twenty largest TNC subsidiaries was not adequately explained by the accelerator, profit or combined models. The result may be attributable to external factors such as the level of political and economic stability in other potential host countries, or other factors not easily accounted for by these models.

The absence of an association between investment and profits once again led to a search for other determinants of inter-firm variations in profitability. Table VII.4 shows mean rates of return on equity and the dispersion of these rates among firms in each size class. No systematic relationship between size and profitability can be discerned. One noteworthy point, however, concerns the data for firms in the smallest class size. The variability of profits (measured by the standard deviation) is highest in this size class.

Table VII.4. Relationship between size and profitability: Indian PMEs, 1972/73–1978/79

Opening size classes		Mean rate of return	Standard deviation of rate of return
I.	<10 million rupees	5.81	11.1
II.	10 to 20 million rupees	8.01	3.8
III.	20 to 40 million rupees	8.31	4.5
IV.	Over 40 million rupees	7.11	7.5

The Public Manufacturing Enterprise

Larger firms enjoy a greater stability in terms of their average profit rates. The relationship between size and profitability was also tested by using linear regression analysis. Once again, no evidence of a strong relationship emerges. This is similar to the results obtained for the TNC subsidiaries sample. For private sector manufacturing enterprises on the other hand there is some evidence indicating that smaller firms are more profitable over time.

Clearly then size is not a prime determinant of inter-firm variations in profitability for the PMEs in our sample. An attempt was also made to relate profitability to the set of variables which describe financing patterns. The main findings are that all measures of profitability are significantly positively related to the internal finance measure and significantly negatively related to the gearing and borrowing ratios. This would indicate that PMEs generally rely on internal resources to achieve high levels of profits. Larger borrowers do not perhaps utilize their funds as effectively and access to credit does not necessarily ensure that existing opportunities to earn profits are realized. It was found that the *growth* of a firm in the public manufacturing sector was significantly associated with high values of the borrowing and gearing ratios. Rapidly growing PMEs had relatively easy access to credit and relied upon it to finance growth. However, since there is no significant positive association between growth and size, PMEs that are large borrowers need not necessarily be the larger firms within the sample.

A general conclusion is that conventional analysis is not a particularly adequate tool to explain differences in levels of profitability of PMEs. Similar conclusions apply to an analysis of the profitability of TNC subsidiaries undertaken in Chapter VI. On the other hand, a number of studies of corporate profitability of private Indian firms has shown a significant association between profitability indicators and financing variables. Thus, conventional theory does seem to provide an adequate framework for an analysis of profitability variations among private manufacturing firms in India.

Finally, an attempt was made to determine persistency of profits in the PME sample. A weak positive association was found between profitablility in the beginning and ending years of the study. The value of a Spearman rank correlation coefficient for firms ranked by profitability in the two years was 0.497. If we compare this estimate with the estimates for TNC subsidiaries and domestic private firms reported in the previous chapter, it is clear that there are no significant differences among the three samples. However, it must be emphasized that the estimates for the TNC subsidiaries and the domestic private firms relate to an earlier period and are not directly comparable with those for the PMEs. If this distinction is ignored, there are some grounds to conclude that a modest persistency of profitability characterizes all three groups of firms in the Indian manufacturing sector. Thus, there are a number of important similarities in the corporate policies pursued by public manufacturing firms and by TNCs.

In conclusion it may be argued that as far as investment behaviour is concerned PMEs, like TNCs, can be induced to participate in the expansion of those sectors that are likely to become increasingly competitive and efficient. Sustained demand appears to be a crucial factor in this regard. It is not high levels of short-term profitability but opportunities to expand sales and fully utilize existing production capacity that are the major influences determining a PME's investment behaviour. As argued in Chapter VI, during the 1950s and 1960s the Indian Government has not been particularly concerned with the expansion of 'efficient' industrial branches. The earlier development plans—particularly those drawn up under the guidance of Professor Mahalanobis—were consciously based on the Soviet model and placed heavy emphasis on the rapid expansion of the capital goods sector. A very large proportion of public enterprises has been located within these industrial branches and their growth has been determined primarily by the Government's abiding commitments to sustain relatively high levels of demand within these sectors. Problems of economic efficiency have become acute. The public sector has not been a large earner of net profits. Moreover, this problem is particularly significant since India has failed to achieve a high rate of surplus mobilization from the agricultural sector as with the case with the USSR. In recent years India has sought to redefine her public sector policy in order to increase the efficiency and competitiveness of the PMEs.

This has involved increased emphasis on the role of PMEs, as exporters. India is developing a competitive position in a wide range

The Public Manufacturing Enterprise

of international markets, including chemicals, steel products, metal manufactures and light electrical machinery. Some PMEs have seized the initiative and significantly expanded their exports. Prominent among these are BHEL which exports thermal sets, boiler equipment, transformers and compressors to the Middle East and the United States; HMT which exports radial drills, grinders, lathes, presses and tractors to the United States and Western and Eastern Europe; and PEC which exports bicycle parts, hand tools, automobile parts and textile machinery to several Asian and African countries. Some Indian PMEs—such as Engineering Projects Ltd., NBCC, and MECON—have emerged as important international contractors and consultancy groups and have won large contracts particularly in the Middle East and Nigeria. Total PME export earnings increased faster than the rate of growth of the country's export trade during the late 1970s.[45]

It is clear, therefore, that Indian PMEs can play a significant role in achieving industrial restructuring in accordance with India's changing comparative advantages. Whether they will be able to do so depends on the Government's industrialization strategy on the one hand, and on the access they can acquire in the world's capital and commodity markets on the other. Usually improved access to world markets can be achieved by expanding co-operation between Third World firms and TNCs. Such co-operation has been growing rapidly. In the case of the Indian PMEs, for example, many Middle Eastern contracts have been obtained due to successful co-operation with Japanese based TNCs.[46] In the next section we examine issues related to PME-TNC co-operation and evaluate the impact of such co-operation on industrial restructuring within the LDCs.

7.4 Problems and prospects of co-operation between transnationals and public manufacturing firms

PMEs have sought co-operation with transnationals for various reasons. In some cases the main objective was to acquire efficient production technologies. In others PMEs have sought export outlets through the distributional and marketing channels controlled by TNCs. It has sometimes been argued that export drives by

PMEs are a serious threat to transnationals. It has been maintained that 'US companies find it increasingly difficult to compete against state owned companies that are not required to earn profits and that receive numerous direct and indirect subsidies from their governments.'[47] In this view, PMEs need have no fear of loss or bankruptcy, no need to pay dividends and enjoy a monopolistic position in product markets.[48] However, export success has been limited by the inability of PMEs based in the Third World to tailor products to suit foreign markets or to commit large sums of money to advertisement and marketing. Export expansion has sometimes been sought through bilateral deals with other state enterprises. For example, agreements between Middle Eastern based oil producers and European state firms regulating the exchange of oil for technology have not been uncommon.[49] Such agreements have also been concluded between TNCs and state enterprises of other Third World countries.

Both TNCs and public manufacturing firms have the capacity to undertake long-term commitments. Short-run profitability is less of a constraint on these firms than on the smaller domestic enterprises. PMEs are particularly inclined to enter into relatively long-term regulator agreements guaranteeing supplies or access to markets. Such arrangements can be used to overcome deficiences created by their inability to achieve vertical integration in production and marketing activities through substantial foreign investment.[50] TNCs are advantageously placed in this respect. In industries where a wide geographical spread is of particular importance, collaboration between TNCs and public manufacturers may be of mutual advantage. Third World producers of petrochemicals and minerals usually maintain links with TNCs which operate as international distributors of these products. Thus, United States Steel is responsible for the world-wide marketing of Venezuelan state-owned iron ore, and the oil products of Middle Eastern state enterprises are usually distributed by transnationals.[51]

Co-operation between PMEs and transnationals is also evident in industrial branches where economies of scale are important yet flexibility has to be maintained. PME managers sometimes find that association with transnationals increases their autonomy with respect to their government,[52] and enhances the ability of their

The Public Manufacturing Enterprise

enterprises to engage in large-scale development programmes on a technological frontier.[53]

There are examples of TNC/PME associations in Third World countries that have existed for a considerably long period. It is worthwhile to examine closely the development of this relationship within a particular industrial branch in an LDC. This will allow us to identify the costs and benefits of long-term collaboration between transnationals and PMEs. We have chosen to look in some detail at the evolving relationship between PMEs and TNCs in the Brazilian petrochemical industry.[54] The industry has grown rapidly since the early 1960s. In 1962 petrochemicals production in Brazil was at a comparable level to that in other LDCs such as India. 'By 1973 Brazil [was] already in a position similar to that of Britain in 1962.'[55] Moreover, the expansion of the petrochemicals industry represented not 'import substitution' but the creation of new industrial capacity. The rapid growth that occurred during the 1960s and the 1970s was the result of collaboration between state enterprises, TNCs and the domestic private sector.

Until the early 1960s the Brazilian petrochemical industry was composed of a state oil monopoly, Petrobras, that controlled oil refining and exploration and several TNCs—Shell and Unilever in particular—responsible for distribution. Other TNCs—Union Carbide, Kopper and Borden and Solvay—dominated the production of petrochemical products. Local firms often used these products to manufacture plastic containers, synthetic textiles and plywood. In the late 1950s it became clear that there was a rapidly growing domestic demand for basic and intermediate petrochemical products. Neither the TNCs nor Petrobras were willing to seize the opportunity and substantially expand production. Local entrepreneurs took the initiative. A domestic group, Capuava, persuaded Petrobras to establish a new wholly owned subsidiary, Petroquisa, which was allowed to enter joint ventures with private firms on a minority basis. Capuava and Petroquisa became partners and built the Petroquimica Unào complex. This firm then established four joint ventures with TNCs, Petroquisa and local investors. These firms were to be the main customers of Petroquimica's output. The firms surrounding the Petroquimica complex organized themselves into a holding company, UNIPAR, in the early 1970s.

The International Economy and Industrial Development

Throughout the 1970s the relative importance of Petroquisa grew while the UNIPAR group of companies faced a series of problems.

> Petroquimica Unào had to pay the price of being a pioneer. . . . Despite the UNIPAR group's best efforts the downstream markets were still not all ready by the time the plant came on stream. . . . [Moreover] other problems entirely independent of petrochemicals had repercussions on the Capuava group's financial position and its ability to sustain its investment in the petrochemical industry.[56]

In 1974 Petroquisa took over Petroquimica Unào and UNIPAR became a minority shareholder. TNCs increased their share of UNIPAR's stock at the expense of domestic capital.

Gaining confidence and experience, the state enterprise pioneered the establishment of new petrochemical complexes in North-Eastern Brazil. A new subsidiary, COPENE, was created. This company was given the responsibility of building up a network of associated firms. These were established through the same strategy of linking state, foreign and domestic private capital that had been adopted in the creation of the UNIPAR complex. A large number of TNCs are involved in the ownership of the new petrochemical group.

> In one company, for example, the stock is shared among a European multinational, a Japanese firm and two local firms; the process they will use is licensed from an American firm. In another case ownership is divided between a Japanese firm, Petroquisa and a Brazilian firm (which) has two major American firms as shareholders; the process to be used is to be licensed from still another American firm. Superimposed on these interconnections is the additional interdependency created by the fact that one firm's ouput are other firms' inputs.[57]

The relationship between TNCs and public manufacturing firms operating in the Brazilian petrochemical industry now seem to be fairly stable. State capital has gained access to sophisticated technology, international finance and management expertise. TNCs have a secure source of raw materials. Moreover, the ability and willingness of PMEs to absorb short-term losses in order to develop the production of basic raw material makes them useful

The Public Manufacturing Enterprise

partners. Finally, collaboration with PMEs usually facilitates TNC dealings with other parts of the state bureaucracy. In Brazil, as in all rapidly industrializing LDCs, the state bureaucracy is deeply involved in the regulation of prices and wages of a large range of markets. Usually PME managers know the existing 'rules of the game' better than their TNC counterparts and can effectively surmount bureaucratic hurdles. TNCs entering a LDC for the first time, or TNCs contemplating expansion in a new industrial branch, find association with PMEs to be of particular advantage.

The establishment of long-term organizational links between TNCs and public manufacturing enterprises on the Brazilian pattern depends upon a number of factors. First of all, the international economic environment is an important determinant of the extent to which a TNC will respond to state initiatives for the establishment of joint ventures. Brazil was advantageously placed in this respect during the 1970s. She sought foreign investment at a time when economic prospects were becoming increasingly bleak in industrialized countries. Brazil had a growing domestic market and a strong repressive regime committed to maintaining a strictly centralized system of wage controls. 'Multinational managers are not likely to mention the repressive capacity of the Brazilian state as a central positive feature of Brazil's good investment climate, but the fact remains that it is essential.'[58]

Furthermore, collaboration between TNCs and PMEs was facilitated by the existence in Brazil of a class of 'burguesia do estado'[59] who managed the state enterprises. This technocratic managerial élite shares the work ethos and the ideology of the TNC boardrooms. The Petrobras administrative system is reported to be as good as that of any major TNC. Brazilian state enterprises are as concerned with maintaining efficient operating practices as are private enterprises in Brazil. This is so despite the fact that PMEs can afford to take a longer-term view of investment prospects and short-term profitability is not a serious constraint.

Collaboration between TNCs and PMEs does not require continuous mediation by the domestic private sector. The development of the Brazilian petrochemical industry has largely left the domestic private investors 'out in the cold'. Although the original initiative for expansion in this field came from a group of private

The International Economy and Industrial Development

entrepreneurs, neither this group nor other companies survived as major producers in the Brazilian petrochemical complex. 'The curious position of the local members . . . is most evident when the roster of participants in the Polo do Nordeste[60] is examined. Only about one third of them have industrial experience in petrochemicals. The rest are banking groups, construction companies or in some cases plastics or textile firms that are the users of the products being produced.'[61] The association of the local business groups is justified on nationalist grounds. In Brazil—a country strongly committed to a capitalist economic strategy—the elimination of domestic private enterprise from the petrochemical sector might give the impression that the state was 'selling out' to international capital.

Bearing these factors in mind, the Brazilian experience provides lessons for other LDCs seeking co-operation between TNCs and public manufacturing enterprises. Many are eager to attract TNCs. India, for example, has recently made substantial changes in its industrial policies in order to permit direct investment by OPEC in key industrial branches.[62] It is clear from our review of the Brazilian experience that the extent to which TNCs can be induced to accept partnership with state enterprises depends on the international environment. TNCs are most likely to be enthusiastic about such arrangements when investment opportunities in the home economies are rather limited. Furthermore, establishment of long-term co-operation between TNCs and PMEs also requires that the government of the LDC is willing and able to create a 'favourable' domestic investment climate. In the Brazilian case, wage restraints were particularly important in this respect. Moreover, co-operation at the enterprise level is also facilitated if the management of the PMEs and the foreign companies shares a common organizational ideology. In other words, both groups must aim at a long-run maximization of profits or growth. It is recognized that PMEs can afford to take a longer-run view of development prospects. This increases their ability to bear short-term losses. As long as commercial viability remains the overriding objective, the capability of PMEs to sustain losses increases their attraction as investment partners from the point of view of the TNCs. Finally, TNCs can be attracted to collaborate with public enterprises if the latter have political leverage within the system and are capable of surmounting

The Public Manufacturing Enterprise

bureaucractic hurdles within the domestic economy.

If these conditions are fulfilled, co-operation between TNCs and public manufacturing enterprise can flourish. An industrialization strategy that emphasizes such co-operation as a corner stone of its development programme is not necessarily efficient or equitable, however. Thus, 'Brazil has no obvious comparative advantage in petrochemicals at all'.[63] The industry's rapid growth was partly due to the strict price controls applied vigorously by the Government. Industrial concentration has been high and inefficiences in production are significant. Moreover, the industry's development had little perceivable impact on the level of employment and income distribution. 'The application of this model [in Brazil] has been accompanied by increasing inequality, rising infant mortality, new outbreaks of epidemic diseases and increasing hardship for large portions of the population.'[64] Whether such costs can be accepted as 'natural and inevitable' in LDCs with a more pluralistic political system remains an open question.

It is clear that TNC-PME co-operation in Brazil was developed in response to growing domestic demand for petrochemical products. On the other hand, the expansion of this industry in the Middle East has been related to the desire of many countries within the region to expand exports. These countries clearly saw the need to allocate investment resources in accordance with their international comparative advantages. Thus, the Second Saudi Arabian Plan (for the period 1975/76–1979/80) envisaged the construction of five very large petrochemical complexes, each capable of producing 500,000 tons of ethylene per year. It also provided for the construction of two new fertilizer plants. The PME in charge of these projects is the Saudi Arabian Basic Industrial Corporation (SABIC) established in 1975. SABIC is in the process of establishing agreements with Mobil, Pecten, Shell, Dow Chemical Europe, and Mitsubishi. Since none of the plants are operational as yet, the terms and conditions of association between SABIC and the TNCs are not finalized. It appears that Saudi Arabia is insisting that most joint ventures be established on a fifty-fifty basis. The insistence on shared management responsibility is particularly strong for export oriented projects. However, TNCs willing to invest in these projects are given generous loans at very low interest rates and, what is more important, potential partners are given the right to purchase extra quantities of crude. This increases the incentive of the oil majors to participate in manufacturing export oriented projects even if these projects are only marginally profitable. Despite these incentives the export oriented projects are moving ahead very slowly and none of the major TNCs have expressed an interest in speeding up the process. Potential political instability is a major factor inhibiting investment expansion. The interest of the TNCs may well pick up if the pioneering ventures prove to be a success or if the perception of political instability turns out to be false in the long run. But at present the outlook for expansion within the world petrochemical industry is bleak.

If the TNCs' interest in hydrocarbon processing industries in the Middle East does not expand, one of two responses may be expected from host governments. They may increase the level of subsidization of feedstock and capital to the foreign investor to the point that the increased costs of transport and construction are entirely offset. Such a policy of subsidization is likely to augment protectionist pressures within western markets; overcoming of these barriers will not be an easy task. Middle Eastern governments will place increasing reliance on 'favourite' TNCs (or TNC conglomerates) to breach tariff and non-tariff barriers. In such a scenario the PME will gradually decline in importance as a source of management control and as a shaper of corporate strategy. It may tentatively be argued that the Saudi approach is likely to be of this type. It seems logical that the TNCs will argue for 'an international division of labour in which the Middle Eastern countries concentrate on the production of the simpler base chemicals'.[65] This will encourage a geographical integration of the petrochemical industry which may provide a stimulus for the gradual removal of marketing barriers.

The other scenario envisages increased friction between Middle Eastern governments and TNCs due to the latter's unwillingness to commit substantial investment to petrochemical plants located in these countries. In this case the PME is likely to increase its influence. Its investment programme is less likely to be conditioned by short-run profitability considerations and marketing opportunities. It is likely to go for large-scale integrated petrochemical complexes since these provide the best opportunity for gaining technological and managerial experience. Its relations with TNCs will remain primarily limited to trading arrangements. This pattern has in the past been adopted by both Algeria and Iraq and is likely to be seriously considered by the revolutionary Government in Iran. Its most serious drawback is that reliance on PMEs will almost inevitably limit the market access of Middle Eastern petrochemical producers in the West. It is therefore likely that Middle Eastern petrochemical producers will seek to penetrate South and South-East Asian markets and to foster regional arrangements. Conceivably, such ventures may be of interest to both oil and chemical TNCs which have a significant investment stake in these areas.

Whatever the pattern of development of the petrochemical industry within the oil rich countries of the Middle East, its expansion cannot in itself ensure that industrialization will lead to an efficient or equitable use of the resource potential of the country concerned. This is most clearly evident in the case of Iran where the rapid expansion of this sector did not lead to a consolidation of the development effort. The captial-intensive technology employed ensured that the vast majority of the labour force did not directly benefit from the expansion of this industry. Unemployment rose and the pattern of income distribution became increasingly unequal during the 1970s.

The integration of the petrochemical complexes within the national economy remains an important task which has not yet been adequately tackled in the Middle East. Thus, backward linkages with the agriculture sector can be developed by encouraging the domestic production of pesticides and fertilizers. The step will ensure that the expansion of the petrochemical industry will have a strong 'spill-over' effect in the rural sector and contribute to an expansion of both agricultural production and employment. This suggests that investing in accordance with a country's comparative advantage requires not only production of the 'right' goods but also an awareness of the impact of this investment upon the rest of the economy. There is a need to deliberately foster national economic integration and to intensify linkages between the expanding industrial branches and the other economic sectors. PMEs may have a crucial role to play in this regard. They can encourage local

The International Economy and Industrial Development

subcontracting and stimulate effective demand in a variety of ways. An expansion of domestic demand is likely to be of interest to TNCs whose investment in most LDCs is in response to expanding domestic market opportunities. If PMEs (and other economic agents) can convince TNCs that increased export opportunities in specific industries can lead to a significant expansion of domestic demand in a Third World country, this may prove a viable basis for envisaging long-term association of a form that reflects the mutual interest of both western countries and LDCs.

Notes

[1] M. Gillis, 'The role of state enterprise in economic development', *Social Research*, Summer 1980, pp. 248–69.
[2] *Ibid.*, p. 254.
[3] *Ibid.*, p. 357.
[4] For a survey of this type of literature, see e.g. R. Turvey, *Economic Analysis and Public Enterprise*, Allen and Unwin, London, 1971.
[5] Choksi, for example, lists no less than twenty-five objectives of public enterprises. See M. Choksi, *State Intervention in the Industrialization of Developing Countries*, World Bank Staff Working Paper No. 341, Washington, 1979, p. 8.
[6] For a survey, see R. Layard, *Cost Benefit Analysis*, Penguin, Baltimore, 1974.
[7] D. Lall, 'Public enterprises', in *Policies for Industrial Progress in Developing Countries*, J. Cody, H. Hughes and D. Wall (eds.), UNIDO/IBRD, Oxford University Press, London, 1980, pp. 219–20.
[8] This is the Little-Mirlees method of evaluating public sector investment. See I. M. Little and J. Mirlees, *Project Appraisal and Planning for Developing Countries*, Heinemann, London, 1974.
[9] See e.g. Stewart and Streeten, 'Little-Mirlees method and project appraisal', *Bulletin of Oxford University Institute of Economics and Statistics*, 1972, pp. 75–91; F. Stewart, 'A note on social cost benefit analysis and class conflict in LDCs', *World Development, 1975*, pp. 31–9; S. Lall and P. Streeten, *Foreign Investment, Transnationsl and Developing Countries*, Macmillan, London 1977, pp. 49–53 and 184–8; and A. K. Sen, 'Control areas and accounting prices; an approach to economic evaluation', *Economic Journal*, 1972.
[10] For qualifications to this statement, see F. Stilwell, *Normative Economics*, Pergamon, Oxford, 1975.
[11] S. Lall and P. Streeten, *op cit.*, p. 186.
[12] This assumes that such a consensus can be consistently articulated by the processes of national politics in LDCs.
[13] K. Marx, *A Contribution to the Critique of Political Economy*, Progress, Moscow, p. 8.
[14] K. Marx, *Capital*, Vol. 1, Moore and Aveling, London, 1886, pp. 148–9.
[15] K. Marx and F. Engels, *Manifesto of the Communist Party*, Progress, Moscow,

1971, p. 46.

[16] *Ibid.*, p. 54.

[17] R. Sobhan, 'Public enterprise and the nature of the state', *Development and Change*, Vol. 10, No. 1, 1979, pp.29–36.

[18] *Ibid.*, p. 29.

[19] Thus J. Stalin, *Economic Problems of Socialism in the USSR*, Progress, Moscow, 1953, argues that commodity production did not exist in the nationalized sector of the Soviet economy, pp. 23–6.

[20] V. I. Lenin, *The State and Revolution*, Progress, Moscow, 1973, p. 71

[21] This is the generally accepted definition of property rights. See E. G. Furubotn and S. Pejovich, 'Property rights and economic theory: a survey of recent literature', *Journal of Economic Literature*, Dec. 1972, p. 1139.

[22] For a contrary view with regard to the USSR, see H. Ticktin, 'The political economy of the USSR', *Critique*, No. 1, 1977, pp. 21–47.

[23] Furubotn and Pejovich, *op. cit.*, p. 1154.

[24] E. Zaleski, *Planning Reform in the Soviet Union*, Chapel Hill, University of North Carolina Press, 1967.

[25] For a detailed description, see V. Stanovic, 'The forms, character and development of self managment in Yugoslavia', in International Centre for Public Enterprises, *Workers Self Management and Participation*, Vol. 1, ICPE, Ljubljana, 1980, pp. 357–455.

[26] On this, see B. Ward, 'Worker management in Yugoslvaia', *Journal of Political Economy*, Oct. 1957, pp. 373–80.

[27] The size of the Workers Council depends on the size of the enterprise.

[28] Stanovic, *op. cit.*, p. 364.

[29] *Ibid.*, p. 384.

[30] *Ibid.*, p. 383.

[31] i.e. public enterprises.

[32] Stanovic, *op. cit.*, p. 365.

[33] *Ibid.*

[34] See B. Bajt, 'Property in capital and in the means of production in socialist economies', *Journal of Law and Economics*, April 1969, pp. 113–41.

[35] E. G. Furubotn, 'Towards a dynamic model of the Yugoslav firm', *Canadian Journal of Economics*, May 1971, pp. 182–97.

[36] J. Dirlam and J. Plummer, *An Introduction to the Yugoslav Economy*, Merrill Columbus, 1973, Chapter 1.

[37] Chapter I of this volume reviews the historical development of Britain and Germany.

[38] Bureau of Public Enterprise, *Public Enterprise Survey*, New Delhi, various issues.

[39] These categories are used by our data source. See e.g. Bureau of Public Enterprise, *Public Enterprise Survey 1978–79*, New Delhi, Vol. 3, 1979, p. 10.

[40] *Ibid.*, various issues.

[41] This is offset by the fact that since 1978 attempts have been made to delegate greater authority to the companies which had been subsidiaries of the Steel Authority of India Ltd. but were reconstituted as independent companies. See Government of India, *Public Enterprise Survey*, 1978–79 p. 1.

The International Economy and Industrial Development

[42] Nine models were estimated.
[43] Described briefly in Chapter VI. See also E. Kuh, *Capital Stock Growth: A micro-econometric Analysis*, North Holland, Amsterdam, 1963, Chapter 2.
[44] Reported in Chapter VI of this volume.
[45] Bureau of Public Enterprise, *op. cit*, vol. 1, 200.
[46] *Ibid.*
[47] K. D. Walters and R. J. Mansen, 'State owned businesses abroad. New competitive threat', *Harvard Business Review*, March-April 1979, pp. 164–71.
[48] *Ibid.*, pp. 164–5.
[49] L. Turner, *Oil Companies in the International System*, London, Allen and Unwin, 1978, p. 180.
[50] Some LDC based PMEs do, however, invest abroad on an impressive scale.
[51] R. Vernon, *The International Aspects of State Owned Enterprises*, Harvard University, 1980 (mimeo), p. 17.
[52] A. Basant and C. Raj, *Public Enterprise Investment Decision in India*, Macmillan, Delhi, 1977, p. 123.
[53] *Ibid.*, p. 127.
[54] The following paragraphs rely heavily on P. Evans, 'Multinationals, state owned corporations and the transformation of imperialism', *Economic Development and Cultural Change,* Vol. 20, No. 1, 1977, pp. 43-64.
[55] *Ibid.*, p. 45.
[56] *Ibid.*, p. 52.
[57] *Ibid.*, p. 54.
[58] *Ibid.*, p. 59.
[59] i.e. state bourgeoisie.
[60] The petrochemical complex in the Brazilian North East.
[61] Evans, *op. cit.*, p. 60.
[62] 'India maps out a new strategy', *Far Eastern Economic Review*, Nov. 7, 1980, pp. 68–9.
[63] Evans, *op. cit*, p. 47.
[64] *Ibid.*, p. 64.
[65] L. Turner and J. Bedore, *Middle East Industrialization*, Saxon House, London, 1979, p. 160.

Chapter VIII

Industrial Restructuring and International Negotiations

Before attempting to draw any general conclusions from the analysis of the foregoing chapters, it is helpful to recall that our conception of restructuring stressed the international (rather than the national) characteristics of the process. This interpretation seems particularly appropriate to manufacturing since, more than any other sector, the degree of international interdependence and specialization is excessive. Today, there are few industrial processes that are not affected in some way by foreign economies. Industries may be dependent on imported raw materials or intermediate inputs, imported capital equipment and technology, foreign labour and management. Alternatively, they may supply foreign markets or find themselves subject to vigorous competition from foreign producers of substitute products. Consequently, the manner in which societies choose to deal with the external sector is crucial to their industrial performance.

A related point, made both explicitly and implicitly in the foregoing chapters, concerns the interrelationship between structural change and industrial policy. Our emphasis on the role of interest groups—industrialists, trade unions and government bureaucracies in various countries—leads us to conclude that their behaviour often provides a nebulous, though important, link between structural changes and policy initiatives. The manner in which vested interest reacts to adjustment pressures influences policy decisions and the resultant pace and extent of structural change. Frequently, a coalition of interest groups succeeds in fashioning new policy initiatives designed as a response to the

The International Economy and Industrial Development

pressures for adjustment associated with structural changes. This direction of causation is contrary to the more typical sequence implied by policy discussions. There, economists usually assume that policy decisions will lead to structural changes (not deter them), either by virtue of the effectiveness of the policies or because they re-enforce existing patterns of change. In practice, both sequences may occur, although in today's global industrial environment the former pattern of causation takes on added importance.

The above description suggests that, in comparison to other economic fields, the manufacturing sector's pattern of development is circumscribed by existing international agreements/mechanisms and national policy decisions having international consequences. This applies regardless of the prevailing causal relationship between structural change and policy making. However, we have made clear that, in our opinion, the influence of interest groups on policy formulation is frequently underestimated. Previous chapters have stressed this interpretation with regard to: a society's choice of a development strategy, the intricate relationships between industrial investment, production and trade at the sectoral and branch levels and the changing patterns of industrial ownership and control.

The influence of interest groups can also be seen in the field of international negotiations whether these pertain to general subjects such as foreign aid, basic needs, etc. or to more specific issues like the Tokyo Round or the Multifibre Arrangement. In this final chapter we address this subject, examining the institutional setting, the relationship between structural change and interest group behaviour in both the West and the LDCs and conclude by looking at the potential role of international negotiations for the restructuring process.

8.1 The institutional setting and industrial realities

The story of the dialogue of the New International Economic Order (NIEO) is not a happy one. Except for a few minor and more technical issues, there has been no real progress, either over the broader range of issues, or on questions pertaining directly to industrialization and trade in manufactured products. This widespread frustration was recently expressed by the Brandt Commis-

Industrial Restructuring and International Negotiations

sion when it called for 'more flexible, expeditious and result-oriented procedures to be introduced without detracting from co-operation within established groups.'[1]

Dissatisfaction is general, extending to the methods of negotiation which are thought to have contributed to past failure in reaching agreements. The Group system which has now consolidated itself as a pattern of alignment divides countries into three groups: the Group of 77 which now includes over 120 LDCs, Group B (western countries) and Group D (socialist countries). China occupies a somewhat separate position. This system, which has dominated many discussions, is based on the presumptions that: (a) there are sufficient common interests within each Group to enable them to arrive, fairly easily, at constructive, agreed positions through internal discussions and, (b) discussions can be simplified by reducing the number of negotiating positions to only three.

The validity of these presumptions has been questioned by the Brandt Commission, in previous chapters of this book and elsewhere. The Groups are by no means homogeneous. Our analysis of growth patterns in LDCs (see Chapter III) suggests that, if anything, the degree of heterogeneity is increasing. Moreover, it is not clear that a common general interest in a NIEO will ensure common interests on specific problems. Regarding industrialization, our analysis of trends in production, export performance and comparative advantages suggests widely divergent experiences among countries at different levels of development. The interests of the NICs are distinct not only from those of other LDCs but are often unique to the specific country. As Killick has argued, 'outside the diplomatic conveniences of international agencies and other aid donors, there is a real sense in which the Third World no longer exits.'[2] If one tries to establish common positions among countries with such divergent prospects, the obvious danger is that agreement can be reached only by adding up the various interests to the different categories of countries, a practice which results in long 'shopping lists' and makes negotiations very difficult to manage.

Problems also exist within Group B, although our empirical analysis suggests that they are somewhat different in nature. Our discussion of neo-protectionism in both its 'defensive' and 'competitive' phases is relevant here. The dispersion of industrial capacity

The International Economy and Industrial Development

has altered each country's approach to questions of international policy and, consequently, has modified the process of policy formulation at the international level. As different countries' shares in world production have changed, so have their capacities to influence international industrial policies. In the case of MVA, such trends are clearly evident from the data presented in Chapter III. Several observers of history have noted that the liberalization of economic relations depends inversely on the degree of equality in the distribution of power among nations.[3] The international distribution of power has become more equal as the relative monopoly of the US in world trade and industrial production has deteriorated. Increasingly, international policy initiatives have become multipolar, based on a system of collegial management in the West. Thus, negotiations pertaining to trade, investment, technology transfer and industrial restructuring are, at least temporarily, more tenuous as the new system evolves.

There are two dangers here. First, the demands of the Group of 77 (in the form of a shopping list) prompt few concessions or counter-proposals unless all members of Group B agree. Second, the positions of the most adamant domestic pressure groups in respective countries will receive undue weight, since the most 'hardline' negotiators will call the tune for the Group as a whole. This usually results in a confrontational situation not favourable to constructive negotiation.

The situation in Group D is somewhat different. Here, the main problem is that these countries maintain a general position of aloofness in the debate. They support the demands of the Group of 77 in most cases, but argue that actual measures of reform and support should apply only to Group B ('the capitalist camp') and not to Group D ('the socialist camp').

The system is further complicated by the existence of regional and trade blocks within each Group. In Group B, for example, the EEC countries must often reach a common position among themselves and then reconcile that view with those of the US, Japan, etc. Once again, advocates claim that the procedure simplifies matters, since the EEC speaks with one voice and the number of divergent positions is reduced. On the other hand, the reconciliation of views with the EEC raises new complications and frequent delays.

Industrial Restructuring and International Negotiations

Similarly with the Group of 77, the regional groupings—in Latin America, Africa, Asia, etc.—must often deliberate among themselves prior to discussion within the Group of 77 as a whole. Even within each regional block there may be sub-divisions, such as the Andean pact. Other affiliations cut across regional divisions, e.g. OPEC, the ACP States, etc.

A further complication is being added to the negotiations by the process of 'politization' of economic debates. Since many discussions are carried out within the UN system and form part of a global NIEO debate, the political conditions within the UN General Assembly—symbolized by the three groupings—extend also to many more technical fora where *prima facie* such political frameworks would seem to be unnecessary. This is further accentuated by the fact that technical agencies such as UNIDO, ILO, FAO, etc., are part of the United Nations system, and the group system in UN debates has inevitably spread to these other organizations as well.

The inherent weakness of universal negotiations involving 150 or more countries arranged in three Groups is that this system results, at best, in a superficial consensus where resolutions are drafted to cover up divergences of views. All participants are left dissatisfied and few, if any, countries regard their commitments as binding. Much of the effort in such negotiations is diverted from substantive issues to questions of semantics and drafting. At worst this method results either in confrontation or 'agreement to disagree'.

There are other considerations which are primarily national in scope but with important consequences for international negotiations. For example, even the realization of perceived national interests is contingent on agreement. Thus, compromises are required between conflicting sectional or industrial interests within the complex political body of the State. Some of these forces may favour a perceived national interest while others do not. The resolution of such conflicts will not necessarily coincide with the perceived interest since the majority view may be poorly organized or less forceful than the contrary position of a minority. This is notoriously true in matters of international trade where the organized interests of workers, employers and regions are nearly always stronger than those of others—consumers, importers, exporters, etc. In such cases, the negotiating process needed is an internal one within the industrial countries, before each perceived national interest can become an effective negotiating position in international negotiations.

A related problem which accounts for the difficulty of realizing positive-sum game opportunities concerns the difference between perceived long-run and perceived short-run interests. The government and community may agree, in the abstract, that long-term national interests would be served by, say, trade liberalization. However, a democratic government can rarely afford to plan beyond the next election, and the short-term difficulties may, in its opinion, cause it to lose the election before the long-run advantages can be realized. 'In the long run we are all dead.' In authoritarian countries, the preference given to short-term interests at the expense of long-term interests, may have reasons other than electoral necessities, but they may be equally weighty. Moreover, any civil service, whether in democratic or authoritarian countries, will have a strong preference for avoiding trouble and 'leaving things alone', rather than encouraging long-term structural changes that create more work, trouble and risks than a policy of catering to existing interests.

8.2 Structural change and interest group behaviour in western countries

In Chapter I we argued that the external sector's role in the development process is partly circumscribed when a society chooses (implicitly or explicitly) the development model to be followed. This choice is subject to the distribution of political power among interest groups on the one hand, and the available choice of technology on the other. Since both sets of forces undergo constant changes, the choice of a development model is not hard and fast. Other observers have noted that, during extended periods of economic prosperity and continuity in growth, the organization of interest groups gains in strength and influence.[4] Our analysis in Chapter III suggests that this is an apt description of conditions in the western world from the years after World War II until the mid-1970s. During that period the ability of interest groups to influence the choice of a development model (and the country's industrial policies) steadily expanded.[5] Their new-found ability began to be tested only as breaks in the continuity of the growth process emerged.

The reasons for these discontinuities are relevant since they partly explain interest group behaviour. We include international shocks to the economic system, such as the action of OPEC, departures from long-term growth patterns, like the slowdown in the West after twenty-five years of expansion, and the gradual emergence of some Third World countries as international economic powers. Other less dramatic but equally important causes of discontinuity may also be cited. First, preceding chapters documented the steady expansion in world trade that occurred between 1950 and 1970. Foreign demand grew more rapidly than domestic demand and, in the process, reduced the effectiveness of traditional means for macro-economic regulation. The resultant uncertainty left governments more amenable to the pressure from interest groups to convert commercial policy into an instrument for regulating the pace of structural adjustment.

Second, long-term employment trends reveal a decline in the manufacturing sector's share in many western countries. While earlier types of employment shifts, e.g. from agriculture to manufacturing or within the manufacturing sector, were easily accomplished, today's displaced workers frequently resist the move from the manufacturing sector to the service sector where employment is growing. These and other circumstances have contributed to a 'mismatch' in the demand and supply of resources, including labour, at the national level. Thus, when adjustment pressures emerge, resources do not immediately flow from unprofitable or contracting activities to new ones with growth potential. Mismatches are reflected in the simultaneous existence of labour shortages in some fields and job shortages in others, together with long delivery delays in certain production processes and surplus capacity in others.[6] Although pressures to adjust may mount, governments— spurred on by other interest groups—are inclined to respond by reducing the pace of structural change and the extent to which industrial restructuring occurs.

Third, interest groups in western countries have yet to fully

The International Economy and Industrial Development

appreciate the long-term consequences of industrial growth and structural change. Our study has shown that in early-to-intermediate stages of development the manufacturing sector tends to grow at a disproportionately rapid rate. Consequently, the prices of manufactured goods fall relative to those for other goods produced by services or agriculture. Between 1965 and 1980 there was a substantial rise in the ratio of commodity prices (including oil) relative to manufactures. Western countries bore the brunt of this shift since they were heavily specialized in manufacturing. Faced with a deterioration in real prices, investors shifted from manufacturing to other sectors. Thus, contraction in some fields of manufacturing was a sensible response to new world price conditions and market structures that reflected changes in comparative advantage favouring non-industrial activities. Various interest groups, however, regarded the contraction of manufacturing (which reflected only one side of the shift) as a seriously damaging trend and lobbied for both macro-economic and industry-specific policies to reverse the trend.

Although the international implications of these disagreements dominate national and international policy debates, there is usually a parallel field of conflict which is purely domestic in scope and receives less attention. One example is the controversy regarding trade in steel that led the US to introduce a new trigger price mechanism, although the interest of American automobile producers, clearly, was not served. Likewise, European efforts to maintain minimum price levels for various petrochemicals are hardly in the interests of European textile producers who depend on these supplies. While many of these issues are of immediate concern to only western industries, we have stressed the fact that neo-protectionist gains quickly spill over. The long-term prospects, if not the immediate ones, of Third World producers will be jeopardized.

Thus, the outcome of international negotiations and policy decisions on specific industrial fields such as these is significant for the restructuring process. Typically, the debate divides into two camps: the neo-protectionist (i.e. Western) side and the pro-restructuring advocates (represented mainly by the Third World). In most instances, however, there are interest groups in the western countries that stand to gain if protectionist solutions were not to prevail. The pro-restructuring forces in these countries obviously include consumers of final products who may be numerous but, frequently, are poorly organized. However, there are other interest groups that are apt to have compatible interests yet they are excluded from such negotiations. These other groups include industries which, through interindustry relationships, are linked to the protected activity along with relevant labour and financial interests as well as portions of the state, regional and national bureaucracies.

There are a number of reasons why such interests have not emerged as effective forces for restructuring. First, governments have made little effort to encourage this sort of approach. Domestic debates have usually matched only the neo-protectionist lobby against policy makers who are prone to support trade liberalization. Second, the gains and costs of organizing an effective lobbying effort vary from one interest group to another. This depends on the size of the industry, firm size, the degree of public ownership and many other factors. Government actions that reduce the cost of lobbying for restructuring purposes or, alternatively, raise the lobbying cost for neo-protectionists would help to alleviate pressure.[7] Third, under present circumstances many potential advocates of restructuring may find it less costly and more lucrative to lobby for protectionist support on their own behalf than to oppose other initiatives that may indirectly penalize them.

8.3 Structural change and interest group behaviour in the Third World

Rapid industrialization entails deep-seated economic and social changes. Since independence, most LDCs have vigorously pursued an objective of 'accelerated' industrial development. This has invariably meant that relations of production within these countries have been profoundly affected. The typical colony had an economy consisting of a large backward agricultural sector dominated by peasant farming. Agricultural production was intended for subsistence, not for exchange. Monetization was minimal and the commercial infrastructure was underdeveloped. An urban sector engaged in

The International Economy and Industrial Development

organizing trade between the agricultural hinterland and the metropolitan centre was also part of the colonial economy. The colony was a supplier of raw materials and was a consumer of industrial products manufactured in the West. There was little scope for domestic manufacturing and expatriate firms rarely played a part in the early industrialization of the LDC. In this respect, the initiative was almost always taken by the domestic bourgeoisie which recognized many activities where domestic industrial production could be efficient and profitable. World Wars I and II provided an added impetus for domestic manufacturing in Third World countries as trade between metropolitan and peripheral countries became increasingly hazardous. The pattern of economic and political administration within the colony did not, however, facilitate domestic manufacturing.

Thus, domestic manufacturers were induced to play an important role in most national independence movements of the Third World. These movements also attracted the support of the peasant masses. Both groups stood to gain from a revision of the economic relationship between the colony and its metropolis. The peasants hoped this would reduce the level and change the terms on which agricultural surplus was extracted from the rural sector. The domestic bourgeoisie hoped that constraints on the growth of domestic manufacturing would disappear. Consequently, independence movements were usually committed to both comprehensive land reforms and accelerated industrialization. In the case of most LDCs, emphasis in the initial phases of independence was on the commercialization of agriculture and import substituting industrialization. As noted in Chapter II, neither policy proved to be particularly successful. The failure of import substitution efforts in Latin American and in many Asian countries prompted planners to pursue industrialization strategies that combined a search for opportunities arising from changing conditions in international markets with policies intended to produce a re-ordering of domestic market preferences.

The priorities of many Third World countries indicate a desire to promote the expansion of branches such as steel and food manufacturing in response to changes in the structure of domestic demand on the one hand, and to encourage growth of export oriented

Industrial Restructuring and International Negotiations

branches such as petrochemicals and electronics on the other. It is relatively easy to identify domestic interest groups that will benefit from an expansion of specific industrial branches. Thus, the military establishment has a vested interest in the development of heavy industry complexes. The newly emergent 'kulaks' stand to gain from the development of industries such as food processing which link agriculture and industry. Domestic producers of light manufactures are likely to profit from an emphasis on export promotion. However, the ability of the various interest groups to influence government policy is not easily discerned. Research into decision-making processes—particularly in the field of industrial policy—has been rudimentary. Relatively little is known about the means by which a section of the political community acquires governing legitimacy and the manner in which this role is sustained within Third World politics. Clearly, a gradual displacement of the pre-capitalist mode of production and the marginalization and proletarization of the mass of the population is taking place in the LDCs through the development of a new institutional infrastructure which is historically unique. Neither the 'nightwatchman' State of the days of the British industrial revolution nor the authoritarian states of industrializing Germany, Japan or the USSR related themselves to civil society in the manner of the 'soft States' of the modern Third World. The 'typical' Third World State is not usually capable of sustaining interest coalitions that are politically viable and can support policies intended to accelerate the industrialization process.

Industrial restructuring in accordance with changing production conditions requires increased economic interaction between non-governmental groups at both the national and the international level. Some LDCs—Brazil, South Korea, Taiwan—have achieved rapid rates of industrial progress. Today these countries are referred to as the Newly Industrializing Countries (NICs) and it is sometimes argued that their association with the OECD countries is likely to be significantly strengthened. Thus, Emilio Fontela foresees the emergence of 'new growth poles' in the OPEC countries and a certain number of NICs having large export receipts and an internal capacity to pursue an industrialization process. A logical sequence, he believes, would include their integration into a

The International Economy and Industrial Development

broader 'industrialized world' together with today's OECD countries.[8] Such an integration would mean an increased level of interaction between producer, consumer and financier interests, both nationally and internationally. The central problem is the extent to which the governments of 'industrially advanced' LDCs can permit groups to bargain without reference to the broader political goals of the dominant political community. The political systems of most LDCs, 'industrially advanced' or otherwise, are highly fragile and political survival is achieved by an adroit balancing of potentially volcanic social and political forces. Development strategies that were worked out over decades can disintegrate within months. This has been the experience of Argentina in the 1950s, Pakistan in the 1960s and Iran during the last decade. The death of Park Chung Hee, the revolution in Nicaragua and the civil war in El Salvador may create pressures that fundamentally alter the political systems of some East Asian and Latin American countries. As a result, the form of these countries' integration into the international economic system may change.

Myrdal has observed that most Third World societies are 'soft States'. Their societies are ruled by political élites incapable of exercising social hegemony and of binding disparate elements together within the national polity. Nationalism itself is an alien import into Third World countries. Traditional institutions—the family, the tribe, the caste, the mosque, the bazaar—remain the foci of social life. In such societies political survival is ensured by putting 'politics in command' (to quote Mao Tze Dong) and by suppressing economic, social and ideological initiative at the level of civil society. Unless a Japanese-like blending of western and local institutions and norms takes root, it is difficult to see how Third World governments can permit domestic groups to operate uninhibitedly at the international level. This is one of the most important causes of the very limited success of regional economic groupings in the Third World.

Moreover, the many restrictions placed upon the operations and policies of public manufacturing enterprises (PMEs) in LDCs show the reluctance of governments to separate issues of political and economic management. As argued in Chapter VII, co-operation between TNCs and PMEs is both feasible and necessary for restructuring in a wide range of industrial branches. Yet in many LDCs—Bangladesh, Egypt, Iraq, Syria, Tanzania—PMEs are instruments of political administration. The dominant political party systematically controls decision-making at all levels within the PME. The political bureaucracy is an equal partner with the technocratic management in such enterprises. Clearly, PMEs such as these have very limited functional independence of the state apparatus. Even in countries such as India, Sri Lanka and Turkey, the government has often intervened to frustrate PME initiatives, particularly in relation to international trade and investment.

Thus, in periods of rapid growth, industrial policy requires a careful blending of the material interests of powerful social groups—a feat that Third World States have, generally, failed to achieve. Their domestic policies, as well as the nature and style of their involvement in international negotiation, are largely determined by the desire to avert the threat of total disintegration through economic upheavals and political chaos.

Given the tenuous circumstances in various LDCs, their participation in international negotiations may constitute an alternative to remedial action at the level of domestic policy. As long as negotiations do not result in substantive policy changes, they entail no substantial political costs. If, however, dominant domestic groups must bear the costs resulting from successful negotiations, the enthusiasm currently evidenced by Third World governments may be dampened. As Chapters IV and V have shown, the structures of industrial output and exports of western countries and LDCs (particularly the NICs) are becoming increasingly disparate. There may be little interest group support in the latter countries for negotiations of a type that integrate their industrial structure with that of the West. Even under these circumstances, however, various LDCs are likely to continue the negotiating process in the hope of (a) extracting marginal concessions and (b) using these fora for symbolic purposes to emphasize the constraining role of the international policy environment (rather than the national policy environment). Obviously the substantive results of negotiations conducted in this manner would be minimal.

It is sometimes argued that in the long run the emergence of non-governmental initiatives, particularly at the international level,

The International Economy and Industrial Development

will be detrimental to the interests of the Third World countries. This is the view of the 'dependencia' scholars who expect that any increase in the level of transactions between North and South will inevitably increase the dependence of the latter upon the former. In their view, the Law of Unequal Exchange ensures an inequitable distribution of the gains from trade. Similarly they assume that the TNC is under all circumstances an agent of the industrialized countries and acts to transfer resources on increasingly disadvantageous terms from the South. The dependency school, therefore, recommends autarchy and isolation and puts emphasis on the achievement of the objective of collective self-reliance. In their view, and in the view of orthodox Marxists, the State is the sole legitimate representative of society and any attempts at direct international negotiation are likely to be subversive.

The State, however, is not capable of formulating and implementing economic policies without developing an understanding with the most dynamic sections of society who see it as serving their interests. An identity of interests between political functionaries, merchants and industrialists sustained British industrial policy during the nineteenth century. Similarly, the Bolshevik party which pioneered Soviet industrialization claimed that it was acting on behalf of the proletariat. Throughout Stalin's rule party propaganda emphasized the material gains of the proletariat since the revolution. The importance of sustaining an alliance between economic interest groups and the political community, even in authoritarian States, is emphasized by current events in Poland. There, the increasing alienation of the ordinary mass of workers from the governing élite has meant a loss of political credibility for the Communist Party and its economic policies.

8.4 Industrial restructuring and international negotiation

Since the inception of UNCTAD in 1964, LDCs have attached great importance to negotiations as a means of changing the international economic system. Their lack of progress is attributable to a more fundamental reason than the procedural problems noted above, i.e. adherence to the Group system, the use of inappropriate negotiating techniques or the selection of inefficient international fora. Essentially, negotiations have begun from the false premise that the LDCs are asking for concessions or sacrifices from the industrial countries on humanitarian, moral or political grounds. That premise does not hold in today's world while the industrial countries suffer from inflation, depression, unemployment, a lack of confidence and instability. Industrial restructuring need no longer be a zero-sum game. Genuine negotiations on restructuring could be a positive-sum game where we can all be better off by re-ordering our affairs differently.

The post-World War II interpretation of mutual interests, presumed that with steady growth in the industrial economies, the benefits were bound to 'trickle down' to the LDCs. Such an interpretation is no longer acceptable to the LDCs and, in any case, it is no longer operational but works in reverse. Just as the growth of industrial countries was supposed to 'trickle down', so now stagflation in industrial countries and their other troubles are 'trickling down' in the form of reduced exports, trade barriers, imported inflation, reductions in aid, etc. Moreover, the present trickle down of trouble seems to be more effective than the trickle down of benefits from growth.

The idea that positive-sum games call for some kind of collective agreement was first put forward by J. M. Keynes in the early 1930s. It was then applied to the domestic scene of industrial countries in a period of depression and unemployment. Domestic Keynesianism had its biggest triumph in western economies after Bretton Woods; it was based on the principle that all partners had an interest in sustained growth and full employment, rather than fighting about shares in a static total of production. Keynes showed that the question of distribution can be dealt with by adjusting the rules of the game so that all participants—workers, employers, government—would be better off than if the depression had been allowed to continue. In this sense, Keynes was the real founder of development economics: he showed that the 'rules of the game' are different (or should be different) for an economy suffering from a labour surplus and unutilized capacities from those in an economy with full employment. In the same way the basic tenet of development economics is that the 'rules of the game' in countries with unlimited supplies of labour should be different from those of industrial countries.[9]

Domestic Keynesianism brought acceptance of the concept of a 'welfare state' in western societies. The idea that the eradication of domestic poverty was not a sacrifice by the better-off members of the community but, on the contrary, was in their own interest when accompanied by full employment and steady growth under stable conditions met with vigorous opposition. It was accepted only after a long struggle and after the upheaval of World War II. Today, proposals for an international welfare economy in which the eradication of poverty in the poorer countries serves as the engine for world growth encounter similar difficulties, given the present state of international organization and international perceptions. Yet the extent of the present world depression and instability and the formidable problems faced by all are equivalent in magnitude to the upheavals of World War II.

If a Keynesian interpretation of mutual interests and interdependence is accepted as the basis of positive-sum games and the foundation of international negotiations, what are the implications for methods of negotiation? One implication concerns the necessity—whether by the summit technique, the UN General Assembly or in some other way—to achieve political agreement on the existence and extent of such mutual interests. This is precisely what the summit proposed by the Brandt Commission was supposed to achieve. Second, it would be desirable to start with areas where the existence of mutual interests is particularly clear and more readily accepted. The difficulty is that, while the presence of mutual interests is widely or even universally accepted in some areas, there may still be disagreements—both within and between countries—about the precise methods of realizing these interests. It is widely recognized that there are many fields in which LDCs and western countries can profit by fruitful co-operation. In a recent publication, Richard Jolly lists thirteen such areas of mutual interest.[10] They include liberalization of international trade, stabilization of commodity prices, maintainance of a growing transfer of financial resources to the LDCs, development of new sources of energy, population and migration policy, ensured supplies of raw materials from LDCs, an acceleration of the pace of the transfer of

Industrial Restructuring and International Negotiations

appropriate technology to the Third World, promotion and regulation of TNC investment in LDCs, etc. In some ways nearly all of these areas are related to the progress of industrialization in the Third World. Like industrial restructuring, these fields have already been the subject of intensive, although not particularly fruitful, international negotiation.

A persistent weakness of negotiations on industry, as well as on other fields of interest, is a tendency to vague and general formulations and resolutions, often made even more obscure by the desire to paper over differences by verbal compromises. Quantitative targets, in particular, have often seemed attractive as a way of countering or avoiding this vagueness. The concrete nature of quantitative targets may, however, be illusionary. A target is only useful if it is either fully accepted on a voluntary basis, or else if it can be enforced; those lacking such attributes may have little practical value. Where such targets are accepted (if not enforced), their adoption may also create moral pressures for implementation although no such pressure existed prior to the negotiation.

In the case of industry, two alternative quantitative measures are available. The better known is the Lima target, according to which the LDCs should raise their share of world industrial output to 25 per cent by the year 2000.[11] A second UN exercise, adopted in connection with the International Development Strategy (IDS), sets targets for the growth of the LDC's GNP and industrial ouput. There is no evidence that the existence of the Lima target itself has led to positive action or agreement on industrial restructuring. On the other hand, the existence of the target and the failure to be 'on target' in an approach to it have served to highlight the need for continuing and intensified international action.

Significantly, the two targets do reflect contrasting philosophies that are also distinguishable in other NIEO negotiations. The IDS target, an actual minimum increase of industrial production, assumes that the end objective is to improve conditions in LDCs without reference to what happens in industrial countries. This line of reasoning is in accordance with the traditional view of interdependence of mutual interests and is compatible with the presumption that the industrial countries constitute the main engine of world growth. By contrast, the Lima target looks at the distribution of industrial power and is based on the view that the relative industrial power of different sets of countries should be changed. In this instance, the redistribution of industrial power is regarded as a pre-condition for sustained improvement in LDCs.

Both quantitative measures can be criticized on other counts. First, they are of a global nature. Hence, they do not directly refer to the distribution of industrial growth among LDCs and ignore the participation of the least developed and poorest countries in any global progress. Second, the targets tell us nothing about the quality of industrialization, i.e. whether the goods produced can serve basic needs benefiting the general population, are luxury goods for a small minority, or if they are capital goods produced using appropriate or inappropriate technology, etc.

Regardless of doubts about acceptability or viability of the Lima target, it is the nature of such an achievement and not the fact of its accomplishment that will govern the Third World's industrial performance. An autonomous effort on the part of LDCs will be required to develop those branches in which they are becoming increasingly competitive and to harmonize economic and social policies in order to maximise the developmental impact of such a pattern of industrial growth.

We have already noted the general limitations of the Group system. Furthermore, the composition of participants is particularly inappropriate for industry—specific negotiations which should include not just governmental representatives but also representatives of national and international business, labour and consumers. Participation of non-governmental groups in UN organizations is, of course, not a new phenomenon—the International Labour Office has included representatives of both sides of industry since its inception. However, western based TNCs, trade unions and consumer associations have, in general, evidenced little enthusiasm to participate in North-South negotiations on either industry or trade issues. Attention must be paid to the task of increasing the interest of non-governmental groups at branch level negotiation.

Negotiations between producers, consumers and financiers based in the industrialized countries and the LDCs in specific industrial branches—such as steel, food manufacturing, agricultural machinery—may well pave the way towards an important political breakthrough in North-South relations on questions of industrial restructuring.

Another requirement for successful industry-specific negotiations is that the representatives of investors, workers, traders, financiers and consumers in a particular industrial branch discuss the whole range of issues relevant to restructuring. In contrast, the present UN system of intergovernmental bargaining artificially segregates issues of trade, investment, transfer of technology and financing. Trade questions are discussed in GATT and UNCTAD, issues of investment and technology may be raised at the UNIDO consultations and financing is the exclusive domain of the IMF and the World Bank. It is inconceivable that any agreement on investment in a specific industrial branch can bring successful results without simultaneous agreements on questions of trade, international pricing and the regulation of restrictive business practices. However, there is little evidence to suggest that the present lack of co-ordination can be easily remedied, given the existence of independent fora. Industry-specific negotiations addressing issues of investment, finance, trade and technology transfer among groups representing producers, workers, financiers and consumers may circumvent the artificial barriers erected between these issues at the international level. Such international initiatives may also by-pass some of the existing political hurdles that handicap current UN-sponsored negotiations.

Turning from the structure of international negotiations to their substance, the almost exclusive concentration on North-South issues is hardly justifiable. The significance attached to this line of negotiation leaves the impression that there is nothing of substance to be gained from other types of dialogue. In some ways, however, more rapid progress could be made by negotiations other than North-South. Two such cases in particular come to mind: one is South-South negotiations and the other is what might be called a global bargain with OPEC.

Taking South-South negotiations first, it is surprising how relatively little has been done to promote fuller economic co-operation among LDCs as part of the NIEO discussions. These countries account for the bulk of the world's population and, in spite of their limited purchasing power, a considerable share of world

The International Economy and Industrial Development

markets. They contain a great variety of resources and conditions and, if the OPEC countries are included, are a capital surplus area. They account for the production of many essential commodities, even apart from oil, and include considerable industrial capacity. The combination of producer agreements for primary commodities, preferential trading systems amongst LDCs and recycling of financial surpluses within these countries, combined with the establishment of a transport and financial infrastructure, could go a long way towards the realization of a NIEO.

From the industrial countries' point of view, there should be no reason to oppose intensified co-operation among LDCs. While industrial countries might be highly suspicious of producer agreements, few if any of the commodity markets seem capable of precipitating the type of price explosion which was seen in the case of oil. Improved recycling of finance within the Third World would relieve the burden on the commercial banking system of industrial countries and contribute to international monetary stability. An expansion of world trade as a result of preferential trading throughout the Third World would increase prosperity and expand Third World markets also for industrial countries, specifically the demand for imported capital goods. Politically, intensive South-South relations would take some of the pressures off the North-South discussions. In any case, the industrial countries having established close collaboration amongst each other, both *de jure* under the EEC and *de facto* through OECD/GATT/MTN, can hardly object to similar co-operation among LDCs. Their official position is in fact to support 'economic co-operation among developing countries' (ECDC).

ECDC would be especially useful in relation to industrialization. Certainly the Lima target cannot be reached simply by producing for domestic markets, or for the markets of industrial countries which may be increasingly protected by trade barriers. Some of the obstacles to ECDC are the lack of a transport, financial and commercial infrastructure oriented towards South-South exchange; the present system is almost entirely oriented to North-South exchanges. Another obstacle is the international network of TNCs. However, with proper regulation and good bargaining, the network could be helpful to South-South interchanges. Although TNCs may be reluctant to support exports from their LDC-based plants to industrial countries where they have their main establishments, they might be quite willing to promote exports from one LDC to another provided that the trade does not interfere with their main operations. The establishment of the necessary infrastructure, although a costly and longer-term development, would seem to be quite feasible if financial resources of OPEC countries were made available.

This last point leads us to the role of OPEC countries. In this area it seems that one of the political pre-conditions towards progress on the lines of the Brandt Report, other NIEO lines or the UN International Development Strategy, would be a global bargain between the western countries and OPEC. For political reasons, western countries are unlikely to agree to the kind of massive resource transfers to non-OPEC (NOPEC) countries implied in the discussion. They reason that such transfers would simply strengthen the recipients' capacity to pay higher oil prices to OPEC. In that case, the transfers would amount to a subsidy for OPEC, a result for which there is neither economic nor political support among the taxpayers of industrial countries. Furthermore, the western fear of provoking oil price explosions prevents, or serves as a pretext for, the rejection of the types of expansionist policies that would boost their demand for the LDCs' products and alleviate protectionist pressures.

A global bargain between the industrial countries and OPEC would best be achieved in direct negotiations between the two groups; North-South discussions of a general nature have not proved useful for this purpose. In the past, OPEC has rejected the consideration of energy as a separate item of discussion outside the North-South dialogue. But the framework proposed here is somewhat different. The basis of the global bargain is to remove the obstacle, or pretext, that prevents western countries from making the resource transfers called for by the Brandt Commission or NIEO programme. The intention would be to benefit the NOPEC countries in two ways: through lower oil prices and via massive resource transfers. At the same time, the proposed bargain is not simply a matter of concessions by OPEC to the industrial countries, but would entail reverse concessions. It will also satisfy one of

The International Economy and Industrial Development

OPEC's most important demands, that of inflation-protected investments for their income surpluses.

Such a bargain would have three elements:

1. OPEC would supply cheap oil (half-price?) to NOPEC countries. This could be done either by differential pricing (of which OPEC has been suspicious in the past) or, if OPEC prefers, by financial rebates, in strict proportion to oil imports on a non-discriminatory basis for all NOPEC countries. It may be noted that Venezuela and Mexico (the latter not a member of OPEC) are already operating such a system in Central America and the Caribbean.
2. The oil price to the industrial countries must be determined and agreed in advance, possibly in real terms rather than in money terms. This is necessary to prevent the resumed economic growth of industrial countries—vital to the Third World as well as the West—from being nipped in the bud by yet another unexpected explosion of oil prices. If prices are fixed in real terms this would, of course, offer additional protections to OPEC against inflation. This second element is more or less in line with the Brandt proposals, although the latter are not clear or concrete enough on this point.
3. In return, the big concession which OPEC should be given is protection against inflation for their surpluses invested in the industrial countries, and possibly also for any surpluses directly recycled to Third World countries. This inflation hedge is so keenly desired that, if offered, OPEC could be expected to co-operate on the first two elements of the package. This would also give an additional incentive to industrial countries to control inflation, a task which would be made easier by a stabilization of oil prices.

The 'global deal with OPEC' can serve as an important step for restructuring world industry in accordance with changing production conditions. It could also provide a means of accelerating industrial investment in energy-poor Third World countries and could also provide the OPEC countries themselves with industrial technology and manpower at costs considerably lower than those in the West.

In conclusion, a concern with international issues should not obscure the need to build interest coalitions at national levels. Any breakthrough in international negotiations must be preceded by protracted negotiations among those interest groups in a nation State that compete to influence the formulation of industrial policy. These groups provide the focus for policies designed to remove obstacles to restructuring or the redistribution of industrial capacity in accordance with changing production conditions. However desirable specific policy options may be in terms of economic theory, their adoption in the real world depends largely on the extent to which politically salient interest groups see these policies as serving their own material ends.

Notes

[1] *North-South: A Programme for Survival*, the Report of the Independent Commission on International Development Issues under the Chairmanship of Willy Brandt, Pan Books Ltd., London, 1980, p. 266.

[2] Tony Killick, 'Trends in development economics and their relevance to Africa', *The Journal of Modern African Studies*, Vol. 18, No. 3, 1980, p. 368.

[3] See Interfutures, *Facing the Future: Mastering the Probable and Managing the Unpredictable*, OECD, Paris 1979, pp. 77–8.

[4] *Ibid.*, p. 82.

[5] For example, the spread of the Welfare State, while helping to humanize growth, has led to an 'oligopolization of social life' where groups organize themselves for negotiations with the government and other groups having different objectives rather than resorting to the market. Social trends such as risk aversion (to protect previously won gains) and the rise of post-materialist values are also best expressed through negotiations of this sort as an alternative to the market.

[6] The possibility of such mismatches is explored by Michael Beenstock, 'The causes of slower growth in the world economy', London Business School, London, 1980 (mimeo).

[7] Examples would be the promotion of importers' associations and the establishment of independent commissions to provide public information on the costs of neo-protectionist initiatives.

[8] E. Fontela, 'International trade and economic growth: outlook for the 1980s', in O. Hieronyml, *The New Economic Nationalism*, Macmillan, London, 1980, p. 167.

[9] This was the term used by Arthur Lewis in his pioneer article on 'Economic development with unlimited supplies of labour', *The Manchester School*, May 1954, pp. 139–91. In this article, Lewis extended the original Keynesian analysis of an economy with excess labour by shifting the emphasis from the domestic scene in industrial countries to the domestic scene in LDCs. This was what we may call 'semi-international Keynesianism'. The step to full international Keynesianism was

advocated in the Brandt Report, with its emphasis on mutual interests and mutual interdependence.

[10] Richard Jolly, 'Mutual interests and the implications for reform of the International Economic Order', in S. Grassman and E. Lundberg, *The World Economic Order Past and Prospects*, Macmillan, London, 1981, pp. 558–81.

[11] For fuller discussion of the Lima target in its various aspects, see H. W. Singer, 'Policy implications of the Lima target', *Industry and Development*, No. 3, Special Issue for the Third General Conference of UNIDO, United Nations, New York, 1979.

Index

Agriculture, 11, 12, 92, 99, 215 in
    Middle East, 293
Aids to industry from Government, 70,
    163
Algeria, 293
Anti-Dumping Practices, GATT Committee on, 161
Argentina, 42, 52, 135, 236, 308
    food processing in, 207
    steel production in, 179
Asian countries' exports, 50
Austria, 188

Bangladesh, 269, 309
Banking in Germany, 23
Belgium, 75
Bergsman, J., 47
Bhagwati Jagdish, 81
BHEL (Indian PME), 285
Bolivia, 269
Borden and Solvay, 287
Brandt Report (Brandt Commission),
    80-3, 298-9, 312
Brazil, 34, 47, 78, 170, 171, 226, 236
    employment by TNCs in, 234
    food processing in, 207
    incentives to export in, 52
    market share analysis, 134-5
    petrochemical industry in, 287-91
    PMEs in, 269, 270
    protectionism in, 42
    sources of growth in, 56
    steel production in, 179
    and US, 51
    value of exports, 59-60

Bretton Woods Agreement, 64, 82, 311
Britain,
    economic growth in, 10-11
    industrialization in, 8
    R and D funds, 49
    social environment in 19th century,
    8-9
    See also United Kingdom
Bukharin, 27, 28
Burma, 34

Cameroon, 170
Canada, 75, 237
Capuava (Brazil), 287
Cargill Corporation, 209
Chemical industry, 172, 183-94
    See also Petrochemical industry
Chile, 56, 110
China, 34
    food processing in, 207
    steel production in, 182
Classical political economy, 16
Clothing industry, 156, 158, 161, 204
    See also Textile industry
Collectivization in Soveit Union, 29-30
Colombia, 52, 56, 136, 170, 171, 236
Colonial trade, 10
Commercial policy practices, 158-9
Commodity composition effect, 132
Common Market (19th century
    German), 19
Comparitive advantage,
    composition of country samples used,
    170
    changes in, 140-52

See also Revealed comparative advantage
Competitiveness effect, 131, 139
Concentration levels in LDCs, 232-3
Constant market share analysis, 130, 131-2
Contraction, limits to, 99
COPENE (Brazil, 288
Cotton industry, 11
Cyprus, 56, 59, 171

Davignon Plan, 69, 178
'Decapitalisation thesis' (TNCs and LDCs), 231-2
Del Monte, 212
Development related to exports, 142-3
Dole, 212
Domestic demand,
  growth in, 117
  in Third World, 54-60
Domestic market size, 123
Dow Chemical Europe, 291

Economic co-operation among LDCs, 315-17
Economic links between countries, 97
Economics, schools of thought, 4-5
Ecuador, 56, 171
Egypt, 42, 56, 60, 170, 171
  PMEs in, 269, 309
El Salvador, 56, 60, 308
Employment, impact of TNCs on, 234-6
Energy costs, 185
Engineering Projects Ltd (Indian PME), 285
European Economic Community, 51, 300
  steel production in, 173
  textile trade in, 199-200, 205
Exchange rates, 71
Export orientation in Third World, 48-53
  impact of TNCs on, 238-9
  state role in, 52-3
Export performance in Third World, 53-60
  related to development, 142-3
Exports of manufactures,
  definition of, 141
  related to growth, 152-64
'External' conditions of production, 3, 139, 297

Fair labour standards, 82
Fertilisers, 193, 293
Fiji, 56
Fontela, Emilio, 317
Food processing industry, 172, 206-17
  luxury foods, 208-9, 211-12
Footwear industry, 156, 158
Foreign Direct Investment Program (US), 69
France, 49, 75, 136, 170
Furniture industry, 156

General Agreement on Tariffs and Trade, (GATT), 64, 161
Generalized System of Preferences, 210
Germany, West, 70
  banking in, 23
  changes in manufacturing, 75
  compared to LDCs, 136
  industrialization in, 16-25
  iron industry in, 20-1
  obstacles to industrialization, 18-19
  political factors, 33
  state ownership of industry, 22-3
  textile industry in, 20
Ghana, 34, 56, 59
Gillis, Malcolm, 269
Greece, 135, 170, 171, 188
Group system of international negotiations, 299-301, 314
Growth rates, industrial, 107-20
  related to export performance, 152-64
Guatemala, 56, 59

Havana Charter, 82
HMT (Indian PME), 285
Honduras, 56
Hong Kong, 50, 78, 134, 138, 170, 199, 236

Index

Imperial Preference System, 61, 64
Import sustitution, 39-48, 54-5, 59, 159, 306
Incentives to export, 52, 60
Income gaps, 106-7
    See also Growth rates
India, 34, 42, 56, 134, 138, 140, 170, 171, 236, 290
    autonomous domestic subsidiaries, 233
    chemical industry in, 190
    food processing in, 213
    PMEs in, 269, 276-85, 309
    steel production in, 179
Indonesia, 34, 56, 213, 269
Industrial organisations,
    changes in, 15
    growth patterns of, 107-20
Industrial restructuring, definition of, 3-4, 34-5
Industry, definition of, 141
Industry, internationalism of, 98
Interest groups,
    in Third World, 305-10
    in West, 302-5
'Internal' conditions of production, 3, 139
International Dairy Arrangement, 211
International Development Strategy, 313
International reform, attempts at, 77-83
International Telephone and Telegram, 209
International trade, historical emphasis on, 8-16
International Trade Organisation, 82-3
Intra-firm trade, 237
Investment, 76, 77
    theory, 252-4
    by TNCs, 225-30, 239, 241
Iran, 56, 293, 308
Iron and steel industry, 173-83
Iraq, 56, 171, 189, 293, 309
Israel, 144, 170
Italy, 49, 75
Ivory Coast, 170

Jamaica, 171
Japan, 49, 75, 82, 136, 139, 170
    comparitive advantage, 143
    and food imports, 210
    petrochemical industry in, 188-9, 191
    steel production in, 173, 175, 179
    textile industry in, 199, 200, 205-6
    trade with US, 63-4
Jolly, Richard, 312
Jordan, 56, 60, 171
Kalecki, M., 246
Kampuchea, 34
Kennedy Round of negotiations, 67, 163
Keynes, J.M., 311-12
Kenya, 171
Killick, T., 299
Kopper (TNC), 287
Korea, 50, 134, 140, 170, 171, 200
Kuwait, 110, 189
Kuznets, Simon, 107-9

Labour-intensive industries, 150, 153, 157, 164
Laos, 34
Latin American exports, 51
    trade, 62
Law of Proportionate Effect, 243-7, 278
Law of Unequal Exchange, 310
Less developed countries (LDCs),
    compared to West, 133-64
    co-operation between, 315-17
    dependance on western markets, 67-8
    domestic industries, 46
    exports, 48-53
    import substitution, 39-48
    manufacturing capacity, 48
    steel consumption, 180
    See Also Third World
Levels of concentration in LDCs, 232-3
Libya, 56
Lima Target, 313, 314
List, frederick, 16-25
    'stages' theory, 17
Long-Term Cotton Textile Arrangement, 198
Long-term and short-term interests, 302

323

Luxury foods, 208-9, 211-12
  See also Food processing industry

Madagascar, 56, 59, 60, 171
Mahalanobis, Professor, 284
Maizels, A., 49
Malawi, 56
Malaysia, 50, 61, 236
Malta, 171
Malthus, Thomas, 15
Management Labour Textile Advisory
  Committee, 198
Manufacture, definition of exports, 141
Manufacturing industries
  changes in, 74-5
  in 19th century, 11, 12
  shares in world output, 96
Market distribution effect, 132
Market size as factor in growth rate, 110
Marxist economic theory, 272-3
MECON (Indian PME), 285
Mercantilism, 17-18
Mercantilist School, 8
Metropolitan capital, 144
Mexico, 51, 52, 78, 135, 138, 170, 171,
  226, 236, 318
  border industries, 237-8
  chemical industry in, 189, 191-2
  employment by TNCs in, 234
  food processing in, 213
  PMEs in, 269
  steel production in, 179
Mill, J.S., 17
Mitsubishi, 214, 291
Mobil, 291
Modes of production, changes in, 35
Monopolization in LDCs, 161-2, 164
Morocco, 233
Most favoured nation (MFN), 67, 68
Multifibre Arrangement, 160, 161, 197, 199
Multilateral bargaining groups, 107
Multilateral Trade Negotiations, Tokyo
  Round, 77-9

Nationalization, 273-4

  in chemical industry, 186-9
  in steel industry, 176-9
  in textile industry, 197-200
NBCC (Indian PME), 285
Negotiations and restructuring, 298-319
Neo-protectionism, 70-1, 72-3, 73-7,
  159, 161
  See also Protectionism
Nepal, 269
Nestlé, 209
Netherlands, 75
Newly industrialising countries (NICs),
  141, 150, 307
  export performance of, 142-3
  steel consumption of, 180
New International Econimic Order
  debate, 298-9, 313
Nicaragua, 170, 308
Nigeria, 56, 171
Non-tariff barriers, 69, 160
Norway, 75, 188

OPEC, role of 317-9
Orderly marketing agreements, 69
Output mix,
  of LDCs, 106
  of western countries, 104-5

Pakistan, 42, 236, 270, 308
Panama, 56, 171
PEC (Indian PME), 285
Pecten, 291
Peru, 213, 233, 234-5
Petrobras (Brazil), 287, 289
Petrochemical industry, 172, 183-4
  in Brazil, 287-91
Petroquimica Unào (Brazil), 287-8
Petroquisa (Brazil), 287-8
Pharmaceuticals, 193
Philippines, 50, 56, 135, 170, 171, 211
Poland, 310
Policy decisions and structural changes,
  297-319
Polypropylene, 187
Portugal, 170, 188
  in 18th century, 13-14

Index

Prais, J., 246
Preobrazhenskii, 26-7
Product composition, 138-9
Product cycle, 145-8
Production orientation, as factor in growth rate, 110, 117, 124
Profitability of TNCs, 249-51
  determinants, of, 254-9, 283
Protectionism, 159, 163, 304-5
  in LDCs, 42-3
  in steel industry, 176
  in US, 69-70
  See also Neo-protectionism
Public manufacturing enterprises (PMEs), 224, 268-94
  co-operation with TNCs, 285-94
  in India, 276-85
  investment, 276, 284
  rate in growth, 278-9
  in Yugoslavia, 274-6

Qatar, 189

Recently developed countries, 144
Reciprocal Trade Agreement Act (1934), 61
Regression analysis, 255
Research and development, 48-9
  in chemical industry, 183-4
Resource-based industries, 149
Resource endowment as factor in growth rate, 109-10, 117, 123-5
Revealed comparitive advantage, 140-1, 142, 150-1
  See also Comparitive advantage
Ricardo, D. 12-16
Russia *See* Soviet Union

Safeguards, 78-9, 81
'Saturation' thesis, 259
Saudi Arabia, 110, 189
Saudi Arabian Basic Industrial Corporation, 291
Schumpeter, 7
Second Saudi Arabian Plan, 291
Shanin, 27-8

Shell, 291
Singapore, 34, 50, 61, 134, 170, 171, 234, 236
Size of TNCs, 243-8
Smith, Adam, 8, 9, 11-12, 15, 224
Social welfare, 271-2
South Korea, 52, 56, 59-60, 61, 78, 236
  employment by TNCs in, 235
  food processing in, 231
  PMEs in, 269
  steel production in, 179
  textiles in, 199, 201
Soviet Union,
  collectivization, 29-30
  first Five Year Plan, 28-9
  food processing in, 207
  foreign trade, 30-1
  industrial development in, 25-32
  industrialisation strategy, 31-2
  'infant stage' of development, 27
  New Economic Policy, 25-6
  PMEs in, 274
  steel industry in, 173
Spain, 170, 171, 188
Specialization, 13-14, 48
Sri Lanka, 56, 170, 269, 309
'Stages' theory, (List), 17
Standard Oil, 209
Steel industry, 172, 173-83
Structural changes in advanced countries, 98-104
  related to industrial policy, 297-319
Sumitoma, Shoji, 212
Sweden, 75-237
Syria, 309

Taiwan, 34, 50, 61, 78, 199, 201, 269
Tanzania, 171, 309
Tariff reductions, 65-6
Tariff setting in LDCs, 41-2, 48
Technology in food processing, 215
Textile industry, 156, 158, 172, 194-206
  outward processing, 203
  synthetic fibres, 203
Thailand, 56, 135, 170, 211, 213, 282
Theories of investment, 252-4

325

Third World,
  chemical industry in, 189-94
  exports, 48-53
  food processing in, 212-17
  heterogeneity in, 119
  interest groups and restructuring, 305-10
  manufacturing capacity of, 48
  steel industries in, 179-83
  textile industry in, 200-6
  and TNCs, 226-30
  and western trade policies, 60-73
  See also Less developed countries
Tinbergen, 80
Tokyo Round of negotiations, 77-9, 163, 210, 211, 262
Trade,
  colonial 10
  in Soviet Union, 30-1, 32
Transfer pricing, 214-15, 258-9
Transnational corporations (TNCs), 149, 181, 223
  as agents of change, 225
  co-operation with PMEs, 285-94
  and food processing, 209, 212
  growth and profitability, 249-51, 280-1
  growth and size, 256
  impact of on growth, 243
  impact of on investment, 230-9
  investment and finance policy, 225-34
  level of international involvement, 236
  patterns of development, 230
  relationships with governments, 225-6
  size and profit, 256
  and the Third World, 226-30
  See also Transfer Pricing
Transport costs, 66
Trigger price mechanism (US), 177-8, 304
Tunisia, 56, 170, 171
Turkey, 56, 59-60, 136, 170, 171, 188

PMEs in, 269, 309

steel production, 179

Unilever, 209, 214
Union Carbide, 287

UNIPAR, 287-8

United Brands, 212
United Kingdom, 75
  steel production, 173
  trade barriers, 69
  See also Britain
United States, 50, 136, 170
  food imports, 211
  food processing, 207
  leadership in international trade, 61-3
  manufacturing, changes in, 75
  political objectives, 63-4, 66
  steel production, 173
  textile trade, 199-200
United States Steel, 286
USSR *See* Soviet Union

Venezuela, 192, 186, 318
Vietnam, 213
Voluntary export restraints, 70

Welfare state, 312
West Germany *See* Germany, West
West Indies, 213
Western trade strategies, 60-73
Williams, E., 10
Wood products industry, 156
World demand, effect on export performance, 130-1, 138

Yugoslavia, 170, 171, 274-6

Zaire, 110
Zaleski, E., 274
Zambia, 56
Zollverein (Germany), 17, 19-20, 24